A Sight Never to Be Forgotten

A Sight Never to Be Forgotten

Eyewitness Accounts of
Union Chaplains at Gettysburg

Nancy Jill Hale

Published by Gettysburg Publishing, LLC
www.gettysburgpublishing.com

Front Cover Images:
Standing: Samuel Witt Eaton
Top row, left to right: Philos Cook, John Ripley Adams, Henry Rogers Pyne, Benjamin A. Chase, Louis N. Beaudry
Bottom row, left to right: Julius Rose, James F. Calkins, Alexander M. Stewart, John B. Seage, Joseph Hopkins Twichell
Back cover image: Paul Henry Wood, (American, 1872-1892) "Absolution Under Fire," 1891, Oil on canvas, 71 1/8 x 101 1/2 in. Raclin Murphy Museum of Art, University of Notre Dame. University Collection, by transfer, 1976.057.
Cover Design by Caroline Stover

Library of Congress Cataloging-in-Publication Data
A catalog record for this book has been requested.

ISBN 978-1-7346276-9-5

Library of Congress control number: 2025043810

Printed and bound in the United States of America

First Edition

Contents

Preface

"I wouldn't be caught dead in a hoop skirt!" Little did I know at the time, but that announcement would lead me into the world of Civil War chaplaincy.

Several years ago, when I was serving a church in New York State's North Country, I was surprised to learn that there was a Civil War reenacting unit that far north (the 118th New York Infantry, the Adirondack Regiment). I attended one of their events and was fascinated by the way the members of the unit strove to portray a historically accurate Civil War army camp. I approached the captain and mentioned that I might be interested in reenacting, but not as one of the women in the group (who wore the large skirts that prompted my remark), but neither did I want to be a soldier who had to carry around that heavy gun and other equipment. The captain asked what I did in real life, and I told him I was a pastor. "Aha," he said. "You can be our chaplain!" "Yes!" I quickly replied, knowing that he had just named what would become the perfect intersection between my vocation as a United Methodist pastor and my passion for the Civil War.

Within a few weeks, I had done some research and purchased a chaplain's uniform, an authentic nineteenth-century Bible, and other pieces of equipment appropriate for the spiritual leader of a regiment. But I wanted to learn more. As a pastor who sometimes struggles with knowing how to care for people in difficult situations and with keeping my own faith strong in challenging times, I wanted to know more about what these men did, what they thought, how they ministered to a regiment of hundreds of men in awful circumstances, how they experienced battle as noncombatants whose primary responsibility was to care for the spiritual, physical, and emotional health of the soldiers while also preparing the men to fight with courage and faith, and how they kept their own faith strong and vibrant in the midst of war. As I started to look at memoirs, letters, and other records left by chaplains, I realized that in many instances, chaplains perceived and interpreted their experiences differently from men whose focus was limited to killing the enemy directly in their front. Those chaplains who remained with their regiments just behind the battle lines had a wide-angle view, while those who remained in the rear to care for the wounded reported the horrors they witnessed with care and tact.

I soon started to study the Battle of Gettysburg and the chaplains who had been there. Although there are books that discuss chaplaincy in the Civil War, and one that focuses on some of the chaplains (both Union and Confederate) who were with their regiments at Gettysburg (*Summon Only the Brave!* by John W. Brinsfield Jr.), I did not find one comprehensive volume that included all those Union chaplains who participated in the Gettysburg campaign or that quoted the many good primary sources written by or about these chaplains. Once I began my research, I discovered letters and diary entries, some of which have never been published, that describe what these men of God experienced and thought and did. I learned that chaplains did much more than just pray for the men and lead a Divine Service each week, which is a common modern perception of chaplains in the Civil War. These men lived with the soldiers, sharing their burdens and their joys, caring for the sick, and burying those who were felled in battle or by disease. Sometimes they picked up a musket to join the firing line, and sometimes they sacrificed their freedom, their health, or even their lives for the sake of the cause and the men in their unit. Their hearts were easily broken by what their men suffered, but they were also inspired by the courage and devotion to duty those men exhibited. Many chaplains proved not only to be extraordinary in the fulfilment of their own duty while in service to the army, but they also accomplished incredible things in their lives and ministry both before and after the war.

The first time I put on my chaplain's uniform, with its heavy woolen frock coat adorned with the shoulder straps of a captain, I was overcome with a feeling of being wholly unworthy to wear it. And as I dove into the stories of these chaplains, I was increasingly awed by their faithfulness to duty and love for their men that made my own ministry seem so inadequate in comparison. But along the way, many of these men have become like friends to me as I related to their experiences and as my respect for their sacrificial service for the sake of others grew by leaps and bounds. I have discovered new motivation and encouragement for my own ministry in these stories, and I hope they will inspire my readers to have greater admiration for the faithfulness of Union chaplains and the significance of their ministry.

Acknowledgments

When this project was nothing more than an idea floating around in my mind, I had no idea about what I was getting into and no concept of the amount of help I would need from friends, historians, research assistants, librarians, and archivists. But all of these, whenever asked, have stepped up to offer their assistance, and I am very grateful for their support.

The staff at several organizations provided biographical information about some of the chaplains in this book, including the United Methodist Archives and History Center at Drew University, the American Baptist Historical Society, the Presbyterian Historical Society, the Lutheran Archives Center, Boston University School of Theology, Olin Library at Cornell University, Beinecke Library at Yale University, Musselman Library at Gettysburg College, St. Lawrence University, Dickinson College, Morris Library at the University of Delaware, McKeldin Library at the University of Maryland, William L. Clements Library at the University of Michigan, Folger Library at the University of Maine, Pattee Library at Penn State University, Archives and Special Connections of the University of Connecticut Library, the Union League Legacy Foundation in Philadelphia, the New York State Military Museum, the Archives of the Susquehanna Conference of the United Methodist Church, the Archives of Michigan, the National Park Service Archives at Gettysburg, the Pennsylvania State Archives, the New Jersey State Archives, the Ohio State Archives, Gale Family Library at the Minnesota Historical Society, the Army Heritage and Education Center at Carlisle, Pennsylvania, and the National Archives and Records Administration.

I received material from several local libraries and local historical societies, including the Greenburgh Public Library in Tarrytown, New York, the Chemung Valley (New York) History Museum, the Tioga County (New York) Historical Society, the Buffalo Library, the Warwick (New York) Historical Society, the Goshen (New York) Public Library, the Crawford County (Pennsylvania) Historical Society, Haverhill (Massachusetts) Public Library, Rancho Los Cerritos in Los Angeles, the Vermont Historical Society, the Rome (New York) Historical Society, Easton Area (Pennsylvania) Public Library, the Three Springs/Saltillo Area (Pennsylvania) Historical Society, and Christ Lutheran Church in Gettysburg.

In addition, I want to thank the many individuals who offered advice and additional information. Authors Mark Dunkelman, Allen R. Thompson, Ron Kirkwood, Michael A. Dreese, George Farr, Martin Husk, John W. Brinsfield, and Eric Wittenberg provided more information from their own research. Ronald S. Coddington kindly sent copies of several chaplain photos. Licensed Battlefield Guides Stuart Dempsey, Jim Hessler, Andy Ward, Richard Goedkoop, and Chris Army granted me access to the Association of Licensed Battlefield Guides library, steered me in the right direction when I couldn't find something, answered my questions, and offered helpful advice.

Other historians who lent a hand were Tim Smith at the Adams County (Pennsylvania) Historical Society, who helped find resources from the society's vast holdings; Steven Roberts, who provided materials regarding his ancestor Henry Seage; Dr. Jennifer Rycenga, who graciously allowed me to cite her unpublished paper about Ferdinand Ward; and Frank Varney, who read portions of my work and offered feedback. Don Madar was instrumental in tracking down information about chaplains' war records; Mark Lawrence Gade made trips to the Michigan Library to find certain records; and James Galasinski visited the archives at St. Lawrence University to access an obscure newspaper article.

Many friends have offered advice, support, and encouragement, including Michael Rinehart, Dr. Rik Scarce, Dr. Lester Ruth, Jim Cassatt, and Pam Cope. I am especially grateful to author and historian Scott Mingus Jr. for his discerning eye and willingness to answer questions about writing and editing.

I would like to thank my sons Kevin and Rick for their support and encouragement and to give a special shout-out to my son Gregory for accompanying me on several excursions to find the gravesites of certain chaplains. And finally, I would like to acknowledge my publisher, Kevin Drake, who caught my vision for this book and shepherded me through the process of researching and writing.

Foreword

Scott L. Mingus, Sr.

Following the April 1861 bombardment of Fort Sumter, men and boys flocked to recruiting stations in cities and towns across the North and South. York, Pennsylvania, was just one example. The U.S. and the Confederate States of America quickly began raising massive numbers of new soldiers.

David Small, the Democratic editor of the Gazette, thundered in an editorial: "The news of the attack upon, and capture of Ft. Sumter, and that the President had called for 75,000 troops, caused a feeling of the most intense excitement, and the pervading topic of the community was, War! War!! War !!!" Similar messages appeared in scores of papers across the now divided country, and the raw recruits began formal training as soldiers.

Often, volunteer preachers and pastors visited various training camps to minister to the men, many of whom were away from their families for the first time. Temptations abounded: hard liquor, gambling, loose women, profanity, and brawling were common in the early days of the war. A new Southern soldier lamented, "If the South is overthrown, its epitaph should be 'died of whiskey.'"

On May 4, 1861, President Abraham Lincoln ordered all regiments in the Union Army to appoint chaplains. He stipulated that the appointees should be ordained ministers of the Christian faith. It would not be until 1862 that Jewish rabbis were added to the formal chaplaincy. Military chaplains received an annual salary of $1,700 and held the same rank as a major. Confederate chaplains, organized at the same time as their Union counterparts, only drew $1.020 in remuneration.

The youngest Union chaplain was the appropriately named George F. Pentecost. He was only 19 years old when he began to minister to the

8th Kentucky Cavalry after his ordination as a Presbyterian pastor in 1864. On the other end of the spectrum was John Pierpont, a Unitarian from Boston who served the 22nd Massachusetts. He was born in 1785. His son James had moved to Savannah before the war. Later famed as the writer of the popular song Jingle Bells, James served in the 5th Georgia Cavalry as a private. One of John Pierpont's grandsons was industrialist J.P. Morgan.

According to military records, 2,154 men served as chaplains in the Union Army during the war. Methodists made up 38% of that number, followed by Presbyterians at 17% and Baptists at 12%. Eleven chaplains were killed in action, with four more being mortally wounded. Several became prisoners of war.

More than one hundred Union chaplains were at Gettysburg. All except one survived the battle. Some left accounts of their experiences in the summer campaign and the war's bloodiest battle. In this book, author Nancy Hale, an ordained United Methodist minister, has mined these accounts to give her readers a glimpse of these men of faith.

Chapter 1:

Introduction

In the afternoon of July 2, 1863, the left of the Union line of battle along the Emmitsburg Road and at the Peach Orchard at Gettysburg was giving way under an assault from several Confederate brigades. Maj. Gen. George Gordon Meade, commander of the Army of the Potomac, ordered reinforcements to support the crumbling line, including the soldiers of the famed Irish Brigade. As the brigade prepared to advance, Maj. St. Clair Mulholland of the 116th Pennsylvania regiment observed what he called *"one of the most impressive religious ceremonies I have ever witnessed."*[1] The men gathered in ranks, turned their backs to the enemy they would soon engage, and faced their chaplain, Father William Corby. The priest stood on a large rock, explained what he was about to do, and noticed that every man *"showed a profound respect, wishing at this fatal crisis to receive every benefit of divine grace that could be imparted."*[2]

Father Corby at Gettysburg (from *The Story of the 116th Regiment Pennsylvania Volunteers in the War of the Rebellion* by St. Clair A. Mulholland)

Mulholland stated that *"while there was profound silence in the ranks of the Second Corps, yet over to the left, out by the Peach Orchard and Little Round Top [. . .] the roar of the battle rose and swelled and re-echoed through the woods, making music more sublime than ever sounded through cathedral aisles."*[3] Father Corby charged the men to confess their sins, urged them to carry out the duty that lay in the fields behind them, and reminded them that a Christian burial would not be offered to any soldier who turned his back on his flag or his duty.

The soldiers then knelt and several officers standing nearby bowed their heads as the priest offered the words of absolution:

> *May Our Lord Jesus Christ absolve you, and I, by His authority, absolve you from every bond of excommunication and interdict, insofar as it lies within my power and you require; therefore, I absolve you from your sins, in the Name of the Father, and of the Son, and of the Holy Ghost. Amen.*[4]

Corby later explained that his absolution was intended *"not only for our brigade, but for all, North or South, who were susceptible of it and who were about to appear before their Judge."*[5]

St. Clair Mulholland would have agreed. He believed that every soldier, having been moved by both *"the eloquence of the good priest"* and *"the incidents of the fight,"* offered repentance that was heartfelt and sincere: *"That heart would be incorrigible, indeed, that the scream of a Whitworth bolt, added to the priest's touching appeal, would not move to contrition."*[6]

Father Corby is perhaps the most well-known Civil War chaplain. Thousands of people have visited his monuments both at Gettysburg and at Notre Dame, where he served as president of the university following

The monument to Father Corby at Gettysburg by sculptor Samuel Murray, dedicated in 1910. (Author's collection)

the war. The monument along Cemetery Ridge at Gettysburg, south of the Pennsylvania Monument near where the Irish Brigade prepared to enter the fray, is the only one to a chaplain on an American battlefield. But he is just one of hundreds of men who served their nation and its soldiers as chaplains.

This book will explore how Union chaplains experienced the Battle of Gettysburg and its aftermath. But first, we will begin with an examination of how chaplaincy became a part of the U.S. Army and look at some of the expectations and challenges faced by chaplains in general.

"To Make Better Soldiers"

Military chaplains have played a role in every American conflict since the Revolutionary War. During the fight for independence, pastors from towns and villages would often accompany their parishioners or neighbors into battle. Early in the war, the militia system was not fully developed, so these chaplains served the soldiers as unpaid volunteers who were not formally recognized by any authority. As the states organized their militia units into brigades and regiments, brigade officers, governors, or state legislatures would choose chaplains who would be paid at a rate determined by each state. Once the Continental Army was organized in 1775, chaplains were slowly transferred from the militia to the army, and Congress adopted a uniform pay scale by which chaplains would be allowed $20 per month. This is the earliest instance of chaplains being recognized by the army.[7]

Chaplains were assigned to accompany troops in subsequent wars, including the War of 1812 and the Mexican-American War (1846–1848). But by 1849, the army reverted to its system of providing chaplains only to military posts, and at the outset of the Civil War, there were only thirty chaplains to serve some 15,000 soldiers. Among other things, these chaplains worked as "schoolmasters" for illiterate soldiers and their children living on the posts.[8] Between 1813 and 1856, only eighty chaplains had been commissioned by the army. The need for a large army in the Civil War required a new system of choosing and assigning a much larger number of chaplains.

The earliest volunteer regiments organized by states would sometimes invite a pastor from the area where the unit was recruited and who was well known to the men to serve as their chaplain, but it was an informal arrangement with no official expectations, pay, or other benefits. On May 4, 1861, only a few weeks after the firing on Fort Sumter, the War Department issued General Order 15; this order allowed for one chaplain for each regiment, with each being paid at the rate of a cavalry captain, which at that time was $1,746 per year. However, because this order was not backed by legislative authority, some army paymasters, who could sometimes be overly cautious about where the government's money was spent, simply refused to pay the new chaplains. So, in July 1861, a bill was introduced during a special session of Congress that codified General Order 15:

> *There will be allowed each regiment one chaplain, who will be appointed by the regimental commander on the vote of the field officers and company commanders on duty with the regiment at the time the appointment is to be made. The chaplain so appointed must be a regularly ordained minister of some Christian denomination, and will receive the pay and allowances of captain of cavalry.*[9]

Although this bill placed the responsibility of electing a chaplain on the field officers, in at least one case the entire regiment was invited to cast votes for their chaplain. Father Joseph B. O'Hagan was a candidate for chaplain in the 73rd New York Infantry in Gen. Daniel Sickles's Excelsior Brigade. O'Hagan noted with some humor, *"a few weeks before I joined them, they had held an election for chaplain: over four hundred voted for a Catholic priest; one hundred and fifty-four, for any kind of a Protestant minister; eleven, for a Mormon elder; and the rest said that they could go to hell without the assistance of the clergy."*[10]

Subsequent debates on this bill included a motion to give chaplains the same compensation as chaplains who had been appointed to army posts, which would have been a lower pay rate than the bill originally proposed. Although this motion was passed, a day later it was reconsidered and withdrawn when one congressman argued that *"the faith of the nation was plighted to chaplains who came out with the regiments mustered into service."*[11] The original bill passed in the Senate and was directed to the House of Representatives.

Some members of the House were concerned about the religious partisanship and anti-Catholic bias that had been prevalent in the years before the war and sought to make sure any bill concerning chaplains would be inclusive. One motion proposed that the commander of a brigade shall have the power to appoint a Roman Catholic chaplain for his brigade if no regiment in the brigade had such a chaplain, and another sought to strike out the phrase that required a potential chaplain to be a member of *"a Christian denomination"* and instead substitute the phrase *"a religious society."* Both amendments were voted down.[12]

Finally, on July 22, 1861, the act was approved without any amendments and with Section 9 recognizing and designating the official role of chaplains as part of the army. Thus, chaplains were understood to hold the rank of captain on the regimental field staff, although it was an honorary rank, not a military rank, and they had no command authority. In addition, and true to army protocol, the chaplain *"shall be required to report to the colonel at the end of each quarter, of the moral and religious condition of the regiment, and offer such suggestions as may conduce to the social happiness and moral improvement of the troops."*[13]

This did not end the debates in Congress about the status, number, roles, and pay of army chaplains. With the war turning out to be a longer and more involved affair than the government first believed it would be, Congress started to take a closer look at potential cost-saving measures, including limiting the number of official chaplains in the army. In January 1862, a congressman from New York introduced a bill to reduce the number of chaplains to one per brigade instead of one per regiment.[14]

This proposal was not well received. Families and friends of soldiers who were fighting in fields or camps hundreds of miles from home knew that the threats to life in an army camp and the dangers of battle would wreak havoc on the faithfulness of their loved ones, which was typically nurtured by a hometown pastor in the bosom of a congregation. The author of an anonymous letter to *The Buffalo Commercial* that same month expressed concerns:

> *During our present war, we have frequently heard expressed by fathers, mothers, wives, daughters and sisters, comfort and confidence in the fact that there are with their loved ones a Christian minister, known to them, to watch their moral when in health, and give them the consolations of the gospel when sick and dying. If a Chaplain's services be at all necessary, then they are necessary for each regiment. To have Brigade Chaplains only, will in our opinion just about nullify all that is useful in the Chaplaincy. It will be spreading religious influence very thin indeed. Under such circumstances the Chaplaincy will become a mere nominal affair.*[15]

During his regiment's time at its winter camp in Falmouth, Virginia, in early 1863, an army captain became convinced that even one chaplain per regiment was insufficient: *"If the reader could use his ears instead of his eyes and listen to what was then said by the soldiers he would soon learn the rank and file dialect of 'the army in Flanders,' and wonder how the Government could be so indifferent to the spiritual welfare of the army, as to allow but one chaplain to a regiment."* [16]

Pastors were concerned about what the young men in their congregations would experience in the army. Chaplain A. M. Stewart was *"unwilling that so many young men, fresh from the quiet pursuits of home, should be so suddenly become exposed to all the destructive tendencies of camp life without some effort and sacrifice to have gospel influences among them,"* [17] so he offered his services as a chaplain just one day after the firing on Fort Sumter opened the war.

Soldiers were also concerned about their separation from the wholesome influences of religious practices and pastors at home, and some of them described the challenges of trying to keep the faith and resist the temptations that thrived in an army camp. When the 2nd Rhode Island Infantry found itself without a chaplain in late 1863, Col. Horatio Rogers *"well understood the fact, that it was unsafe for men, who were face to face with death, and who were beyond the restraints of stable society, to be without the influence of religious service and instruction [. . .] A chaplain was required."* [18] 1st Lt. Elijah Hunt Rhodes of the same regiment agreed with his colonel: *"Soldiers are not the worst men in the world, but they are very careless in regard to matters of religion [. . .] we hope to have a chaplain soon."* [19]

Men of the 154th New York Volunteer Infantry lamented the loss of their chaplain, Henry D. Lowing, who resigned due to poor health in December 1863.[20] The regiment did not receive a new chaplain until ten months later, during which time the soldiers tried their best to hold worship services and prayer meetings on their own. In a letter home, Pvt. Emory Sweetland of the 154th assured his family that despite many *"contaminating influences"* in camp, *"I am trying to be a Christian. I find it rather hard sometimes."* [21] Others in the regiment

1st Lt. Elijah Hunt Rhodes of the 2nd Rhode Island Infantry bemoaned the absence of a chaplain for his men. (Library of Congress)

noted the importance of participating in a religious atmosphere and gathering for worship and religious study in the army because these practices helped them resist the temptations of army life. One private complained to his sister that *"there is no Sunday in the army."*[22] In his letters, Sweetland noted how religious men were sustained by *"faith [that] enabled them to endure, their reliance on the prayers of the families, and the opportunity for them to band together in worship."*[23]

A private in the 33rd Massachusetts Infantry admitted that *"as a general rule army life is not conducive to religion; it rather tends the other way."*[24] But he also confirmed the value of religious observance when it was possible:

> *The religious services in our log chapel were closely attended every evening. I think there were quite a number of genuine conversions (as we Methodists call it) among the men of the rank and the file besides some few of the officers; besides there were quite a number of both classes who were formerly religious but had fallen away somewhat, who were now reclaimed and pledged themselves to a prayerful life. A marked change was noticeable in the moral life of each of them.*[25]

Following the normal rhythms of Sunday worship and other religious activities, and especially prayer, could help men feel more connected to those at home and to the religious training of their youth, but the pattern of army life did not always allow for such regular observances. Father Corby noted that one reason he offered his general absolution on the battlefield at Gettysburg is because the Irish Brigade had been marching steadily for two weeks, and he had not had opportunities to observe mass during that time.

THE JOURNAL.

Coudersport, Pa.

Wednesday, Feb. 18, 1863.

Army Christian Association.

WHEREAS, it becomes necessary for us in order to counteract the evil influences by which we are surrounded, and for the promotion and advancement of the cause of Christianity, and to heighten our moral and social standing; therefore,

1. *Resolved* That we unite ourselves together as a body of Christian brethren under the name of "The Christian Association of the One Hundred and Forty-Ninth Regiment, Pennsylvania Volunteers."

A resolution from the 149th Pennsylvania Infantry to form the "Army Christian Association Resolution" in which the soldiers would provide spiritual care for each other in the absence of a chaplain. (from *The Potter Journal and News Item*, Feb. 18, 1863)

Sometimes men had to take the matter of spiritual care into their own hands. The 149th Pennsylvania Infantry (the "second Bucktails") did not have a chaplain for the first ten months of their service until the Rev. James Calkins joined the unit in June 1863. But in the absence of a spiritual leader, fifty members of the regiment signed a resolution proclaiming themselves as members of "The Christian Association of the One Hundred and Forty-Ninth Regiment." These men vowed to care for each other's spiritual well-being, to avoid *"profanity, card playing, and those amusements often resorted to by soldiers in the army,"* and to faithfully *"encourage, counsel, and advise each other in the discharge of our duties, and thereby watch over one another that we do not go into forbidden paths."*[26] Elijah Hunt Rhodes of the 2nd Rhode Island Infantry noted the *"considerable religious interest"* in the regiment and *"had been active in keeping up a Sunday school in the Regiment, whenever it was at rest, and otherwise in directing the attention of as many officers and men as he could interest to religious subjects"*[27]

Chaplains also recognized the dangers of being separated from home and hearth, as Chaplain Louis N. Beaudry of the 5th New York Cavalry reflected on life in an army camp:

> *How few of [the soldiers] are able to stand up to the early principles taught them. Take a man away from respectable female society, and the sacred influences of home, and he gravitates rapidly toward barbarism. Men who were not respectable but normal at home, but also strictly and consistently religious, here soon became gamblers, profane, thieves, prostitutes and opposers of all that is good.*[28]

Chaplain H. Clay Trumbull of the 10th Connecticut Infantry believed that the men in a regiment appreciated their chaplain's presence whether in camp or on the battle line, where they *"felt stronger if one whom they looked to as God's representative was near them,"* and he cited one rough-hewn captain who said, *"We count our chaplain as good as a hundred men in a fight, because the men fight so much better when he's with 'em."*[29] An anonymous chaplain voiced his concern in a letter that was printed in his hometown newspaper: *"Nothing will so much inspire a soldier to nobler deeds of daring as the impression of fighting in a righteous cause, sanctioned by the prayers and presence of a pious Chaplain."*[30] However, some chaplains saw an advantage to ministering to those who were away from familiar associations and habits. Chaplain Alonzo Quint of the

Chaplain H. Clay Trumbull of the 10th Connecticut Infantry noted the significance of a chaplain as "God's representative." (from Trumbull's *War Memories of an Army Chaplain*)

2nd Massachusetts noted that the relationship and communication *"between minister and soldier is free and familiar–far different from that in the stereotyped localities where the parishioner sleeps in his hired pew. The crust which grows over men at home is broken [and] men are not ashamed to acknowledge their need of God's help."* [31]

Failure to observe the sacred nature of the Sabbath was another matter of concern to both chaplains and soldiers. Col. Robert McAllister of the 11th New Jersey was *"convinced of the wickedness of working on the Sabbath day–either in peace or war."* [32] Chaplain Stewart of the 102nd Pennsylvania Infantry complained that there is *"no Lord's day in times of war. The need for all this common use of holy time may seem in place to military men; yet have I not been able to discern why it could not be in general avoided."* [33] He noted one Sunday morning that *"preparations for public worship [were] made. At ten o'clock, however, the bugle suddenly sounded to strike tents and be ready to march."* [34] Stewart even blamed the devil for the inability to hold regular worship on Sundays:

> *Certain is it, however, that oftentimes we have more services of a purely military kind to perform on [the Sabbath] than upon other days. Knowing that the devil is a philosopher, as well as a consummate military chieftain, the matter may be accounted for as follows. This subtle and very notable deviser, Satan, on Friday or Saturday, starts the secesh on some new enterprise, which generally results in putting us in motion by Sabbath. Sure it is, we have no Sabbath in camp–nothing to distinguish it from any other day of the week.* [35]

Finding Suitable Chaplains

Although Congress expected chaplains to be "regularly ordained ministers," candidates were not required to show credentials proving that they were, indeed, duly ordained. Some men were attracted to the prestige of being an army officer and receiving a good salary without having to drill and fight. So, men with no credentials at all applied for, and sometimes received, commissions as chaplains. In addition, some chaplains in the first few months of the war were simply good friends of the colonel and had little or no theological training or even any religious background. Other candidates who applied for chaplain commissions were either unable to find churches at home to serve or had been ousted from the ministry. One of President Lincoln's secretaries, W. O. Stoddard, noted that this lack of suitable clergy to fill chaplaincy positions provoked Lincoln to the point of admitting, *"I do believe that our army chaplains, take them as a class, are the worst men we have in the service."*[36] Capt. Henry Blake of the 11th Massachusetts Infantry was candid in his criticism:

> *The chaplains of the army, those that should be the types of its purity, were commissioned without regard to their moral qualifications; and, as a class, exerted a debasing influence upon the soldiers so that it was generally impossible to perceive any distinction between the man of God and the man of sin.*[37]

Finding suitable chaplains had become a sore point for Lincoln, but sometimes political considerations overrode even Lincoln's discretion. In one case, the president was determined to see a certain man appointed as a chaplain, but Secretary of War Edwin Stanton considered the man undesirable and repeatedly rejected Lincoln's appeals:

Secretary of War Edwin Stanton rejected a petition from President Lincoln to appoint a man as a chaplain. (Library of Congress)

Dear Stanton: Appoint this man to be chaplain in the army. A. Lincoln.

Dear Mr. Lincoln: He is not a preacher. E. M. Stanton.

Three or four months elapse, evidently, and then we have:

Dear Stanton: He is now. A. Lincoln.

Dear Mr. Lincoln: But there is no vacancy. E. M. Stanton.

Dear Stanton: Appoint him a chaplain at large. A. Lincoln.

Dear Mr. Lincoln: There is no warrant of law for that. E. M. Stanton.

Dear Stanton: Appoint him anyhow. A. Lincoln.

Dear Mr. Lincoln: I will not. E. M. Stanton.

And he didn't.[38]

On December 16, 1861, the War Department issued General Order 108, which specified the appropriate uniform for chaplains, including a *"plain black frock coat with standing collar, and one row of nine black buttons; plain black pantaloons; black felt hat, or army forage cap, without ornament. On occasions of ceremony, a plain* chapeau de bras *may be worn."*[39]

However, some chaplains, perhaps especially those who were not suitable for the position and yet coveted the chaplain's rank of captain, were dissatisfied with this plain, unmilitary-like dress code that did not include shoulder straps or other insignia of rank, and they wanted more recognition—and a commensurate salary—for their service to the army.

Chaplain John N. McLeod of 84th New York Infantry in the plain uniform specified for chaplains. (Library of Congress)

Early in 1862, a group of Protestant chaplains assembled in Washington to discuss a petition that would organize chaplains into graded ranks (lieutenants, captains, majors, lieutenant colonels, colonels, and brigadier generals), and each chaplain would be paid according to his rank. In addition, the petition included the proposal that chaplains should wear military uniforms with the insignia of their rank embroidered on the breast of the frock coat.[40]

Chaplain Alonzo Quint of the 2nd Massachusetts Infantry described the feelings of the chaplains in his division regarding the flaunting of rank: *"The shoulder-straps, gilt buttons, and swords, on some chaplains, have always excited the ridicule of army officers. The less a chaplain assumes to be a military man, the better. His influence is that of a Christian minister. As to rank, due respect, etc., a chaplain needs no military rank, nor exacted salutations."*[41]

The plain uniform for chaplains was not required, so chaplains were free to dress in a way that was comfortable and acceptable to them. Some chose to wear civilian clothes either because they believed a chaplain should be identified by his character and not his outward appearance, or at the behest of his denominational superiors, who sometimes frowned on their ministers wearing any kind of military

Chaplain Gordon Winslow of the 5th New York Infantry in full dress uniform, with shoulder bars, sash, and sword. (Library of Congress)

Chaplains of the Ninth Corps near Petersburg, Virginia, about 1864. Chaplains wore a variety of military or civilian clothes. (Library of Congress)

dress. But some chaplains chose to wear the full trappings of their rank as captain, including an ornamental officer's sword. Occasionally, this proved beneficial, as in the case of Chaplain Frederic Denison of the 1st Rhode Island Cavalry, who described an advantageous experience during the Battle of Bull Run in August 1861:

> *I had the fortune to pick up six full armed rebel soldiers of Jackson's corps, and to take them with me into our lines and hand them over to the provost. Then I appreciated and found the full justification of my uniform and sword. The captives took me to be a captain of the line with a squad of cavalry at my heels.*[42]

While military dress proved advantageous for Chaplain Denison, in at least one incident wearing the full military uniform proved lethal for a chaplain during the Battle of Gettysburg; his story is found in chapter 2.

Unqualified and unskilled chaplains, and those more interested in rank and salary, proved to be poor candidates for the office and outright negligent in fulfilling their duty and caring for the state of their men's spirits. An officer in the 22nd Massachusetts Infantry bemoaned his experience with such chaplains early in the war:

> *The custom had been to commission, very often, those who had no standing in religious circles at home, and who had been, in many cases, ordained to the ministry for the purpose of being eligible to the coveted positions. This mercenary element would remain with the army in winter quarters, and discharge their nominal duties in a perfunctory way. But when the fighting commenced and they could render inestimable services in caring for the wounded in numberless ways, they would resign, almost en masse. There were notable exceptions to this rule, and those who were faithful are remembered with profound respect and gratitude by those to whom they ministered and by the veterans who knew them. At least seventy-five per cent of the chaplains commissioned during the first year of the war were practically unfit for their work.* [43]

Chaplains such as this caused the demoralization of troops who counted on having a strong spiritual guide among them.

One soldier shared his experience about how a poor chaplain caused great harm to his faith:

> *A stumbling-block.*
>
> *My two young sick friends had been persuaded to lie down, and were now fast asleep, side by side with the wounded. But where was the Chaplain? What had become of him? He had escaped with the earliest dawn, without so much as inquiring whether the men were dead or alive. This was the conduct of a man who professed to be a faithful follower of Him who went about doing good! This was a man whom I had reverenced and loved as a brother in Christ. Oh, what a stumbling-block that man was to my soul; for weeks and months Satan took occasion to make this a severe temptation and trial to me. I was tempted to judge every Christian by that unholy example, and to doubt the truth of every Christian experience which I heard related from time to time. But, thank God, by God's grace I was enabled to rise above this temptation.*
>
> *My doubts were gradually removed, and my faith in Christians re-established; but I never sufficiently recovered from my feelings of disgust towards that particular Chaplain to ever again be able to persuade myself to listen to a sermon delivered by him, or to attend any religious meeting at which he presided. I always looked upon him afterwards as "one who had stolen the livery of heaven to serve the devil in"; a mere whited sepulcher, and unworthy the sacred name of a minister of the Gospel.*
>
> *Oh that he might realize that these were wartimes, and that consequently it was out of the question for Chaplains in the army, especially in time of battle, to*
>
> *"Be carried to the skies on flowery beds of ease;*
>
> *While others fought to win the prize, and sailed through bloody seas."*

From *The National Tribune*, November 10, 1898.

Congress first sought to rectify the problem of deficient chaplains by attempting to drastically reduce the pay rate, with the assumption that lower pay would weed out those inferior chaplains who were seeking an easy salary. But this bill never came to a vote, so Congress passed a bill that tightened the requirements for chaplains by requiring candidates to submit proper credentials and recommendations to be considered for the chaplaincy:

> *No person shall be appointed a chaplain in the United States Army who is not a regularly ordained minister of some religious denomination, and who does not present testimonials of good standing, with recommendation from either some authorized ecclesiastical body, or not less than five accredited ministers belonging to said religious denomination.*[44]

To further strengthen this effort to provide high-quality chaplains to the army, the legislation included instructions to regimental commanders to *"inquire into the fitness, efficiency, and qualifications"* of chaplains, and *"to muster out of service such chaplains [...] who have not faithfully discharged the duties of chaplains."*[45]

These instructions were not always followed because they gave commanders latitude in evaluating chaplains that they were otherwise reluctant to lose, and because the "duties" of chaplains had never been clearly spelled out by the government or the army. However, this legislation did help improve the quality of chaplains as the war progressed. In addition, by changing the language of the earlier act of July 1861—*"a minister of some Christian denomination"* to *"a minister of some religious denomination"*—the congressional act of July 1862 cleared the way for the first Jewish chaplains to serve the Union army.[46]

The 1862 act also included a provision that *"the compensation of chaplains should be one hundred dollars per month and two rations a day when on duty."* [47] One chaplain strongly protested the order for chaplains to be paid only when on duty. As commissioned officers, he argued, they should be entitled to the same privileges as other officers. However, he pointed out, the solicitor of the War Department had decreed that, unlike other officers, the man who has proved himself an accredited minister of Jesus Christ shall not be compensated when on leave for any reason, even to accompany the remains of a soldier home for burial, or to visit a soldier's family, or to be treated for illness or injury.[48]

Despite all these legislative acts, neither the army nor the War Department ever clearly outlined the duties of a chaplain. Yet chaplains were expected to *"enhance the effectiveness of the troops by encouraging them, demonstrating their cause, and stimulating their patriotic loyalty."*[49] For the most part, chaplains worked out their duties and responsibilities according to their desire, as men of the cloth, to care for both the physical and spiritual well-being of the troops, sometimes with the help and guidance of their commanders, and sometimes not. At least one regimental commander wanted to clearly define the duties of his chaplain.

Lt. Col. Charles Tilden of the 16th Maine issued these orders in January 1863:

> *The Chaplain of the Reg't shall have the personal charge, control, and supervision of the postal affairs of the Reg't, attending to the receipt, delivery, and prompt transmission of the regimental mails. He shall receive letters at all times from the officers and soldiers of the Regiment, and shall be supplied with postage stamps to sell to the officers and soldiers who may desire to purchase them. The Chaplain shall have the charge of the religious concerns of the Reg't, visiting the sick in camp or hospital at least once daily and conducting the public religious services of the Regiment. He shall also be an assistant to the Maj. In the sanitary department, reporting promptly to the Maj. all matters requiring attention.*[50]

Unfortunately, many chaplains did not receive guidance or support from either the army or their commanding officers. Chaplain James

Lt. Col. Charles Tilden of the 16th Maine Infantry clearly laid out his expectations for his regiment's chaplain. (Maine Historical Society)

Chaplain James Junius Marks of the 63rd Pennsylvania Infantry was frustrated by the lack of support from the army and his commanding officers. (from *The Peninsula Campaign in Virginia* by Rev. J. J. Marks, D. D)

Junius Marks of the 63rd Pennsylvania Volunteer Infantry expressed his frustration:

> *In many cases, some of the best [chaplains] have suffered months of martyrdom, and nowhere can the chaplain look in hope for help, the government giving him, indeed, his commission, but not assigning his duties, nor compelling the other officers of his regiment to help and sustain him in his work. Their duties are prescribed, definite, and minute; but for him, all is uncertainty.*[51]

Chaplain Edward P. Stone of the 6th Vermont Volunteer Infantry lamented his lack of usefulness in the army:

> *It w[oul]d not do any good I suppose, for me to try to tell you how little there is to encourage me here in the army. No chaplain that I have talked with feels certain at all times that it is of any use for chaplains to be here. Some of them have been here for a month or two without an opportunity to hold a single meeting of any kind or do anything else as a minister (. . .) We can do nothing but pray.*[52]

In a speech given fifty years after he first enrolled as chaplain of the 72nd New York Infantry, William Eastman remembered this feeling of futility:

> *In a little world of most accurate order, where every man's duties and position are absolutely prescribed the chaplain alone has no definite position and no prescribed duties. In a sphere where everything is concentrated on one sole end, he alone finds himself of no direct use towards that end and apparently superfluous.*[53]

Chaplain Frederic Denison of the 1st Rhode Island Cavalry was discouraged to learn that a chaplain had *"no appointment or recognized place . . . on a march, in a bivouac, or in a line of battle; he was a supernumerary, a kind of fifth wheel to a coach, being in place nowhere and out of place everywhere."*[54] The State Military Historian for Massachusetts shared the sentiments of these chaplains:

> *In a little world ruled by clockwork, where in the ordinary camp routine each man had his precise position and every hour its prescribed duties, the chaplain alone held a vague and indefinite place, and had to fill his own hours and lay out his own plan of work. This left his whole sphere of usefulness to be determined by his personal qualities. To the man of strength and tact, this*

freedom was an advantage, and he often created for himself a position of vast influence; but the weak or tactless man found himself pushed aside, the mechanism provided no place for him such as it created for all others; he degenerated into the mere postmaster of the regiment or the caterer for the officers' mess. It was fortunate if actual demoralization did not follow.[55]

One chaplain sought the help of his colonel in trying to infuse some "religious feeling" into the men, with perhaps some unexpected results:

> *One of the Michigan regiments in the Army of the Potomac was brigaded with a Pennsylvania regiment into which their chaplain had infused considerable religious feeling, and several had been baptized. This feeling also prevailed to some extent in other regiments of the brigade but had not taken effect in the Michigan regiment. The chaplain referred to, having the welfare of the Michigan regiment at heart, conceived the idea of calling on the colonel, a soldier from his youth and every inch a man, gruff but brave, not sudden and quick in quarrel, nor full of strange oaths, but bearded, like the Pard; gaining reputation even in the cannon's mouth. Consequently the chaplain waited upon him, calling at his tent and finding him, stated that several members of other regiments of the brigade had recently experienced religion, and [this Pennsylvania chaplain] had baptized fifteen the previous day; remarking also that he was very desirous of a like result in the Michigan regiment, but unless the Colonel made some effort in that direction the regiment would be left behind in the matter. The colonel, a little nettled at what he considered over-zeal of the chaplain, and especially at the idea of having his regiment suspected even of being slow or behind in any respect, started to his feet, called the sergeant major, and hurriedly said: "Give my compliments to the adjutant and direct him to detail immediately with orders to report to the chaplain here, twenty men for baptism; my regiment shall not be beat in any way by any regiment in the brigade." The chaplain gave him one serious look and left quick.*

From Michigan Adjutant General's Office, *Michigan in the War* (Lansing: W. S. George & Co., 1882), 373.

The United States Christian Commission recognized this situation as a failure on the part of the chaplaincy system. Its report given in early 1863 stated, *"the law under which chaplains are appointed defines no position, gives no protection, and prescribes no duties; so that the best men are liable to discouragement under unfavorable local influences."*[56] The solution, said the report, was to supplement the existing army chaplain system by enlisting volunteer chaplains and lay delegates for a period of two to three months from every city or large town, by supplying the vacant pulpits by a system of rotation among other local clergy, and by using commission funds to help defray any expenses the chaplain might incur. The plan was to have one minister and one lay delegate in each brigade so that even those brigades with few or no chaplains would have some kind of spiritual care. Although the commission did send several hundred lay delegates into the field, there is no evidence that this plan to recruit short-term chaplains was successful.

Because of the lack of clear directives regarding a chaplain's duties, two clergymen wrote manuals to help their colleagues. In 1863, the Rev. J. Pinkney Hammond, a chaplain assigned to the general hospital at Chester, Pennsylvania, was frustrated by the lack of army directives regarding the duties of chaplains, so he wrote a booklet designed to help chaplains determine *"the exact routine of labor which, in addition to the public religious services of the camp or hospital, would render the chaplain most useful to those entrusted to his spiritual care."*[57] His 280-page book proposed to *"offer a few suggestions, and to point out certain channels of usefulness which experience has proved to be effective,"*[58] and included everything from army regulations regarding the appointment, pay, and qualifications for chaplains, to an extensive list of duties and suggestions for how to keep soldiers occupied with beneficial games and pastimes.

That same year, the Rev. W. Y. Brown, a chaplain at Douglas Hospital in Washington, wrote another small work upon the subject *"that would 'bring the work [of chaplains] within the requirements of the Army Regulations.'"*[59] Both Hammond and Brown strongly urged chaplains to avoid certain "carnal" duties, as Brown described:

> *A thousand and one matters, which are entirely foreign to the duties of his office, will be constantly pressed upon the attention of the chaplain, and which he will do well to avoid. He is not a common-carrier, an express-man, a post-boy, a claim-agent, a paymaster, a commissary, a quartermaster, an undertaker, a*

banker, a ward-master, a hospital-steward, or a surgeon; and he must not assume the duties of these several officers, although they will be constantly urged upon him. As a rule, he should avoid all matters not legitimately pertaining to the duties of his office.[60]

But many chaplains, especially those who were most respected by the men in their regiments, ignored this advice and did whatever they could to care for the spiritual, physical, and emotional welfare of their soldiers.

Regardless of what the army or the commanders did or did not dictate, chaplains realized that their primary duty was the spiritual well-being of the men in their regiment. They attended to that duty by leading the Divine Service on Sunday mornings, offering the sacraments of Holy Communion and Baptism, providing Bible studies and prayer meetings during the week, offering prayers at dress parades, providing counsel for the men, and visiting the field hospital to minister to the sick and the wounded. Dedicated chaplains soon discovered that many tasks did not fall under the heading of "spiritual care" but were still of much benefit to the soldiers, such as delivering incoming mail and posting or "franking" outgoing mail; writing or reading letters for those who were sick, injured, or illiterate; writing letters to inform families of the deaths of their soldiers; teaching illiterate soldiers to read and write; and providing reading material in the form of religious tracts, pocket Bibles, or any books that might encourage or teach the men.

Sunday morning mass in the Arlington Heights camp of the 69th Regiment of the New York State militia led by Father Thomas H. Mooney, June 1861. (Library of Congress)

Chaplain T. R. Beck of the 13th New Jersey faced some challenges while serving as the regimental postmaster:

> *There had been no mail for several weeks and the boys were getting impatient to hear from home. They fairly pestered the life out of the chaplain to know when the mail would be in. He couldn't go anywhere or attempt to do a thing without meeting some one with the inquiry about mail. There is a limit to the endurance even of clergymen. Getting tired of answering questions the following notice was posted outside the chaplain's tent:*
>
> *"The chaplain does not know when the mail will be in."*
>
> *The boys didn't like this. It was shutting them off too summarily. Finally a wag got a piece of charcoal and made an addition to the sign.*
>
> *All the boys tittered when they saw it, but sneaked out of sight when they saw Colonel Carman approaching. He gave one glance at the sign in front of the tent, and then stuck his head in the opening.*
>
> *"Say, Cap," said he, addressing the chaplain, "what sort of a notice is this you have out there?"*
>
> *"Oh," replied he, "the boys are bothering me so much about the mails that I thought I would post a general answer, so that they may all read it."*
>
> *"But isn't the language rather rough?" inquired the colonel.*
>
> *"It's all right, isn't it?"*
>
> *"Just look at it and see how it reads, Cap."*
>
> *The chaplain stepped out, bareheaded, and this is the sign that met his astonished gaze:*
>
> *"The chaplain does not know when the mail will be in–neither does he care a damn!"*
>
> *That sign came down, and never again did anything of the kind appear in front of his tent.*

From Joseph E. Crowell, *The Young Volunteer* (New York: G. W. Dillingham Co., 1906), 69)

Another important task that some chaplains undertook was delivering the soldiers' pay to their families at home. Chaplain William H. Stevens of the 148th Pennsylvania once traveled to Harrisburg with a muslin bag under his arm containing $75,000 in cash, bound in small packets, all of which Stevens successfully delivered to the correct parties.[61]

Many chaplains (and their regimental commanders) believed that there were three dangerous threats to the morale, discipline, and readiness of troops in camp: the sins of profanity, drunkenness, and gambling. Chaplain H. Clay Trumbull taught his soldiers that having the necessary courage in battle depended on being free from these sins: *"When a soldier is called to face death as a servant of God he must keep himself from evil, so that he may be near to God and trustful in him. Thus pure and thus trustful, he may be fearless and courageous."*[62] Some chaplains sought to eradicate these moral failings by strict measures. Regarding the use of swear words, Chaplain Richard Eddy of the 60th New York Volunteer Infantry suggested to his regimental commander that *"since profanity is such an inexcusable and yet such a heinous sin, that those who use it shall be subjected to the penalty prescribed in the Articles of War."*[63]

Chaplain John Chandler Gregg of the 127th Pennsylvania Volunteer Infantry would have been pleased to see an extreme penalty exacted against two "secesh" Virginians who turned out to be professional gamblers. When these gentlemen strolled into the Union camp and took advantage of the more naïve soldiers, Chaplain Gregg said he wished

A group of officers drinking and playing cards in camp.
(Library of Congress)

that these men (and all their kin) would have been given *"a coat of tar and feathers before mounting them [on a rail]. This would have made a good Sabbath sermon on the sin of gambling and its consequences."*[64]

H. Clay Trumbull took a more lighthearted (and most likely, more successful) approach toward the evils of profanity. As he walked along the picket line one day, he told the men:

> *"I just want to say that the Colonel has detailed me, the chaplain, to do whatever swearing is necessary on this round of picket duty. So if any of you think there is a call for something along that line, just send for me, and I'll attend to it." The men themselves would enter into the spirit of this arrangement, and they would call a man to order if he swore on the picket-line: "Mind your business there! Don't be doing the chaplain's work!"*[65]

As many chaplains realized, a bit of humor could go a long way to get through to the soldiers.

Chaplain T. Scott Bradner of the 124th New York "Orange Blossoms" took his responsibility to curtail swearing among the men very seriously. In a letter home, Sgt. William Bailey of Company K wrote, *"Some of the boys that did not swear when at Goshen are getting so they can do it with out much trouble now. I think they do it because the Col. and other officers do sometimes. I know it is the nature of some, but I am happy to say, it is not mine. You never hear our little Capt. or first Lieut. swear, not a word."*[66] Bradner decided to focus on the poor example set by Col. Van Horne Ellis. *"When [the chaplain] sermonized about the evils of profanity, he made it a point to stand close to [the colonel], who apparently got the message. Soldiers noted that Ellis' intemperate language seemed to be improving. On Sunday, October 5 [1862], Bradner was in especially good form, reading from the 34th Psalm and from Proverbs. Hitting his stride, he 'gave it to them big for swearing.'"*[67]

Soldiers spoke most highly of those chaplains who were not proud or flashy in their religion, who did not take advantage of their

Col. Van Horne Ellis of the 124th New York Infantry, who was known for his tendency toward profanity, was chastised by Chaplain T. Scott Bradner. (Library of Congress)

rank, and who could adapt their religious sensibilities to the realities of serving in the army. William Putnam, the chaplain of the 160th New York Infantry, noted that some people thought *"the office and work of a chaplain in the army in the War of the Rebellion was either only a sinecure, or else an uncertain or unknown quantity. It may have been such in some cases that failed for lack of adaptation to the situation and surroundings."*[68] When the 145th Pennsylvania Volunteer Infantry was enduring its hard marches to Gettysburg, Chaplain John H. W. Stuckenberg would often walk beside the men and allow an exhausted soldier to ride his horse. Chaplain Charles L. Hagar of the 118th New York received very high praise from Maj. John Cunningham: *"Our Chaplain is more than a 'Sunday man,' is busy in making himself useful every day. Comforting the sick, writing their letters, cheering the discouraged and 'home-sickers,' caring for our mail and giving much of willing and needed service."*[69] In addition, officers and soldiers alike would greatly admire any chaplain who would not think that it was beneath his religion to carry some whiskey to give to injured men, especially on the battlefield.

Because chaplains were noncombatants whose primary concern was the well-being and morale of the troops rather than their ability to drill, shoot, and follow orders, they held a unique place in their regiment, as Chaplain Trumbull of the 10th Connecticut described:

> *[The chaplain] was a commissioned officer, yet without command. He could be welcomed alike by a major general or by a second lieutenant without the fear of any seeming incongruity of association. Yet he could be among the enlisted men as one entirely with them in sympathy, without any thought on the part of either that he was stepping out of his sphere or crossing the line which divided commissioned officers as a class from enlisted men as a class.*[70]

In addition, tending to soldiers who were wounded or dying gave chaplains access to the intimate and religious thoughts and feelings of the men, for it was in these moments that a man's faith, or lack of it, or desire for it, would often be expressed. Thus, chaplains were well situated to discern the "moral and religious condition" of the men in their care and to understand what the soldiers were thinking and feeling before, during, and after battle.

Despite being noncombatants, some chaplains chose to fight alongside their men. The Military Historian for Massachusetts believed that frustration over the lack of support and direction from the army and their superiors would stifle *"the very spirit of adventure, [which] having no legitimate channel,"* would lead some chaplains to seek out risky and dangerous situations.[71] Other chaplains were driven to pick up a musket and go into battle out of a sense of solidarity and loyalty to their men. At least one chaplain was killed in action while fighting with his regiment.

In December 1862, Chaplain Arthur Buckminster Fuller of the 16th Massachusetts was compelled by ill health to ask for a discharge from his duties. He received an honorable discharge on December 10. The next day, a call went out for volunteers to cross the Rappahannock River into Fredericksburg, which was held by well-concealed Confederate infantrymen and sharpshooters. Although Fuller was under no further obligation to the army, he volunteered to go with other members of his regiment to make this dangerous crossing.

> *He volunteered, musket in hand, and crossed the river in safety; but fell soon after entering Fredericksburg, pierced with two bullets, the one entering his chest through his arm upraised to discharge the musket, the other piercing his hip. A third bullet struck his breast laterally, tearing his coat and vest, but inflicting no wound.*

The men whom Fuller had accompanied came under the same heavy fire and were ordered to fall back, leaving the chaplain's body lying on the streets of Fredericksburg until another regiment was sent forward an hour later and was able to retrieve him. Unfortunately, Confederate soldiers had had time to rob his body of the few precious things he had planned to carry home.

From *Chaplain Fuller; Being a Life Sketch of a New England Clergyman and Army Chaplain* by Richard F. Fuller (Boston: Walker, Wise, and Company, 1864).

Chaplain Arthur Buckminster Fuller of the 16th Massachusetts Infantry was killed while fighting alongside his men at Fredericksburg in December 1862. (from Chaplain Fuller; *Being a Life Sketch of a New England Clergyman and Army Chaplain* by Richard F. Fuller)

Many chaplains came from a church in a town or city where a regiment was recruited, so they had preexisting relationships with the soldiers' families and often assumed a paternal attitude toward these young men who were far from home, many for the first time.[72] This gave chaplains opportunities to develop intimate relationships with soldiers in a way that was not possible or advisable for other officers. Soldiers would be more willing to share thoughts and feelings with their chaplains that they might be reluctant to share with their commanders or even with each other. By reason of being commissioned officers who could at the same time mingle and speak freely with the soldiers as comrades, and who could be trusted by virtue of their pastoral office to keep confidences, some men would use their chaplain as a sounding board for everything they believed was unsatisfactory regarding their commanders or their government. And sometimes, chaplains would relay these grievances via letters to the editors of newspapers back home, often including their own frank observations about the army, its commanders, and the condition of the fighting men and the challenges they faced. Chaplains felt free to do so because they sat outside the chain of command and had no authority to issue orders, and thus were not amenable to the United States government or the War Department like other enlisted men and officers.[73] Unlike commanders, who answered to their superiors or to their state patrons, and thus had a vested interest in producing reports that would shine the most complimentary light on their units, chaplains were accountable to a different flock, namely the families of the wounded and slain soldiers, the parishioners who would one day welcome them back to their churches, and denominational superiors, all of whom would expect the highest degree of truthfulness from these men of the cloth.

Most chaplains also knew they answered to greater authorities than those in the army, and would have agreed with Father Thomas Scully, the chaplain of the

Father Thomas Scully of the 9th Massachusetts Infantry claimed a higher authority than even the president! (Library of Congress)

famed 9th Massachusetts Irish regiment, when he proclaimed, *"I have a higher rank than the president or the congress of the United States can give to man! I labor in the service of God. He is my paymaster."*[74]

And chaplains knew that their God would certainly hold them accountable to the accuracy and veracity of their writings.

Chaplain William R. Eastman of the 72nd New York Volunteer Infantry summarized the place, role, and significance of chaplains in a speech he delivered fifty years after the war:

> *In one word, the significance of the chaplaincy was this: that the government offered to each regiment one man to be a friend to every man. While other officers might be good friends, this man was to make a business of kindliness. Not a commander, not a fighter, not hemmed in by any rules or any rank; left to himself to reach men by their hearts if he touched them at all, and by their hearts to make them better soldiers; a man to be sought in the hour of need; to stand for truth, purity, and all righteousness; for honorable living and hopeful dying; and having done all to stand by, in the spirit of service, according to the pattern of the Master.*[75]

In all of this, chaplains had to learn, usually through a baptism of fire, how to be in ministry in situations for which they were thoroughly unprepared, including a heated and distressing religious atmosphere in which clergymen and congregations had taken up opposing and seemingly unreconcilable sides.

Although chaplains were not called to face the dangers of the front line or picket post, all of them shared the collective pain of battle and its gruesome aftermath. Some of them sacrificed much on the altars of war and their duty to God and the soldiers. Physical wounds and disease affected a few, cutting short their time of enlistment. Spiritual and emotional wounds affected many others as they watched their men enter the fray only to be brutally cut down and unceremoniously buried without even the benefit of a prayer uttered over the body. Some chaplains left the pastoral ministry after their time of service in the army, and at least a few were documented to have experienced what we would call post-traumatic stress. Chaplain Stuckenberg's depiction of how soldiers feel and think after a battle may also describe how chaplains were affected by what they experienced:

> *What they have seen and heard is indescribable, but it haunts them till the day of their death–and they are changed beings, and can*

never again be what they were. Thought has been busy, hurried, distracted and anxious; feeling has been excited, deep, and intense, and painful; and an impression has been made that can never be effaced, and which must either lead a man nearer to God, or petrify his heart.[76]

Above all, most chaplains did their best to hold fast to their faith that God was working out his purposes even if those purposes were hidden from ordinary men and required so many to suffer and die. At least a few chaplains sacrificed more than others, including their lives and their personal freedom.

The Theological Climate of the Mid-Nineteenth Century

The years leading up to the Civil War created a theological crisis as clergy and churches in the North and the South became increasingly polarized over political and social issues, especially slavery. By 1845, the three largest Protestant denominations—Methodist, Presbyterian, and Baptist—had split into Northern and Southern denominations that supported the causes of their respective sections. Southern clergy could cite passages of scripture that seemed to clearly condone (or at least tolerate) slavery, but those in the North needed to find ways to interpret the Bible to support the cry for abolition. While clergy in both the North and the South pounded their pulpits and proclaimed their interpretation of

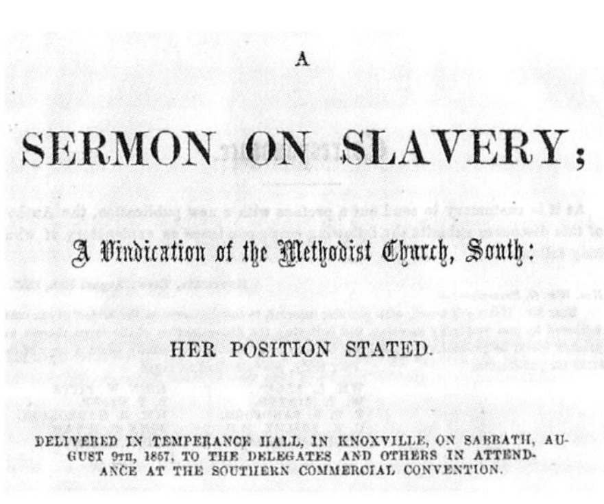

A

SERMON ON SLAVERY;

A Vindication of the Methodist Church, South:

HER POSITION STATED.

DELIVERED IN TEMPERANCE HALL, IN KNOXVILLE, ON SABBATH, AUGUST 9TH, 1857, TO THE DELEGATES AND OTHERS IN ATTENDANCE AT THE SOUTHERN COMMERCIAL CONVENTION.

Pastors in the South preached sermons that defended slavery as a divinely ordered system and railed against the abolitionists in the North. (Library of Congress)

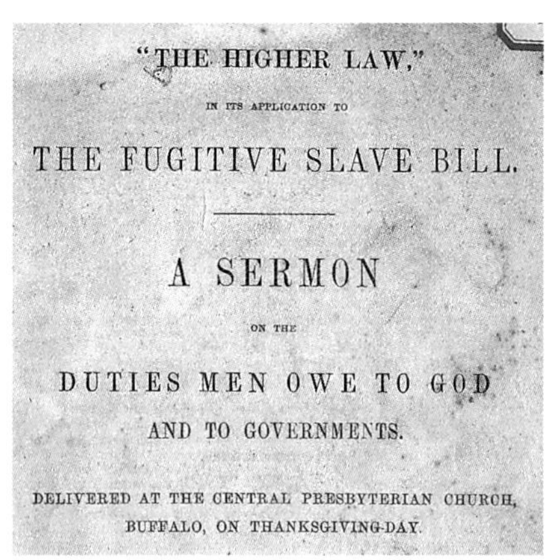

"THE HIGHER LAW,"

IN ITS APPLICATION TO

THE FUGITIVE SLAVE BILL.

A SERMON

ON THE

DUTIES MEN OWE TO GOD

AND TO GOVERNMENTS.

DELIVERED AT THE CENTRAL PRESBYTERIAN CHURCH, BUFFALO, ON THANKSGIVING-DAY.

Pastors in the North preached against slavery and cited "the Higher Law." (Temple University Digital Collections)

scripture, which affirmed that God was on their side, chaplains faced the challenge of preparing men for the rigors of campaign and battle.

Some chaplains saw the coming battle as a religious war or even a crusade. At the outset of the war, Chaplain A. M. Stewart affirmed that *"the present war is, in many of its aspects, a religious one. It is a battle for truth and righteousness–for liberty against despotism."* [77] In a letter requesting appointment as a chaplain, he argued that it was vitally important to remind soldiers of this religious nature of their nation's cause because *"those who fight for a religious principle are mighty in the day of battle."* [78]

In the context of these religious principles, secession was considered not just rebellion against the Constitution, but also against the nation that had been established to carry out God's divine purposes. From the earliest settlements in this New World, people believed they were carrying out those purposes by establishing a nation given to them by God. Puritan leaders reminded those who would settle in this land in the 1630s that their undertaking was a divinely ordained mission.

In early 1861 before the war broke out, the Rev. Francis Vinton preached a sermon in which he declared the sanctity of the nation: *"The people of these United States, under the Federal Constitution, are ONE NATION, organic, corporate, divinely established, subject to government, and bound in conscience to obedience. Disloyalty to the Constitution, is, therefore, impiety toward God."* [79]

Theological considerations aside, chaplains quickly learned to adapt their ministry to the realities of army life in camp, campaign, and battle. Thoughtful chaplains realized that the kind of sermons and forms of care and comfort that worked well among their parishioners at home were not suitable for men in an army. As Chaplain Trumbull noted,

> *Old sermons, preached in the quiet of home life, or in the self-seeking struggles of business and money-getting activities, were not adapted to the needs and trials of men who had left home behind them, and were living and dying in self-sacrificing devotion to their God-given government and their loved and imperiled country.* [80]

Rev. Francis Vinton spoke out in defense of the nation he loved. (*The Vinton Memorial* by John Adams Vinton)

As far as many chaplains were concerned, appeals for patriotic devotion to the nation's divine cause or chest-thumping calls to put down the rebellion did not prepare soldiers to fight as well as did the assurance of God's ever-present help and promise of a heavenly reward for faithful duty. However, not all chaplains, especially at the beginning of the war when the quality of chaplains was poor, were adept at giving messages that would inspire the soldiers. At least one chaplain simply pulled an old sermon from his "barrel" without thought to how it could benefit men in an army: *"The preacher took an old piece of faded yellow manuscript and (. . .) discussed <u>infant baptism</u> and closed with an earnest appeal, touchingly eloquent, to <u>mothers</u>! (. . .) I'm sure there wasn't a mother in the regiment (. . .) and not more than two or three infants!"*[81]

The bias, or agenda, of chaplains concerning battle was not a single-minded focus to direct the soldiers in their duty to annihilate the enemy while dodging flying pieces of lead, but to ensure that the men would have strong faith that would enable them to face the dangers of the battlefield, trusting in what Chaplain William R. Eastman of the 74th New York Infantry called a "hopeful dying" if they were to fall.[82] Chaplains did this by assuring the soldiers that Divine Providence was in control of all things, including the outcome of battles, which enabled the soldiers to do their duty trusting that whatever happened was God's will. As Chaplain Trumbull preached, *"success in every righteous conflict depends on God."*[83] Chaplains also reminded the men that God's will was inescapable. If God destined a certain man to fall at a certain time, there was no way to avoid that divine edict.

Chaplains appealed to the belief system that was nurtured by the Second Great Awakening. This was a religious revival that occurred in the early nineteenth century and was grounded in an evangelical theology that emphasized the possibility of personal redemption from sin and the promise of an eternal reward in heaven, as opposed to the Reformed idea of predestination, which taught that God alone chooses who is "destined" for salvation. Chaplains helped the men to understand that even though they might die because God's will ordained it, they could trust that through personal repentance and faith, they would receive salvation and entrance into their heavenly home.

The emphasis on death and dying came naturally to chaplains; in their pastoral ministry they would have had much experience with it among their parishioners. *Ars moriendi*, the art of dying well, had been a bedrock of Christian teaching and practice since the Middle Ages,

This is a small oil sketch of a 15- by 20-foot fresco in the former Camp Curtin Memorial Methodist Episcopal Church in Harrisburg. The church was built in the 1890s on the site of a Union army recruiting and training camp, and when it was expanded in 1915 it was dedicated as a memorial to all Civil War–era soldiers. Civil War orphan and artist C. Day Rudy was commissioned to paint this mural for the sanctuary. The image of Christ appearing to a fallen soldier represents what chaplains wanted to give their men: assurance that even if they fell in battle, Christ would be with them to comfort them. (Susquehanna Conference United Methodist Church Archives)

and it still held a prominent place in the nineteenth-century American religious environment. But in the army, chaplains perhaps found more urgent reasons to teach this art and to help soldiers face death with hope and not fear. Sermons and bedside exhortations and private counsel focused on removing the fear of death so soldiers could perform their duty trusting that no matter what happened, and especially if they fell, they could, indeed, die well and gain the promised heavenly reward. Soldiers *"needed to be both willing and ready to die,"*[84] and it was the duty of chaplains to provide them with both the will and the readiness. Good dying would also assure family and friends at home that their loved one died without fear or despair. As Chaplain Trumbull noted, *"a Christian soldier can anticipate that with a measure of restful satisfaction, and his loved ones can look back upon it with a sense of its exalted fitness."*[85] Helping soldiers readily accept the possibility of death (for the sake of cause, nation, and God) would also even the moral scales of killing: *"Focusing on dying rather than on the killing enabled soldiers to mitigate their terrible responsibility for the slaughter of others."*[86] Finally, trusting that their comrades died "well" could help soldiers through the aftermath of a battle by giving some sense of meaning to these deaths.

One poignant scene of dying well occurred at the bedside of a young soldier from the 2nd Massachusetts Infantry at a field hospital at Gettysburg. He had been shot in the lung and lingered two weeks under the care of an unnamed "soldier-loving chaplain" who kept reminding the boy of the faith and love of Jesus that he had earlier professed to the chaplain.

> *On being told he was dying, he said, half-conscious, chanting in measured cadence, "I've–got–to–die." This he repeated many times; and then in cadence still more thrilling, "I'm–willing–to–die [. . .] I'm prepared–better prepared" than some of his fellow soldiers at the point of death like himself, who had been thoughtless and irreligious. With these broken words–"better prepared–better prep," his lips refused further utterance [and] his pallid features glowed with seraphic radiance, and his spirit soon passed away.*[87]

By contrast, a lack of faith might leave soldiers to die not well, but in the throes of doubt and anxiety. Chaplain John H. W. Stuckenberg described how the thought of dying affected the soldiers in his care:

> *Just before entering the field of battle, the conscience of a man, not altogether dead to religion, is unusually active. He will ask himself*

how his account stands with his Maker, in whose presence he may soon be called to appear. The past will roll its burden of sin upon him, and hang heavily on his soul. His besetting sin will stand between him and his God to disturb his peace. Then, if ever, there will be keen anguish of soul, deep regrets and an earnest desire for purity of heart.[88]

The chaplain's task was to ensure that a man would not need to enter the fray with the "burden of sin" hanging upon him, thus preventing both his ability fight well and, if necessary, die well. When Father William Corby offered his famous general absolution to the Irish Brigade before they advanced into the Wheatfield at Gettysburg, this was his purpose: to ensure that the men, Roman Catholic or not, would know that if they were to fall, their sins would be forgiven and they should have no fear of death or damnation.[89] As one Confederate soldier proclaimed, *"Christians make the best soldiers, as they would not fear the consequences of death as others would."*[90] Many Union soldiers likely felt the same way. And although a man might be a good fighting man without the assurance of faith, the lack of it could cause a soldier to face death not with the hope of eternal peace, but with anger and agitation of the spirit:

There are sounds in battle more fearful than the shrieking of shells, the whistling of bullets, the rattling of musketry, the thunder of cannon, the unavailing cries for help, and the groans of the wounded and dying; they are the horrid oaths uttered there by the wounded and dying, sometimes polluting the lips with the last breath with which the soul passes from the body to the judgment seat of Him whose name he profaned.[91]

For some men in the ranks, their chaplains represented both God's presence among them and God's sanction for their cause:

There were times when the very presence of the chaplain with his regiment on the eve of battle, or while already under fire, was inspiriting to officers and men, who were encouraged to feel that they had God's blessing while one of God's representatives was immediately with them.[92]

Although most chaplains believed that being "God's representatives" among the soldiers meant honoring their position as noncombatants, there were a few who were willing to do anything asked of them, including taking up arms and joining the men in the line of fire. When Chaplain Stewart proposed his services to the 102nd Pennsylvania Infantry, he assured the regimental commander that *"should you require me to wield the sword or handle the rifle, I would have no hesitancy."*[93] Chaplain Lorenzo Barber of the 2nd U.S. Sharpshooters (a unit of renowned marksmen) had been recruited because of his superior skills with a rifle and became known as the "Fighting Parson." His courage under fire inspired his men: *"That chaplain practices what he preaches. He tells us what we should do and goes with us to the very front to help us in battle."*[94]

The theological crisis created by the war affected almost every aspect of the lives of many soldiers and their families. Even President Lincoln, who was by no means a staunchly religious man, recognized this theological crisis created by divisions and debates within the Christian community. In his second inaugural address, he acknowledged the challenges faced by all faithful people:

> *Both read the same Bible and pray to the same God, and each invokes His aid against the other. It may seem strange that any men should dare to ask a just God's assistance in wringing their bread from the sweat of other men's faces, but let us judge not, that we be not judged. The prayers of both could not be answered. That of neither has been answered fully. The Almighty has His own purposes.*[95]

The unique challenge for chaplains was to sustain the men in their regiments and to strengthen their faith and courage until those divine purposes were finally worked out, no matter how much blood and suffering it might cost along the way.

In October 1889, Gen. Joshua L. Chamberlain, who had commanded the 20th Maine Infantry at Gettysburg, gave a speech at the dedication of the Maine monuments on that battlefield in which he said, *"In great deeds something abides."*[96] Years after the war, Joseph Sanderson, former chaplain of the 3rd Pennsylvania Artillery, reflected on that abiding essence of the chaplains' service:

> *I submit that among the wholesome results wrought into our nation by and through the Civil War, there was a strongly marked moral fiber woven into the soldier, and by example extended into our citizenry, due to a larger extent than it is ordinarily conceded, to the good offices of the ideal chaplain.*[97]

Some chaplains left memoirs, some authored regimental histories, and a few wrote letters to family, friends, and newspapers describing their experiences. The stories of some chaplains are all but lost to history, with only fragmentary information about their lives and their service, but the existing accounts reveal the distinctive way chaplains reported what they saw and did before, during, and after a battle. According to Allen Thompson, *"history [. . .] is the memory of the perception of events"* and this perception varies according to the *"biases, experiences, time, [and] physical viewpoint"* of each individual.[98] Chaplains' perceptions and assessments were influenced by several aspects of their position, their sense of duty, and their physical location during a battle.

First, chaplains held a unique position within their regiments and enjoyed special relationships with the soldiers in their care. Unlike other officers, they had access to the intimate thoughts, feelings, and expressions of faith of the soldiers, all of which shaped their viewpoint during a battle and its aftermath. In addition, many of the quotes from chaplains in this book come from letters written immediately following the battle or other event. Their personal memories were still fresh and had not been diminished by the passing of time. And most of their letters were composed while the chaplains were still working in the field or in the hospitals, so their descriptions of what they saw and heard (and smelled, in many cases) were well-grounded in the scenes that surrounded them. Finally, as noted, the chaplains' unique bias or agenda as a spiritual presence and guide rather than as an officer with command authority affected the ways they understood and processed what they experienced.

Of the more than 275 Army of the Potomac infantry and cavalry regiments involved in the Gettysburg campaign, only about 134 had chaplains with them during the battle.[99] In the following chapters, we will meet some of these men and see how their accounts can help us better understand not only the Battle of Gettysburg and its aftermath but also the unique perspective of chaplains. As Chaplain William Eastman noted, *"many men who undertook the service [of chaplain] fell short, perhaps far short of their opportunities; but many also gained for themselves much love and a good name and a share in the final triumph."*[100] The stories of the chaplains who were at Gettysburg reveal that most, if not all of them, gained that good name through the courage and faithfulness they demonstrated while serving their men and their cause during those brutal three days of fighting and their aftermath in July 1863.

The following chapters cover each of the seven infantry corps and the cavalry corps of the Army of the Potomac, and only those forty-nine chaplains who left a record of some kind about their time at Gettysburg are included in their respective chapters. The names of those chaplains for whom no personal record of their service could be found are included in the appendix.

"The Chaplain at Gettysburg" by William A. Smith. (US Army Chaplain Museum, Fort Jackson, SC)

Chapter 2:

The First Corps

CORPS COMMANDERS:

Major General John Fulton Reynolds
Major General Abner Doubleday
Major General John Newton

The First Corps was the first infantry unit from the Army of the Potomac to arrive at Gettysburg on July 1, 1863. It was part of the left wing of the Army of the Potomac, which also included the Third and Eleventh Corps, with Maj. Gen. John F. Reynolds acting as wing commander.[1]

Most of the corps spent the night of June 30 camped about five miles south of Gettysburg. It was ordered to advance in the morning to support the two brigades of Brig. Gen. John Buford's cavalry division that were positioned about a mile west of the town. Two brigades of the First Corps reached the fields west of town by midmorning and immediately went into action to the north and south of the Chambersburg Pike.

As Reynolds shouted, *"Forward men, forward for God's sake, and drive those fellows out of the woods,"* the Iron Brigade (the First Brigade of the First Division) dashed into Herbst's Woods and collided with the advancing Confederates.[2] Moments later, Reynolds was killed by a minié ball that entered the back of his head, and Maj. Gen. Abner Doubleday assumed command of the field.

Reinforced by four more brigades that arrived by midday, the First Corps formed a line along McPherson's Ridge from Herbst's Woods south of the pike toward Oak Hill to the north, where they were assaulted by Confederates advancing from both the west and the north.

Maj. Gen. John F. Reynolds was killed soon after his men went into battle on July 1. ("The Fall of Reynolds," Library of Congress)

The Union troops held their positions throughout the afternoon until they were overwhelmed by elements of four Confederate divisions and were finally pushed back through town about 4:00 p.m. The shattered remnants of the corps rallied on Cemetery Hill along with the Eleventh Corps, which had fought north of town that afternoon. For the next two days of the battle, one division of the First Corps was on Culp's Hill supporting the Twelfth Corps, and the other two divisions were positioned along Cemetery Ridge to support the Union center, where they played a role in repulsing Confederate assaults on July 2 and 3.[3]

Over the course of the three days, the First Corps suffered a casualty rate of more than 49 percent, the highest of any Union corps, with most of those casualties occurring on July 1. Although these troops had been forced to retreat that day, they had fought hard to hold back the Confederates while the rest of the army rushed toward Gettysburg, and, along with the Eleventh Corps, they formed the basis of the "fishhook" position of the Army of the Potomac that was one of the keys to the eventual Union victory.

FIRST DIVISION:

Brigadier General James S. Wadsworth

First Brigade:

Brigadier General Solomon Meredith

The Iron Brigade had won its moniker for the way the soldiers demonstrated steadfast courage under fire at the Battle of South Mountain in September 1862. At Gettysburg, the brigade rushed into Herbst's Woods on the morning of July 1 and collided with Confederate troops, pushing them back west of Willoughby Run. Occupying an exposed position for most of the day, the Midwesterners of the Iron Brigade held on stubbornly until the crushing weight of fresh Confederate troops forced them back. They retreated slowly toward the Lutheran Theological Seminary, holding their line until the entire First Corps line fell back through town about 4:00 p.m. On July 2 and 3, the Iron Brigade occupied the western slope of Culp's Hill, facing north, where they were not actively engaged.[4]

Of the five regiments in the western brigade—the 2nd, 6th, and 7th Wisconsin, 19th Indiana, and 24th Michigan—three of them had chaplains with them at Gettysburg, all of whom left a written record of their service.

Samuel Witt Eaton, 7th Wisconsin Volunteer Infantry

Samuel Witt Eaton was born on his family's farm in Framingham, Massachusetts, on December 25, 1820. After completing his theological studies, he was licensed to preach by the Congregational Church in 1844. Having determined to devote his life to work in the Mississippi Valley, he settled in Lancaster, Wisconsin. He married Catherine Elizabeth Demarest in 1847 and was ordained as an evangelist a year later. After several years of

Chaplain Samuel Witt Eaton of the 7th Wisconsin Infantry. (Wisconsin Historical Society)

ministry, he was compelled by failing health to return east. After recuperating, he traveled in Europe for a year and then resumed his parish ministry in Lancaster in 1858.

Edward Dwight Eaton, Samuel's son, described how his father came to be chaplain of the 7th Wisconsin Infantry:

> *When the war had been waged for about a year there was an unexpected crisis in the home of the pastor. An official letter from the Seventh Wisconsin Regiment, at the front of the Army of the Potomac, brought word that the soldiers of the regiment had been asked to express their choice for a chaplain and they had voted for the Lancaster minister who many of them knew and honored; an invitation was extended to him by the authorities to accept the chaplaincy of the regiment, which had already won distinction as one of the four regiments constituting the famous Iron Brigade, which General Grant afterwards was to value so highly and praise so unreservedly.*
>
> *There could be no question as to what answer should be made to this invitation. Friends and parents of the boys at the front were eager to have such ministry for them. "You have a call now, if you never had one in your life before," said Mr. Barber [a friend and church member], with characteristic mingling of humor and emotion. The members of the church were sure they ought to spare their pastor for this patriotic service, and not less sure that their minister's wife could keep things going in the church during his absence; and the war might not last more than a few months longer. So the quiet scenes of pastoral life were exchanged for the vivid experiences of camp and battlefield.*[5]

Edward Dwight Eaton, son of Chaplain Eaton.
(from *Commemorative Biographical Record of the Counties of Rock, Green, Grant, Iowa and Lafayette, Wisconsin*)

In July 1862, Eaton was commissioned as chaplain of the Seventh, and he remained in service with the regiment until the end of the war, seeing the men through several bloody battles. Eaton became a respected chaplain among the Wisconsin regiments in the Iron Brigade, which *"had varying experiences with their chaplains [and] the Seventh fared the best."*[6]

Eaton composed a manuscript that described his experiences from the time he was mustered into the regiment until he was mustered out in July 1865. He touches only briefly on the actual Battle of Gettysburg but wrote more extensively about the things he saw in the succeeding days and weeks.

Eaton's account of the Gettysburg campaign begins on June 12, when he recounted a sad event that took place during the march north:

> *I witnessed the execution of John P. Woods of the 19th Indiana, for desertion. A chaplain knelt with him, and he offered a penitent prayer. He would have preferred not to have had his arms confined, but Lieutenant Rogers could not take the responsibility of permitting it. His breast was laid bare, and was pierced by several shots, and he fell backwards from his coffin. The Lieutenant, observing that he moved, ordered others to fire, and his brain was pierced. We left immediately, while men were hastily digging the grave.*[7]

Execution of Private Woods of the 19th Indiana Infantry, June 12, 1863, for desertion (from *History of the Twenty-Fourth Michigan of the Iron Brigade* by O. B. Curtis)

The narrative picks up again on Sunday, July 4, the day after the battle: *"This day is made more illustrious than before by our great victory, accomplished by the fighting of the last three days. My regiment moves with the army, but I remain to care for the wounded."*[8] Eaton described coming across a corporal from his regiment who suffered from a mortal abdominal wound:

> *I found him reading a testament which I had given him, and which, though badly soiled, afforded him true comfort. He became interested in religion last winter, and has tried to live a Christian life since. On my first visit, he said that he should not wish to get well, if he knew he was prepared to die. On my last, early in the day on which he died, he assured me that he did not fear to die, and seemed pleased that he was almost home. I call again in the afternoon, and find the glassy eyes of the morning closed.*[9]

Eaton's good friend Lt. Col. John B. Callis was gravely wounded on July 1, and when the colonel's wife learned the news in a letter from Eaton, she rushed to Gettysburg. In a letter to his own wife, Eaton wrote: *"It is pleasant to be able to show the grave of James Gow to Mrs. Callis in a Presbyterian church yard, while so many have been buried in an open field and so many cannot be identified by any inscription. Men are here searching for the bodies of friends; one man offers $20 for the discovery."*[10]

A few days after the battle, Eaton ministered to a distraught father:

> *A Mr. Alcorn came from his home beyond Pittsburgh, and took up the body of his son, which had been buried, and had it interred in a lot which he purchased in the Gettysburg cemetery, together with the body of a son of his friend. After I had offered prayer at the grave, Mr. A and a remaining son embraced each other and wept. The three young men all belonged to battery B.*[11]

Lt. Col. John B. Callis of the 7th Wisconsin Infantry, a good friend of Chaplain Eaton, was seriously wounded on July 1. (Minnesota Historical Society)

Before Eaton left Gettysburg to rejoin his regiment in Virginia, he reflected on the battle in which more than 60 percent of the men in his brigade were counted as casualties:

How remarkable the favoring Providences connected us to this battle: much cool, wet weather for the march and battle, and for the wounded; the 1st Corps, with the 11th, arriving just in time to check the enemy before he had gained the strong position which we subsequently occupied; these corps giving battle almost recklessly and being repulsed, which put us on the defensive in a strong position, and made the enemy the attacking party; General Ewell neglecting to follow us to the heights on the day that he gained the advantage, affording time for the other corps to come up, and for fortifying.

The question was whether the wall of living flesh would stand immovable, like the stone walls behind which some of our men were posted, and which had been partly built by them, or whether those living stones would recoil at the shock of so many hundreds of cannon and thousands of muskets. The heroism of some regiments, fighting until nearly annihilated, was scarcely inferior to the most remarkable Greek valor. The 2nd Wisconsin, of my Brigade, was reduced from two hundred and forty-seven enlisted men to thirty-four. Co. C of that Regiment numbered after the battle but two.[12]

Eaton visited the field where his regiment fought on July 1 and recorded his thoughts about the battle scars left on the landscape:

Trees, dead or wounded, told how fierce the struggle had been. A fortnight after the battle the groves looked as if a fire had run through them, their part of the foliage being dead, innumerable small withered branches or hanging down, and those which had been entirely shot off almost formed a carpet on the ground in some places. Some large oaks had died in consequence of receiving so many rifle shots. The tops of trees had been broken off at points where they were from six inches to a foot in diameter, and in some instances were hanging down and in others lying on the ground. On our left there was a tree, probably about two feet in diameter, which a shell had passed entirely through. The trees were riven as by lightning.[13]

Although the Army of the Potomac had gained the victory, Eaton wondered if the cost in human lives was worth it: "*On rejoining my Regiment on the Rappahannock it was affecting to reflect that so many members of the soldier congregation with whom I commenced my labors a year ago, are of the dead. What measure of activity could satisfy one where men die so fast.*"[14]

The Grand Review of the Army of the Potomac, Washington, May 1865, with banner from schoolchildren welcoming the "Heroes of the Republic." (Library of Congress)

At the grand review of the Army of the Potomac in Washington in May 1865 following the Confederate surrender at Appomattox, Eaton and his comrades were profoundly moved by what they experienced:

> *What affected us most was to see the children of the public schools in spring attire, at the North Portico of the Capitol, with wreaths and bouquets and flags. They sang the Star Spangled Banner, the Battle Cry of Freedom, and Victory at Last. We had not been accustomed to children in the army, and the sight made some of our men weep.*[15]

Eaton's service to the men at Gettysburg received praise from Col. William W. Robinson, the commander of the 7th Wisconsin, who acknowledged the chaplain in a report to the governor:

> *I must here be allowed to bear testimony to the valuable services of our very worthy Chaplain, Rev. Samuel W. Eaton. During such times as we have just passed through, as well as the quiet times in camp, he promptly and cheerfully attends to the sick and wounded, and freely performs any other necessary duties compatible with his*

position, and does not hesitate to follow us to the battle-field in the performance of such duties.[16]

Edward Eaton, the chaplain's son, also commended his father's courageous service: *"At Gettysburg in his ministrations to the wounded he so exposed himself that his colonel felt constrained to order him off the firing line."*[17]

His duty to his nation and the men in his regiment fulfilled, Eaton returned home on July 14, 1865, realizing that *"an experience of three years in the army may well enhance one's estimate of woman and society, of wife and children, of housekeeping and cookery, and of peace."*[18] After the war, Eaton resumed his ministry and served the church at Lancaster for another twenty years. In 1886 he accepted the call of the Congregational Church at Roscoe, Illinois, where he served for sixteen more years. In the autumn of 1903, he moved to Beloit, Wisconsin, to be near his son. Samuel Witt Eaton died at the age of eighty-four at the home of another son in Newton Highlands, Massachusetts, on February 9, 1905. He and his wife, Catharine Elizabeth, had four sons, two of whom followed their father's footsteps into the ministry, while the other two became physicians. Mrs. Eaton died in February 1904.

Just before the Battle of Fredericksburg in December 1862, Chaplain Eaton sent a letter to a newspaper that included a typical observation of a chaplain who was aware of the spiritual and moral health of his men:

> *On the eve of battle a soldier will sometimes put his pocket book into the hands of the Chaplain with a word and a tear, or a manner which expresses more than both. At such a moment hearts touch that had hardly recognized their kindred humanity before. Refinement does not separate itself from rudeness; even the pious and the profane have some heart throbs which are similar. In the immediate presence of a great common danger a man is simply and only a man, except as trust in the Mighty One makes him greater; and it is found and felt that the most unworthy have something of their humanity left, to which possibly the good may yet make its appeal not in vain.*[19]

There is very little biographical information available for Thomas Barnett. He was born in Ohio on July 17, 1833, and became a Methodist pastor. He accepted the position of chaplain for the 19th Indiana in April 1863. Amazingly, while the Battle of Gettysburg was still raging on July 2, Barnett found time to compose a letter to the *Indianapolis Journal*, the only example of his writing regarding Gettysburg that could be located:

Chaplain Thomas Barnett of the 19th Indiana Infantry. (Archives of the United Methodist Church)

> *Editor Journal: Permit me to drop a word of information to the many friends of officers and men of the 19th Indiana Regiment, through your valuable paper.*
>
> *I could not exaggerate the bravery of the officers and men. They, without an exception yet known, were all found at their respective posts, and although led immediately into a murderous fire, without time to adjust their pieces, yet they stood up boldly and manfully. Colonel Williams was in the thickest of the fight from the commencement and could be seen, frequently in the advance of the regiment, making observations for the success and safety of his men. He very narrowly escaped twice, a ball passing through his hat and another struck his side, and was prevented, doubtless, from killing him by a pocket map which it struck, penetrating his coat and nearly through his map, lodging in the last fold. The Colonel has never taken the ball out of the map, but keeps it as it was.*

Col. S. J. Williams of the 19th Indiana Infantry was saved from death when a minié ball was stopped by a folded map in his pocket. (Library of Congress)

Lieut. Col. W. W. Dudley fell severely if not mortally wounded early in the day, while urging forward his men. Major John M. Lindley was severely wounded in the hand, the ball striking his hand and saber. While waving his saber over his head another ball struck him on the cheek, just grazing the skin. The Major, we hope will soon recover. Adjutant George W. Finney was slightly wounded.

The Surgeon and First Assistant Surgeon are in the hands of the rebels.

Fears are entertained that the Assistant Surgeon, Dr. A. B. Haines, has fallen, or is wounded. I will append to this a list of names of officers killed and wounded in the fight of the first day of July, 1863. [20]

After listing those names and the total number of casualties among officers and enlisted men, he ends his letter by stating that the regiment *"went into the fight with about 300 men, all told, and came out with 69, all safe."* [21]

One year after Gettysburg, on July 2, 1864, Barnett wrote a letter of resignation stating, *"out door speaking has so impaired my vocal organs that I am unable to speak loud enough to be heard by even a small congregation in the open air. I can not continue to perform the duties of a Chaplain longer with any degree of benefit to the Regiment."*[22] He left the ministry around the same time, supposedly while being investigated for unnamed charges, then attended the Washington University School of Medicine in St. Louis, Missouri, and moved to Kansas to practice medicine.[23] He was active in the local chapter of the Grand Army of the Republic (GAR) and local politics. He died on May 19, 1904, and is buried in Fort Scott, Kansas. Just weeks after his death, he was honored with a resolution from the GAR that recognized his

devotion to duty whether as a soldier in the celebrated Iron Brigade upholding his Country's flag or as a Christian Minister, faithful in word and example to his sacred calling, or as a physician shrinking from no labor in the alleviation of human suffering, or as a public officer performing every duty with fidelity and courage, or as a husband and father, kind, gentle, and loving. [24]

William Chittenden Way, 24th Michigan Volunteer Infantry

William Chittenden Way was born in Livingston County, New York, on July 31, 1824. As a young man, he held jobs in several businesses, including a printing office, clothing store, and daguerreotype establishment. In August 1845 he married Eliza M. Lane and they had three children, one of whom died in infancy. He entered the ministry as a Methodist preacher in 1857, was ordained in 1861, and, according to his colleagues, *"was a genial, common-sense man, with a keen appreciation of human nature and a relish for humor [. . .] spiritual and devout, and yet destitute of cant and sanctimoniousness."*[25] In August 1862, he accepted a commission as chaplain of the newly organized 24th Michigan Volunteer Infantry.

The men of the 24th were latecomers to the Iron Brigade, joining the other four midwestern regiments in late September 1862 after the brigade had become severely reduced in numbers by heavy fighting in several battles. With their new uniforms and their standard forage caps, the Michigan men stood in stark contrast to the battle-scarred veterans of the other regiments and their well-worn uniforms and distinctive black slouch hats. As new troops that had never seen battle, the men of the 24th were not warmly welcomed into the Iron Brigade, even though they brought a much-needed influx of almost 900 fresh men to the ranks.[26]

Chaplain Way was much loved by the men in his regiment. One of the regimental historians considered Way to be *"one of the great fighting padres of the war, one who took good care of his men."*[27] When the regiment set up camp near Falmouth, Virginia, on the Fitzhugh Estate in May 1863, they named the site Camp Way in honor of their chaplain. The soldiers described the area as *"a most beautiful spot, well supplied with wood and water, and by far the pleasantest camping ground of the regiment yet."*[28]

Early in the morning of July 1, Way asked that the regiment be assembled for prayer

Chaplain William Chittenden Way of the 24th Michigan Infantry spent several weeks after the battle caring for wounded soldiers in hospitals around Gettysburg. (Library of Congress)

before resuming their march toward Gettysburg. He *"stepped in front, as up and down the ranks the famed black hats, feathers sweeping low, were doffed by hushed soldiers. In stentorian tones, the chaplain called upon the God of battles, the Saviour of far-flung lines of infantry, to bless the troops and bring victory to their righteous cause, commending the souls of his listeners to their Father in Heaven."*[29] As he prayed, *"cartridges and hardtack were distributed among the men [since] time was precious and not to be lost."*[30]

Way acted as a correspondent to the *Detroit Advertiser and Tribune*, and his letters kept the people back home informed about the condition and situation of the men in the regiment. For weeks following the battle, Way remained in Gettysburg to care for the wounded at the general army hospital at Camp Letterman. During that time, he wrote several letters to the *Advertiser and Tribune* in which he provided updates on the condition of the wounded and the situation in and around Gettysburg. He visited every hospital, trying to assemble as accurate an account as possible of those who had been wounded or killed. On July 7 he sent an extensive list of the casualties and added:

> *It is sad indeed to look upon the decimated ranks of one of the bravest regiments that ever left the Wolverine State. Gettysburg is to-day one vast hospital, and, as a general thing, our wounded*

After the battle, Chaplain Way ministered to the wounded at Camp Letterman, the general army hospital on the York Pike east of Gettysburg. (Library of Congress)

are doing well–fast recovering from the effects of their wounds. The Court House–a fine building–the College, Seminary, churches, school houses, warehouses and private dwellings are filled with the wounded suffering soldiers. As soon as it was known that we had gained possession of the town again, and the rebels were retreating, citizens began to return and the wants of the wounded supplied, as far as the very meagre stock of the citizens would allow.[31]

Way also lauded private citizens who had opened their homes to provide lodging for the wounded, such as David Wills.[32] The chaplain expressed regret that he was *"not able to give you the names of many others, who perhaps will never receive a full reward for their noble deed here, but, I hope, will hereafter from the hands of Him who says: 'Inasmuch as ye have done it unto one of the least of these, my disciples, ye have done it unto Me.'"*[33]

Way's letter continues:

The work of burying the dead has been slowly progressing. Squads of Confederates have been detailed under guard, to bury their own dead. I went upon the field with two of our own regiment and buried many of our own fallen brave, and while there saw the evidence of a species of vandalism, which would disgrace a savage nation. Our dead were robbed of everything, and in very many instances were stripped of their clothing, and in every instance their shoes were taken.[34]

Years after the war, a veteran from the 24th recalled Way's devotion in caring for the dead:

Our honored chaplain [. . .] was compelled by the exigencies of that awful fray to go out with spade in hand and cover with a modicum of friendly dust the unburied heaps of his slain comrades. [O]ne day after the battle, while the chaplain was ministering to the wounded, he learned that thirty bodies of his regiment were lying unburied on the battle-field where they fell. He picked out two men who were but slightly wounded, and they went a mile and a half to the field and buried their comrades.[35]

On July 15, Way sent another letter to the *Advertiser and Tribune* and noted he was *"struck by the universal cheerfulness of those who have been wounded, and especially those who have suffered the loss of limbs by amputation–and there are scores of them. As a general thing the 'stumps' are doing finely."*[36] He went on to describe the situation in the hospitals and to complain about the quality of some nurses while praising others:

> *In the town, the hospitals have assumed an air of comfort and cleanliness. The bundle of stray or hat, and 'gum blanket' have given place to the soft straw bed, with clean woolen blankets and cotton sheets [. . .] The various associations have an abundant supply of almost everything the soldier requires, which is being distributed lavishly, and there is no reason why a single Union soldier should want, if surgeons, and especially nurses, do their duty.*
>
> *I wish every hospital were supplied with competent nurses. It is too often the case that those who are always falling out on the march, manage to get detailed as hospital attendants, and are absolutely good for nothing. There are a great many good nurses, men who are good soldiers and used to attending to the sick. The faithful soldier, wounded, demands our best efforts and sympathies.*
>
> *It is but just to give the members of our "regimental band" the credit due them for their efforts as nurses in the hospitals. None have been more assiduous in their attendance upon the suffering and wounded soldiers. I have seen them thus engaged, and know of their faithfulness.*[37]

By the middle of July, Way reported that the town of Gettysburg was *"filled to overflowing with sightseers and sad-hearted relatives, the one in search of curiosities, the others in search of some loved one who is suffering from wounds received in the most sanguinary battle of the war."*[38] The chaplain also recounted a special visit he and surgeon Alexander Collar made to a citizen of the town:

> *We called upon the old patriot, Mr. [John] Burns, the other day, and found him quite comfortable. It will be remembered that Mr. Burns is the man who, though passed seventy, shouldered his musket and went to the field, and fought with the "Old Iron Brigade." He is made up of the right kind of stuff. Let his name be recorded in history, as an example of matured patriotism. He was wounded three times, but none of his wounds are very serious, and he is getting on finely, and hopes to get another crack at the rebels.*[39]

Way ended his letter of July 15 with a poignant image:

John Burns, the "old patriot" who picked up his old flintlock musket and joined the Union soldiers on July 1, was visited by Chaplain Way while recuperating at his home in Gettysburg. (Library of Congress)

> *It is saddening to stand near the office of the Express Company and see the coffined remains of scores and even hundreds, being sent to their former homes to be buried among friends. Many are dying, and it is almost impossible to get a coffin for their remains, so great is the demand for them.*[40]

On August 7, Way sent another dispatch to the newspaper. By this time, the various hospitals were running more efficiently except for *"one thing, which has come to my knowledge I object to stoutly, viz: crowding Union and rebel soldiers in one tent together. The men do not like it and the feelings of many citizens are outraged by it. This difficulty will be remedied soon."*[41] In addition, he remarked that *"many of the rebels are loud in their praises of the Yankees for the kind manner in which they have been treated. Some, however, are sullen, and receive every attention as thought it was their due."*[42] By contrast, he related

> *the revolting fact that two or three Union soldiers were lying in a barn about three miles from town. The barn belongs to a Mr. Cunningham, a true Union man, and is being used for a rebel hospital. These wounded men were found to be in a sad and neglected condition, having laid on a bundle of hay for four weeks with broken thigh bones, and that, too, without being set or care for properly. The rebel surgeon in charge of the hospital seemed to be a humane man and rendered as an excuse for their condition, he had nothing to do with it.*[43]

Way expressed his frustration by noting that the rebels *"receive the same care and treatment as our own men, which contrasts strangely with the treatment received by our men, who are prisoners, lower down in Dixie."*[44]

By early August, the demands of caring for the wounded were beginning to wear heavily on Chaplain Way. In a letter to Capt. Albert M. Edwards, who was with the regiment in Virginia, Way admitted,

> *I had rather be with the regt. but can do our own boys much more good here than I could there. I have buried the only soldiers here that have been buried decently and have given every one of our boys a Christian burial. Some days I have buried three in one day but this only once. At our hospital, the Express Office, all are doing well with one or two exceptions, and ours is the only hospital where they have religious services during the week. We have worship here every morning and eve–and the boys like it. For a day or two I have not been well. I have been with the wounded so much that I smell blood and the wound smell all the time and it would be a relief for me to go to the Regiment, but my duties are in some respects Mother of Conscience.*[45]

He rejoined his regiment by mid-September 1863 and remained in service with them until the unit mustered out on June 30, 1865. After the war, he returned to pastoral ministry and served several congregations in Michigan. Way was active in the Regimental Association and played a role in the effort to place monuments to the Michigan regiments at Gettysburg. He gave the invocation during the Michigan Day at Gettysburg ceremonies.

Way received accolades in both the regiment's official report and in the report of the Michigan state agent at Washington. In his report, Col. Henry A. Morrow wrote: "*Chaplain William C. Way was early in attendance at hospitals and rendered valuable services. He remained in attendance on the wounded for several weeks after the battle, and both officers and men speak in the highest praise of his kindness and efficiency.*"[46] The state agent reported from Gettysburg on July 12, 1863:

> *Chaplain Way is always busy. He seems to be known personally by nearly all the boys in the division to which he belongs. As he goes the rounds among the boys, one says, "Chaplain, did you write to mother for me?" Another says, "Chaplain, our Surgeon is so busy, I fear he cannot get to me for a long time; will you please look at my limb and see if all is right?" The Chaplain calls for water and soap, takes out his scissors and pins, and dresses it himself. Thus he labors.*[47]

In the years immediately following the war, Way's "*nervous system became so impaired that he was quite seriously affected thereby, often fearing that insanity might befall him. These sad fears often rested as a terrible nightmare upon his mind.*"[48] In 1892, he requested to be placed on the "superannuated" (retired) list of pastors and went to live with his daughter in Michigan. He died on September 3, 1896, and is buried in Woodlawn Cemetery in Leslie, Michigan.

The Ryder family of Livonia, Michigan, had two sons serve at Gettysburg. John was in the 24th Michigan Infantry and was killed on July 1. Alfred served in the 1st Michigan Cavalry and was mortally wounded on July 3. Chaplain Way wrote three letters to the Ryder family to inform them of John's death and of Alfred's serious condition.[49]

On July 9, he told the family John had fallen but assured them that he "*had buried him with my own hands,*" and informed them that Alfred "*does not expect to live. He is wounded through the left lung, and it is with some difficulty that he breathes . . . He gave me his testament [pocket Bible] to give to his mother. He has carried it with him through the war so far . . . In regards to dying he seems to be feebly resigned and said, 'The Lord doeth all things well.'"* Way said that Alfred looked forward to *"exchanging this battling world for a better home above . . . he hoped to meet you all in heaven."*

Three days later, Way wrote to the family again:

> *I am happy to inform you, that notwithstanding the expressed opinions of several surgeons to the contrary, your son Alfred is decidedly better to-day. I saw him this afternoon and learned more of the character of his wound, and find that he is not in so much danger from his wound as from an injury of his spine occasioned from a fall from his horse . . . Dr. Johnson the Medical Director has much more hope of him. He seems quite cheerful and has good care . . . he knew of nothing that he wanted that was not furnished except a mother's care.*

Way also assured them that he *"missed John and have marked his grave so that I shall know it, and will have it marked so that any one else can find it."*

Alfred's father came to Gettysburg to care for his son, and Way wrote to Mrs. Ryder on July 18: *"You husband is here and in attendance with Alfred who is very low and from all appearances is sinking fast. I see that he grows weaker every day. Mr. Ryder spoke about writing and I know that he did not want to leave Alfred and I volunteered to write for him."* Way assured the boy's mother that *"Alfred seems to be so patient, so calm, so considerate"* and *"John is in heaven . . . joining in the praises of the church triumphant. I think Alfred will join him soon."*

Pvt. John Ryder and his brother Corp. Alfred Ryder served in the 24th Michigan. On July 1, John was killed in action and Alfred was severely wounded and died three weeks later. Chaplain Way wrote letters to the Ryder family to inform them about their sons. (Wayne [Michigan] Historical Museum)

Chaplain Way gave the invocation at the dedication of the monument to the 24th Michigan Infantry at Gettysburg on June 12, 1889. In this photo, Way is seated next to the monument, facing to his left. (Sons of Union Veterans, Department of Michigan)

Second Brigade:
Brig. Gen. Lysander Cutler

Brig. Gen. Lysander Cutler's brigade led the First Corps on the march to Gettysburg and was the first Union infantry unit to engage the Confederates. On the morning of July 1, they first formed a line straddling the Chambersburg Pike, but before noon, all the brigade's regiments moved north of the pike. After being pushed back by a Confederate attack, they resumed their original position until new threats from rebels to the north on Oak Hill proved to be overwhelming. Cutler's men reformed to the left of the Second Division troops, then withdrew when the rest of the First Corps line began to break. The brigade spent July 2 and 3 on Culp's Hill, repelling Confederate attacks on the night of the second and the morning of the third.[50]

Of the six regiments in this brigade, which included the 7th Indiana, 56th Pennsylvania, and 76th, 84th, 95th, and 147th New York, none had a chaplain with them at Gettysburg.

SECOND DIVISION:
Brig. Gen. John C. Robinson
First Brigade:
Brig. Gen. Gabriel Paul

Brig. Gen. Gabriel Paul's brigade arrived on the battlefield in the late morning of July 1 and formed the corps reserve by the Lutheran Theological Seminary until they were ordered to the far right of the corps line near Oak Hill and the Mummasburg Road. They assisted other regiments in holding off Confederate attacks from the west and the north, but pressure from the larger rebel forces pushed them back with the rest of the First Corps. One regiment in the brigade, the 16th Maine, was ordered to cover the retreat and paid dearly for its service, counting 131 men as casualties out of the 298 they took to Gettysburg.[51]

On July 2, the brigade was in reserve along Cemetery Ridge and was sent farther south late in the afternoon to help defend against the Confederate assaults, but by the time they reached the area, the rebels had already started to retreat. They were then sent to East Cemetery Hill to help repel another attack but again arrived after the Confederate tide had turned back. July 3 found the brigade supporting batteries on Cemetery Hill, facing the town. One last time, the men were sent to assist their comrades, this time in holding off the Pickett-Pettigrew-Trimble charge, but they arrived to see the rebels already retreating. They stayed in the area and skirmished with the enemy until the next day.[52]

Four of the five regiments in the brigade, the 13th Massachusetts, 16th Maine, 94th and 104th New York, and 107th Pennsylvania, had chaplains with them; only two of those left records of their service at Gettysburg.

Philos Goodrich Cook, 94th New York Infantry

Philos Goodrich Cook was born in Constable, New York, on August 10, 1807, and was raised in New York and Vermont. After graduating from Middlebury College in Vermont, he moved to Buffalo and became a teacher. He attended Auburn Theological Seminary and was appointed chaplain at the state prison in Auburn for three years, then became pastor of the Ludlowville Presbyterian Church. He returned to Buffalo in 1856, where he made his home for the rest of his life. In 1840, Cook married Clarissa C. Tottingham, and they had two sons and three daughters.

Chaplain Philos Goodrich Cook of the 94th New York Infantry. (courtesy of The Horse Soldier)

Philos's son George, a lieutenant in the 21st New York Infantry, was wounded at the Battle of Antietam, and the elder Cook went to Sharpsburg to care for him. While he was there, Cook met Col. Adrian Root of the 94th New York Infantry. Root mentioned they had no chaplain and asked Cook if he would serve in that capacity. Cook went back home, enrolled in the 94th, and stayed with the regiment until it mustered out in July 1865.[53]

Throughout his service, Cook served as a correspondent for several newspapers in New York. In a letter to the *Buffalo Christian Advocate* dated June 30, Cook apologized for not replying promptly to the editor's request for information and reported that the regiment had been on the move almost constantly for the preceding two weeks. They reached Frederick, Maryland, on June 28 then advanced two days later toward Emmitsburg *"at a very rapid rate–causing much complain [sic] among the troops, the distance being nearly 25 miles."*[54] Cook gloomily noted that

> *[m]uch of the time it has rained day and night, causing the roads to be muddy and the marching exceedingly fatigueing [sic] and exhausting to the men. None but those who have experienced it can know the discomforts and fatigues of a week's marching in mud and rain–every thread of clothes upon the person and in knapsacks wet through and through. Having no opportunity to dry, you must wear them by day and sleep all night in damp and wet clothes. But these are only the incidents of war and must be borne as best they can be. It will add nothing to ones [sic] comfort and enjoyment to complain.*[55]

On July 14 and 15, Cook composed letters describing the regiment's entry into the battle:

> *On the morning of the memorable 1st of July 1863, the 94th marched from Emmetsburg [sic] to this place, arriving about 12 o'clock. As the battle had been progressing for some two hours, and the commander of the (1st army) corps had been killed, and the*

demand for reinforcements seemed urgent, the 2nd Division were ordered forward into the conflict without time for rest or food. It was a sad and awful moment as the regiment filed by, and the parting word of cheer was exchanged in the felt certainty that to some it was our last parting on earth.[56]

Never shall I forget my emotions and the expression on many countenances of the boys as we exchanged words and glances while they passed by me to encounter the perils of the battle-field. I tried to say an encouraging word and cheer them on to their fearful work. In general they seemed cheerful and resolute.[57]

Once the regiment had gone into line of battle, artillery shells began bursting nearby and Cook and the other noncombatants were compelled to retreat to a safer place. The surgeons had selected a nearby house for a field hospital, but it proved to be too close to the firing, so Cook moved further to the rear to an open field where he

had a good view of some portions of the field; soon the Union boys advancing along the skirt of the woods up through a field of corn, and disappeared again in the woods. Then commenced the rapid discharge of musketry, producing in the hearer feelings of sadness and fear, more akin to terror than anything else. On the right of our troops, beyond a piece of woods, I could distinctly see long lines of rebels moving through a field of wheat for the purpose of flanking their opponents. How anxious I felt! What fearful foreboding, I cannot tell.[58]

From his vantage point near Oak Ridge, Cook watched the movements of the brigade:

Moving to the right a few hundred yards along the skirt of a piece of woods, and then advancing an 1/3 or 1/4 of a mile through an open field and woods, they came in sight of the enemy. Here they lay down behind a fence from whence they sent forth their missives of death with terrible effect; the enemy fell by scores and after a short resistance began to retreat. Had our boys remained here or near that position longer, they say they should have held the enemy in check, and inflicted great damage upon him, with very small loss to themselves. But being ordered to charge across the open field they advanced from behind their breast work, but had not gone far before they found that a large force of the enemy were flanking them on the left. In fact they were soon between two fires, and were obliged to retreat to the lower side of the woods where they had first entered this part of the field. Here they again rally and form line of battle, and give the enemy volley after volley, with terrible effect–mowing them down, as they found on visiting the ground afterwards, by thousands. But though the brave fellows did all that was possible for skill, courage and determination to do, it was found impossible to hold their ground. The odds against them were too great, at least three to one![59]

View of Oak Ridge leading to Oak Hill, where Chaplain Cook watched his men fight on July 1. (Library of Congress)

After watching these "thrilling scenes" for an hour or so, Cook rode into the center of town to find the division hospital. He stopped in front of Christ Lutheran Church on Chambersburg Street and saw the area filled with groups of three men—two uninjured men bringing in one wounded soldier. An officer shouted for those who were not wounded to return immediately to their regiments, but Cook doubted that many of them obeyed the order. He also noticed that *"a long line of rebel prisoners were just entering the yard in rear of the church–a saucy, rough looking set of fellows."*[60]

Inside the church, he *"found great confusion [. . .] no system or plan of action seemed to prevail. Many were dropped in the passages, preventing others from finding a place for depositing their charge when they could be cared for and made comfortable."*[61] After laboring in the church for an hour, he noticed signs that the Union troops were being forced back through town: *"The street was not only filled with stragglers covered with blood, dirt, and gunpowder, but several regiments passed in regular order, showing conclusively that the army was falling back.*"[62] He watched in horror as the men

> *found themselves under the necessity of retreating between two lines of the enemy for nearly half a mile! Many a poor fellow was made to bite the dust while passing between these two lines of fire. The retreat was in the direction of the town, and, as many of the enemy reached the town from different directions sooner than our boys, they had no difficulty in capturing large numbers just before or soon after they entered the town. In fact, the boys were too much exhausted to make good their escape.*[63]

As he stood by the church, he knew that the enemy was close at hand, and *"after some moments of deliberation as to whether I should remain and be taken prisoner or make my escape, I concluded on the latter, mounted my faithful steed and was soon pushing my way through the crowd towards Cemetery Hill."*[64] Once there, Cook depicted the scene as the remnants of his division gathered under their tattered, battle-scarred regimental flags:

> *How sad we felt when we saw who and how many were not present you can better imagine than I describe. Our Colonel, 8 Captains, 4 Lieutenants and 278 of our brave boys were among the missing. Yet, notwithstanding these sad facts, we could not but meet each other with a smile and congratulations as we thought or spoke of hair-breadth escapes. I cannot tell how thankful I felt that my messmates and dear friends, Major Moffett and Adjutant Scoville, had been spared. How the latter laid his head against my horse as we met, and wept for joy, and many others with glistening eyes could only exclaim: "Oh! Chaplain, we are here, but it's a wonder that any of us are alive!"*[65]

The exhausted men slept on their arms that night, safe among the rest of their corps. The regiment spent the next two days of battle in support of another division and, although they did not engage in battle, they suffered under *"the most tremendous shelling that was ever witnessed several hours on the third day without flinching."*[66]

When Col. Adrian Root was taken prisoner (along with many others in the 94th), he was taken to see Confederate general A. P. Hill, who offered him either immediate parole or exchange at Baltimore once the rebels had captured that city. In a letter home, Root said he *"thought of the hundreds of our wounded men in the rebel lines, and asked permission to attend to their wants, and offering to be personally responsible for a detail of prisoners, if they could be given me."*[67] Root's request was granted, and he and 150 other men of the 94th declined the ordinary parole, which would send them to a parole camp with other Union prisoners, and were instead assigned to collect wounded Union soldiers from the field. They placed these men in and around a barn and then cared for them as best they could with what little supplies were available.

Col. Adrian Root of the 94th New York Infantry (center) was taken prisoner on July 1 and declined ordinary parole for himself and his men. (Library of Congress)

When the regiment left Gettysburg in pursuit of the Confederates, Cook stayed behind, saying that he *"felt it my duty to remain with the prisoner boys, and do what I could for their comfort while I remain here. What disposition will be made of them it is not yet possible to say. They are very uneasy and anxious to have the matter decided. Until regularly exchanged they feel unwilling to take up arms against the Confederates. And yet well informed military men regard their parole as a nullity."*[68]

In addition to caring for these prisoners, Cook also spent time visiting the hospitals and conducting religious services in both the division hospital at Christ Lutheran and for the rebel wounded at the hospital at Pennsylvania College (the present Gettysburg College). On the same day the regiment left Gettysburg, Cook and Colonel Root started for Washington, where Root planned to advocate for his "paroled" men at Gettysburg since their parole did not conform with current army orders. But after speaking with another officer on the way, Cook decided to return to both care for and work beside the prisoners. Cook noted that although many citizens in Gettysburg and from other Northern cities had come to help, *the work of caring for the multitude of sufferers from the terrific conflicts of the 1st, 2d and 3d inst., is, humanly speaking, endless. There are ever and anon some–yea, too many–uncared for and suffering for the want of sympathy and nursing [. . .] During the late heavy rain several of the poor fellows who were lying outside upon the ground, were carried off and drowned by the swollen stream near by.*[69]

Cook noted that the *"scenes of sorrow and anguish on the part of the friends of the wounded and dead who are constantly arriving in search of loved one, are numerous and harrowing beyond description."*[70] He depicted one such scene in poignant detail:

A lady sits near me who arrived from Elma day before yesterday in search of her son, who was wounded on the 2d day of the battle. Soon after her arrival a messenger came from the hospital–four miles distant–saying that the young man could survive but a short time. It was nearly 9 o'clock P.M. when the mother arrived at the tent where her some, with eight others, lies upon the bed of straw groaning out his precious life. He was indeed but too near the end of his pilgrimage. He expired at 5 o'clock in the morning. What were the emotions of that mother during the few hours of consciousness that remained to her child, who but a mother in similar circumstances can tell?[71]

Chaplain Cook remained in Gettysburg until July 16, then returned to his regiment near Rappahannock Station, Virginia. When he rejoined his comrades in the 94th, he was

happily disappointed in the demeanor of the troops. After the severe and exhausting labors of the previous three weeks and the disappointment which I knew they experienced in not having been permitted to attack and destroy [Confederate general Robert E.] Lee's army at Williamsport, I expected to find the men low spirited and grumbling at the prospect of re-entering upon the hated soil of Virginia. But so far as I can judge from appearances, the men are in good spirits, and I have heard no mutterings or complaints at the prospects before them. While the rank and file of the army wished and hoped to attack the Rebs at Falling Water and were confident of their ability to beat them, and thus as they believed virtually destroy the Richmond army they seem to submit with a much better grace than I feared they would to the judgment and direction of the "Powers that be."[72]

President Lincoln had called for a Day of Thanksgiving, Praise, and Prayer on August 6, 1863, for the victories at Gettysburg and elsewhere. Cook and the other chaplains of Paul's brigade held a religious service that day, which *"left the assembly with a higher appreciation of the war, its past, present and future, what has been accomplished, what remains to be done, and the spirit in which it should be prosecuted."*[73]

After he finished his duty with the 94th, Cook returned to Buffalo where he served as a missionary for the Young Men's Christian Association and helped organize a church in a building that had been constructed during the war as a shelter for invalid troops. He also established a charity organization, a reading room, and other local missions. At the age of 87, he contracted a severe cold. He died on June 26, 1895, and is buried in Fairlawn Cemetery in Buffalo.

Ferdinand De Wilton Ward, 104th New York Infantry

Chaplain Ferdinand De Wilton Ward of the 104th New York Infantry. (Brinton Family Papers, Morris Library Special Collections, University of Delaware)

Ferdinand De Wilton Ward was born in Bergen, New York, in 1812. After graduating from Union College and Princeton Theological Seminary, he married Jane Shaw in 1831. In 1836, the Wards sailed to India to serve as missionaries, but they found the climate and the challenges of living in a different culture too difficult, and they returned to America in 1847. Ward accepted the pastorate of Central Presbyterian Church in Geneseo, New York, where he ministered for a total of twenty years before and after the Civil War. He was also involved in the American Bible Society and published tracts and books. The Wards had five children; two died as infants while they were in India, and one daughter and two sons survived to adulthood.[74]

In the summer of 1861, Brig. Gen. James Wadsworth, a prominent citizen of Geneseo, organized the 104th New York Infantry (later called the Wadsworth Guards).[75] The regiment left for the war in February 1862, and Ward followed them a few months later intending to *"minister to the men and to provide readers of the Livingston Republican with accounts of how their sons and brothers, fathers and husbands were fairing at the front."*[76] Ward was commissioned as chaplain on July 17, 1862, just in time to watch the regiment fight in the Battle of Cedar Mountain. As the weeks went by, Ward grew weaker, enfeebled by an intestinal illness that had first affected him in India. He was ordered home in mid-September, but he found his temporary assignment to a church there unsatisfying, and he decided by the end of the year to return to his regiment, a decision lauded by the editors of the *Republican*: *"We are glad for the sake of the brave boys who are now lying sick and wounded. We shall miss you, Dr. Ward, but go where duty calls you–go with our wishes and our prayers."*[77]

By late June his ailments had returned, and during the march toward Gettysburg he often had to ride in an ambulance, dehydrated and unable to sleep. However, he attended to his duty in the aftermath of the battle. In mid-July, he and the regimental surgeon were on detached service at the division hospital at White Church south of Gettysburg. Noting that he was aware of *"the painfulness of false rumor,"* he provided an extensive and carefully researched list of those who were wounded and killed and acknowledged the vast number of the regiment's casualties: *"this catalogue will be painfully enlarged as time passes on. It will be observed that the loss of officers is specially great [and] in due time there will be a thorough re-organization, if not consolidation, of the Regiment."*[78]

The German Reformed "White Church" south of Gettysburg was a First Corps hospital in which Chaplain Ward tended to the wounded. (Mt. Joy Township)

In a letter written in mid-August, Ward described what he saw and heard during the battle:

> *I was so near as to hear the yell which attends such attacks and hear the sharp musketry. At Chancellorsville I counted seventy booming of cannon each minute, but here they were countless. No word more perfectly describes the scene and results than Satanic. I visited the entire battle ground, and the trees look as if*

a sirocco has passed over them, their vitality departing through the perforations made by shot and shell and ball. And the lonely graves–fields covered with them. Sad scenes![79]

Ward also wrote that during his two weeks at the White Church hospital, he witnessed *"scenes far more numerous and agonizing than those at Bull Run and Chancellorsville. About four hundred wounded officers and privates–Union and Confederate–were gathered in a barn and under tents."*[80] He and each of the three other chaplains in the division were assigned special duties, with his being to attend to the dying and bury the dead:

> *I committed twenty-four to their hastily dug graves (twelve Union and twelve Confederate). A plain board with name, company and regiment, marks the spot where lies buried, coffinless and shroudless, the form of a loved husband, son or brother. Better this than the condition of thousands lying in piles upon the rocks where was made what is regarded the most fearful charge ever known in our national history.*[81]

In the same letter, Ward defended the honor of the men in his regiment against vague charges of "idleness":

> *The 950 who passed through Washington sixteen months ago, are reduced to less than 90! And where are the absent ones? At Gettysburg 25 officers and privates were killed; 86 wounded; 94 prisoners and missing [. . .] If the 104th is not entitled to the name of a hard working and patriotic regiment, I know not where such an one is to be found. That there have been instances of cowardice and desertion cannot be denied; but as a body they have ever manifested a spirit of obedience, activity and heroism.*[82]

Ward ended this letter by expressing his understanding of the army's purpose and the nation's cause and the need to continue the fight regardless of the cost:

> *When speaking of peace as that which this army desires, it should not be understood as "peace on any terms"–very far from it; but peace consistent with the claims of truth and righteousness and the constitution. "Oh that I could see a battle," says the tarrier at home. "I have seen one and do not wish to see another," says the warrior. But it is not on the battlefield alone that the soldier*

suffers. It is an uninterrupted series of sacrifices from the hour he leaves home till he returns to its quiet retreat and social intercourse. We shall welcome the conscripts, but we anticipate for them many a sad hour. They must come or all is lost, but joyous will be to them the day when their services are no longer needed on the tented and battle field. Many thanks for the Union. To no one is it more welcome than to the Chaplain of the 104th.[83]

A week later, he wrote to his daughter Sarah and described

the great mental suffering arising from [. . .] our reduced numbers. Some 60 to 70 on parade rather than 600 & more. It depresses greatly. The officers almost all gone. It is sad, sad–so small a parish–so little to do. All these things create an almost intolerable sadness–shall I say, homesickness. Perhaps I ought not to name [these feelings]. They are unsoldierly, childish. I hope that I am not wholly useless.[84]

In the middle of July, Ward had described the extreme pressure he was experiencing: *"I have no time, strength, nor heart to recall and narrate what I have seen during the last two weeks. Oh, what weariness, yea, exhaustion of body and spirit!"*[85] This strain, combined with his already poor health, led Ward to ask for a discharge for disability in November 1863. He returned to his pulpit in Geneseo and resigned in 1873 to serve as a district superintendent for the American Bible Society. After his wife died in 1886, Ward moved to Switzerland to find relief for his failing health. He died there on August 11, 1891, and is buried in Temple Hill Cemetery in Geneseo, New York.

Second Brigade:
Brig. Gen. Henry Baxter

Henry Baxter's brigade brought up the rear of Robinson's division on the march to Gettysburg, and when they reached the battlefield, they were at first held in reserve near the Lutheran Seminary. Soon they were ordered to extend the Union line north of Cutler's brigade and along the Mummasburg Road to bridge a gap between the First and Eleventh Corps. Baxter's line formed a salient, or right-angle bend, along the road and the regiments were exposed to enemy attacks from two directions. The brigade helped drive back the first assaults and captured a number of prisoners, but as more Confederate troops joined the fray, the entire First Corps line could not withstand the pressure of the superior rebel forces and gave way. Baxter's men spent most of July 2 in the Union line along Cemetery Ridge. That evening they were sent to East Cemetery Hill to support the Eleventh Corps against the rebel attack, but they were not ordered to advance against the foe and spent an uneasy night on the hill resting on their arms. On the morning of July 3, the brigade was sent to Culp's Hill to support the Twelfth Corps, then returned to Cemetery Hill early in the afternoon. After the Pickett-Pettigrew-Trimble charge was repulsed, some of the regiments skirmished with Confederates on the ground between the two army lines.

There were six regiments in the brigade: the 11th, 88th, and 90th Pennsylvania, the 12th Massachusetts, and the 83rd and 97th New York. Chaplains accompanied four of these regiments to Gettysburg and three of them wrote about their experiences.

William Henry Locke, 11th Pennsylvania Infantry

William Henry Locke was born in Baltimore on March 28, 1828. His family moved to Pennsylvania when he was six, and as a young man, he worked as a printer until he felt called into the ministry. He was licensed to preach by the Pittsburgh Conference of the Methodist Episcopal Church in 1852 and served several churches in western Pennsylvania. He married Margaret Loor in 1856, and they had three sons, two of whom preceded him in death, and three daughters.

When the war broke out, the 11th Pennsylvania (soon to be called the "Old Eleventh" to distinguish it from the 11th Pennsylvania Reserves) was among the first to respond from the state. They mustered in on April 23, 1861, as a ninety-day regiment, then reorganized in July for a three-year term. By November, the field staff positions were filled and Locke became the regiment's chaplain.[86]

Soon after the war, Locke wrote a history of the regiment, noting how being chaplain provided him a special advantage in recording events:

> *The duties of the writer did not require him to carry either sword or musket, and the story he here tells is made up from a note-book*

never absent from him, whether in camp or on the march. When the original record–sometimes made during a halt along the roadside, and sometimes in the midst of battle–better tells the story, that record is inserted, day and date.[87]

In mid-June, as the brigade moved north out of Virginia, Locke noted that the 11th *"began its march northward with two hundred and eighty-eight men, scarcely a third of the number with which it had marched southward a year before."*[88] He described the long, hot marches, including one that lasted nineteen hours, and mused that *"General [Henry] Halleck once said that the great want of the Army of the Potomac was legs. He will be glad to learn that we have come into possession of those valuable appendages, and know how to use them."*[89] But despite the burdens of their marches, *"everywhere along the route the troops were greeted with demonstrations of delight. It was so new to us, who had always been received with frowns, or a look of contempt, or in sullen silence, to be met with smile of welcome"* from citizens in Maryland.[90]

On June 30 when the First Corps reached the Pennsylvania state line, *"a new class of emotions was awakened in every heart, that could only find expression in the hearty cheers there given for the good old State."*[91] Once they crossed into Pennsylvania, they received the news that Maj. Gen. Joseph Hooker had been replaced as commander of the Army of the Potomac with Maj. Gen. George Gordon Meade, and Locke reflectively wrote,

Unaccounted for, and to them unaccountable, the removal of General Hooker was accepted by the rank and file as the expression of doubt and uncertainty, in the high places of government, as to the issue before us; and with an army less patriotic or less intelligent the effect would have been full of disaster. But there comes an hour, in the experience of every true soldier, when he feels that victory depends not so much upon the commander as on himself–on his own fidelity to duty. Such an hour came to the Army of the Potomac, and each man was nerved for the work before him.[92]

Maj. Gen. George Gordon Meade assumed command of the Army of the Potomac just days before the Battle of Gettysburg. (Library of Congress)

As the First Corps moved toward Gettysburg on July 1, Robinson's division was still three miles from town when the soldiers heard distant artillery fire. Locke recalled *"how that first gun–the invariable prelude to battle–always startles the nerves, and sends the heart on a double-quick motion! But as cannon answers to cannon, the nerves become accustomed to the unusual sound, and the heart comes back again to its steady beat."*[93] When the brigade took its place in the battle line, Locke noted that with each repulse of the enemy, the men shouted, *"We are Pennsylvanians, and have come here to stay."*[94] Robinson's division held firm until both the First and Eleventh Corps were overwhelmed by rebel attacks in their front and at their flanks, and were forced back through the town.

The division surgeons had set up a hospital at Christ Lutheran Church on Chambersburg Street earlier in the day and Locke was there when the Union troops retreated through town:

> *Basement and auditory, chancel and choir, the yard in front, the yard in rear [. . .] crowded with the brave men of the Second Division, wounded and dying. We were going in and out among these, when the broken and flying battalions of the Eleventh Corps came streaming in from the right. It was a sight never to be forgotten. Crowding through the streets, and up the alleys, and over fences in utter ignorance of whither they were going, every moment increased the confusion and dismay. To add to the terrors of the hour, the enemy gained possession of the town, and firing rapidly into our retreating ranks, shot and shell mingled their horrid sounds with the groans of the dying thus stricken down.*
>
> *But the retreat was not all confusion. The same noble corps [the First Corps] that had so successfully maintained its ground of the left, when resistance was no longer possible, fell back in solid phalanx. And though "Cannon to the right of them, Cannon to the left of them,*

Christ Lutheran Church on Chambersburg Street, where Chaplain Locke was caring for the wounded when he was caught behind enemy lines on July 1. (Courtesy of Lester Ruth)

Volley'd and thunder'd," shoulder to shoulder they marched, rank after rank halting to fire upon the advancing foe, and then closing up again with a daring coolness.[95]

Locke did not follow the retreating troops but remained at the Lutheran Church, and as the rebels took command of the town, he was caught behind the enemy lines and became a prisoner. He learned that the three Confederate corps commanders had arrived in town, so he knew that the entire rebel army had concentrated in the area.[96] But he knew nothing about his own troops: *"There was no one to tell us of the Union army, whether its other corps were near enough to come to the support of the First and the Eleventh holding Cemetery Hill [. . .] No word that a single man had been added to the brave few that bore the brunt of yesterday's fight, came to our ears; and when the battle commenced, shortly after noon of Thursday, it need not be concealed that there were painful fears of the issue."*[97] Locke spent an uneasy night in Gettysburg as *"the enemy in town passed the night in riot and feasting."*[98]

In the morning, the rebels formed new battle lines in the streets, and Locke noted that if he and the other Union prisoners *"could have known that throughout the night one corps after another had been arriving"* on the field, they *"would have accepted that bright morning as the harbinger of final success."*[99] A Confederate captain came into the hospital and told Locke, *"Your troops occupy a strong position at the upper end of the town [. . .] but I'm sure they won't be there long."*[100]

Throughout July 2, Locke cared for the wounded at the hospital while listening to the almost incessant *"roar of artillery and the rattle of small arms"* that did not cease until night came.[101] Those working at the hospital were concerned about the men who were wounded in the days' fight; when the rebels gained control of the town, they had seized the medical supplies of the Union surgeons for use with their own wounded. But foremost in the minds of all the Federals caught behind the Confederate lines was the question, *"did [the army] hold its position throughout the fight, or were its ranks broken and scattered?"*[102] Locke recorded an encounter with a Confederate officer that evening:

> *we inquired [. . .] how the battle had gone. He was not at all inclined to be communicative, and only in answer to a direct question did he say that we still held our lines unbroken. There was a faint dawning of hope. We knew that nothing less than the entire Potomac Army could resist such an attack as had been made during the day by the combined Southern forces.*[103]

Fighting resumed on Culp's Hill on the Union right early on the morning of July 3, and once it ended a few hours later, there was

> *an ominous quiet. It was not the quiet of inaction, but like that which precedes the storm. It was beyond human endurance that such fighting as had characterized the last two days could continue longer. And there was a changing of troops and a moving of artillery that indicated preparations for the final assault. The enemy was boastful as ever. Our taciturn friend of the day before, accompanied by one of two others, came again into the hospital. They had been making observations from the church steeple, and the prospect of success made him more talkative. "Everything," said he, "is going just as we wanted it."* [104]

When the cannonade before the Pickett-Pettigrew-Trimble charge began around 1:00 p.m., Locke thought *"it seemed as though ten thousand furies were let loose at once. Shells of all sizes and shapes went howling over the town like demons escaped from perdition, tainting the very air with sulphurous [sic] smoke and smell."* [105] Locke, along with others, climbed the church steeple and watched the rebel lines moving from the west, toward Cemetery Ridge. *"In splendid order did they come, three columns deep, with every flag unfurled and flying in the breeze."* [106] But once the Federal cannon opened on the Confederate lines, the field was covered in dust and smoke and Locke could see no more of the battle.

Blinded from knowing what was happening on the field, Locke said *"it was a fearful afternoon. The wounded men lying in the yard, and able to help themselves, crawled into the house. It seemed safer there, because less distinctly did the unearthly sound that filled the air strike upon the ear."*[107] By evening, after the worst of the battle had been spent, Locke noticed an *"evident uneasiness among the Confederates. No shouts of victory ran along their lines; there were no congratulations among officers and men, so natural if success had crowned their efforts."* [108] He watched as Confederate wagons were loaded and rebel wounded were quietly removed from the hospital, until, at nightfall, *"scarcely a Southerner was to be seen"* in the town.[109] When one Union soldier in the hospital offered his belief that the Confederates were falling back, Locke saw *"a brave Michigan volunteer, whose right arm had been amputated near the shoulder, held up the other, as he said: 'This is all I have now, doctor, but for a victory here, I would give this one, too!'"* [110]

Throughout the evening, Locke saw anxious faces at the windows of the houses and buildings in town as they observed the rebels moving away from town in the direction they had come. But after dawn on July 4,

> *a good, strong line of Federal skirmishers was seen advancing boldly through the street. One clear, shrill cheer was given, which, quick as thought, was repeated by a hundred voices. Instantly houses that had been closed for three days and looked deserted, were thrown open, and doors and windows crowded with faces beaming with hope and joy. Many of the wounded in hospital crawled to the doors as best they could, and though in some instances only in feeble strains, welcomed the morning with shouts of victory.*[111]

Locke described his experience of being among the Confederates in Gettysburg:

> *During the three days that the rebels held possession of Gettysburg, for representatives of Southern chivalry they displayed the grossest ruffianism. Stores were broken open and pillaged of their contents, and private cellars robbed to replenish their knapsacks. They came in the hospital, taking from the wounded men shoes or caps, or whatever article of clothing suited their fancy. Two soldiers fought over a sword taken from the side of a captain too badly wounded to offer resistance, and the dispute was only settled by the interference of an officer who, happening in at the moment, appropriated the coveted weapon to his own use.*[112]

Locke also wrote about a Confederate quartermaster who *"made himself especially conspicuous on the streets for loud talking and boisterous threats of firing the town, and making of Gettysburg a second Fredericksburg."*[113]

Locke recalled the ways he had seen Southern women devotedly care for their wounded soldiers after previous battles, but, by comparison, he noted,

> *nothing we had ever seen could exceed the devoted attention of a few noble women of Gettysburg. From that first dreadful day to the last, they were angels of mercy, always coming at the auspicious moment; braving alike the bullets that were flying through the streets, and the shells that were bursting overhead, and the leering look and coarse remark of an exultant foe, to carry comfort and succor to the wounded and the dying.*[114]

On July 4, many of the Union wounded in town were quickly removed to hospitals that had been established south of Gettysburg out of fear that the retreating foe might send a few shells into town in retaliation for their humiliating defeat. Once this task was completed, Locke went off in search of his regiment, which he had not seen since the morning of July 1. He discovered that out of the 212 officers and men that had been present for duty at the opening of the battle, only 79 had reached Cemetery Hill.

Locke rejoined his regiment as they began their pursuit of Gen. Robert E. Lee's army on July 6 and reported that the troops were in excellent spirits, at least until the rebels crossed back into Virginia on July 14:

> *After all our marching and planning, the rebels have eluded us. With his army little better than a mob, General Lee has succeeded in making a safe passage of the Potomac. Where his capture was regarded with so much certainty, there could not be anything else than great disappointment at this unexpected result (. . .) Another of those mistakes has been made so fatal to the permanent success of the Potomac Army (. . .) Nothing now remains but to follow the enemy through Virginia, where the advantage of roads, position, and everything else will be in his favor.*[115]

Locke resigned his commission as chaplain on December 9, 1863, and soon returned to pastoral ministry, serving Methodist Episcopal churches in Pennsylvania and Ohio. He asked to be added to the retired list of pastors in 1904. He and his wife lived with their son, then with their daughter, and while on a visit with another son in Brooklyn, Locke died on June 15, 1905, and was buried in Sewickley, Pennsylvania.

Horatio Stockton Howell, 90th Pennsylvania Infantry

Horatio Stockton Howell was born near Trenton, New Jersey, on August 14, 1820. After graduating from Lafayette College and Union Theological Seminary, he entered the ministry in the Presbyterian Church in 1846. He married Isabella Grant that same year, and they had two sons and one daughter. In 1853, he was called to serve the Presbyterian Church at Delaware Water Gap in northeastern Pennsylvania, where he also ran a private school for boys. On the counsel of his dear friend and mentor, the Rev. James P. Wilson, Howell became a staunch abolitionist and decided to enroll as the chaplain of the 90th Pennsylvania Volunteer Infantry; he mustered in on March 13, 1862. Once he assumed his duties as chaplain, Howell preferred to wear the full military uniform, including the shoulder straps and dress sword of his rank as captain.

Chaplain Horatio S. Howell of the 90th Pennsylvania Infantry was killed on July 1. (Presbyterian Historical Society)

On July 1 at Gettysburg, Howell dutifully went to the hospital in Christ Lutheran Church on Chambersburg Street. Late that afternoon, he stepped out to the front porch of the church just as the Confederates were chasing the retreating Union soldiers through town. One rebel stopped at the foot of the steps and, thinking Howell was a Union officer and thus a good "catch," called on him to surrender. Howell tried to explain that he was a noncombatant, but the impatient rebel shot and killed him. Since we have no record from Howell, we must turn to the writings of others who can testify to his service as chaplain and to his killing.

Sgt. Archibald Snow of the 97th New York Infantry was with Chaplain Howell when he was shot and killed at the Lutheran Church. (Library of Congress)

There are at least four written accounts by eyewitnesses of the event that differ slightly in their details. The first comes from Sgt. Archibald Snow of the 97th New York (in the same brigade as the 90th Pennsylvania), who had been shot in the jaw and was having his wound dressed at the hospital that afternoon. Snow said he had just walked out the door of the church behind Chaplain Howell when "the advance skirmishers of the Confederates were coming up the street on a run." One of them,

> *placing one foot on the first step [. . .] called on the chaplain to surrender; but Howell, instead of throwing up his hands promptly and uttering the usual, "I surrender," attempted some dignified explanation to the effect that he was a non-combatant, and as such was exempt from capture, when a shot from the skirmisher's rifle ended the controversy. A Confederate lieutenant, who came up*

at this time, placed a guard at the church door, and to the protests of the surgeons against shooting a chaplain, replied that the dead officer was armed, in proof of which he pointed to the chaplain's sash, and light, rapier like sword belted around the chaplain's body.[116]

Another witness was Mary McAllister, who lived across the street from the church. She shared her memories of the event with her friend May Gerlach Hoffman in 1903, who carefully recorded McAllister's words, and the account was printed as a serial article in *The Philadelphia Inquirer* in June 1938 for the 75th anniversary of the battle:

> *[W]hen six or seven rebels came riding up the street firing and yelling, [. . .] they halted at the church to say something to the wounded men on the high church steps who had gathered themselves out of range of the firing, and in a few minutes a pistol went off and we saw they had shot a man. He was down then; and when we looked, he was lying with his head toward us on the pavement. And those men on the steps said: "Shame! Shame! That was a chaplain!" Those on horseback said: "He was going to shoot." But the wounded men said: "He was not armed." They had many words and then they rode off again, shooting as they had come. A surgeon came over the next morning and he said: "We regret terribly about our chaplain. He was one of the best men." They had carried him into the yard and buried him. His name was Rev. Horatio S. Howell.*[117]

Howell's body was later moved to Green-Wood Cemetery in Brooklyn, New York.

Chaplain Howell's gravesite in Green-Wood Cemetery, Brooklyn, New York. (Author's collection)

The third account comes from Pvt. Harry Hunterson of the 88th Pennsylvania Infantry, who had been instructed to escort a wounded Confederate prisoner to the hospital at the Lutheran Church:

> *When I brought my prisoner up the street to the hospital the Chaplain [Reverend Howell] was standing outside at the fence. I started up the steps, and when I got on the top step I*

turned around and saw a rebel run up on the other side of the street, with his gun at right shoulder shift. When he got nearly opposite he brought his gun down to a ready, and I thought he was going to fire at me, so I pulled my rebel around in front of me, and as I was backing in the door, pulling him in, the rebel across the street fired and killed the Chaplain. Other rebels came along, and stole the boots off the Chaplain's feet.[118]

The final account is from Lt. Charlie Potts of the 151st Pennsylvania, who reported that after taking some of his wounded to the division hospital at the church and supplying them with water, he *"went to the front just in time to see the Chaplain of the 90th Penna. killed, while standing in the doorway of the church. In company with two others, we picked him up, but he had been instantly killed, the ball entering his mouth and taking an upward course through the brain."*[119]

In September 1889, the veterans of the 90th gathered in Gettysburg to dedicate both their "Boulder" monument on Cemetery Ridge, which marks the area where the regiment was engaged on July 2, and the monument to their chaplain in front of Christ Lutheran Church. Howell's good friend, the Rev. Dr. William Aikman, gave the oration at the dedication ceremony, in which he described the incident at the church that day:

All day long there has been coming the mournful procession of ambulances and stretchers, as the wounded were borne to the rear, a rear soon to become the front of battle. That procession rightly finds its way to this spot, and just as it ought to be this church becomes a hospital, to which the wounded are brought. The yellow flag is floating languidly in the hot July air, over yonder porch. The Chaplain has been doing his work of gentle ministration to the sufferers within, assisting at the instant a surgeon in dressing the wound of a soldier who had had an artery of his leg shot away. He hears the shots and confusion of the retreat, and says to the surgeon "I will step outside for a moment and see what the trouble is." He has scarcely taken his place on the steps by the side of a surgeon, looking at the backward sweep of the battle, as it showed its ragged edge on the street, when round yonder corner rides a rebel cavalryman, in the reckless excitement of the hour. He sees the group above him and levels his carbine at the church porch;

chaplain and surgeon insignia are not regarded, probably not seen; they do not stay his hand nor turn his eye. The fatal ball sharply sings, passes the surgeon's head, strikes the face and tears through Howell's brain. In an instant he passes out of life and this place becomes forever consecrated by his blood.[120]

The monument to Chaplain Howell was the first one placed on a battlefield in memory of a chaplain killed in the service. It is shaped like a pastor's reading desk and holds an open Bible in bronze with the inscriptions:

> *In Memoriam. Rev. Horatio S. Howell, Chaplain 90th Penna. Vols.; was cruelly shot dead on these Church steps, on the afternoon of July 1st, 1863.*
>
> *"He delivereth me from mine enemies; yea, thou liftest me up above those that rise up against me." –Psalms xviii, 48*
>
> *"He being dead, yet speaketh." –Hebrews xi, 4.*

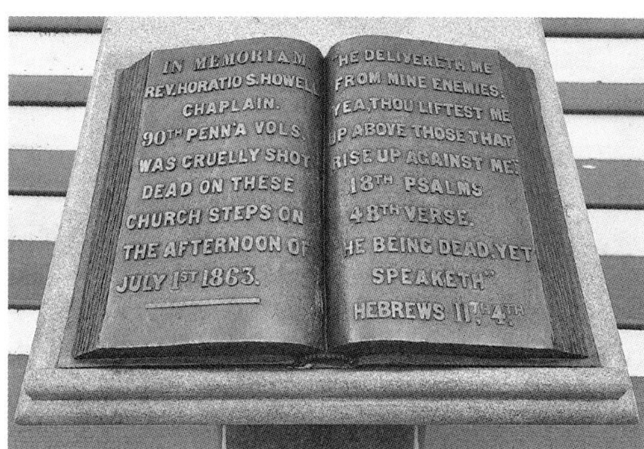

The monument to Chaplain Howell at the base of the steps of Christ Lutheran Church was dedicated in 1889. (Author's collection)

John V. Ferguson, 97th New York Infantry

John Van Epps Ferguson was born on August 22, 1829, in the town of Ohio in Herkimer County, New York. After attending Fairfield Seminary, he taught school for a few years and then went into business. In 1853, he married Ann Catherine ("Kate") Abeel, and they had three children. Poor health compelled him to leave his business, so he decided to study medicine but soon felt a call to the ministry. He was ordained into the Methodist Episcopal Church in 1856 and served several churches in upstate New York. At the outbreak of the war, he traveled throughout Herkimer County and gave patriotic speeches that inspired men to enlist in a new regiment, the 97th New York Infantry. In March 1862, he was mustered in as the regiment's chaplain.

Chaplain John Ferguson of the 97th New York Infantry. (Northern New York Methodist Episcopal Church Minutes)

In late 1862, the men of his regiment had presented him with an engraved officer's sword, but, in contrast to Chaplain Howell, Ferguson wore the sword only once because he said he had *"not love of Style, fuss & feathers enough to wear it much."* [121]

Throughout his time of service, from March 1862 to July 1864, Ferguson wrote letters home to Kate and his sons, three of which describe his experiences at Gettysburg. On July 11, 1863, he told Kate *"I am still well & remain at this place trying to do what I can for reliving* [sic] *the sufferings of the poor wounded soldiers."* [122] The regiment's colonel, Charles Wheelock, had been wounded during the fight on July 1, and Ferguson related the story of Wheelock's experience:

> *I have the pleasure of informing you that Col. Wheelock has escaped from the Rebs & has safely returned after being two days in the mountain with no food before he dare venture to a house as Rebs were on both sides of the Mountain. He escaped while passing through a forest in the dark night by lying down just at the side of the road & the guards didn't miss him.*
>
> *Col Wheelock's sword & a part of the flag staff captured by our regiment were saved by a Lady Miss Carrie Sheads the principal of the female academy who lived in a house in which Col Wheelock stopped as the Regt were falling back. She hid them from the Rebs who followed the Col into the house by covering them in the folds of her dress. I yesterday went with the Col. over the battlefield & to the house & obtained the sword & highly prized flag staff.* [123]

Col. Charles Wheelock of the 97th New York Infantry was wounded on July 1. Chaplain Ferguson helped him recover the sword he had hidden in a local home during the retreat. (New York State Military Museum)

Chaplain Ferguson accompanied Col. Wheelock to the Sheads House to recover his sword. (Tyson Brothers)

Ferguson ended this letter by noting that *"some of the rebel dead are not buried yet but they are using the rebel prisoners for that purpose."*[124] He said he expected to remain at Gettysburg for some time and expressed confidence that *"things look brightly & hopeful now. Though I don't expect Lee's army will be all destroyed, that's impossible, I do think it will be greatly damaged, our forces are after him."*[125]

On July 28, Ferguson stated that he had not heard anything from the regiment since they had left to pursue the Confederate army, but he expected to return to his unit soon since the division hospital was being dismantled, with the wounded being sent to the Camp Letterman general hospital. Some of the more seriously wounded could not yet be moved, including Lt. Frederick Henry Beecher of the 16th Maine in the same brigade, the nephew of the great abolitionist preacher Henry Ward Beecher. Ferguson related sad news about Lt. Rush P. Cady of the 97th, who *"died last Friday of his wounds, his mother was here caring for him. She felt very deeply his death for he was a noble young man & fine officer. They had him embalmed & took him home to Rome [New York]. She was very grateful to me & others for our care & attention to him."*[126] The chaplain also explained why one captured soldier might not have written home to his wife: *"He may not have taken his parole as many did not for they must go right back into the army as no parole except at Richmond is respected by our Government & many went on to Richmond."*[127] He told Kate that he hoped for *"peace within a year, but we must no doubt have some more hard fighting,"* and asked her to kiss the boys for him.[128]

Ferguson did not return to his regiment immediately as he had expected. Instead, he wrote on August 8 that he had stayed to help the regimental surgeon, but he and the surgeon had just received their orders to report to the regiment in Virginia. He was *"not expecting but two or three more large battles to end this war & if enough conscripts are sent on soon these will be decisive & not very severe."*[129] In his next letter from

Rappahannock Station, Virginia, dated August 25, Ferguson lamented that *"conscripts & more substitutes are daily arriving but we have received none as yet. The conscripts are generally good men but the substitutes are mostly Old Sogers."*[130]

In his final letter home on October 6, 1864, Ferguson wrote, *"Of course I feel very anxious to get home & be again with my family but I would like to see the fatal, final blow struck first."*[131] But he would have to watch that final blow from afar because he mustered out of the army just a few weeks later. He returned to New York and served Methodist Episcopal churches in upstate New York until he retired in 1870. Kate died in 1882, and Ferguson married Helen M. Dodge in 1886. He died after a prolonged illness in Utica, New York, on August 1, 1905, leaving behind Helen and one surviving son, the Rev. Raymond H. Ferguson. He is buried in Little Falls, New York.

At the funeral for Rev. Ferguson, a friend and fellow veteran, Rev. W. R. Helms, who had served in another regiment in the same brigade, offered a eulogy that aptly captured Ferguson's character as a chaplain, as reported in the August 5, 1905, edition of the *Utica Daily Press*:

> *Mr. Helms . . . referred to the wounding of a lieutenant belonging to [his] company. Looking for him, he came across the wounded man and the chaplain to the hospital. The latter greeted the newcomer but said he could not arise from his knees to take him by the hand, for he was holding the artery which had been cut and from which, otherwise, the soldier's life blood would ebb. The chaplain was spattered with human blood, but he held on like the hero that he was and, when relieved by the doctor, was so weak that he could not use the hand which had performed such faithful service for some time. This merely shows what the real chaplain is like. Mr. Helms' remarks were touching and showed a side of the character of Mr. Ferguson that was unsuspected by many, that of the bravery which counts for so much.*

THIRD DIVISION:

Maj. Gen. Abner Doubleday / Brig. Gen. Thomas Rowley

First Brigade:

Col. Chapman Biddle

When General Reynolds was killed early in the battle on July 1 and Maj. Gen. Abner Doubleday rose to command of the First Corps, Brig. Gen. Thomas Rowley assumed command of the Third Division and Col. Chapman Biddle took over for Rowley in the First Brigade of the division. The brigade was the last infantry unit of the corps to reach the battlefield, arriving around midday, and was ordered to form behind and south of the Iron Brigade. At the far left of the Union line in a large open field, the brigade advanced to Willoughby Run to try to find shelter from the incessant Confederate artillery fire. After evicting some rebel skirmishers from a barn in their front, the brigade moved back along the Fairfield Road toward the seminary, then were shortly ordered back to their original position along McPherson Ridge. By midafternoon, two fresh lines of Confederates approached, overlapping the brigade's left, and they were soon ordered to withdraw to the seminary, where they made a valiant stand until, like the rest of the First Corps, they were overwhelmed by the superior numbers of the foe and fled to Cemetery Hill. On July 2 and 3, the brigade was in support of the Second Corps along Cemetery Ridge.

The brigade included the 80th New York (also known as the 20th New York Militia), and the 121st, 142nd, and 151st Pennsylvania regiments; only two regimental chaplains from this brigade were at Gettysburg, and neither left a record of their experiences there.

Second Brigade:

Col. Roy Stone

Stone's Brigade, known as the "Second Bucktail Brigade," consisted of green troops who had never been under fire. They arrived on the field via the Emmitsburg Road and ran across the fields to Seminary Ridge, where they were ordered to throw their knapsacks and blanket rolls in a pile and advance toward McPherson Ridge. They formed a line to the right of the Iron Brigade, facing west, but once Confederates appeared on Oak Hill to the north, two regiments aligned along the Chambersburg Pike. The 149th Pennsylvania rushed the railroad cut in their front and drove back a Confederate advance but soon came under enemy fire from three directions and were forced back. These regiments were the last Union units to leave the McPherson Ridge line. Along with Biddle's brigade, the Bucktails formed a final line of defense in front of the seminary until they could hold no longer and then joined the rest of the First Corps in the retreat through town. The brigade spent most of July 2 in support of guns on Cemetery Hill until they were ordered to the left in the evening where the Union line was under fierce attack. The Bucktails did not engage that day, but some of them were able to recover two abandoned Union guns near the Emmitsburg Road. On July 3, the brigade was behind the Second Corps line along Cemetery Ridge and played a role in repulsing the rebels during the Pickett-Pettigrew-Trimble charge.[132]

The Second Bucktail Brigade comprised three Pennsylvania regiments: the 143rd, 149th, and 150th. Only the latter two had chaplains on their rosters at Gettysburg, and the writings of only one have been located.

James F. Calkins, 149th Pennsylvania Infantry

Chaplain James Calkins of the 149th Pennsylvania "Bucktails." (Library of Congress, Lindquist Family Collection)

James Frederick Calkins was born in Painted Post, New York, on March 27, 1816. He graduated from Union College in Schenectady in 1841 and then attended Auburn Theological Seminary. After graduation, he accepted a call to the Presbyterian Church in Wellsboro, Pennsylvania, where he was ordained in September 1844. A few weeks later, he married Maria Louis Hanford; they had two daughters. In early 1863, there was a diphtheria epidemic among his parishioners, and although he had also contracted the disease, he still cared for his church members and performed thirty funerals in two months. As he was convalescing, he was unable to preach, and he requested a leave of absence from his parish so he could enlist as chaplain of the 149th Pennsylvania Regiment, known as the "Second Bucktails." His illness had delayed him from joining the regiment right away: *"I had held for several months a commission as Chaplain of the 149th Pa. Volunteers. As soon 'after sickness,' as I was able to preach I occupied the pulpit, resigned the pastorate, told them I should start that week for the Army of the Potomac. The Church protested that I would die if I went. I went in May and stayed until the end of the War."*[133] He joined the regiment just weeks before their brutal fight on July 1, during which they suffered a 74 percent casualty rate.

It is interesting to note that the 149th had been without a chaplain since its organization in August 1862, and the lack of spiritual guidance fell hard on some of the soldiers. In February 1863, some forty-three members of the regiment formed the "Christian Association of the One Hundred and Forty-Ninth Regiment, Pennsylvania Volunteers," in which the men agreed to gather regularly for prayer, counsel and advise each other, and *"discard all those things which are calculated to detract from the Christian character."*[134] The arrival of their new chaplain was heralded with much pleasure, at least among the members of the Christian Association, and Calkins soon became a beloved addition to the regiment.

One week after the Battle of Gettysburg, Calkins felt compelled to write a letter to the *Wellsboro Gazette* because he had been watching in vain

> *to find something published approaching the truth regarding the position and suffering of the 3d Division, 2d Brigade, and especially the 149th Regt (. . .) It is now a week after the battle. I have worked as faithfully as all the means in the Regt would allow, to gather the facts in detail. The farther I go in the investigation the more am I convinced that the records of this awful war, sanguinary as they are, do not show a parallel to the fearful havoc and determined bravery of our troops under Gen. Reynolds, and Gen. Doubleday on the first day of the Gettysburg fight. I have waited to see if the facts would not teach the public at some more impartial hand than my own, but in vain. That Wednesday's fight was a prize fight on the part of the enemy; a surprise fight on our part. It revealed the position of the foe and enabled Gen. Meade to assume that masterly defense which ensured us the victory. In fact the first corps by general consent held the key to the success of*

> *our army, And it fell upon the boys of the Bucktail Brigade to lay their hands on that key. They turned, flinching not till they had fully unlocked the door which revealed to us the enemy, though their brave companions were falling around them like grass before the scythe. None of them had ever been in front and under full fire before. They were worn down from marching on the uncertain track of the enemy for three weeks. Many of them went sore footed, and all of them weary, into the fight. But they were on their own soil. Pennsylvania sounded good to them. Its cool air and springs, its fresh butter and milk, above all, its memories of home, dear home, inspired them; Cool as veterans of old campaigns, they fought and fell (. . .)*
>
> *By their side stood the 143d Pa. Vol's, commanded by the gentlemanly Colonel Dana of Wilkes Barre, and the 150th Pa. Vol's, commanded by Colonel Wister, once a captain in the old Bucktails, equally they stood to their post, till there was no longer any object, or possibility of holding it, and then all fell back through the streets of the city, swept by the bullets of the enemy.*[135]

Although there is no evidence that Calkins was, like Chaplain Locke, caught behind the lines at the division hospital, his letter suggests that he was an eyewitness to what happened there during the three days of the battle:

> *Dr. Humphrey, our efficient surgeon-in-chief of the division, had established his hospital in the Catholic Church, and soon with all his wounded and dying men, fell into the hands of the enemy. But unmindful of the change of guards at the door, and caring not whether they wore Gray or blue coats, he went on with his bloody but humane task. They took his horse, and those of his assistant physicians. But what are horses at such a time. The changed countenances of the Rebel officers in those hospitals, during the three days, as they climbed the belfrey [sic] and came down again, now brightening up, and*

Chaplain Calkins may have spent the three days of the battle caring for the wounded in St. Francis Xavier Roman Catholic Church in town.
(St. Francis Xavier)

> *then enlongating inch by inch, till the barbers had to charge a quadruple price for shaving them, was a very instructing scene. When the battle was still raging, so eager were the wounded in the hospital to be doing something, those that could hobble out on their crutches went from house to house, and to every possible place that could hide a rebel, and marched out the gray backs to the guard. Nothing could be more ludicrous than to see one of these limping soldiers marching along the streets, commanding an armed rebel to walk before him, and he with nothing but his crutch to help himself with. While our friend, Dr. Humphrey, was thus passing through the streets, a dutchman told him there was a rebel stealing his horse. The Doctor found him; a fat 180 pound gray back, and took him in charge, marching him to the guard, not thinking till he had delivered him up that his antagonist was armed to the teeth, while he had no weapon.*[136]

Calkins ended his letter by including a lengthy list of casualties and affirming that *"many instances of personal courage have come to my knowledge, but it is difficult to mention those details without disparaging others of equal merit, and without being tedious to those friends for whom this article is prepared that we forbear."*[137]

Calkins remained with the Bucktails for the rest of the war and mustered out with them on June 24, 1865. Returning to his parish at Wellsboro, he continued to minister there until 1879. He then spent ten years as pastor in another church until failing health led him to retire to Geneva, New York, where he died on November 10, 1893. He is buried in Wellsboro, where he had spent a total of 36 years ministering to *"all the flock in the wide wilderness"* of northern Tioga County.[138]

Third Brigade:
Brigadier General George Stannard

Stannard's brigade, called the Second Vermont Brigade, consisted of five nine-month regiments from Vermont that had been assigned to the defenses of Washington and had never been in battle.[139] On June 30, the brigade was rushing to Gettysburg and two of the regiments were left at Westminster, Maryland, to guard the First Corps wagon train. The other three regiments arrived on the field in the evening of July

1 and were sent south of Cemetery Hill behind the remnants of their corps. On July 2, the brigade was moved to a gap in the Union line just south of the Copse of Trees, where they helped the Second Corps troops stem and turn back a rebel assault. Then they advanced toward the Emmitsburg Road and helped recapture four Union cannon on the way. The Vermonters played an important role on July 3 by forming a line from which they fired on the flanks of the rebels during the Pickett-Pettigrew-Trimble charge, thus helping to break up the Confederate assault. Only three regiments in the brigade, which included the 12th, 13th, 14th, 15th, and 16th Vermont, had chaplains with them at Gettysburg, and only two wrote about their time with the regiments.

William Stevenson Smart, 14th Vermont Infantry

Chaplain William Smart of the 14th Vermont Infantry. (Vermont Historical Society)

William Stevenson Smart was born on March 10, 1833, in Johnstown, New York. He attended the Washington Academy in Cambridge, New York, then traveled to San Francisco to study law. He was admitted to the bar in 1856 and practiced law in San Francisco. He then studied theology at Xenia Theological Seminary in Pittsburgh and Union Theological Seminary in New York. He married Sarah Juliet Chipman on September 8, 1858, and the marriage produced three sons. Smart was ordained in 1861 and served the Congregational church in Benson, Vermont, which granted him a leave of absence for nine months so he could serve as chaplain of the 14th Vermont Infantry. He mustered in on October 12, 1862.

Smart wrote a letter to the *Rutland Herald* on July 4, 1863, following the fight at Gettysburg:

> *We have had one of the severest battles of the war, and have won a great victory. After two days of fighting we have driven the enemy before us. The 2d Vermont Brigade were in the thickest of the fight. They occupied one of the most important positions near the centre of the line and were yesterday under the hottest of the fire. Veterans could not have displayed more coolness or made more dashing charges.*[140]

After including a list of casualties, he noted that, as of the date of his letter, the total number of killed, wounded, and missing from the three Vermont regiments that had been engaged was 330. He ended his letter by proclaiming *"Our brigade marched 130 miles in seven days and went into the fight the next day much fatigued, but with their courage and patriotism undiminished. Let us join on this our national anniversary in thanksgiving to Almighty God, the All-Wise Disposer, for our success, and commend to His mercy the suffering and bereaved."*[141]

At the regimental reunion on July 4, 1887, in Fair Haven, Vermont, Smart gave an address in which he recalled the experiences of the 14th at Gettysburg, including its hardships:

> *The perils of war are by no means confined to the battle field. We lost more men on the march to Gettysburg than we did in the battle. We left Wolf Run Shoals on the Occoquan River [in Virginia], June 25, with 723 men. We mustered only 500 men when we stood on Cemetery Hill. Two hundred and twenty-three of our comrades had fallen by the way from the utter exhaustion of their strength. In the battle we lost 100 men, and when we reached Funkstown in the pursuit of Lee, there were not 300 men ready for duty. This was the work of two weeks. So melts an army under the inexorable demands of a campaign.*[142]

Maj. Gen. Abner Doubleday of the First Corps thought highly of the Vermont boys. (Library of Congress)

Smart recognized the "good fortune" of being placed in such a position that their service was conspicuous and meritorious enough to deserve mention by General Meade in his official report of the battle. Smart praised the Vermont men and their reputation as fighters:

> *General Doubleday had no cause to regret the confidence with which he received the Brigade into his division. He was reported to have said when we reached Gettysburg, and others showed some hesitation about accepting us as we were raw troops who had never been in action, "Where are they from?" "They are from Vermont." "Well I will take them. The Vermont boys always*

fight well." Well, boys, you did fight well; and I may say it, who was only your chaplain, and so not entitled to any praise or honor, of the battle field, but the honor of serving and praying for such brave men.[143]

Before closing his address with an overview of the war and its causes, Smart offered these timely words of warning:

> *I do not suppose you are ignorant of the cause which led to our great war [. . .] To many it is a part of your personal history. But a generation is coming who must learn it by a study of the past. We know, because we have lived through the long struggle, that slavery caused the war, and that the removal of that great wrong from the constitution of our country is one of the fairest fruits of the contest. But the generation who know this as a part of their own past are rapidly going. A great epoch in the life of the nation is closing in the departure of those who helped to make it great.*[144]

Smart mustered out with the rest of the regiment at the end of July 1863. He served as pastor at a church in Albany, New York, for twenty-two years, then served another church in Brandon, Vermont until 1905. Sarah died in 1911, and Smart died in Burlington on April 29, 1912. They are buried in Cambridge, New York.

Alonzo Webster, 16th Vermont Infantry

Alonzo Webster was born on January 27, 1818, in Weston, Vermont. Called to preach at an early age, he was admitted into ministry with the Methodist Episcopal Church in 1837. He married Mary Jane Weed in 1840, but she died just two years later, and he took a second wife, Laura Peaslee, in 1844. They had two sons and one daughter.

Chaplain Alonzo Webster of the 16th Vermont Infantry. (Claflin University)

Webster served numerous churches throughout Vermont before the war and worked as an agent for the American Bible Society, chaplain of the Vermont Senate, and chaplain of the state prison at Windsor. He accepted a commission to be chaplain of the

16th Vermont in October 1862, and after serving out the regiment's nine-month term, he enlisted in the 6th Vermont Infantry as its chaplain in October 1863 and served for one year. He was also the owner and editor of the *Vermont Christian Messenger*, and he used this position to write articles that kept the people at home informed about the regiments.

On July 5, two days after Gettysburg's conclusion, Webster sent a letter to the *Messenger* in which he lamented that *"we are so unfortunate that at a time when we have much we wish to write, to be without the material and time to do it. We left our baggage trains between this and Emmettsburg [sic] and have not seen them since. They have on board all our materials for writing, blankets, food, and in fact, all we have to make camp life endurable."*[145] He then described the actions of the Vermont brigade during the three days of battle:

> *By a forced march we arrived here on Wednesday, just at night, and found the battle of the day still raging [. . .] We were immediately marched upon an eminence against the town, in front of the centre of the rebel lines of battle, and took our position, and then slept upon our arms. Thursday opened with skirmishing along the lines, but the terrific fire of artillery, and the deadly strife of battle did not again commence until about 2 o'clock in the afternoon. The rebels had posted their batteries where they could rake our centre, and for a while, the roar of artillery shook the earth, and shot and shell were hurled with fearful screams through the air on their mission of death and ruin.*
>
> *The Vermont troops stood the fire with a cool, unflinching courage that would do honor to old veterans. The three regiments in the action, are said never to have flinched or wavered during the whole contest. They made charges with the greatest success, amid scenes of the greatest peril, and it was said no troops could possibly, under any circumstances, do better than those of our brigade in this fight.*[146]

Webster described what he saw after the Confederates retreated on July 4: *"We now have possession of the hard fought field, strewn thickly with the rebel dead, they not having time, or not caring to take the pains to bury them. An entirely different spirit is manifested by our forces."*[147] He also declared that

> *there is no question of their [the Confederates'] defeat in this mad attempt to invade the north (but) we pay dear for our victory. Our*

> *heart bleeds for our suffering wounded, and all is being done that can be under the circumstances, to make them comfortable. No person can appreciate the fearful horrors of war save those who witness the unsightly wound, and untold horrors and suffering which it inflicts."*[148]

Webster claimed that as the rebels retreated, they spiked several Union guns that had been in front of the Vermont troops, but this was never verified. Webster also lauded the First Vermont Brigade, *"having marched thirty-two miles that day. They came upon the field just in time to save our left wing, which was then being heavily pressed (. . .) we have reason to thank God for his mercy and grace. Through His blessing our national arms are destined to triumph."*[149]

In a second letter, written on July 8, Webster reported that he did not accompany his regiment as they moved toward Frederick, Maryland, in pursuit of the enemy, but remained at Gettysburg to serve as chaplain for the division hospital, where *"we have some six hundred of the 1st army corps, 3d division. Only a small number can find any accommodations in the houses here. They lay in barns, tents, and sheds, with a little straw under them to add to their comfort."*[150] He and the regimental surgeons who stayed behind did not know how long it would be before they could join the regiment on their way home, but in the meantime, they were doing all that could be done under the circumstances to care for the wounded. Webster and the surgeons rode across the battlefield on July 7, taking in the carnage:

> *Many miles were swept with the awful storm of battle, and the field were still strewn with the implements of war, dead horses, and still some of the rebel dead remain unburied. The face of the country is marred and trodden by the contending armies; the ground ploughed, and trees torn by the force of deadly missiles. The stench was intolerable, and it will be long ere the traces of this battle will disappear from the scene of strife.*[151]

He wrapped up his letter by apologizing for not writing more because there were so many wounded men who asked him to write letters to friends and family.

Webster wrote another letter on July 15 reporting that he had no information about the whereabouts of his regiment but could only assume that they were in pursuit of the Confederates. He also noted that it had been *"impossible for us here to get any mail, or reliable news since the battle. The Government now controls the railroads into this place, and the only business appears to be that of carrying the wounded and getting them transported to places where they can receive due care and attention."* [152] Almost all of the wounded of his brigade had already been sent away, and he expected

> *the Sixteenth Regiment will soon be relieved from service and at farthest will report at Brattleboro during the coming week. It is hoped that even before this, the fate of the rebel army will be decided, and it now appears to us, that we have good reasons to anticipate its overthrow. If this can only be done, it will add in no small degree to our joy as we return home from this brief service, which is closing amid stirring events of great magnitude to the country. We shall return with joy, and yet with sorrow. We sorrow for the noble dead that have fallen by sickness and battle, and have thus sacrificed their lives in the noble cause so dear to us. We deeply sympathize with their kindred, who will never enjoy the pleasure of meeting their friends again on earth. All honor to the dead, who thus die for the country, and all comfort to the friends who mourn their loss. It will give us joy to see our friends and homes again, and to know that our conduct as soldiers, has brought no dishonor to our native State, and that we have done something to defeat a defiant foe, and turn back from the free States the boasting army of the South, who were bent upon the invasion of our homes, the dishonor of our flag, and the destruction of our Government.* [153]

Webster submitted an article for his paper on July 28 after the regiment had finally arrived in Vermont, *"weary and worn by toil and danger, [and] glad to rest from the tiresome march and daily toil of the soldier's life."* [154] He noted that the division hospital had been broken up on July 18, and at that time,

> *eighteen thousand wounded had been sent away, and it was thought that at least as many more were awaiting transportation. It will be observed that this included a part of the rebel wounded. A large number of wounded came on the same train with us to Baltimore. It was gratifying to witness the careful attention given to supply their wants at the various stations where we stopped. Refreshments were gratuitously provided to an ample extent (. . .) We judged from appearances that a change for the better had come over the people in Baltimore since the breaking out of this war.* [155]

In addition, he noted that *"as we passed on through Maryland and Pennsylvania, we were greeted with unexpected demonstrations from the people, who thronged the roadside in every village we passed, waving flags and handkerchiefs, in marked contrast with their appearance when we were passing through there to the seat of war."*[156] The regiment and those returning from detached duty in Gettysburg serendipitously met in Baltimore, where many of them received the first mail delivery since being in camp in Virginia. The 16th comprised the last of the nine-month Vermont men to be mustered out of service, and Webster said they all expected *"to know again the freedom of civil life, where 'red tape,' and the drill and the burdens of the soldier's mechanical life, shall be among the things that were."*[157] He ended by recognizing those who paid the ultimate price for their service, and by trusting *"that the blood of these patriots may give new life to the Republic."*[158]

In a final article about the Gettysburg campaign, published in late August 1863, Webster felt compelled to refute some information he had seen in other papers claiming some of the wounded Vermonters had suffered needlessly from a lack of proper and attentive care:

> *When the wounded were being brought in to our hospitals, the surgeons connected with the Vermont brigade, worked two nights in succession, taking for themselves little or no rest or sleep during this time. Our surgeons evidently had not only professional skill for their business, but feeling hearts, and working hands, in the discharge of their onerous duties. The Vermont Brigade at the Battle of Gettysburg, were included in the first army corps, and unfortunately for us, a large number of the surgeons of this Corps, were taken prisoners on the first day of the fight, when the rebels gained possession of the town. This threw a greater amount of labor and responsibility upon the surgeons of our brigade, for the two succeeding days of that terrible conflict.*[159]

He ended this editorial with a personal reflection on his experience:

> *War is a fearful scourge, and no person distant from the scenes of the bloody field of battle, can form any just idea of its unsightly horrors, and multiplied woes; but even the dark and frowning cloud of war has a silver lining, in the sympathy of man for his suffering brother, and in the efficient arrangement of our government and voluntary associations, to reach with cordials and care, the bleeding victims of this national strife, whether they be friends or foes.*[160]

While Webster was with the regiment on the way to Gettysburg, he experienced a personal tragedy when his daughter Hattie died of diphtheria on June 30 at the age of six, and he was not able to attend the funeral. But his grief must have been partially assuaged by the fact that his son Dan Peaslee Webster, age 16, was with him during his time of service to help care for the sick and wounded, especially at Gettysburg. Dan went on to become a doctor.

After he mustered out of the 16th, Webster accepted a commission in the regular army and was stationed at the post hospital in Montpelier, Vermont. In 1865, he was sent to South Carolina to work as a missionary among freed slaves and to organize a Methodist Episcopal church there. He helped found and was the first president of Claflin University at Orangeburg, South Carolina, and served as editor for several publications. His wife Laura died in 1885, and he married his third wife, S. O. Purdom, a year later. He died in his native state of Vermont on August 1, 1887, and is buried in Brattleboro.

Webster was the first president of Claflin University in South Carolina, which offered for the first time in that state higher education regardless of race or religion. (From *History of Higher Education in South Carolina* by Colyer Meriwether, 1889)

Chapter 3:

The Second Corps

CORPS COMMANDERS:

Major General Winfield Scott Hancock
Brigadier General John Gibbon

The Second Corps of the Army of the Potomac marched more than thirty miles on June 29th and reached Uniontown, Maryland, at 10:00 p.m., where they stayed in camp the next day. On July 1 they arrived in Taneytown around 11:00 a.m. but were able to rest for only two hours until they were ordered to continue toward Gettysburg. They stopped about three miles south of town by 4:00 p.m. and went into bivouac for the night. At dawn on July 2, the corps set out again and reached the battlefield by 7:00 a.m. After changing positions several times, they were finally inserted into the Union line along Cemetery Ridge with their right connecting with the Eleventh Corps just west of the summit of Cemetery Hill and their left connecting with the Third Corps north of Little Round Top.

Late in the morning of July 2, some Second Corps regiments engaged Confederate troops to gain control of the Bliss Farm, which sat between the lines and provided a good position for the skirmishers of whichever army could maintain possession. Later in the day, one division of the Second Corps was sent to support the Third Corps troops in the Wheatfield while elements of the other two divisions were sent to confront the Confederate attacks along the Emmitsburg Road and to hold the center of the Union line along the northern part of Cemetery Ridge. With support from some First Corps regiments, the line held despite a brief breakthrough by some determined Georgians.

On July 3, the Second Corps endured the great cannonade before the Pickett-Pettigrew-Trimble charge, and then successfully, but bloodily, defended its position along the Angle and around the Copse of Trees against the Confederates who had made it that far in the charge.

FIRST DIVISION:

Brigadier General John C. Caldwell

First Brigade:

Colonel Edward Cross / Colonel H. Boyd McKeen

The soldiers of Col. Edward Cross's brigade arrived on the field at Gettysburg on the morning of July 2 and assembled en masse on Cemetery Ridge near the center of the Union line. The men enjoyed a leisurely morning, but when fighting broke out along the lines of the Third Corps that afternoon Cross's men were the first troops to enter the fray in the Wheatfield. Two of the brigade's regiments held their position in the center of the Wheatfield for about half an hour until they were pushed back by overwhelming numbers of enemy troops. The other two regiments were protected by tree cover and a stone wall and held firm until about 7:00 p.m., at which time they were relieved by another brigade. About an hour earlier, Cross had fallen and Col. H. Boyd McKeen of the 81st Pennsylvania assumed command of the brigade. That night, the brigade built breastworks along the position they had held that morning, which gave them protection from the great cannonade the next day. On July 5, the brigade joined the pursuit of the Confederate army.

The brigade included four regiments: the 5th New Hampshire, 61st New York, and 81st and 148th Pennsylvania. Three had chaplains with them at Gettysburg, but we have a record of service for only one of them.

William Henry Stevens, 148th Pennsylvania Infantry

William Henry Stevens was born in Shirleysburg, Pennsylvania, on December 12, 1831. While working as a plasterer, he felt called to the ministry and was licensed to preach by the Methodist Episcopal Church in 1854. He married Margaretta Sheffler on February 18, 1858, and they had five sons, two of whom died young. Stevens was serving two churches in Centre County, Pennsylvania, in 1862 when his parishioners asked him to recruit part of a company that was assigned to the 148th Pennsylvania Volunteers. Stevens mustered in on August 16, 1862, as second lieutenant of Company H.

Chaplain William Henry Stevens of the 148th Pennsylvania Infantry. (Three Springs - Saltillo Historical Society)

No sooner was the regiment organized than Stevens was summoned to the quarters of Col. James A. Beaver, who was seeking a chaplain for the regiment. Although there were several applicants for the position, the colonel asked Stevens, *"Lieutenant, which would you prefer, to retain your present position with the possibilities of promotion or become Chaplain of the Regiment?"* Stevens replied, *"My business is preaching, I would rather be Chaplain,"* and Beaver told him, *"Then go sell your sword and buy a Bible."*[1]

Col. James A. Beaver of the 148th Pennsylvania Infantry wanted a good chaplain for his regiment. (US Army Heritage and Education Center)

No documents or letters written by Stevens have been located, but we can learn a bit about his experience at Gettysburg through the words of his son Emory in his "Story of the Chaplain" in the regimental history.[2] Here is Emory's recollection of his father's stories about Gettysburg:

> *During the race with Lee for Gettysburg, on the first day of the battle, the Regiment made thirty-five miles; the heat was intense and the dust several inches deep, rising and settling everywhere and filling eyes, ears and throat. Much of the afternoon of that day his horse was at the disposal of the foot-sore. The Regiment neither knew where they were marching nor what was transpiring in their front. Toward evening he stepped out of the column, and from an old man near the road, learned that a great battle was being fought and that one of the Union Generals had been*

killed. This was the first news the Regiment received of Gettysburg where so many of their number were to fall. A few minutes later an orderly passed asking for General Hancock, and still later the escort bearing the body of General Reynolds was met.[3]

Like most chaplains, Stevens despised the use of profanity and would chastise those who uttered profane oaths, but he made an exception on July 3:

> *The only time he ever heard anything savoring of profanity, that was not utterly repulsive to him was during the great artillery duel of the third day. He was with the reserve artillery, which was parked near Rock Creek. It seemed to him that everything was being blown to pieces and at the rate the reserve was being hurried to the front, there soon would be none left. A Lieutenant in charge of a field piece came back; two horses were dragging the gun, one wheel of which was gone, the axle being supported by a rail. As the Lieutenant was coupling to a new gun the Chaplain ventured to ask:*
>
> *"Lieutenant, how is it going up there?"*
>
> *Sharp and emphatic the answer came, "Oh, we're just giving them h—."*
>
> *The Chaplain felt relieved, and if General Sherman's definition of War is correct, the Lieutenant's answer described the true situation.*[4]

Stevens had close encounters with two generals at Gettysburg, one Union and one Confederate. On July 2, when Confederate brigadier general William Barksdale was mortally wounded during his brigade's advance on Cemetery Ridge, he was captured and carried to the Jacob Hummelbaugh farmhouse, just down the Taneytown Road from General Meade's headquarters, where Stevens "*assisted in the care of General Barksdale [. . .] as also in his burial under the little peach tree, near General Meade's headquarters.*"[5]

When Confederate general William Barksdale was mortally wounded on July 2, Chaplain Stevens helped care for him at the Hummelbaugh House on Taneytown Road. (Library of Congress)

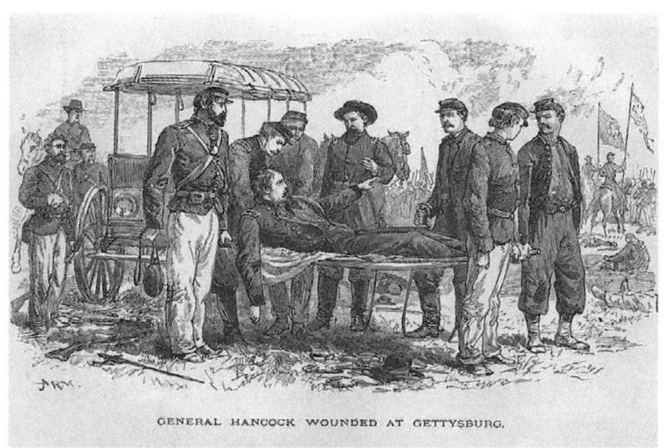

Stevens was present when Maj. Gen. Winfield Scott Hancock was brought to the corps hospital after being wounded on July 3. (from The life of Winfield Scott Hancock: Personal, Military, and Political, 1880)

On July 3, Union Second Corps commander Winfield Scott Hancock was wounded near the end of the repulse of the Pickett-Pettigrew-Trimble charge when a shot hit his saddle and forced a nail from the saddle tree into his groin. Stevens was present in the corps hospital when surgeons were examining the wound, and he noted that when the nail was discovered, *"the remarks made by the General when told of the discovery were not exactly religious."*[6]

On the morning after the battle, a group of men from the 148th were gathering up wounded Confederates lying between the lines. Stevens was offering food to a Confederate officer who said that the men in his regiment came north expecting to fight

> *a few militia and home guards and only realized what was before them, when on the morning of July 2d, they saw the butterfly of the Second Corps and knew that that meant the Army of the Potomac was in their front. This officer refused to be exchanged when the opportunity was presented, said that it was useless to fight longer and that he had enough of it.*[7]

Later that day, *"the Chaplain counted five dead rebels, each shot through the forehead, behind a rock, in front of the Regiment's position in the second day's fight, bearing awful testimony to the marksmanship of the command."*[8]

In April 1863, the regimental officers presented their chaplain with a magnificent and very large saddle horse named Jim, which became Stevens's constant companion for the rest of the war. Because Jim was so big and flashy, he was prone to being taken by other soldiers (or waggoneers) who needed a good horse. On the evening of July 2,

> *Jim was left in the rear of Cemetery Ridge, while the Chaplain went to the line to minister to any in need of his services. When he*

returned, Jim was gone, a cavalry officer having appropriated him. He was recovered the next day. The officer at first with a good deal of bluster and many threats refused to surrender him, but when he discovered that the Chaplain, who had only a fatigue suit on, probably ranked him, quickly quieted down and meekly listened to a lecture on horse stealing.[9]

Stevens became severely ill in the spring of 1864 and was sent to a hospital in Washington where doctors were convinced he would not survive. He was furloughed in September and sent home to die, but with tender care from family and friends and, according to Emory, with the help of some radishes, Stevens recovered and rejoined the regiment six weeks later.[10]

The 148th fought its final battle at Farmville, Virginia, two days before the surrender of General Lee's army at Appomattox on April 9, 1865, and they mustered out on June 3. After the war, Stevens returned to his ministry, but with his health compromised, he asked to be put on leave for a few years to recover from both the lingering illness and the strain from his army service. He was elected to the Pennsylvania House of Representatives as a Republican in 1888 even though he had not sought the office; he refused reelection in 1890. Margaretta died in 1895, and a year later Stevens married Catherine Linn, the widow of his friend and colleague Rev. Hugh Linn. In 1901, Stevens retired from both political service and active ministry, and he died on June 10 of that year in Shelby, Iowa. He is buried in Three Springs Cemetery, Huntingdon County, Pennsylvania.

Second Brigade:
Colonel Patrick Kelly

After hard fighting in every campaign since Bull Run in 1861, the famed "Irish Brigade" was greatly reduced in numbers and was the smallest brigade in the Army of the Potomac, with three of its regiments fighting together as one unit. They arrived at Gettysburg with the rest of the Second Corps on the morning of July 2 and formed to the right of Cross's brigade along Cemetery Ridge. They entered the Wheatfield to the right of Cross and remained on Stony Hill until Confederate troops nearly surrounded them, and the brigade fell back in some disorder. That evening, the survivors gathered in their former position on Cemetery Ridge. Early on July 3, they built breastworks and remained behind them all day until they helped repel the far right of the Confederate advance (the brigades of Cadmus Wilcox and David Lang) during the Pickett-Pettigrew-Trimble charge. That evening, they repaired their breastworks in anticipation of another attack that never came, and late in the afternoon on July 5 they began to march after the Army of Northern Virginia.

At its formation in late 1861, the Irish Brigade consisted of six regiments and five Roman Catholic priests as chaplains. By the time of Gettysburg, only Father William Corby remained to serve as chaplain for the small brigade, which included the 28th Massachusetts, 63rd, 69th, and 88th New York, and 116th Pennsylvania regiments.[11]

Father William Corby, 88th New York Infantry and Irish Brigade

William Corby was born in Detroit, Michigan, on October 2, 1833. He enrolled in Notre Dame University at the age of nineteen and was ordained a priest on December 25, 1860. When his religious superior called for volunteers to serve as chaplains in 1861, he resigned from his professional duties and headed to Washington, where he was assigned to the 88th New York Infantry and became part of the Irish Brigade. Corby left a memoir in which he recounted his experiences with the brigade throughout their term of service.

On June 29, Corby noted that the Second Corps *"made the longest march [. . .] by infantry of any department during the war,"* a total of 34 miles.[12] When some soldiers became exhausted and declared they could not continue, others urged their comrades on by repeating the rumor that "Little Mac" (Gen. George B. McClellan) was back in command of the Army of the Potomac, which Corby noted had a good effect on the men. Late that night, Corby described a tired marching army:

Father William Corby served as chaplain of the Irish Brigade. (Notre Dame Archives)

> *As a rule, not a voice is heard. Fatigue and drowsiness, added to a rather weak and faint feeling, indispose men to converse, and by*

silent consent each one discontinues conversation. The click of a large spur, the occasional rattle of a sword, and other mechanical movements are the only sounds heard above the slow, steady tramp of the line and the heavy tread of the few horses that carry mounted officers. Even these mounted officers frequently dismount and walk to avoid being overpowered by sleep and to save themselves from falling from the horses. Many, many times I had to do so.[13]

While the corps was resting at Taneytown, Maryland, on July 1, *"a courier came up at break-neck speed, his horse panting and covered with foam. He announced that fighting was going on at Gettysburg [. . .] and at once we resumed our march. We had about thirteen miles to go."*[14] The corps arrived late in the day and were posted along Cemetery Ridge. The next day, Corby described the flurry of activity going on around the corps:

The two great contending forces watched each other keenly with beating hearts and anxious expectation of what result might follow the pending struggle. Generals are in a "brown study," staff officers and orderlies are dashing along the lines from left to right and from right to left, carrying orders. On the flanks the cavalry and light artillery are on a sharp look-out, and all are astir. One can hardly imagine the stupendous task it is to dispose a large army of tens of thousands of men and hundreds of cannon to advantage.[15]

The priest turned his thoughts to the citizens of Gettysburg and could *"scarcely imagine the trepidation of these poor people [. . .] Many fervent prayers were said and holy vows pronounced, no doubt, especially on the nights of the first and second."*[16] Once it became obvious that the brigade would be sent in to support the collapsing Third Corps line in the Wheatfield, *"at this critical moment [the chaplain] proposed to give a general absolution to our men, as they had had absolutely no chance to practice their religious duties during the past two or three weeks, being constantly on the march."*[17] The priest then offered his famous "absolution under fire" and the men dutifully followed their bright green flags into the fray.

Corby was surprised by the effect of his absolution. A week after the battle, a captain he knew not to be particularly religious approached him while on the march and said, *"Chaplain, I would like to know more about your religion. I was present on that awful day, July 2, when you 'made a prayer,' and while I have often witnessed ministers make prayers I have never witnessed one so powerful as the one you made that day in front of*

Father Corby offering absolution at Gettysburg on July 2. (from *The Story of the 116th Regiment Pennsylvania Volunteers in the War of the Rebellion* by St. Claire Mulholland)

Hancock's corps just as the ball opened with 120 guns blazing at us."[18] Corby noted *"one good result of the Civil War was the removing of a great amount of prejudice. When men stand in common danger, a fraternal feeling springs up between them and generates a Christian, charitable sentiment that often leads to excellent results."*[19]

Corby was invited by the surviving members of the brigade to attend the twenty-fifth anniversary of the battle, an event he called *"one of the grandest and most interesting sights of my life. The emotions that filled my breast when I met the surviving officers and men once more on the field that drank in the blood of so many of our dead companions may be more easily imagined than described."*[20] The former chaplain gave an address to the crowds, and *"at first I got on reasonably well, until, looking over our illustrious and numerous band as it appeared at Alexandria, Va., in the fall of '61. I happened to make this statement, 'Here is what is left of us; where are the others?' when I filled up very unexpectedly and could not speak for several minutes. I had struck a very tender chord."*[21]

While at Gettysburg for the anniversary, Colby paid homage to the priest at the Roman Catholic church in Gettysburg, the Rev. Joseph A. Boll, who had visited the battlefield immediately after the battle a year before he was ordained as a priest. When the steeple of the church was being repaired years after the battle, the carpenter found a Southern bullet embedded in a timber, and Rev. Boll gave it to Father Corby.[22]

Rev. Joseph A. Boll found a Confederate bullet in the steeple of St. Francis Xavier Church and presented it to Father Corby. (St. Francis Xavier Church)

Photo of the newly erected monument to Father William Corby by photographer William H. Tipton, circa 1910. (Gettysburg National Military Park Library)

After the war, Father Corby returned to his teaching duties at Notre Dame University, where he served as vice president and then president. After spending time at Sacred Heart College in Wisconsin, Corby returned to Notre Dame and oversaw a campus rebuilding program following a devastating fire in 1879. He died on December 28, 1897, and his casket was carried to his burial place in Notre Dame's Holy Cross Cemetery not by fellow priests, as was the custom, but by Civil War veterans, and he was afforded full military honors.

In 1910, a monument to Father Corby was dedicated at Gettysburg, the only one to a chaplain on an American battlefield. The statue is assumed to have been placed on the rock on which the priest stood when he offered the general absolution, but some accounts differ from the generally accepted circumstances about the monument's placement (see sidebar).

Third Brigade:
Brigadier General Samuel Zook

The brigade under the command of Brig. Gen. Samuel Zook arrived with the rest of the Second Corps troops on the morning of July 2 after an exhausting night march that included only a few brief stops. By 10:00 a.m., the brigade was positioned on Cemetery Ridge behind the Irish Brigade, and the men were finally allowed to rest. Later that afternoon, they marched toward the Wheatfield to add strength to the Third Corps' defense against the Confederate attack. As the brigade moved near Stony Hill, Zook was mortally wounded while the unit faced heavy fire. Along with the Irish Brigade on their left, they repelled one rebel attack before their line was broken by the advance of other Confederate troops approaching on their flank, and they fell back to the position they held that morning.

Zook's men did not engage in the fighting on July 3 and spent the next two days resting and burying the dead. Out of the four regiments in the brigade, the 52nd, 57th, and 66th New York and the 140th Pennsylvania, only the 52nd was accompanied by a chaplain.

Fourth Brigade:
Colonel John Brooke

Brooke's brigade reached Gettysburg early on July 2. After remaining east of the Taneytown Road for a while, they formed with the rest of their division on Cemetery Ridge. The brigade was the last of Brig. Gen. John Caldwell's units to enter the fray in the Wheatfield that afternoon. With Cross's brigade on their left and the other two brigades on their right, Brooke's men entered the Wheatfield with their line reaching almost from one side of the field to the other. After stopping to fire at Confederates at the southern edge of the field, they were ordered to advance up a rugged ledge into the Rose Woods, moving beyond the rest of the division. At the top of the ledge, the brigade engaged Confederate troops in their front and on both flanks. None of the division's other brigades were moving up in support, so Brooke's men had no choice but to pull back amid heavy fire. Colonel Brooke was wounded during the fighting. The brigade lined up along the Wheatfield Road until they were relieved by Fifth Corps troops and could return to their original position on Cemetery Ridge.

On July 3, the men constructed breastworks in the morning, but when the Pickett-Pettigrew-Trimble charge surged forward that afternoon, the rebels veered off to the north and out of range for Brooke's men. The brigade did capture some Alabama soldiers when they made their ill-fated advance toward the end of the Confederate charge. Brooke's men buried the dead and rested for two days and finally left the field in pursuit of the rebels late on July 5. Three of the five regiments in the brigade—2nd Delaware, 27th Connecticut, 64th New York, and 53rd and 145th Pennsylvania—had chaplains with them, but only one recorded his experiences.

Chaplain John H. W. Stuckenberg of the 145th Pennsylvania Infantry. (from *I'm Surrounded by Methodists*)

John Henry Wilbrand Stuckenberg was born on January 6, 1835, in Bramsche, Germany. His father and sister emigrated to the United States in 1837, and the rest of the family followed two years later. They settled first in Pittsburgh, Pennsylvania, and then in Cincinnati. Stuckenberg graduated from Wittenberg College in Ohio in 1857 and remained there for one more year to complete his theological studies. After serving a Lutheran congregation in Iowa for a year, he traveled to Germany to pursue a doctoral degree at the University of Halle.

When the Civil War broke out, Stuckenberg returned to America and accepted a position as pastor of a new congregation in Erie, Pennsylvania. Stuckenberg encouraged his parishioners to answer President Lincoln's call for more troops in July 1862: *"He was very anxious to enlist his services on the side of the north, and pleaded its cause as worthy of every man's support. He regarded it as his duty to be an example to the people of Erie by joining the army as a chaplain, which would enable him to perform the task for which he was most qualified."*[23] Stuckenberg enlisted as chaplain of the 145th Pennsylvania Infantry on September 10, 1862.

During his time of service, Stuckenberg kept a journal that detailed the events he witnessed, including the Gettysburg campaign, and in January 1864 he gave a lecture on the subject. [24] While describing the hard marches leading toward Pennsylvania, he noted how much the soldiers wanted to leave Virginia, where they had felt very unwelcomed. They crossed into Maryland on June 26th and faced more long marches until they arrived in Uniontown on June 29, where Stuckenberg noted the men *"were completely worn out and they needed all the 30th for rest."*[25] The regiment marched through Taneytown on July 1 and *"looked anxiously forward to our entering our own beloved state–Pennsylvania–crossed the line with much pleasure, heard reports of an engagement at Gettysburg and of the death of Gen. Reynolds whose body was conveyed past us in an ambulance."*[26] They bivouacked in a field a couple of miles south of Gettysburg that evening, glad for the chance to rest, but uneasy because they did not know the disposition of the enemy in their front.

On the morning of July 2, their officers *"exhorted those under them to do their duty faithfully, and that perhaps the impending battle might end the war."*[27] The brigade was massed in columns by regiments near the center of the Union line on Cemetery Ridge. They watched the Irish Brigade participate in Father Corby's act of absolution, and then Stuckenberg led his regiment in a prayer:

> *Seeing the Irish brigade bowed in prayer and feeling deeply impressed with the idea that many might enter the battle never to return, I asked permission of Col. Brown to hold worship before entering the battle. He willingly acquiesced. "Attention" was called. After a few remarks we joined in prayer. The occasion was a very solemn one–it was the last prayer in which some of our regt joined.*[28]

Then, "*I lay with the regt till about noon, when becoming hungry, I started to hunt my horse which had been sent to the rear with my provisions [. . .] I was very tired and after dinner lay down to rest. But immediately the heavy thunder of cannon was heard on the front. This was about 3 P.M.*"[29]

When the rebel artillery opened,

> *I jumped up, took my canteen and some bandages and hastened to go to the regiment. But coming to the top of a hill the shells fell rapidly between the regt. and myself, and I thought it folly to expose myself. I remained on this hill for a while, attending to some wounded men, watching the prisoners who came in and the fight generally as much as possible. But soon my position became too much exposed. The shells came nearer and nearer, some exploding just in front of me. One struck the ground a short distance before me and threw its pieces and earth and rocks high in the air. Some shells fell near the place where my horse was. A kind of panic seized the "bummers" [those soldiers who shirked their duty to be on the battle line] and others–all who hurried farther back. The hospital was moved hastily. I moved my horse, took him farther back to the side of a hill under cover of some high rocks. Leaving my horse there in charge of some of our regt. I went to assist the wounded.*[30]

While at the hospital, Stuckenberg saw the regiment's colonel, Hiram L. Brown, suffering terribly from a wounded arm, and Brig. Gen. Samuel Zook of the same division, who was mortally wounded.

Colonel Brown asked Stuckenberg to find the regiment's adjutant, John Black, who had been badly wounded, and the chaplain found him at the Eleventh Corps hospital, where he *"was willing and ready to die and longing for death to relieve him. I asked him whether he had any words for his parents? 'Tell them,' he replied, 'that I fell in a noble cause . . . I have been a bad boy . . . but God is merciful.'"*[31]

As night fell, Stuckenberg and one of the surgeons left the hospital to try to find more wounded men of the regiment on the battlefield:

> *We soon came to a house full of wounded men, with only one or two well ones to wait on them. We went on farther, over fields & rocks & stone walls & through woods not knowing whither our course would lead us. We met few soldiers, heard but little noise. The very stillness was fearful & oppressive. A dread came upon us as I neared the ground where the desperate fighting had taken place in the afternoon. At any moment I might stumble on some corpse or fall over some wounded man. We frequently stopped to listen for groans, but heard none till we came to another house.*
>
> *I asked for the wounded of our regt. and found one man answering to my call. I passed through between the wounded men outside the house, entered the house, with great difficulty passed in the dark through a room in which were some wounded men, & entered another room. On a bed suffering terribly lay Forbes of Co. G, wounded through the breast. He begged us to dress his wounds, but as there was no candle to be had, this was out of the question. I gave him some whiskey to stimulate him and then left the many wounded at their house (no physicians to attend them, no candle even, though they were taken away as fast as the ambulance could carry them) and went further to the front.*
>
> *Back of the house we saw the first corpse. Scarcely had we passed it when a bullet from the rebels whistled past us and warned us to proceed no further. Nor could we have gone much further, for our picket line was but a short distance in front of us. In again passing the house we had just left we heard subdued, but constant groaning near the barn. I found a rebel there, seriously wounded, who gave no answer to the question, whether I could do anything for him? he being perhaps unconscious and near his end. In passing from the field we learned that a wounded man was lying all alone in the woods. We carried him to a place where he*

could easily be found, and sent a stretcher for him. We went back to the hospital, where I found quite a number of our wounded. I then went to bed. Seldom had I been so tired. Nature had endured all it could and now coveted the balmy restorer–sleep.[32]

On the morning of July 3, Stuckenberg visited the hospital again and found many wounded men lying on the bare ground with no shelter. Then he *"soon started to the front to see the regt. It was very small–66 men and officers, commanded by Captain Oliver. Though saddened by their heavy loss, they were in good spirits because they had driven the rebels and taken 75 or 100 prisoners."*[33]

After a while, he returned to the hospital to rest but was soon roused by the sound of fighting on Culp's Hill, behind the hospital. He heard Union artillery firing from a nearby position, and he

ascended a rocky hill–it was composed of large masses of rocks–to the middle one of the three batteries. Gen. [Henry] Slocum [commanding the Twelfth Corps] was here, in person directing the firing. A short distance before us was a round hill [Culp's], covered with trees. On the side of the hill nearest us, the smoke was seen rising in columns from the forest–there the fighting took place. The rattling of musketry was constant, rapid & terrific. The columns of smoke indicated the progress of the fight. It also served to indicate the position of the rebels to the artillerists. The shelling was rapid and must have produced terrible havoc in the rebel ranks.[34]

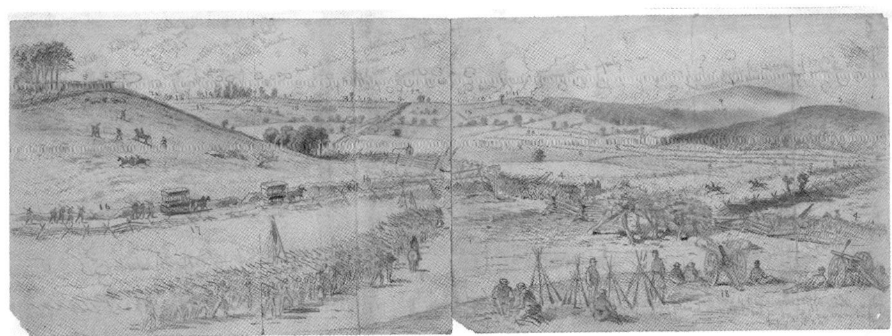

Chaplain Stuckenberg climbed Powers Hill on July 3 to watch the Union batteries in action as they fired toward Culp's Hill. In this sketch from Edwin Forbes, Powers Hill is to the far left. (Library of Congress)

The division field hospital, which had been located at the Granite School House not far from the Twelfth Corps hospital at the George Spangler Farm, came under fire from the cannonade on July 3 and was moved about three-quarters of a mile south to the banks of Rock Creek. Stuckenberg reported:

> *for hours I searched ineffectually for [the hospital]. I was faint & sick. The heat was almost insufferable. I walked till I gave out, put wet leaves in my hat & rested–walked on again, obtained some coffee & a cracker from H. Hays of our regiment, started for our hospital again, which was in the woods, on the side of a hill, on the right bank of Rock Creek. I found Genl's Hancock & Gibbon there, both wounded, and thousands of other men & officers of our own corps. And more were constantly being brought in. Of our regiment there were many scattered about in different hospitals & some were on the field of battle in the hands of the enemy.*[35]

Just before he started to search for the Second Corps hospital, Stuckenberg came across Capt. John Hilton of Company K lying on the ground with a shattered leg. Because he was in extreme pain, the captain refused to be moved to the new hospital location. The surgeons told Stuckenberg that the young man had no hope of recovery, and the chaplain asked if he might break the news:

> *My task was a delicate, unpleasant and sad one. When I told him that probably his wound would be fatal, he told me he had feared it, but it seemed he never so fully realized it as then. His eyes filled with tears, deep emotions were traced on his youthful countenance, he cast a glance upward & lay silent. "Chaplain, what does it take to constitute a Christian?" He was very anxious about his soul. He had been piously trained, had been a good boy, it seems, but for some years had been rather careless. After conversing awhile on the subject of religion, he spoke about his mother & sisters. Were it not for them death would be easy. He loved them tenderly & wanted to live for their sakes. His deep feeling moved me deeply–he was overwhelmed with emotion–he, his servant, and I, all of us wept. He said he did not want to be taken to the hospital–he must die anyhow and would as soon die where he was as anywhere else. "Bury me," he said as if utterly hopeless of recovery, "under this tree." His leg has since been amputated & strong hopes are entertained of his recovery.*[36]

On July 4, Stuckenberg walked across the ground where the regiment had fought two days earlier and saw *"Guns, bayonets, & bayonet scabbards, cartridge boxes, & cartridges, haversacks & canteens were thrown and scattered in all directions. Among the dead we soon recognized those of our own regiment . . . They were carried to an apple tree, under whose shadow they fought. I offered a prayer and left the bodies there to be buried."*[37] As he started back to his regiment, the major of the 64th New York asked him to hold services for his regiment since they had no chaplain. Stuckenberg recalled,

> *I did so immediately after leaving our dead. The men were behind their breastworks, I stood in front of them. Brisk skirmishing was going on all the time, and rebels as well as our men could be seen running and firing. A rebel flag was also seen at the edge of the woods. Worship at such a place, at such a time, with fearful scenes just enacted & being enacted, was very solemn. I thanked God that we had been spared, prayed for the many wounded & remembered the relatives and friends of the killed. The solders felt deeply & many were moved to tears.*[38]

He planned to hold services for his regiment, but a rebel battery opened on some skirmishers near the position of the 145th. One shell struck directly in front of them, and the chaplain was advised to go to the rear.

Stuckenberg returned to the relocated Second Corps hospital and was heartbroken by what he saw, including some wounded who were lying in the mud with nothing to shield them from the rain. He went on to describe in gruesome detail the horrors he witnessed:

> *What a hospital on or near the field of battle is can only be known by those that have seen one. There were between 2000 and 3000 wounded in 2nd corps hospital. In 1st Division there were two operating stands, where the Surgeons were constantly consulting about operations and were performing amputations. Heaps of amputated feet & hands, arms & legs were seen lying under the tables and by their sides. Go around among the wounded and you witness the most saddening and sickening sights. Some are writhing in pain, deeply moaning and groaning and calling for relief which cannot be afforded them. The finest forms are horribly disfigured & mutilated. Wounds are found in all parts of the body. Here lies one with his leg shattered, the flesh torn by a shell, nothing*

but shreds being left. There lies one shot through the abdomen, the intestines protruding–his life cannot be saved, perhaps even opium gives him but little temporary relief. He is but waiting to die. Here lies one with his arm almost severed from his body–waiting for amputation. There lies one young and once handsome shot through the face and head–his eyes swollen shut & covered with a yellow, putrid matter, his hair clotted with blood, his jaws torn, & a bullet hole through each cheek. Some of the wounds are dressed, some not. From some the blood still oozes, in others maggots are perhaps found. Perhaps they are poorly waited on, there not being nurses enough. No physician may have examined their wounds and dressed them. Their physical wants may not have been attended to. They long for home & their friends, but they cannot get to the one, the other cannot come to them. Through neglect, perhaps, they die. They are buried in their clothes, without shroud, without coffin, perhaps without religious services and a board to mark their resting place. The hospital soon becomes foul, especially in summer–the stench sometimes being almost intolerable. Medicines may be scarce, the food unpalatable–perhaps scarce. Near the battle field of Gettysburg the barns for miles were filled with wounded, many of whom had neither surgeons, nor nurses, nor food.[39]

The regiment left Gettysburg on July 5 and camped at Two Taverns until July 7. Stuckenberg was sick and weak and he traveled to see a friend in nearby Littlestown who helped him find a comfortable place to rest. On July 7, Stuckenberg and his friend loaded their saddlebags with provisions and headed back to the hospital. Although he wanted to stay and care for the wounded, he and all the other chaplains of the division except one were ordered to return to their regiments. He and his friend rode south across the battlefield and noticed that some of the dead rebel soldiers had been hastily buried, but others were lying on the ground waiting for burial. *"The stench was fearful, almost intolerable. The bodies, some horribly mangled lay there five days exposed to the sun–black rotting, full of worms."*[40] As he finally started for Taneytown to join his regiment, he noted *"with what feelings I left that field! We had suffered severely, but ours was the victory."*[41] When he rejoined the 145th, he *"felt somewhat lost . . . and somewhat homesick, for so many of my dearest & best friends in the regt. were absent."*[42]

Although he was profoundly devoted to the men in his regiment, Stuckenberg's heart was always with his parishioners in Erie, who had been without a pastor for a year. Perhaps he was moved by a letter from the church he received in September 1863: *"On Sundays we are rather dull at present. Reading sermons [provided by Stuckenberg] is regarded with but little favor by most of our members, and the attendance consequently [is] slender."*[43] He tendered his resignation on September 28, citing both the needs of his parish and also the fact that because the brigade had been reduced to the size of a regiment, the two remaining chaplains would be sufficient to care for the men's spiritual needs.

He ministered in Erie until 1865 when he moved to Germany for more study. He returned to the United States and organized a Lutheran church in Pittsburgh and taught at Wittenberg College in Ohio. On October 27, 1869, Stuckenberg married Mary Gingrich, a longtime friend in Pittsburgh. In 1880 they traveled to Berlin, where he was a popular lecturer and pastor. The Stuckenbergs returned to the United States in September 1894 and settled in Cambridge, Massachusetts. He and Mary took more trips to Europe and in May 1903 while in England, Stuckenberg died during surgery for a throat condition.

The Stuckenbergs had lived in Gettysburg for a while and became closely connected to Pennsylvania (now Gettysburg) College, which received his papers as a bequest. He is the only Civil War chaplain buried in Gettysburg National Cemetery, and Mary, who died in 1935, rests beside him.

Chaplain John H. W. Stuckenberg later in life. (courtesy of Musselman Library, Gettysburg College)

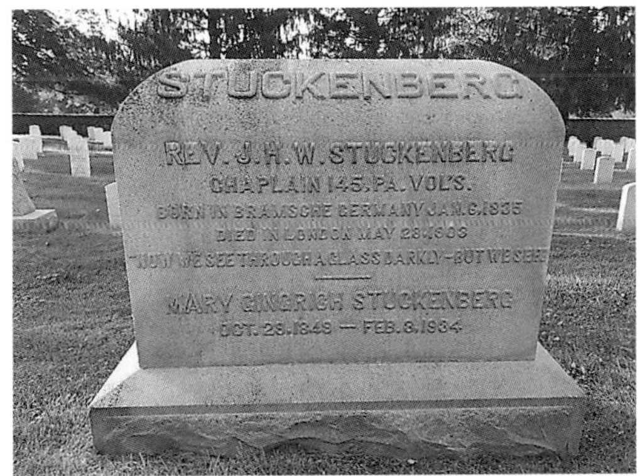

The grave of Chaplain Stuckenberg in Gettysburg National Cemetery. (Author's collection)

On January 6, 1864, Rev. Stuckenberg gave a speech in Warren, Pennsylvania, about the Battle of Gettysburg. After describing the prayer that he offered on July 2, he reflected on what he had come to recognize in his men:[44]

> *On the battlefield just before entering the battle, men think and feel as they never thought and felt before, and men there pray who never prayed before. They are, before the action, fully conscious of the danger to which they will be exposed. I have seen the bravest men grow pale, their lips quivering and frames trembling as they stepped up to me, some to bid goodbye, other to give me letters or money or watches to send to their friends in case they were killed. Their feelings can only be experienced, never described. Home rises before the mind with its peace, its joys and its loved ones. The probable chances of life and death are carefully weighed. Eternity looms up before the mental vision, and seems fearfully near. Life and death, time and eternity assume a terrible reality, as never before. Thought is quickened and comes in lightning flashes through the mind; the feelings are intensified, the heated blood courses feverishly thro[ugh] the veins, swollen as if they would burst; years are lived in minutes.*
>
> *The whole being seems endowed with a superhuman power–some, actuated by the principle of right and Liberty, revealing the divine, while those who are actuated by hatred and revenge become demons. There may be some fear in the heart before the battle. "There goes a brave man," said the Duke of Wellington as he saw a man pale and tremulous as he charged on a battery. And he was brave because he could face the cannon while fully conscious of the danger. Generally, after the first volley, all fear vanishes. There is no time to think of the danger. All the power of thought and emotion and will are intensely bent on one object, to conquer the foe, and there is no room left for the thought of danger or the emotion of fear. So absorbed is the mind by this one object and so intent on accomplishing it, that a kind of frenzy possesses the soldier while in battle. All ideas of time vanish–hours becoming like a few minutes. Sometimes neither the bullets nor shells with their unearthly sounds are*

heard. The sight of the dead and wounded does not affect him as in calmer moments. And the excessive labor produces no fatigue at the time. But when wounded and still exposed to danger, his helplessness engenders fear, the fatigue of the fearful exertion is felt; with the wounds comes fever, and with the fever a burning thirst.

He finished his speech by affirming,

We saw at Gettysburg what our soldiers can and will do. Duty is the motive that led them into the army and a righteous cause inspires them in battle. They are inured to hardships and suffering and bear them unmurmuringly. They are brave and determined, as only freemen can be. Talk not to them of giving up the contest, before the great end for which they fight is accomplished. The hope of the rebels from the beginning has been, that the North would become impatient and give up the contest.

The army believes firmly in the guidance of God, and all they need to make them successful is: a hearty support of the people of the North. And if we at home do our duty–banish everything that is mean and contemptible in spirit; banish all petty differences; and rise as one man with one heart & one mind to a full sense of the magnitude of the struggle & of the world-wide and never ending importance of the result; then the limits of rebel rule and tyranny will constantly be contracted until it shrinks to nothing; the states will return to their allegiance; the rebel rag will be held up to all liberty-loving people for contempt and execration; from every flag-staff in every village and county in the country, from every American vessel including the pirates on the sea shall wave in a purified flag the Stars and Stripes; our soldiers shall be welcomed to their homes with tears of gratitude & joy, and from this nation reunited and regenerated shall ascend shouts of joy which the nations of the earth shall hear–as the doom of the tyrants that wished our destruction and of slavery and oppression everywhere, and as a sound of hope and a call to courage to all who wait longingly for the Sun of freedom to shine upon them.

SECOND DIVISION:

Brigadier General John Gibbon

First Brigade:

Brigadier General William Harrow

Brig. Gen. William Harrow commanded a brigade of four regiments: 1st Minnesota, 15th Massachusetts, 19th Maine, and 82nd New York. Like other Second Corps brigades, Harrow's brigade reached Gettysburg on the morning of July 2 after long and hot marches and spent a quiet morning in line along Cemetery Ridge north of Caldwell's division. When the Confederates advanced against the Third Corps that afternoon, Harrow's brigade was piecemealed out in support. Two regiments, the 15th Massachusetts and 82nd New York, were sent to the right end of the Third Corps line on the Emmitsburg Road, north of the Codori Farm; both lost their commanders when they were forced back by the rebel attack. The 19th Maine was sent out to support a battery that was overrun by Confederate troops, and they, too, were forced back. The 1st Minnesota was ordered to plug a gap in the Union line by countercharging against a brigade of Alabamians, and although they kept the rebels from advancing any further toward Cemetery Ridge, they paid heavily for their heroic charge.

That evening, all four regiments returned to the position they held just a few hours earlier and helped care for the wounded. The next morning, the brigade was moved a bit to the west behind a stone wall. After enduring the cannonade that preceded the Pickett-Pettigrew-Trimble charge, the regiments watched as the Virginians from Pickett's Division first marched toward them, then obliqued to the Union right and approached the brigade (Alexander Webb's) to the north of the Copse of Trees. Harrow's men were ordered to advance quickly to the scene of the fighting, and they did so in a great mass. They engaged in brutal hand-to-hand fighting, helped stem the Confederate onslaught, and captured several Confederate flags and many prisoners. After helping to bury the dead and resting on July 4, they joined the rest of the Army of the Potomac as it left Gettysburg on July 5.

The 19th Maine and the 1st Minnesota had chaplains with them, and the latter wrote letters describing his experience.

Francis Asbury Conwell, 1st Minnesota Infantry

Francis Asbury Conwell was born in Seaford, Delaware, on November 8, 1812. In 1820, his family moved to Indiana, where Francis served as the first postmaster in the new town of Laurel. When he was thirty-eight, he decided to follow in his father's footsteps and enter the ministry in the Methodist Episcopal Church. He was licensed to preach in 1838 and sent to Fort Wayne in 1840 to serve a congregation that was at that time "out of all civilization."[45] He married Mary Mercy Fingland in 1849, and they had two sons and two daughters. In 1855, he moved to Minnesota and served congregations in and around Winona until he enlisted as a chaplain in the 1st Minnesota Infantry and was mustered in on October 15, 1862, at Bolivar, Virginia.[46]

On July 2, 1863, the regiment was ordered to charge against the Alabama brigade of Brig. Gen. Cadmus Wilcox, and even though the Minnesota boys were greatly outnumbered, they bought enough time for more Union troops to be brought in to secure the line on Cemetery Ridge. But their courageous action cost them dearly, with many officers being wounded or killed.

Capt. Nathan S. Messick of Company G found himself in charge of the remnant of the regiment but was killed the next day during the Pickett-Pettigrew-Trimble charge. Chaplain Conwell wrote a poignant letter to Messick's widow on July 13:

> *Dear Sister Messick:*
>
> *Your husband, Capt. Messick, passed many and great dangers in leading his company through hard fought fields of blood, and on the 2nd of July he escaped, while all around him fell, and he became the head and commander of the regiment, and nobly led them forward to bleed, die, and conquer. But just as victory was perching upon our banner, he fell! Oh yes, my sister, he fell! And with him hundreds of others fell–general, brigadiers, colonels, and men of all rank, fell. But the living pressed the battle sorely and to the overthrow of the insolent invaders.*

Chaplain Conwell wrote a poignant letter to the widow of Capt. Nathan Messick to inform her of his death in action on July 3. (Gale Family Library)

I know Sister Messick how delicate and difficult is my task in attempting to offer my heart felt condolence for this painful bereavement of you and your fatherless children; and should be speechless only for the book that issues from the God of all consolation until you find promises for you, and them.

Be of good courage and the Lord will strengthen thy heart.

On the 4th of July we laid away the remains of that brave and honorable soldier, in a grave literally dug out of the rock on a high, dry point, near Rock Creek, about two miles south east of Gettysburg.

We had religious service, and not an eye or heart but was melted. It appeared like the funeral of our regiment; 48 had died; 184 were wounded; 97 were still in the field fighting.

Well such is war!

The way to glory is the way to blood. Your husband has left a good name for honor, courage and devotion to his family and friends.

So far as I know his relation with me and with every other man in the command was pleasant and friendly. When I last saw him, which was very shortly before he fell, knowing my danger better than I did, he first ordered me off my horse, then in ten minutes ordered me to retire from the line to the rear.

I looked back in pity, prayer and care on the small but brave boys then left; and when next I saw the Regiment it was reduced to the number of a company.

Good bye sister, pray for us still. We are now hovering round the flying rebels, and expect soon to be in the deadly strife on the banks of the Potomac. God save my little band, and give us success, victory and salvation for Jesus sake.[47]

In his quarterly report to his commander, dated October 1, 1863, Conwell seemed to be almost overcome by the effects of the battle on his regiment. He recalled that

the quarter opened with the dreadful fight of Gettysburg and as it was our painful duty on the 4th and 5th of July to read services, bury the dead, and move carefully over acres of wounded men, I could but feel and think my work was done. My brothers and sons were gone: our regiment was no longer a power on the earth, but lying upon, or sleeping in its bosom. On visiting the front lines, and finding ninety-five still there, faint but pursuing, I re-devoted myself to the faithful ones who "never loose [sic] a flag or a gun."[48]

In the same correspondence, he noted that when the regiment was sent to New York City in mid-August to help calm the situation there in the aftermath of the draft riots, *"we spent ten days in delightful, social and religious privileges with the citizens of Brooklyn. The effect was good, ennobling and rejuvenating the jaded officers and men of your command."*[49] He also complained that *"a number of papers to whom I sent paragraphs did not publish."*[50]

Conwell's health had long been a concern and challenged him throughout his service in the army. Although there is a discrepancy in the date of the following event (see note), it demonstrates the fortitude and faithfulness Conwell showed in his duty:

[W]hile the regiment lay in camp near Mine Run the chaplain went to Washington to get pardons for some deserters and when he came back the deserters were sitting on their coffins ready to be shot. The train being late, he ran from the train to the camp and was so exhausted that he fell right down with the pardon in his hand and after that I never saw him well. Either he was hurt internally or his nervous system was so shattered that he was unable to get around although he did not feel disposed to go to the hospital he was sick enough to go.[51]

Conwell mustered out of the regiment on May 5, 1864, and returned to Winona in very poor health. He moved to Evanston, Illinois, and worked as a financial agent for the Seaman's Bethel Home in Chicago. He evidently missed serving in the army, and in 1870, he applied for a position as a post chaplain in the regular army, stating his *"hopes of living and dying in the U.S. Army."*[52] He put his life on hold, selling his house and taking a temporary job for a seamen's mission agency, as he waited to receive notice of his application. Even though colleagues, state senators, and even President Ulysses S. Grant offered recommendations for him, congressional approval of his application dragged on for several years. He asked to be considered for some other government office or work, but he finally withdrew his application in 1875 because he was approaching the mandatory retirement age for service in the U.S. Army and learned *"there was no prospect of my success."*[53] Conwell died after a prolonged illness on January 9, 1885, in Evanston and was buried in Graceland Cemetery in Chicago.

Second Brigade:
Brigadier General Alexander Webb

Also known as the Philadelphia Brigade, this unit included four regiments: the 69th, 71st, 72nd, and 106th Pennsylvania. Brig. Gen. Alexander Webb had been given command of the brigade only a few days before the Battle of Gettysburg, and he tried to instill much-needed discipline in the ranks and pushed them hard during the marches north, covering 35 miles on June 29. After resting the next day, they continued north and bivouacked behind Little Round Top on the night of July 1. They marched toward the Union lines early on July 2 and took position to the right of Harrow's brigade along Cemetery Ridge. The 69th was sent to the stone wall while the other three remained in support behind the crest of the ridge. When a Georgia brigade threatened to break the line in their front, the other three regiments were ordered forward; although some Georgians managed to breach the wall to the left, the Pennsylvanians held firm in their position and pushed the rebels back.

One regiment, the 106th, was sent to Cemetery Hill after dark on July 2 to support the Eleventh Corps in their defense against a Confederate attack, although they arrived too late to participate in the action. Another regiment, the 71st, was sent to Culp's Hill to reinforce the Twelfth Corps, but a sudden and unexpected nighttime attack by rebels caused the commanding officer of the 71st to order them back to Cemetery Ridge.

That night, Meade told the division's commander, Brig. Gen. John Gibbon, to expect an attack against his front on July 3, which proved true. The three regiments still left on the ridge (all but two companies of the 106th remained on Cemetery Hill) prepared for the Confederate charge. They watched as the Virginians of Pickett's Division headed straight for them, then sprang up from behind the stone wall and unleashed a deadly volley. But the Confederates still surged forward and Webb's line broke as some rebels climbed over the wall. With support from surrounding Union troops, the Confederate assault was finally halted and driven back. After resting on July 4, the brigade moved in pursuit of the Confederates on July 5.

Only one of the Philadelphia Brigade regiments, the 72nd Pennsylvania, had a chaplain with them during the battle, and he left no record of his time at Gettysburg.

Third Brigade:
Brigadier General Norman Hall

Norman Hall's brigade reached the field with the rest of Gibbon's division early on July 2 and was positioned on Cemetery Ridge between the brigades of Harrow and Webb, with two regiments along the stone wall and the other three in support. During the Confederate attacks that afternoon, two of the brigade's five regiments were sent forward to try to close the gap left when Caldwell's division was advanced to the Wheatfield. Although these regiments were forced back, the rest of the brigade held the line along the wall or remained firm in support.

The next day, while Virginians from Pickett's Division marched toward the brigade, all five regiments were moved closer to the wall and next to the Copse of Trees. Like the other brigades in this area, they poured withering volleys into the Confederate lines and eventually charged toward the Copse, where the breakthrough was taking place, and engaged the rebels in close combat. When other Union regiments came up in support, the rebels were successfully driven back.

None of the regiments in Hall's brigade, which included the 19th and 20th Massachusetts, 7th Michigan, and 42nd and 59th New York, had a chaplain with them at Gettysburg.

THIRD DIVISION:
Brigadier General Alexander Hays

First Brigade:
Colonel Samuel Carroll

Col. Samuel Carroll commanded the "Gibraltar Brigade" which included the 4th and 8th Ohio, the 7th West Virginia, and the 14th Indiana regiments. The brigade led the Second Corps march to Gettysburg, and on the evening of July 1 it camped near Powers Hill along the Baltimore Pike. Early on July 2, they moved to Cemetery Ridge and took position to the right of Webb's brigade, near the Brian Farm. In the midafternoon the 8th Ohio was sent out toward the Emmitsburg Road, where they skirmished with some Confederates, eventually driving them back.

Later that evening, the rest of the brigade was sent to East Cemetery Hill to help repel the attack there by rebel forces from Maj. Gen. Jubal Early's Division, who had overrun the artillery on the hill and were driven off by fierce close-up fighting and a bayonet charge.

These three regiments remained at the base of Cemetery Hill through the next day while the 8th Ohio remained in its forward position toward the Emmitsburg Road. During the Pickett-Pettigrew-Trimble charge, this regiment was perfectly situated to pour volleys into the flanks of the far-left units in the rebel line, causing them to break, and eventually, surrender by the hundreds. The rest of the brigade joined the 8th that evening, and they spent July 4 tending to the dead. They left with the rest of the army on July 5.

Three of the four midwestern regiments were accompanied by their chaplains, but none left a written record of their service at Gettysburg.

Second Brigade:
Colonel Thomas Smyth

Col. Thomas Smyth commanded a brigade of five regiments: the 1st Delaware, 12th New Jersey, 14th Connecticut, and 108th New York. The 10th New York Battalion served as the provost guard for the division. Joining the rest of their division on Cemetery Ridge on the morning of July 2, they were massed to the right of Carroll's brigade and in support of a battery. The brigade moved to relieve units of the First Corps that had been arrayed along the ridge the night before. Throughout the day, three of Smyth's regiments skirmished with Confederates over control of the Bliss Farm property, which lay squarely between the opposing lines and changed hands several times. By the end of the day, Confederates had seized control of the large brick barn, and Smyth's men pulled back to the stone wall and used fence rails to strengthen their position.

The Bliss barn continued to change hands on the morning of July 3, until Brig. Gen. Alexander Hays ordered the barn and house burned. The brigade rested behind its fortifications until the Confederates began their advance following the great cannonade that afternoon. The Union soldiers had been cautioned to hold their fire until the rebels came close, so once the line of Brig. Gen. J. Johnston Pettigrew's North Carolinians reached the fences along the Emmitsburg Road, Smyth's men poured volleys into them. Once the rebel charge was broken, some of Smyth's men leaped over the wall to capture prisoners and battle flags. Off to the brigade's left, Webb's brigade was in danger of being overrun, so Smyth ordered his men to fire into the flanks of the Virginians, which helped stop the charge. The men rested on July 4 and left Gettysburg on July 5 in pursuit of Lee's army.

Three of Smyth's regiments had their chaplains with them during the battle; two of those chaplains wrote about their experiences.

Thomas Grier Murphey, 1st Delaware Infantry

Thomas Grier Murphey[54] was born in Kent County, Delaware, on March 26, 1817. After graduating from Andover and Amherst Academies, he attended Princeton Theological Seminary, completing his studies in 1843. The following year, he was ordained in the Dover Presbyterian Church in Dover, Delaware, and he married Elizabeth W. Kimberley, with whom he had six children. He served both as a pastor and as principal for a girls boarding school until 1861, when he mustered into the 1st Delaware Infantry on September 24 as its chaplain. He remained with the regiment throughout their term of service and mustered out on July 12, 1865.

Shortly after the end of the war, Murphey wrote the regimental history and he noted in the preface that *"most of it was written on the field, during active operations of the army."*[55] Steady marching took up the last two weeks of June 1863, ending on July 1 at Taneytown, although even then, *"the troops were entirely ignorant of our destination, or the whereabouts of the enemy."*[56] However, the sounds of battle soon reached their ears, and the body of General Reynolds was carried past the anxious soldiers. They were ordered to move out but their steps *"became more steady and solemn as we heard the booming cannon, and saw the smoke of battle rolling up in black columns against the sky. As usual, the conversation in the ranks ceased . . . and scarcely a sound was heard except the steady tramp of*

Chaplain Thomas Grier Murphey of the 1st Delaware Infantry. (Library of Congress, Liljenquist Family Collection)

the moving column."[57] They bivouacked that night three miles south of Gettysburg and early the next morning they reached the town and took position near the center of the line of battle just west of Cemetery Hill.

The Bliss Farm stood directly in front of the 1st Delaware's position and about halfway between the opposing lines. Confederate skirmishers were in the barn and taking shots at Smyth's brigade. Shortly after arriving on Cemetery Ridge, some of the Delaware men were sent forward to drive out the enemy and take command of the barn, but they were driven out themselves by a reinforced enemy skirmish line after about an hour.[58] Chaplain Murphey described one of the tragic casualties that occurred as the men fell back:

> *Captain M. W. B. Ellegood was mortally wounded and fell on the field. As the enemy's line passed over, a Rebel soldier seeing the captain not yet dead, raised his musket to bayonet him, but his commanding officer called on him to desist and threatened to run him through if he ever knew him to injure a wounded or fallen foe. Captain Ellegood was a conscientious soldier, and fought from a sense of duty. But few dreaded a battle more than he, none entered more promptly, or fought better, when duty called him into action. Besides being a brave soldier he was a good Christian man. He knew from the first that his wound was mortal, and waited with patience and resignation for the end to come.*[59]

As the battle over the Bliss buildings continued throughout the day, Murphey noted *"there [were] serious apprehensions"* that Union troops near Round Top could not hold their ground, and *"orders were given detailing*

This bronze panel on the 12th New Jersey monument shows the fighting at the Bliss Farm. (courtesy of Nelson Widell)

certain medical officers to remain with the wounded if it should be necessary to fall back."[60] At the end of July 2, *"one inquired of another as to the result of the fighting; nothing seemed to have been gained or lost as to advantage, and we rested that night where and as we could, anxiously awaiting the result of the next day."*[61]

He reported that while field hospitals were being moved farther from the line of battle on July 3,

> *there burst over and around the barn, in which our division wounded were, a terrific storm of shells. Men who had seemed utterly unable to move aroused themselves, and crawled to some other place, as they supposed, of safety, or at least of less danger. Horsemen, footmen, and wagons, rushed wildly across the field, or down the road, under cover of the hill in the place of danger, rather than out of it. The confusion, haste, and alarm of each one alarmed the rest, and altogether the scene was both amusing and frightful. The shelling endangering the hospital, did not last long, and appeared to be the result of the concentrated fire upon our batteries on Cemetery Hill. Yet, for several hours the shells came howling over the hill and falling in the field. Before night all the wounded were removed to new place on Rock Creek. All that night, and the day and night following, our ambulances were busy bringing in the wounded. When, finally, all were in the little grove, containing some two or three acres, was literally filled with the victims of the demons–treason–rebellion–war.*[62]

Murphey was ordered to remain behind to care for the wounded after the army left to pursue the Confederates on July 5. Although some medical officers also stayed in Gettysburg, Murphey noted that many civilians and members of the United States Christian Commission and volunteer aid societies brought much-needed food, clothing, medical supplies, and assistance. He noted that *"the most useful were married and single ladies, who, prompted by the goodness of their hearts, came from their comfortable homes to undergo the discomforts and toil of a field hospital to relieve the sufferers. Many a blessing was invoked on them for their kindness."*[63] Although *"the best spirit seemed to animate the great majority of those who came with their stores and willing hands,"* there were those *"whose sympathies were for the Confederates alone, and gave all they brought to them, and did nothing for others. We had a corresponding class from Philadelphia, who declared they would not give a cup of tea to a Rebel to save his life."*[64] This situation necessitated an order that *"nothing should be carried to the wounded of either party by their friends, and everything was deposited in the store-house to be distributed indiscriminately by authorized persons."*[65] Surgeons would provide wounded soldiers of either army with comparable care, the only distinction being Union soldiers would receive priority when cases were similarly urgent.

While surgeons worked to amputate shattered limbs, Murphey was assigned *"the duty of burying the dead. An idea of the scarcity of assistance and of the mortality may be inferred from the fact that, although every effort in our power was made to inter the dead, they accumulated, and lay for days unburied. At length we were obliged to call in assistance from another Division Hospital."*[66] He also noted that *"each chaplain gave his especial attention to the wounded of his own regiment, and to those of other regiments having no chaplain lying nearest his own . . . There was not a wounded man of the First Delaware who was not provided for and made comfortable."*[67]

Murphey had the opportunity to care for and speak with wounded Confederate soldiers, and he discovered to his surprise that there was *"as large a proportion of Christian men as in our own army."*[68] This led him to reflect on the nature of duty and religious faith:

> *It is the duty of every one to respect and honor those who rightfully rule over us and to support the legal Government under which he lives. But loyalty is not religion, and though rebellion against a good constitutional Government is sinful and incompatible with true piety, yet where and who is the Christian man thoroughly loyal to his God? And if a man may be a Christian though not sinless, or in all things obedient to the Divine Government, may not another be a Christian though a political heretic?*[69]

The Christian Commission arrived in Gettysburg and set up tents at Camp Letterman in late July. Commissioner Andrew Cross was an old friend of Chaplain Murphey and they met while caring for the wounded. (Library of Congress)

His conversations with rebels also yielded other interesting revelations: *"Many of them expressed their gratitude and surprise upon receiving the kindness which was shown them. It far exceeded what they expected."*[70] He spoke with them about *"the uselessness and inhumanity of continuing the contest, and charged upon them the real authorship of the war, which [they] did not deny. Some admitted it, and blamed South Carolina for it. Others even boasted that they fired the first gun and commenced the war."*[71]

Murphey summed up his thoughts about the battle and the pursuit of Lee's army:

> *The fruits of the battles on the 1st, 2d, and 3d of July, 1863 at Gettysburg, were appalling. Although, when the official reports were compared, the numbers of killed, wounded, and prisoners were not greatly unequal, the fact of a decided Union victory was admitted on all hands, and, notwithstanding our losses and grief on account of them, all loyal hearts were cheered. On the morning of the 4th the pursuit of the retreating foe was commenced, and strong hopes were entertained that they could not recross the Potomac.*
>
> *A heavy rain which fell, swelling the river, strengthened these hopes. They had re-crossed it after the battle of Antietam . . . They could not escape this time, it was confidently asserted. But they did recross, and . . . the disappointment of the loyal people was intense, and many yet wonder why it was permitted, especially with former examples before us. There may be those who know, we do not.*[72]

Chaplain Murphey and Assistant Surgeon J. W. McCollough were released from their duty at Gettysburg on August 1, and they left to rejoin the regiment in Virginia. The 1st Delaware, having seen action from October 1862 to the end of the war, was present at the surrender at Appomattox Courthouse in April 1865. Murphey described the pride and joy among the soldiers when told of the surrender, but he sadly noted that Brig. Gen. Thomas A. Smyth, who had commanded the regiment and then the brigade, was wounded during the last skirmish of the regiment on April 7, and he died on his way home at almost the same time Generals Lee and Grant were signing the document of surrender on April 9.

After the war, Murphey served for eleven years as a missionary among freedmen at Amelia Courthouse, Virginia. He died of spinal meningitis on January 9, 1878, and is buried in the Old Presbyterian Cemetery in Dover, Delaware.

Not much information is available about the early life and education of Henry Smith Stevens. He was born in Cromwell, Connecticut, in 1833 (some sources say 1832), and graduated from Madison College (present-day Colgate University in Hamilton, New York) in 1852. By 1858, he had returned to Cromwell and was serving as pastor of a Baptist church. He married Eliza Hoyt in 1859, and they had one son in 1861. In July 1862, Stevens mustered in as chaplain for the 14th Connecticut Infantry.

Although we know little about Stevens before his service in the army, he left quite a bit of information about his experiences with his regiment. He kept a diary during his three years as chaplain (which was incorporated into the regimental history that he published in 1906), wrote the souvenir booklet of the regiment's reunion at Antietam in September 1891, and gave a lengthy oration at the dedication of the regimental monument at Gettysburg in 1884. The quotes used here come from the latter source, which he gave while standing with the survivors at the location of the monument on the ridge where they were positioned on July 2 and 3. He addressed them, sometimes in the present tense, and described the actions of the regiment in detail.

Stevens recalled the long marches toward Pennsylvania during the latter part of June, during which the men learned that George Meade had replaced Joseph Hooker as commander of the Army of the Potomac. The chaplain noted:

> *The news of the change of commanders, though a surprise, did not disconcert the men of the Union Army. The next great battle was to be won by the sturdy, unconquerable courage of our men, and by the harmonious cooperation, for once, of officers of all grades, all having but one object–the defeating and driving from our Northern soil the invading rebel hordes. The Union troops at Gettysburg were simply invincible.*[73]

At 3:00 p.m. on July 1, as the regiment advanced toward Gettysburg after resting for a short time at Taneytown, Maryland, Stevens reminded the men,

> *as you advanced your steps were quickened by the sounds of battle coming to you on the throbbing air; and groups of stragglers, skulks and shirks, relating, as usual, marvelous stories of disaster, met*

you. You gave them, as was their due, derision and jeers for their stories, but the sight of wounded men and prisoners and smoke-begrimed cannon passing to the rear told you that real work had been done. You knew that work was before the old Second Corps, and not without some longing to meet the pretentious, arrogant invader on Northern soil, you pressed on and by nightfall were close to Gettysburg.[74]

Stevens recalled that once they arrived at Gettysburg, *"that night, on picket near the Baltimore pike, your minds conjuring up the possibilities of the days before you, was not an unpleasant but rather restful one."*[75] The next morning, after resting in an open field along the Taneytown Road, Stevens reminisced,

> *You took your assigned position on yonder grassy slope; by no means then forecasting that this ridge on which you were for the first time resting was to become, and in part through yourselves, one of the most renowned places history names, or probably shall ever name. We remember the interest we took, when strolling to the summit of the ridge, in watching our sharp-shooters at their work, and the fascination there seemed in it in spite of its cruel character. We remember, too, how the bravery of our new Division Commander [Alexander Hays] impressed us, as we saw him riding along posting the line of skirmishers, and giving them instructions in a voice distinctly audible to all of us. This novel sight of a Division Commander in such a position, and so coolly and indifferently exposing himself to the fire of the enemy's marksmen, inspired a wonderful courage into your hearts.*[76]

Stevens recalled the challenges of those who spent the night on picket duty: *"You of Companies A. and F. who were well to the front on the picket line, found the position by no means a pleasant one, because of the proximity of the rebel pickets and their pertinacity."*[77]

Chaplain Stevens spoke highly of the inspirational courage of Brig. Gen. Alexander Hays, the division commander. (Library of Congress)

Stevens sadly recollected two incidents of the morning of July 3. The first was

> *the finding of Corporal Huxham by a comrade when a relieving squad came up. He was resting against the fence, apparently taking aim, but really dead; shot through the head, with his face toward the foe and his hand upon his weapon. Alone, far from all loved ones, fulfilling his oath of loyalty, the brave, faithful spirit passed from his body by the swift leaden messenger sped by a traitor's hand.*[78]

The second incident involved

> *a wide-awake rebel gunner, [who,] desirous of disturbing the slumbers of some of us trying to get some rest on this ridge, sent a shell which struck and exploded a caisson of Arnold's Battery, close to our left. The rebels cheered and yelled all along their line for a mile or more. The spunky Arnold, by whom as an Artilleryman the 14th were ever after ready to swear, soon had the wreck cleared away, and sent an answering shot. That first shot exploded a rebel caisson, and then it was the turn of our men to cheer; and cheer they did for several minutes, from Round Top to Cemetery Hill.*[79]

Other regiments from Smyth's brigade had been involved on July 2 and 3 in the skirmishing at the Bliss Farm. But it was the 14th Connecticut that ended the fight by capturing and then burning the buildings on the morning of July 3. Stevens noted that *"there has been with some, we find, a question as to who, on the 3d of July, performed these deeds; but every man of the 14th who was here on that day is ready to take oath that upon our regiment was imposed the task and to our men belongs the honor; and we put your claim upon the monument we unveil here this day without fear of disproof."*[80] Stevens then recounted the events of that morning that he claimed the men would *"ever refer with great and just pride"*:

> *During the forenoon of the 3d it became evident that the enemy must not longer be allowed to use those buildings, and the duty was devolved on the little 14th, minus its two companies on the skirmish line, to retake and "hold" the barn and house. You . . . remember with what beating hearts you moved up to the right of your position . . . and then started on your peril-fraught undertaking. As soon as you appeared within range you were "sighted" by all the*

sharpshooters in the buildings and the skirmishers in front of you, and as you could not under such circumstances properly charge in any sort of formation, you were wisely directed to "scatter and run" for the barn; but many dropped before getting there. . . . The enemy's skirmishers within range, increased until they outnumbered you nearly three to one, were closing in upon you; the sharp-shooters had a bead on every head, hand, or foot that appeared outside of the buildings; and the rebel artillery was dropping shells among you through the roof of the barn, and it seemed to you that you must be annihilated or captured unless another regiment came to your relief. But you had been ordered to "hold" the buildings, and hold them you must as long as any of you were left there alive.

You with willing hands soon applied the torch (many blazing wisps of hay) in various places and left the buildings to the flames. Like brave men that you were, you bore all your dead and wounded with you, and though many dropped by the enemy's bullets on the return, you took them all up and brought them to your own lines.

All honor to the men of a depleted regiment who, performing so perilous an exploit, were so manly and humane withal that they would not leave one of their dead or injured comrades in the hands of the enemy![81]

Stevens shared an episode of that July 3 morning which he claimed few in the regiment had witnessed:

Bright little "Jeff" of Co. F. was fatally shot on the charge. He was dashing ahead well to the front, and one of his comrades heard him shouting to some who seemed to be laggard, "Come on, you cowards!" when he was struck near the shoulder by a musket shot, the ball passing down into his chest. He was borne to this ridge, a little to the rear of this position . . . As soon as he saw us . . . he called in a loud voice, "O, Chaplain, come here!" We hastened to him, and, dropping upon one knee at his side, took his hand. His frenzied grasp and the contortions of his countenance told the agonies of pain he felt. Wishing to draw him out, we, still holding his hand and stroking his forehead, said, "What shall we think of you, Jeff?" With a startled expression he looked up, when, seeming to comprehend the significance of the words and tone, he spoke: "Tell my mother–tell–my–" and was gone. Brave young Jeff! A few minutes ago plunging into the thickest of the fray where duty bade, a genuine hero, and now, with death's hand on him, his heart full of tenderness . . . he turns his thoughts toward that one whose heart is yearning most for him, and with that dearest, sacredest name borne by mortals upon his lips, passes away.[82]

After a lull in the action, Stevens reminded the soldiers that many of them were trying to rest or find food or were scribbling notes home when they heard

the friendly English Whitworth, far at the enemy's left . . . Other bolts from other guns followed quickly . . . Who can fitly describe that awful pounding of those two hundred rapid, fierce-firing cannon? The solid earth trembled with the concussion, and the air seemed filled with hurtling, whizzing shot and bursting shell. The storm seemed sufficient to blast everything that had life on these opposing hillsides. You betook yourselves immediately to the shelter of your wall. What could you do, you infantrymen, but crouch and bow down behind its friendly, partial protection? The enemy was at long range, and you could not strike back; you could only endure and wait, and like brave men keep your places and take mangling or death, if such were to be your fate, during this merciless hammering.[83]

Then, as the great cannonade ended, Stevens said the men watched in awe as

that long, strong line of rebel infantry advance[ed] to the attack. You have all called it magnificent. You all admired the immensity, the showiness, the steadiness, the momentum of it. But fascinating as the view of it was to you as soldiers who could admire and appreciate grand and precise military display, to watch in admiration only was not your legitimate business just at that moment. That line meant business, serious business for you. It was the true bolt of the preceding cannon thunder–lightning, mischievous, terrible, fatal as to its purpose and effort concerning you; and you, by your daring and courage, must ward it off and quench it, or woe to you and to the Union! While our artillery are playing into it, gashing the ranks in ghastly fashion, you are preparing to play your part –the most important part–in arresting it.[84]

Stevens carried the survivors back to that momentous afternoon by painting a vivid picture of all they experienced:

On July 3, acting corps commander Brig. Gen. John Gibbon told the men of the 14th Connecticut that they must hold their line to the last man. (Library of Congress)

> *Your rifles (how many of you blessed the fates that you had the "Sharpes" that day!) you rest, ready charged and cocked, upon the wall, beside which you kneel after partially rebuilding it. The contents of your cartridge boxes you cooly empty upon the ground beside you, ready for instantaneous handling. Grimly and eagerly you watch the oncoming foe,–that immense wave of human vitality, purpose, and power. . . . General Gibbon, Acting Corps Commander, rides past, and you hear him say: "The fate of the whole army now rests with you. Don't fire until you get the word; then fire low and sure! We must hold this line to <u>the last man</u>!"*
>
> *They reach the fence, and quick the command, "Fire!" "Fire!" "Fire!" rings along the line, and with emotion of inexpressible thrill you press the triggers and your rifles outblaze. That frontal, formidable line melts away as snowflakes that fall upon the sea.*
>
> *But the heavy supporting columns close in upon them on either flank and remnants of the lines form anew, a still formidable force. They are over the fence now, pushing this way and firing upon you as they come. Wild impulse assumes control of you, and you spring to your feet regardless of danger. Your officers shout to you enthusiastically. Your remembrance of occasions when the rebels had you at disadvantage makes ecstatic this opportunity to get even, and more than even, with them. You shout: "Now we've got 'em!" "Sock it to the rebels!" "Fredericksburg on the other leg!"–and other things that we will not repeat here.*
>
> *At the left of yonder angle a desperate struggle is enacting. The rebels . . . have broken over the wall, and pressing back the infantry, are among the guns. Your commander . . . shouts to you, "Left oblique, fire!" At once your rifles play into the crowd, and presently they fall back. Up at the right a similar contest is waging.*

. . . The order rings out: "Right oblique, fire!" and your rifles play in that direction with like results. So have you helped your fellows.

Now comes the moment for a counter charge. The Captain of Co. A. springs over the wall; his men and others quickly follow. The men in front resist a little, but see the game is up. Retreat to their own distant line is impossible. They fling down their arms, and some drop upon the ground crying excitedly, "Don't fire! We surrender!" Prisoners are gathered in like berries from the bush, and battle-flags enough to make a whole brigade happy.[85]

In his souvenir booklet for the regiment's reunion at Antietam in September 1891, Stevens said the final scene at the end of the Confederate charge was "indescribable":

Poor wounded wretches, scattered or lying in heaps, over the fields and in the road far in front, were writhing in agonies or straightening out in the last death shiver. Some unhurt ones who dared were running with all their might to reach their own lines. Some of Armistead's men, pressed out beyond the angle in front of our men, were daringly grouping for some resistance, or flinging themselves upon the ground with Pettigrew's men, while a sizable group still clung to the front of the angle for protection and maintained their firing. Those upon the ground, now thoroughly bereft of hope and filled with fear, raised handkerchiefs, that looked like leaflets fluttering in the breeze, and waved them above their heads, crying out mightily for quarter.[86]

Stevens recalled that by July 3, 1863, the regiment that consisted of ten full companies at the beginning of its service had been reduced in size to barely one company. When one Confederate soldier stepped over the stone wall in front of the 14th on July 3, he asked, *"'Where are your men?' And when told they were here, said, 'I mean those you had here who gave us such volleys as we advanced?' When assured that all were here except the disabled, he said, with emphasis, 'My God! We could have gone through as it was if we'd known how few you were!'"*[87]

Finally, the chaplain noted the contrast between the emotions of that *"hour of glory [when] wounds, hunger, home-longings, prospective hardships and dangers were all lost sight of in that supreme hour of your victorious rejoicing"* and the ache of how *"the cries of the wounded in their agonies, way in your front, smote your hearts with pain."*[88]

In his souvenir booklet, Stevens affirmed,

> *If anyone asks what gave us the victory at Gettysburg we unhesitatingly reply, the stern, unflinching courage of our men and the signal unity of purpose and thorough devotion of our commanders. Said to the writer one blood-covered man just out of the vortex of flame and death at the left on the second: "I never knew our men to fight as they do today–they cannot be whipped." The words of Goodell of the Fourteenth, who, brave fellow, fell dead, his head pierced by a musket ball, soon after uttering them: "I would rather be killed than beaten today!" expressed the common sentiment of our men.*[89]

Stevens resigned from the chaplaincy on December 22, 1863, and resumed his ministry at a church in Brooklyn, but soon accepted an appointment in the Pension Bureau in Washington, where he remained for twenty-five years helping to identify and care for the graves of Civil War soldiers in various locations, including Andersonville, the site of a former prisoner of war camp where many Union soldiers died. Stevens was also active in GAR circles for many years and was chaplain of the General George G. Meade Post No. 5.

Stevens's wife, Eliza, died in 1864, and he married Julia W. Gregory two years later. They had no children. He died on July 18, 1913, and is buried in Arlington National Cemetery in Virginia. Julia is interred next to him.

Third Brigade:
Colonel George Lamb Willard

George Lamb Willard's brigade entered the Gettysburg campaign wanting to redeem themselves from their reputation as "the Harper's Ferry Cowards." In September 1862 they had been posted at Harper's Ferry and had been among the more than 12,000 Union soldiers who were captured by Confederate general Thomas "Stonewall" Jackson in his advance through the Shenandoah Valley during Gen. Robert E. Lee's first invasion of the North. After being taken prisoner, the brigade, which was commanded by Col. Isaac Trimble, was paroled and sent to Camp Douglas in Chicago, a prisoner of war and training camp. In November, the brigade was officially exchanged and sent to serve in the defenses of Washington, D.C. When the brigade was called to join the Army of the Potomac as it moved toward Pennsylvania, it was assigned to the Second Corps and placed under the command of Col. George Lamb Willard. In addition, the men in the four regiments of the brigade had never seen battle, save for their brief experience at Harper's Ferry, so their Second Corps comrades viewed them with suspicion and scorn. They had much to prove at Gettysburg, and so they did.

The hard marches of the Second Corps were all the more difficult for these men who had not been conditioned to such strenuous work. They reached the Taneytown Road south of Gettysburg about 9:00 p.m. on July 1, then continued to Cemetery Ridge early the next morning. When the Confederates advanced toward the Union lines late in the afternoon of July 2, division commander Brig. Gen. Alexander Hays sent Willard's brigade to help stem the rebel tide. The regiments charged against a Mississippi brigade while yelling, "Remember Harper's Ferry!" and halted the Confederate assault and recaptured the cannon that had been overrun by the rebels.[90] Their victory came with a high cost, including the loss of Colonel Willard. As the brigade was moving back toward Cemetery Ridge, an artillery shell hit him in the face and killed him instantly. Col. Eliakim Sherrill of the 126th New York assumed command.

On July 3 the brigade suffered through the Confederate artillery barrage and then opened fire on the rebels from behind a stone wall during the Pickett-Pettigrew-Trimble charge. As the rebels began to falter, Willard's men jumped over the stone wall and captured hundreds of prisoners. They had indeed redeemed their soldierly reputations and honor at Gettysburg.

Three of the four regiments of the brigade—the 39th, 111th, 125th, and 126th New York—were accompanied by their chaplains, and all wrote about their service.

John Nelson Brown, 111th New York Infantry

Rev. John Nelson Brown was born in Milford, New York, on August 16, 1818. He left home at the age of thirteen to learn the harness maker's trade but soon felt a call to ministry and began more formal education. He graduated from the Poultney Academy in Vermont in 1840, entered the ministry in the Methodist Episcopal Church the next year, and served several churches throughout upstate New York and northern

Pennsylvania. He married Eliza A. Graham in 1842, and they had two sons. In 1862, *"he answered his country's call and 'for three years,' to quote his own language, 'my principal bed was the ground, with an army saddle for a pillow, and the heavens for a covering, with occasionally a heavy sheet of rain or a coverlid of snow as an extra luxury.'"*[91] He mustered into the 111th New York Infantry on August 20, 1862, and remained with the regiment until they mustered out on June 4, 1865.

Chaplain John N. Brown of the 111th New York Infantry
(*Genesee Conference Methodist Episcopal Church Minutes*, 1895)

Brown evidently kept a diary during his term of service, but it cannot be located.[92] However, he did have quite a bit to say about his experiences at Gettysburg in speeches he gave at the regimental reunion at Gettysburg in June 1888 and in Auburn, New York in October 1888. As he began his speech at the first meeting, he recalled,

> *I never made but one speech in Gettysburg, and none of the people of Gettysburg heard that. It was not made in the village, but out about a mile, near Ziegler's Grove, while standing on a stone wall in front of my regiment just before we made the charge on the second of July, 1863, and in the midst of a terrible storm of rebel shells that were falling up us like hail. I stood on that wall and made a speech to the men of the 111th, but neither the people of Gettysburg nor of the world ever knew anything about it, for my voice was drowned . . . by the louder and more eloquent voice proceeding from the throats of more than two hundred cannon.*[93]

After assuring the men that their service at Harper's Ferry was not in the least cowardly and stating he had never regretted being there with the men and had never been ashamed of them, he returned to Gettysburg:

> *I recollect that in that first charge, on the 2d of July, our first color-guard fell, wounded. He called to the second to take the flag and bear it onward. As he did so he was instantly killed. The third grasped it, and he fell mortally wounded, and the fourth seized the falling standard, and raising it aloft, bore it onward to victory. Such was the spirit and bravery of our men, and such the baptism of fire experience by the Old Third Brigade.*[94]

At the reunion held in Auburn, the chaplain gave an oration that was "loudly cheered":

> *Can I ever forget the evening after the terrible battle at Gettysburg had been ended? I went out over the field to look for the boys of 111th, on the spot where they made the immortal charge which has made the names of the 111th renowned forever? As I called them, name by name, one answered here and another, but there were some voices I never heard again. As I was riding by one poor fellow, I saw by his uniform that he belonged to the 111th but I could not tell who he was for he lay upon his face. Dismounting, I turned him over and beheld the brave and generous Proseus, that brave and gallant fellow whom the boys all loved as a brother. Proceeding a little farther, I also found the body of the heroic Lieutenant Granger lying far within the enemy's lines. Just as the rays of the evening sun were dying away in the west, gilding the surrounding hills with beauty but adding only horror to the battlefield, I made my way back to camp and brought twenty ambulances to the field. These were filled and refilled and not until 2 o'clock the next morning did our ghastly labor end.*[95]

Throughout the night of July 3, Brown *"did most excellent service in burying the dead, in marking their graves, and in caring for the wounded."*[96] He remained at Gettysburg until July 29, when he and the regimental surgeon left to rejoin their regiment.

Brown's ministry with the regiment drew high praise:

> *He was known as the personal friend of every soldier in the command. He could exhort, reprove, and rebuke with such kindness and force as to show himself to be a friend to the good and a terror to the wicked at one and the same time. His services were of such acknowledged value as to be considered indispensable to the discipline of his regiment, whether in camp or on the field of battle.*[97]

Although there is no evidence that Brown picked up a musket in battle, he was called the "fighting chaplain," perhaps because he preferred to stay with the men near the firing line and remained with the regiment throughout its three years of service.

Chaplain Brown mentioned that when he visited the national cemetery at Gettysburg years later, *"I wept as I gazed upon those innumerable graves,"* then proclaimed, *"on the field of Gettysburg I would erect a monument worthy of their valor and glory, a monument whose shaft shall be the first to kiss the sun as it rises over the eastern hills in the morning, and the last to bid the God of day good bye at night."*[98]

After the war, Brown returned home and served a succession of churches throughout western New York.[99] He retired from active ministry in 1891, saying that over fifty years, he had served twenty-one churches, two terms as a presiding elder, and three years as chaplain. Although retired, he continued to preach until the week before his death on August 4, 1895. He is buried in Union Cemetery, Livonia, New York.

An article in the Auburn (New York) *Democrat* in 1912 relates the following story about Chaplain John N. Brown and the Harper's Ferry debacle:

> *After the surrender Stonewall Jackson came riding through the camps on his little sorrel, and seeing our chaplain and recognizing his rank from his uniform said, "Chaplain, your people must go home, you have no business here."*
>
> *"We will," the good chaplain replied, "when you lay down your arms and cease your opposition to our government."*
>
> *Jackson looked at him and said, "Chaplain, what is your name?"*
>
> *"I would not dare tell you my name, Sir."*
>
> *"Why not?"*
>
> *"It may be enough for me to say, that my name was once a terror to all Virginia, indeed may I say, to the whole South, and right here at Harper's Ferry."*
>
> *Jackson said, "Well, really I am now quite curious to know what it is."*
>
> *"General! My name is John Brown." Jackson laughed and rode on.*
>
> *The "other" John Brown, of course, was hanged in Harper's Ferry in 1859 for capturing the U. S. arsenal and trying to incite a slave revolt.*

Confederate general Thomas J. "Stonewall" Jackson met Chaplain Brown at Harper's Ferry. (Library of Congress)

Ezra DeFreest Simons, 125th New York Infantry

Chaplain Ezra DeFreest Simons of the 125th New York Infantry. (from *A Regimental History: The One Hundred and Twenty-Fifth New York State Volunteers* by Ezra Simons)

Ezra DeFreest Simons was born in Troy, New York, on July 10, 1840. His parents died when he was young, and he was raised by the Rev. George Colfax Baldwin, a Baptist pastor in Troy. He began to study for the ministry but interrupted his preparations to enlist in the 125th New York Infantry as a private in Company D on August 13, 1862. Just two weeks later, he was promoted to commissary sergeant, and a month later he was captured (and quickly paroled) along with the rest of the brigade at Harper's Ferry. In February 1863, the regiment's chaplain, Joseph L. Barlow, was forced to resign because of poor health. The regiment's officers petitioned New York governor Horatio Seymour that Simons receive a commission as chaplain. This petition was necessary because Simons had not yet been duly ordained, as the U.S. Army required of any potential chaplain. However, Simons was commissioned by the governor on March 3, 1863, and immediately took a leave of absence to go home to Troy to be ordained as a Baptist pastor. He returned to the regiment in Centreville, Virginia, and brought with him fifty fatigue hats donated by a woman from Troy, which were much appreciated by those members of the regiment who received them.

Simons wrote the regimental history, which was published in 1888. He described the regiment's encampment near Centreville during the spring of 1863, where they were assigned to the outer defenses of Washington, as *"golden days of soldiering . . . the poetry of a soldier's life, with all the benefits and but little of the band of outdoor life, which in its better features was truly wholesome."*[100] That idyllic experience of soldiering moved toward its end as the Army of the Potomac marched past Centreville on its way north in the middle of June. Simons recalled that as the veterans of that army passed by, they were *"shaming us, as the old soldiers named us, 'bandbox and white-glove' soldiers, while we envied them as veterans. But, white gloves were soon to be things of the past, and the band-box was to be forever laid aside, as we became parts of that greatest Army of the Republic, the sharers of its toils, mingling blood with that of its heroes and identified in honor and destiny with its triumphs."*[101] On June 24, the regiment and the rest of the brigade joined the Army of the Potomac on its march. After suffering through long marches for which the men were physically unprepared, including one day's march of thirty-three miles when men fell out by the hundreds, the regiment arrived at Gettysburg on the evening of July 1. Then, early the next morning, the regiment

> *was in the line of march of the Second Corps moving upon the field. As we neared this, an ambulance, with stretcher at side, turned out of the road into a field. The stretcher was half covered with blood. The sight awakened a sense of the bloody work at hand. Be it remembered, that, although the regiment had been in service from August, 1862, until July, 1863, Harper's Ferry was its only record of service, and that was for the most part bloodless. . . . we were taken to the left of the centre of the main line, and placed on the left of Cemetery Hill, with the Bryan house and Ziegler's Grove to our right. The bands were playing down in the field. This was one of the very few times when any music was heard on battle-field, save that of cannon and rifle, of shot and shell. In time of action men were needed for other purposes than to make pleasing music; and the musicians were utilized "to bear away the wounded, and to cover up the dead."*[102]

Simons realized that their position enabled them *"to see most of the conflicts which followed; and, during the progress of these, could note the waving of the signal flags on Little Round Top, where was stationed a part of the signal corps. We were in position, too, to have part in much of the fighting; and at the decisive point to aid in bearing the brunt of the battle."*[103] The men watched as their comrades in the 39th New York (Garibaldi Regiment) were deployed as skirmishers in front of the brigade:

> *And now they pass down at our right . . . into the field . . . Brave fellows–brave or stupid, which is it?–there they stand in open field, and the crack of rifles is heard. The rebels are down behind the fence and are sheltered. "Drop, Garibaldis!" Yes, they did drop, one after another, as the bullet did its work. Some to rise not again; and here come some of the poor fellows with shattered jaws and maimed limbs and cut faces.*[104]

There were batteries to the left and right of the brigade, but they didn't fire until midafternoon when *"from over by the Seminary comes hurtling a shell. Right over our heads it flies; and battery to left replies with quick, sharp note, and its shell explodes amid the smoke of the rebel gun. Beautiful piece of artillery practice, that. 'Boys, lie down!' The men are on the ground under the iron hail which now rattles over our heads."*[105]

At the dedication of the regiment's monument at Gettysburg in 1888, Capt. E. A. Hartshorn recalled, "At Harper's Ferry, Chaplain Simons, then commissary sergeant of the regiment, came to me in the thickest of the rebel cannonading and requested me to show him how to load and fire a rifle." [106] While there is no evidence that Simons fired any weapon at Gettysburg, he felt a need to be with his regiment in the heat of battle. When the brigade was ordered to move farther south along the Union line to help stem the tide of the rebel attack late on July 2, Simons advanced right along with them and provided his eyewitness account:

> *It was now about 7 o'clock in the evening of a long, beautiful, warm, July day. As we moved down into the strife the writer looked to the west. The sun was sinking low, and the heavens were ablaze with its splendors, in marked contrast with the lurid fires of death towards which we were marching. We were halted amid the smoke in front of some swale–a new growth of trees–in which we could see, dimly, because of the smoke covering the field–men moving. The brigade was dressed on the colors, an unusual thing under such circumstances. Our men commenced to fire, but the word was shouted: "Firing on your own men!" Upon which the command was given by Colonel [George Lamb] Willard: "Cease firing!" Officers, as did the writer, rushed in front of our line repeating the order. But the interval permitted the enemy to reload, and we speedily learned our mistake. A man to the left of the writer fell in an instant prostrated by a bullet. Then, doubt removed, the men await no order, but press on, firing as they move. On we rushed with loud cries! on–with bullets whizzing by our ears, as if messengers from the cold, icy regions of the dead–with shells screaming and cannon-balls tearing the air, like so many fiends bent on destruction: now bursting above and around us; now ploughing the ground at our feet and laying many of our noble men low in death or bleeding with wounds: on, on, we rushed, through storm of fire and death, thundering above and darting around us like the thunder and lightning of heaven: on, driving the rebels*

before us, mortally wounding General [William] Barksdale at the head of the rebel force, who in vain sought to lash and lead his men forward, and who died in our hands.[107]

For Simons and many men of the 125th, this action of July 2 defined their Gettysburg experience and redeemed them from the sobriquet "Harper's Ferry Cowards." And, perhaps because Simons participated in it so closely, he wrote another vivid and artistic description of his experience:

> *But, look! The fire is creeping towards us along the Emmettsburg [sic] road! See in the fields how the panting giants are wrestling! Their breath is aflame. Now one is pressed back, and now the other is forced to knee. "Help!" and down the hillside towards the combatants we march. The sun is declining behind the hills in the west. The birds start up and fly away, singing in sweet discord with the hoarse music of battle. We are down on the bloody arena. Back, Third Corps; forward, the Second! Oh, it was grand!–awfully grand!–as with loud, brave cries we press them . . . as the rebel line is driven back, broken and scattered. Blaze artillery from the hill beyond in our faces; sting, like serpents, bullets through the air; but, as night sets in, the living of our men rest in victory, as the dead sleep in a triumph henceforth unbroken by the turmoil of earthly strife.*[108]

Like many chaplains, Simons probably retired to the field hospital after the fighting on July 2. His account of the events of July 3 evidently came from his conversations with Capt. Samuel C. Armstrong. That morning, the 125th was back in its position near Ziegler's Grove. A detachment of the regiment under the command of Capt. Samuel C. Armstrong was on the skirmish line west of the Emmitsburg Road, near the Bliss Farm.[109] Simons noted that these skirmishers

Chaplain Simons lauded Capt. Samuel C. Armstrong for his handling of his troops on July 3. (Library of Congress)

> *hugged the ground, for the firing was hot, the rebels pouring in a flank fire on the picket-line, from the houses of Gettysburg, killing and wounding some of our men. About noon,*

Captain Armstrong withdrew the line for rest to the reserve station on the Emmettsburg [sic] road; and at this point they were under the artillery fire which preceded Pickett's charge. The shot and shell from both sides passed over their heads. Noticing a lull in the cannonading, Captain Armstrong looked around and saw the Confederate lines marching grandly down the slope towards our men. He immediately ordered the entire picket-reserve and all whom he could muster–about seventy-five all told–to fall in, and led them on the "double-quick" about three hundred yards down the Emmettsburg road, to get at the enemy in flank.

Finding a rail fence at right angle to their advancing line, some sixty or seventy yards from their extreme left, he posted his men along the rail fence. They took position unflinchingly; and, resting their rifles on the top of the fence, took deliberate aim and poured a murderous fire into the rebel flank, comprising [General J. Johnston] Pettigrew's men.

To the Eighth Ohio has been given the credit for the flank fire which contributed efficiently to this result. But, distinct record should go into general history of Captain Armstrong's brave and skillful part at that important point of the battle. From Captain Armstrong's position the Confederate dead could be seen lying in heaps. Hundreds of the charging line prostrated themselves on their backs in the Emmettsburg road, and waved their hats and handkerchiefs in token of surrender. Some of the bravest rushed close to the main Union line, and fell a few yards away. Of the five officers who served with Captain Armstrong in his brave action, which aided in the great victory secured, he was the only survivor.[110]

The night of July 3 brought heavy rain to the battlefield, which only increased the suffering of the wounded and the burdens of the surgeons and chaplains who cared for them. Simons ended his chapter on Gettysburg by recalling,

Dreadful was the night which followed. The rain now fell as in torrents. The densest darkness filled the woods by the creek, as the sad cries–the very wailings of the wounded peopled the air with images of distress. That night, given to the care of hundreds of suffering men–Confederates and Union men mingled–remains a dark, dread memory. . . . Rock Creek, in that night of storm, overflowed its banks, and the ground where the wounded were lying was flooded. The men were hastily moved, some of them being taken from a foot depth of water. The writer had opportunity then to witness the bravery of men whose valor was equally manifested in enduring suffering as on battle-field.[111]

Simons remained at Gettysburg to serve in the hospital until the end of July when he was relieved by David Demers of Troy, who arrived to care for the six remaining wounded men of the 125th. Demers wrote that the chaplain *"felt much relieved when I arrived, as he felt it his duty to be with the regiment."*[112]

Once he rejoined his men, Simons continued to serve beside them in battle. He helped rally the men when a line was in danger of being broken, served on the skirmish line at Ream's Station, Virginia, and was at the front on April 15, 1865, when General Lee surrendered his army at Appomattox. In honor of his battlefield courage, he was commissioned as adjutant on July 13, 1864, but at the request of the men in the regiment, he chose to remain as their chaplain. Simons served as a correspondent to the *Troy Daily Times* for the remainder of the war and often sent letters home asking for donations of mittens, caps, reading materials, and "singing books" for use in his chapel services.

After the regiment mustered out in 1865, Simons returned to Troy and served a church for two years before moving to San Jose, California, where he married Genevra L. Barnes in 1868. The couple returned east, and Simons served as the first pastor in a newly organized Vail Avenue Baptist Church in Troy. He also served churches in New Jersey and New York City, where he died on June 28, 1888, at the age of forty-eight. An honor guard consisting of several survivors of the 125th escorted his coffin to the church in New York City for his funeral and then back to Troy for his burial in Oakwood Cemetery. He left behind his wife and five children.

Chaplain Ezra Simons died four months before the dedication of the monument to the 125th New York Infantry at Gettysburg on October 3, 1888. In his regimental history, he affirmed to the survivors that *"the price paid in blood was none too great for the fruitage to the Nation and the world."*[113] (From *New York Monuments Commission Final Report on the Battlefield of Gettysburg*, 1900)

Theodore Spencer Harrison (he preferred to use his first initial) was born in 1820 in Poughkeepsie, New York. He was licensed to preach in 1844 and, after six years of scientific and theological studies, was ordained and began his ministry in the Baptist Church. When the war broke out, he was pastor of a church in Dundee, New York, and he helped to recruit for the 126th New York Infantry. On August 2, 1862, he resigned as pastor, enlisted in the regiment as a private, and was soon appointed sergeant of Company B. Once the regiment was officially organized three weeks later, he was appointed chaplain and was selected to receive the regimental colors that were presented by a ladies' organization in Geneva, New York.

Chaplain T. Spencer Harrison of the 126th New York Infantry. (Library of Congress, Liljenquist Family Collection)

Harrison had taken leave from the regiment for illness but returned on June 13 just in time for the long march to Gettysburg. After the battle, Harrison sent a letter on July 6 to a newspaper back in New York, writing, *"Dear sir: Here you will find a list of killed and wounded of the 126th. I send it to you in order to relieve the painful anxiety of friends. Our regiment has won imperishable laurels, and gained a place in history for time to come, though at a fearful cost."*[114] Harrison then lists the names of those who were wounded or killed, including Lt. Col. Eliakim Sherrill, who was a friend of the chaplain. His letter continues,

Lt. Col. Eliakim Sherrill of the 126th New York Infantry was a friend of Chaplain Harrison and was killed during the Pickett-Pettigrew-Trimble charge on July 3. (Library of Congress)

> *This list is as complete as I could make under the pressure of circumstances. . . . A hard fought battle, but a complete success for the army of the Potomac. Large numbers of the wounded rebels brought in. Their dead left, a great number of them for us to bury. So completely demoralized were they*

that many of them when attacked by our boys, gave themselves up. I understand that their officers made their men believe that we were green militia, but said they found out the mistake. I guess they did. What is left of us are in good spirits and are now marching forward on the pursuit of our flying foe. The prospect is that Lee will regret ever having come North. God be praised for this success.[115]

In a private letter, Harrison wrote, *"July 4th. Two hundred and forty-six of our Regiment are killed or wounded. The battle-field is covered with the slain. The hospitals overflow with wounded. Scores are crying for help. All over the field ghastly corpses stare at you. . . . July 6. Ordered to follow the Regiment. The sick and wounded to be removed."*[116]

Chaplain Harrison was one of only three officers out of the original thirty-nine who were still in service by the time the regiment mustered out. The author of the regimental history noted that *"many soldiers can testify to the kind offices and attentions of Chaplain Harrison in their behalf when maimed and bleeding they had been borne from the ranks where they fell in battle, and when prostrated by sickness or wounded they were lying in the hospital."*[117]

In August 1864, Harrison was detached for duty at the division hospital and then returned to the regiment the following May. When the regiment mustered out in June 1865, he went back to New York. Over the next five years, he served three churches before he fell ill with rheumatism and died on March 14, 1870, leaving behind his wife Sarah Ann Crouse and two daughters. He is buried in Hillside Cemetery in Dundee, New York.

Chapter 4:

The Third Corps

CORPS COMMANDERS:

Major General Daniel E. Sickles
Major General David B. Birney

The Third Corps of the Army of the Potomac was the only corps that was not commanded by a West Point graduate. Maj. Gen. Daniel Sickles was given command of the corps in February 1863 but took a leave of absence after the Battle of Chancellorsville. He returned to the corps at Frederick, Maryland, on June 28. Two days later, army commander George Gordon Meade ordered the corps to move to Emmitsburg and guard the town.

When fighting broke out at Gettysburg on July 1, Maj. Gen. Oliver Otis Howard, who took command of the field after the death of General Reynolds, ordered Sickles to hurry his corps forward. Knowing that he had been expected to stay at Emmitsburg, Sickles left two brigades there and ordered the rest of the corps to Gettysburg.

When the bulk of the corps arrived south of Gettysburg, it spent the night in bivouac near the lower end of Cemetery Ridge, with orders to prolong the line of Maj. Gen. Winfield Scott Hancock's Second Corps and place its left near or on Little Round Top. Concerned about the high ground in his front that dominated the line he was expected to hold, Sickles consulted with senior officers and then assumed the responsibility of moving his corps into what he believed would be a stronger position. The brigades moved forward in increments, until they were in position by about 3:00 p.m. The new line ran along the Emmitsburg Road, then turned sharply east at the Sherfy Peach

Orchard and continued toward Devil's Den. However, the corps did not have enough men to properly defend this line, and there was a large gap between the troops in the Peach Orchard and those on Stony Hill to the west of the Wheatfield. Even with additional infantry support from other corps and artillery support from the artillery reserve, Sickles was unable to withstand Confederate attacks coming from the west. His line finally broke late that afternoon, and the corps lost heavily. It spent the rest of the battle in the rear of the Union line, with some units being called up to support the front line on July 3.

A shell fragment struck Sickles in the leg on July 2, and he was carried off the field about 6:30 p.m. Surgeons quickly amputated his leg, and he was soon taken by train from Union Bridge, Maryland, to Washington to recover.

FIRST DIVISION:

Major General David B. Birney

First Brigade:

Brigadier General Charles K. Graham

After enjoying the visit of some ladies at their camp near Taneytown, Maryland, on the evening of June 29, the brigade marched toward Emmitsburg and was ordered to advance quickly to Gettysburg on July 1. After an exhausting march, during which they passed civilians fleeing their homes, the men of the brigade settled in for the night near the Trostle Farm. The soldiers were up early on July 2, knowing that they would be called to enter the battle that had begun the day before.

Graham's brigade occupied the salient at the Peach Orchard, where they were vulnerable to attack from two sides. After enduring artillery fire in their exposed position for two hours, they were attacked by South Carolinians and Mississippians from the south and the west, and Graham's brigade started to crumble until it finally collapsed, suffering the highest casualty rate (49 percent) of any brigade in the corps.

The brigade joined the rest of the battered and disordered Third Corps in the rear of the Union line. Two regiments moved to support a battery near the Copse of Trees during the Pickett-Pettigrew-Trimble charge on July 3, and that night, the men were ordered to pick up guns from the fields around them. After caring for the dead and wounded for two days, they joined the rest of the army in its pursuit of the enemy on July 6.

The brigade included six Pennsylvania regiments: the 57th, 63rd, 68th, 105th, 114th, and 141st. Only the 57th had a chaplain, and he left no record.

Second Brigade:
Brigadier General Hobart Ward

Hobart Ward's brigade reached Emmitsburg midafternoon on July 1. As the men were preparing to go into bivouac they received orders to continue to Gettysburg. Like Graham's men, they were passed by terrified people fleeing Gettysburg. Early on July 2, one regiment and some sharpshooters were sent on a reconnaissance to see if enemy troops were in the woods opposite the corps line. There they ran into some Alabama troops, and after a brief but sharp fight Ward's men were returning to the brigade when they were ordered to stay near the Emmitsburg Road as skirmishers.

That afternoon, the rest of the brigade was assigned to anchor what would be the left flank of General Birney's division, the Third Corps line, and the entire Army of the Potomac. The six regiments plus two attached units of sharpshooters were positioned from the southern end of Houck's Ridge, just north of Devil's Den, to the woods at the southeastern corner of the Wheatfield. When the Confederates began their advance, some of them encountered Ward's sharpshooters, who fell back slowly, firing as they went.

One battery was located near the end of Ward's line, which drew the attention of attacking Confederates. As men from Texas, Arkansas, and Georgia pushed toward the ridge and the guns, Ward's men were overpowered, despite desperate countercharges and receiving reinforcements from another brigade. Eventually they fell back as three of the Union guns were overrun and captured. The survivors spent that night north of Little Round Top; they were sent the next morning to support batteries along Cemetery Ridge, although they did not participate in the repulse of the Pickett-Pettigrew-Trimble charge. Several of the regiments were on skirmish duty on July 4, and the brigade returned to its original position near the Weikert Farm on July 5 before joining the army in the pursuit of Lee's forces on July 6.

The brigade included the 3rd and 4th Maine, the 86th and 124th New York, the 20th Indiana, the 99th Pennsylvania, and the 1st and 2nd United States Sharpshooters. Of these, all but the 99th Pennsylvania and 1st U.S. Sharpshooters were accompanied by their chaplains, and we have records of three of them.

Stephen Freeman Chase, 3rd Maine Infantry
Benjamin A. Chase, 4th Maine Infantry

Stephen and Benjamin Chase were brothers, ministers, and chaplains in different Maine regiments. Unfortunately, only scant information can be found about their service in the army.

Stephen Freeman Chase was born in Unity, Maine, on September 13, 1836. Little is known about his education, but he was ordained in 1859 and served a Methodist Episcopal church in Maine. The next year, he married Ellen M. Doe, with whom he had five children. He mustered in as chaplain in the 3rd Maine Infantry on March 23, 1863.

Chaplain Stephen Freeman Chase of the 3rd Maine Infantry.
(Maine State Archives)

After the Battle of Gettysburg, Freeman was assigned to duty at the Third Corps hospital, which was in various houses and barns along the Taneytown Road. On July 10, he sent a letter to the editors of a Maine newspaper in which he praised the regiment and offered consolation for those at home:

> *I purposed, during our twenty-two days' marching campaign to give you some account of its vicissitudes and incidents, but I have no heart to do it now, and it is not of this that the friends of the Third wish to hear. Matters of a deeper interest absorb our attention now. Our emotions are of mingled sadness and grateful rejoicing. A fearful battle, great in slaughter, but glorious in victory, has been fought. Of the patient, energetic endurance of our men on the tedious march, and of their valor in the desperate conflict, too much cannot be said in praise. The overwhelming*

repulse of the enemy, with fearful slaughter, and the haste and confusion of his flight, attest the invincible energy, so long lying latent in the "Army of the Potomac." Let it be no longer asked whether this army is ever to accomplish anything. Once surely it has driven the enemy from before it, and proved itself competent for something beyond "masterly inactivity." We are sad as we think of the lost and suffering ones, but rejoice, with inexpressible gratitude to God, at the victory He hath given us. The glorious "Fourth" accumulates importance and renown. Vicksburg and Gettysburg on that day make second declaration that this land shall be the home of Freedom.

Success seems attending us at every point, and the nation is called to thanksgiving.

But I took my pen, not to write a letter but to give information to the friends of the 3d Maine. I sympathize deeply with the many who are bereaved, or filled with deep solicitude for their friends who have shared in the casualties of the recent bloody battle. The Third never suffered so severely or fought more nobly. Only a small fragment is left.

There is much that might be of interest of which I would be glad to write, but I have not time. I have been two days catching odd moments enough for this desultory note and for revising and getting as correct as possible, the subjoined list of casualties [which the newspaper had printed the week before].

Those who find the names of their friends among the wounded have our assurances that we shall spare no efforts for their comfort and recovery. Our labors have been very continuous and exhausting yet most cheerfully rendered. . . . Let us hope and pray that this sanguinary strife will soon cease, and the nation come forth as gold tried by fire.[1]

Freeman wrote another letter to his sister Lizzie on July 24:

Much of interest has transpired not only with us but all through the land. Some of the most desperate and bloody conflicts of the war have been fought and its most glorious victories won. Vicksburg and Gettysburg unite to declare, a <u>second time</u> on the <u>now doubly glorious</u> Fourth, that this land shall be free from the rule of tyrants. Great has been the rejoicing of the Land–<u>deep</u> should be its gratitude and loud its praise to the God of Battles. The scenes

I have here witnessed will ever be fresh in memory and cause me to desire to witness no more of war's horrors.

The battlefield is being visited continually by people from all parts of the county and present many a wonder to the eyes unused to war.

My health has been good through the labors and exposures of the long march, the battle, and subsequent days, till quite recently, were quite exhaustive and I became pretty well jaded. Our labors are not now so severe and our fare and accommodations are better and I am getting to feeling quite energetic.

When the army moved, the General [J. Hobart Ward] detailed me to remain here as Chap'n of our Corps hospital. Dr. Hildreth, surgeon of my regt. and my "chum" ever since I have been in the army was detailed "Surgeon-in-Charge" of the Corps hospital–so we are still together and as he is a very nice man, I am happy to be able to enjoy his fellowship.

We are hoping soon to join the Army so as to be "in" at the taking of Richmond or whatever may be done.[2]

In December 1863, Freeman served as a recruiting officer and encouraged the veterans to reenlist. He spent time in a hospital in Washington, D.C., for a wound he received in May 1864 during the Wilderness campaign and resigned on June 28, 1864. He returned to Maine and then transferred to the Southern New England Conference of the Methodist Episcopal Church to continue his ministry, serving churches in Topsfield and Salem, Massachusetts. In 1878, he turned in his ordination papers and studied dentistry. He opened a practice first in Boston and then in Newtonville, Massachusetts, where he lived for the last thirty-six years of his life. He died on March 31, 1920, at his home and is buried in Newton Cemetery. His wife had died in 1912, but he was survived by four of his daughters.

Benjamin A. Chase was born on June 16, 1833, in Unity, Maine. While studying in Newbury, Vermont, he felt a call to enter the ministry. He continued his education and was admitted as a deacon in the Providence Conference of the Methodist Episcopal Church in 1860. He enlisted in the 4th Maine Infantry on June 15, 1861. In late 1862, while on a trip home, he married Carrie M. Rich on November 15 and unsuccessfully attempted to recruit men to fill out the depleted ranks.

There is no record of Benjamin's time at Gettysburg. He mustered out of the regiment on July 19, 1864, and returned to New England, where he served churches in eastern Maine and Rhode Island. In 1872, he gave a lecture on the history of the regiment at a reunion that was very well received by the veterans and their families, but, unfortunately, was never published. Perhaps he had planned to do so, but he died just two years later, on August 17, 1874, at the age of forty-one while serving his church in East Cumberland, Rhode Island. He left behind his wife and four young daughters and is buried in Pond Cemetery in Unity, Maine.

Chaplain Benjamin A. Chase of the 4th Maine Infantry. (Maine State Archives)

Lorenzo Barber, 2nd United States Sharpshooters

Lorenzo Barber was born in Berkshire County, Massachusetts, on April 9, 1821. As a youth, he became a member of the Providence Conference of the Methodist Episcopal Church, and after completing his theological education at Concord Biblical Institute and Boston University, he was a professor at various institutions, including the New York Conference Seminary. In 1852, he married Charlotte Dewey, who died in 1860, leaving him one daughter, Eva. Barber joined the Troy (New York) Conference in 1857 and served the church at Albia. In December 1861, he was recruited to serve in the 2nd Regiment, United States Sharpshooters because of his renown as a marksman.

Chaplain Lorenzo Barber of the U.S. Sharpshooters. (from *Berdan's United States Sharpshooters in the Army of the Potomac*)

Barber quickly gained a reputation as the "fighting chaplain," and even soldiers in other regiments stood in awe of his prowess. A private from the 124th New York Infantry who served in the same brigade as the sharpshooters wrote, *"The sharpshooters Have A Buly Chaplain He takes his Rifel And goes in Ever Fight With the Boys And if He gets sight on A Rebel it is Shure Death to Him For he is as good A shot as they Have.*"[3] A sergeant in Barber's regiment proclaimed, *"I think the men are scarce that have killed as many Johnnies as [Barber] has. He gets his gun up to his face then says 'God have mercy on your poor Soul' & lets her go & down comes Mr. Johnnie. I wish the army furnished more such men. He is known all through the Corps as the fighting Chaplain."*[4] The regimental historian of the 124th New York noted that during a skirmish at Wapping Heights, Virginia, in late July 1863, *"Chaplain Barbour [sic] of the sharp-shooters–one of the best shots in our army–who, with his trusty rifle in hand moved with the skirmishers, soon caught sight of a Confederate marksman posted in the top of a tree, and by several carefully directed shots so demoralized the poor fellow that he dropped his own gun, descended to the ground begging for mercy and ran into our lines declaring that the first bullet had taken off his hat and that the next two had singed his hair."*[5] The historian of the sharpshooters wrote that Barber *"practices what he preaches. He tells us what we should do, and goes with us to the very front to help us in battle."*[6]

Barber served as a correspondent to newspapers in Troy, New York, but there are no letters from him regarding the Battle of Gettysburg, perhaps because he was not with the regiment during the battle. In late June, he demonstrated his daring and cunning when he went to Washington to retrieve the Sharpshooters' mail, a typical responsibility for chaplains. On his way back to the regiment, he passed through Emmitsburg, where *"he was 'surprised' by a large force of [Confederate general J. E. B.] Stuart's cavalry, as he was bringing to the regiment a week's mail, and while his captors were looking over the contents of the mail bag, he slips out one side and jumps upon one of their finest looking horses and 'skedaddles' into camps, tells us the sorrowful tale, but we feel repaid for the loss of our mail, by the escape of our Chaplain."*[7] The historian of the U.S. Sharpshooters added, *"I understand he brought along with him two prisoners, however he managed to do it."*[8] Barber and the mail were evidently captured sometime around June 30 and he returned to the regiment on July 5.

A few weeks later, Barber was wounded in the leg while he was on the skirmish line during the Battle of Mine Run, Virginia, and he was taken to a hospital in Alexandria. The following year, he underwent surgery to remove the bullet that had never dislodged from his leg and had caused him severe pain. At some point, he married his second wife, Marion Williams, perhaps when he was home recovering from his surgery. They had no children together. He returned to duty in November

1864, but never fired another shot with his regiment; he served solely as chaplain. He was discharged on February 18, 1865.

After the war, Barber left full-time ministry but served as a local preacher for various churches while also working as an insurance agent in Troy, New York. Known locally as the "Fighting Methodist Parson," his use of his telescopic rifle drew great crowds for his services. Barber's final and sadly ironic trial came on April 9, 1882, when he was hunting with a friend. While climbing over a fence, his gun discharged and he was hit in the stomach. He died five days later and is buried near Troy, New York. One of his men summed up his service to the regiment: *"We have learned to regard him as a Christian and a friend; a brave soldier in the service of his country, and a faithful and zealous minister in the service of his God."*[9]

Third Brigade: Colonel Regis de Trobriand

On July 1 the brigade commanded by Col. Regis de Trobriand marched to Emmitsburg to guard against a Confederate attack from the west, while the rest of the corps headed toward Gettysburg. In the early hours of July 2, the brigade was ordered to immediately rejoin the division, which it did by about 10:00 that morning. When the Third Corps was ordered forward to form a new line in the afternoon, de Trobriand's men took position between Ward's and Graham's brigades and occupied the Stony Hill and the southern border of the Wheatfield. Two regiments were detached to support Graham in the Peach Orchard, and another was sent to reinforce Ward near Devil's Den. Those that remained in the Wheatfield and Stony Hill area successfully held off repeated Confederate attacks until reinforcements from the Fifth Corps that had arrived earlier began to pull back, leaving de Trobriand's men in danger of being surrounded. After falling back to the north end of the Wheatfield, two regiments were sent back in to stem the Confederate tide that was threatening to sweep the field. When Second Corps reinforcements arrived, de Trobriand's men could finally withdraw. They spent the night near the Taneytown Road and then moved to the position they had taken the previous morning. Unfortunately, this left them vulnerable to the cannon fire that preceded the Pickett-Pettigrew-Trimble charge. They were sent toward the Copse of Trees to support a battery and watched as the Union boys repulsed the Confederates at the Angle.

The brigade returned to its original position and spent the next two days caring for the wounded. Although most of the Army of the Potomac left the field on July 6, de Trobriand's men joined the pursuit early the next day.

De Trobriand's command included the 3rd and 5th Michigan, the 17th Maine, the 40th New York, and the 110th Pennsylvania regiments. Three chaplains accompanied the regiments, but none left writings that could be located.

SECOND DIVISION:

Major General Andrew A. Humphreys

First Brigade:

Brigadier General Joseph B. Carr

As the men in Brig. Gen. Joseph Carr's brigade marched toward Emmitsburg on July 1, they could hear the distant sound of artillery to the north. After resting for two hours, they quickly continued to Gettysburg along with Brig. Gen. William Brewster's brigade. A wrong turn in the dark brought them close to the Confederate line, and the two brigades had to quietly backtrack until they regained the correct route. They reached the bivouac area of the First Division by about 2:00 a.m. of July 2.

Sickles ordered Carr's brigade to take a position along Emmitsburg Road, extending Graham's line from the Peach Orchard. The right of Carr's line was separated from Hancock's line back on Cemetery Ridge, creating a large gap between the two corps. Carr's men were ordered to lie down during the artillery barrage that preceded the Confederate attack, and they listened as the sounds of battle to their left grew louder. When the attack came to their position, the men found themselves overwhelmed by rebel forces approaching from both the south and the west. Despite making a desperate stand, the brigade was soon overpowered and was ordered to fall back to Cemetery Ridge. Some soldiers turned to fire on the enemy as they pulled back to a position near the Taneytown Road.

Early on July 3, orders came for the brigade to join the rest of the Third Corps farther in the rear, and then to go to the right to support Union batteries that were coming under fire from Pickett's men. At the end of the day, Carr led his men to their original position, where they remained until they were sent toward Emmitsburg early in the morning of July 7.

The 1st, 11th, and 16th Massachusetts, 11th New Jersey, 12th New Hampshire, and 26th and 84th Pennsylvania (guarding trains at Westminster) composed Carr's brigade. Chaplains were present with four of those regiments, but only one recorded his experiences at Gettysburg.

Warren Handel Cudworth, 1st Massachusetts Infantry

Chaplain Warren Cudworth of the 1st Massachusetts Infantry (U.S. Army Heritage and Education Center)

William Handel Cudworth was born in Lowell, Massachusetts, on May 23, 1825. Although raised in a Congregational church, he entered the Unitarian fold when he was hired to serve as the organist in a local church. He graduated from the Phillips Academy in Andover in 1845 and from Harvard Divinity School in 1851. He was ordained on March 17, 1852, and began his lifelong ministry at the Unitarian Church in East Boston, where he would serve for thirty-two years.

Just one day after news of the attack on Fort Sumter reached his congregation, Cudworth went to the Massachusetts State House to offer his services as chaplain. On May 27, 1861, he was commissioned as the chaplain of the 1st Massachusetts Infantry. When he went into camp with the regiment, he sent a notice of resignation to his church, but the congregation wouldn't hear of it and convinced him instead to find someone to fill his pulpit until he returned from the war. Before leaving, he advised his parish to use the funds they had raised to build a new church for the benefit of soldiers' families instead.

Cudworth wrote and published the regimental history in 1865 and much of the following is taken from his work.[10] He was critical of those chaplains who chose to take up arms and fight with their men, and in a letter to a friend, he wrote, *"I have no sympathy whatever with fighting chaplains, and think that they prostitute their office by doing so. So I hold that no clergyman should enter the service except as a chaplain, and then remain strictly a non-combatant."*[11] In the preface to the regimental history, he affirmed (with customary humility in referring to himself in the third person), *"The author of the following history volunteered his services as chaplain in the First Regiment from no love of warfare, but simply because, with all his heart, he believed in 'Liberty and the Union' . . . Being a chaplain, with an assigned place in rear of the column or line of battle, thither he always went, and there he always staid."*[12] He noted his information in the history came from both his own eyewitness experiences and the also the reports of the wounded as they were brought to the rear.

During the army's march toward Pennsylvania, Cudworth sent a letter to his mother describing the regiment's situation:

> *We arrived here on Saturday night, leaving Falmouth a week ago last Thursday, and have marched over a hundred miles, sometimes all night, till, having overtaken the enemy, we are watching him, playing off and on, endeavoring to distract his attention, divide his forces, and, should we find a favorable opportunity, attack him at some weak point. It is impossible to foresee where we next may go, but in my opinion, neither Lee nor Hooker intend to risk a general engagement if it can be avoided, but will try by moving about to out-general each other.*[13]

After several days of hard marching, the regiment finally reached Taneytown on June 30. Cudworth noted the friendliness of the citizens in Maryland, who waved flags and provided food and milk at reasonable prices. He recalled that one little girl *"seemed never weary of shouting in her shrill, childlike way, 'Three cheers for the Union!' and when one of the soldiers responded, 'Three cheers for you, little girl!' she answered quickly, 'Three cheers for you, too, sir!'"*[14]

From their bivouac near Emmitsburg on July 1, the men heard heavy firing from the north and west, which they had expected all day. As the 1st marched toward the sound of the guns, *"Large numbers of Dutch farmers were passed on the road, sitting with their families on the fences fronting their estates, gaping at the troops moving by; and the able-bodied men among them received any thing but complimentary salutations, as the weary troops plodded along to defend the lives, rights, and property of such creatures."*[15]

When Brig. Gen. Andrew Humphreys's division took the wrong road on the way to the battlefield on July 2, they came very close to running into Confederates who were at the Black Horse (Bream's) Tavern. (Library of Congress)

Cudworth recalled the almost disastrous march of the division on the evening of July 1:

> *Approaching the neighborhood of Gettysburg after dark, a mistake was made in the roads, which led the division directly through the enemy's lines, and within a few hundred feet of thirty pieces of their artillery. The mistake was discovered by the capture of a sergeant of a rebel battery at supper in one of the houses, when the column faced about, and quietly retraced its steps. The right road was soon found; and, at two o'clock in the morning, the jaded soldiers threw themselves upon the ground, under the shadow of Round Top Hill.*[16]

It is likely that Cudworth was near the front on July 2, at least until he received orders to go to the rear to care for the wounded. Hence, the chaplain confused some details in his account of the fighting (see footnote):

> *Information was brought in by the cavalry at noon that the rebels were massing in front of our centre and left for an assault in force. Gen. Sickles immediately moved his corps forward to an elevated plot of ground under cover of Round Top, and deployed skirmishers along a line of fences running nearly parallel with the Emmetsburg [sic] road. He had hardly finished the disposition of his troops, when the enemy emerged from the woods in solid lines, and began a rapid advance. Observing the change made in the Union front by Gen. Sickles' manouvre, however, they obliqued a little to the left, and resumed their advance. The skirmishers were scattered before them instantly; but the line of battle stood firm. Artillery*

and infantry were so posted, that every shot would tell; and the first fire made such fearful havoc in their ranks, that they came to a halt. Closing up the gaps, they again moved forward, firing volley after volley as long as the regiments remained sufficiently unbroken to retain their organization, and then loading and firing each man for himself, wherever he happened to be. Their advance was steadily resisted for over an hour by the third corps, assisted only by the batteries upon Round Top, and a few guns on the left, when Gen. Sickles fell back to his first position along Cemetery Ridge; having the fifth corps upon his left, and the second on his right.[17]

Most likely, Cudworth had retired to the hospitals in the rear soon after the fight on July 2 commenced and stayed there throughout the remainder of the battle. Hence, his description of the Pickett-Pettigrew-Trimble charge came to him secondhand and contains many errors. However, he offered recollections of his experiences in the hospitals, which are more reliable, yet still overstated in some ways. He recalled one story that had been related by a soldier in the hospital:

As one of our wounded men was lying in a barnyard, whither he had limped to avoid the flying balls, a column of retreating rebels came through, on their way to the rear. One of them remarked, in his hearing, that he was disgusted with the whole thing.

"Why not stop, and give yourselves up?" asked the wounded Federal.

"The Yankees would kill us."

"Pshaw! whoever told you that lied."

"What do you know about it?"

"Why, I'm a Yankee, and know how the Yankees treat their prisoners."

"Are you sure they would not hurt us at all?"

"Sure? Of course I am, or I would not tell you so."

"Well, what shall we do?"

"Leave your guns here, go out in front and shake a white handkerchief, and they will stop firing to let you come in."

"What do you say?" was the inquiry among the rebels of each other; and, as a result, over two hundred of them turned back, and surrendered themselves prisoners of war.[18]

Cudworth reported that at the end of the day on July 3,

> *While along their lines all was silence and gloom, in ours all was merriment and rejoicing. Bands played national airs in fortissimo style; men cheered at any thing and every thing in the excess of their enthusiasm; and unrestrained hilarity ruled the hour. Even the wounded and bleeding sufferers in the hospitals seemed to forget their pain in the great joy our triumph universally afforded. The writer remembers two men in the third corps hospital, who said they were glad of and gloried in their wounds, if they had aided in the achievement of victory; and several, who could not speak, looked the assent and sympathy their pale lips were unable to utter.*[19]

After spending two days working in the hospitals, Cudworth reported on *"Tuesday, July 6th, orders came to the First Regiment to pack up in readiness for a move. The wounded were left in charge of Surgeon Whiston, until they could bear removal to some regular hospital; and the dead of both sides buried, with suitable inscriptions on the rude head-boards designating their graves."*[20] The regiment moved off in pursuit of the Confederate army, with their beloved chaplain beside them, and he noted the spirit of the men: *"The defeat of Lee twice in succession had given the Federal soldiers an importance, in popular estimation, which was seen and felt wherever they moved. The feeling was universal, that the rebels had made their last invasion of Union soil, and that their power was on the wane. Hence many who had been non-committal, while it remained uncertain which side was going to conquer, at once declared for the North, when there was no longer any doubt."*[21]

On July 12, the regiment was camped near Williamsport, Maryland,

> *where orders were received to be in readiness for an assault upon the enemy. At that time it was raining in torrents. The Potomac was unusually high and swift, and thanks went up to Heaven for the rain, almost as numerous as the drops that came down. It was felt to be impossible for Gen. Lee to ferry his forces across the river, and it was known that one of his bridges there had been destroyed. All that seemed necessary was an assault, to compel his vanquished and retreating army to surrender. Never were soldiers seen so eager for a battle, so impatient to be allowed to engage the enemy. Being held where they were from the 12th to the 15th, while the rebels were so near they could see their pickets in the neighboring woods and on the adjoining hills, some of our soldiers actually wept, they*

were so desirous of the one grand, final conflict which might end the whole war, and release them from the privations and sufferings of another campaign in Virginia.[22]

But it was soon discovered that the Confederates had *"escaped from the clutches of Gen. Meade, greatly to the mortification and disappointment of his soldiers, who were thoroughly persuaded that it could have been conquered entire, had they been permitted to make an assault as soon as they arrived. Sorrowfully, therefore, the next day, the column was formed for a continuation of the march, now destined to stretch into Virginia again."*[23]

Cudworth remained with the regiment until they mustered out on May 28, 1864, when their three-year term of service expired; he had been with them the entire time except for a brief visit home at the time of First Bull Run. He returned home to great fanfare from his congregation in East Boston, where he picked up his ministry, served as chaplain for the Department of Massachusetts, Grand Army of the Republic,

The Confederates retreated across the Potomac River near Williamsport on July 13 and slipped away before the Union army could attack. (From *Frank Leslie's Illustrated Newspaper*, August 1, 1863)

This sketch shows Chaplain Cudworth with an officer at Wapping Heights, Virginia, during the pursuit of the Confederate army in late July. (from *History of the First Regiment Massachusetts Infantry* by Warren Cudworth)

and became a popular lecturer for temperance associations around eastern Massachusetts. On November 29, 1883, while Cudworth was participating in a community Thanksgiving service at the Maverick Congregational Church, he paused in mid-prayer, uttered, *"I . . . must . . . stop"* and fell to the floor, the victim of a fatal stroke at the age of fifty-eight.[24] A large gathering of veterans, from his regiment and others, filled the church during his funeral and served, along with the regimental drum corps, as an escort to Woodlawn Cemetery, where he was laid to rest. Cudworth had never married.

Second Brigade:
Colonel William R. Brewster

Col. William Brewster commanded a brigade that had been organized at the beginning of the war by Daniel Sickles and was named the Excelsior Brigade. Originally consisting of five New York regiments, a sixth joined the brigade in 1862. Along with Carr's brigade, the Excelsiors reached Emmitsburg in the afternoon of July 1, expecting to camp there for the night. But two hours later, they were ordered to Gettysburg and reached the field about 2:00 a.m. after their wrong turn and countermarch (see above).

On July 2, the brigade was positioned behind the Third Corps line along the Emmitsburg Road to serve as a reserve. When Confederate forces started advancing on the Union line from the Peach Orchard, the Excelsiors formed a line facing south, but the rushing tide of the Mississippians was too strong, and all but one regiment broke for the rear. The 120th New York held its ground behind a stone wall until they, too, were overwhelmed. The shattered brigade fell back and regrouped behind some Second Corps units on Cemetery Ridge, where it spent a restless night.

The next day, the Excelsiors joined the rest of their division in supporting batteries near the front lines but did not participate in the repulse of Pickett's men. After spending two days caring for the wounded, the brigade joined the rest of the Third Corps in pursuit of Robert E. Lee's army on July 7. Five of the Excelsior regiments, the 71st, 72nd, 73rd, 74th, and 120th New York, had chaplains at Gettysburg, but the 70th New York did not. Only one of those chaplains left a written record of Gettysburg, while a second left a legacy of faithful service that was lauded by others.

Joseph Hopkins Twichell, 71st New York Infantry

Chaplain Joseph Hopkins Twichell of the 71st New York Infantry. (Joseph Hopkins Twichell Papers, Beinecke Rare Book and Manuscript Library, Yale University)

Joseph Hopkins Twichell was born on May 27, 1838, in Southington Corners, Connecticut. After graduating from Lewis Academy, he entered Yale in 1855, and then Union Theological Seminary four years later, where he was a classmate of William Eastman, who became chaplain of the 72nd New York Infantry in the Excelsior Brigade, and where Twichell and his friends were steeped in abolitionism. Although Twichell was not yet ordained, Daniel Sickles recommended him to a friend who was recruiting a new regiment. Twichell enlisted in the Jackson Regiment (later renamed the Second Excelsior, and then the 71st New York Infantry) on April 29, 1861, and was mustered in on July 18. He had written a letter to his father on April 22 explaining his intention to volunteer as a chaplain:

> *If you ask why I fixed upon this particular regiment, composed as it is a rough, wicked men, I answer, that was the very reason. I saw that the companies of the better class of citizens were all attended by chaplains, but nothing was said about these. There, I thought, is a place for me.*
>
> *So far as I can find out, my risk of physical injury, in any event, will be slight. If my life is lost, it will be given just where it could not be refused in caring for the sick, in maintaining discipline not by violence, and in the pursuit of peaceful ministrations, such as may soften in some degree the asperities of war. My Bible, tracts, and a few books will constitute my weapons.*
>
> *You know how I have often thought myself fitted by nature to influence this class of men. If I may judge by a little experience, I shall expect by a cautious study of ways and means to gain confidence, then influence and to do good. I should not expect a*

revival, but I should expect to make some good impressions, by treating with kindness a class of men who are little used to it.

Another thing. Nothing is more repugnant to a civilized sense than the burial of a man as though he were a dog. This it is the privilege of the chaplain to prevent.[25]

After serving with the regiment for almost two years, Twichell traveled home to Southington, was ordained on January 30, 1863, and promptly returned to his duty with the regiment.

Twichell kept up a regular correspondence with his family throughout the war. On the eve of the Battle of Gettysburg, he wrote to his mother from the regiment's bivouac near Taneytown, Maryland, and described the Third Corps' long marches:

We are all tired out and had been allowed insufficient rest, never halting until dark and being aroused before sunrise almost every night . . . I have walked a large part of the way, unable to endure the sight of men dropping with fatigue or treading with pain on account of blistered feet while I sat in a saddle. Many such a one has my good Garryowen [his horse] borne on his able back since we left Falmouth. One circumstance has operated greatly to mitigate our discomfort and revive our drooping spirits, and this is our meeting friends and receiving friendly greetings. The set Virginia sneer and frown are left behind. Here another mood prevails. The farmers as we passed had pails or tubs of fresh, clear water at their gates and the loyal kitchens of their wives yielded abundance of good bread–but better still are the smiles, and waving flags and cheers with which they meet us . . . altogether we are refreshed in the inner man.[26]

Twichell also noted the return of General Sickles, who had been recuperating from a wound he received at Chancellorsville, recalling that the general *"received a most complimentary welcome. Great cheers swelled along the lines as he rode by and all hands feel relieved at his return."*[27]

Twichell wrote a lengthy letter to his sister Sarah Jane immediately after the battle in which he assured her that he was safe but that the battle had been terrible, *"one of the hardest fought, if not the hardest, of the war . . . Another libation of blood has been poured out to Liberty. Thousands of souls have been called to sudden judgment–thousands of homes are desolated."*[28]

Twichell reported that on the morning of July 2 he had visited with friends from the First and Twelfth Corps, then returned to his regiment to find that the Third Corps had advanced from the position they held that morning:

> *Following, I overtook it, formed in line of battle with the rest of the Brigade, preparing to go forward. After a look and a little talk, the bugle sounded and with a firm step with colors flying, the bravest men in the army marched into the open field. It was a splendid sight. Far to the right and left the dark lines of infantry moved on, with the artillery disposed at intervals, while the stillness was unbroken save by the scattered fire of skirmishers in front. My eyes and heart followed the flag which I love best and I stood unsuspicious of danger, but full of anxiety.*
>
> *Of a sudden, from the left, a point not apprehended as concealing the enemy, a battery opened upon us the most terrific fire I ever witnessed. The first shell struck not more than two rods behind where I, with several other non-combatants, were standing, expecting to see it begin from the front. We all retired rather precipitately to the partial shelter of a brick barn hard by [the Trostle barn], and there remained until our artillery silenced the guns that had opened. It was awful. For half an hour it raged incessantly. Grape, canister, solid shot and shell whizzed and shrieked and tore past us. The trees near by were torn and dismembered . . . A fragment of shell killed two chickens within a rod of where I sat. Every moment I expected to be struck, but at length perceiving that our soldiers had advanced further up the field, the fire was diverted from that point and we were released. I never experienced a deeper sense of deliverance.*

Chaplain Twichell and others probably sought refuge from the great cannonade on July 2 behind the Trostle Barn. This photo shows the many horses that were killed during the battle. (Library of Congress)

We retired a little and then the wounded began to come in. One of our boys was brought to us with both legs gone. Poor fellow, he lived but a few minutes, having given me his wife's address and commended his soul to the mercy of heaven. Before he expired, a battery from the front again rendered our position unfit for a hospital. The doctors went still further back and . . . I followed them. All the afternoon the battle continued with great violence.

The rear was one vast hospital. The wounded were everywhere, and scenes of sickening horror were presented on every side. The fortunes of the day were of varied aspect. At times we were forced back, but generally the appearance was hopeful. Both sides fought with the utmost desperation. At nightfall it was plain that our arms had gained an essential victory. The plan of the enemy–to turn our left flank–was foiled, although he held portions of the field–the more deplorable because we could not get at our wounded.

At a little before sunset the sad intelligence spread that Gen. Sickles was wounded. He had been the master spirit of the day and by his courage, coolness and skill had averted a threatened defeat. All felt that this loss was a calamity. I met the ambulance in which he had been placed, accompanied it, helped lift him out, and administered the chloroform at the amputation. His right leg was torn to shreds, just below the knee–so low that it was impossible to save the knee. His bearing and words were of the noblest character. "If I die," said he, "let me die on the field," "God bless our noble cause," "In a war like this, one man isn't much," "My trust is in God," were some of the things he said. I loved him then as I never did before.[29]

When General Sickles was wounded on July 2, Chaplain Twichell administered the chloroform for the amputation of the general's leg. Sickles is shown here with brigade commanders Joseph Carr and Charles Graham near the site on the Trostle Farm where Sickles was struck by a solid shot. (Library of Congress)

Twichell noted that he had spent all his time, from the evening of July 2 until July 4, among the wounded, and their sufferings touched him deeply: *"The fortitude with which they bear their terrible sufferings moves me almost to tears . . . I leave nothing undone that I can think of to assuage their pains. My own conscience and their gratitude furnish sufficient incentives."*[30]

He left the Third Corps hospital for a while on July 4 to help bury the dead who had been left on the field:

> *In a pouring rain we performed the last sad offices for the fallen and left them in soldiers graves. We found five of our wounded. They had lain 2 nights on the ground–three of them with broken legs–suffering God alone knows how much. It was the most terrible battlefield I had ever beheld. The stench was almost unendurable and the dead lay everywhere. In one place more than 30 were gathered together and the look of their bloated, blackened corpses was a thing to murder sleep. I saw where two confederate officers had tried to screen themselves behind a stump, but a shell passing through had taken off both their heads. I grieve for our poor boys. We had none to spare and now can hardly be called a regiment.*[31]

He noted that several officers had been wounded or killed but proclaimed that *"the Army of the Union has fought as if appreciating its Cause. The accidents of war are dreadful, but the fruits of such a war as this amply pay the cost. We have undoubtedly gained a victory. God be praised! The army will probably be set in motion again tomorrow, for the enemy has gone. May the day be hastened when war shall cease."*[32]

After caring for the wounded in the corps hospital for two weeks, Twichell visited friends about ten miles from Gettysburg, from where he wrote to his brother Ned:

> *Owing to the scarcity of surgeons–as few as possible having been left behind–much more than usual has devolved on Chaplains. . . . Within three days the condition of our hospital has much improved. Nearly all of the slightly wounded have been sent away, making more room for the bad cases, and assistance has reached us in the shape of stores, nurses and surgeons sent by the authorities and benevolent persons of various cities.*
>
> *I intend to start for the regiment in two or three days. If another battle takes place soon, as is probable, I wish to be with my regiment. I have not heard from it since it went away from*

Gettysburg. I shall never forget this hospital. It has been a scene of great sufferings, also a place in which the love of God and the preciousness of redemption have been strikingly manifested. . . . All the country round about is a graveyard–not an acre for miles but has some mark of death left upon it, yet if it only brings the blessing, we will rejoice.

I have been considerably among the confederate wounded. Thousands of them were left in our hands and they fared miserably. Many were not taken from the field till the fourth day. The Confed. surgeons left with them were too few to care for a twentieth of the number–we had more of our own than we could attend to, and the poor creatures had to suffer and die for want of care. Nearby us is a barn, within and around which were 150 of the wretches, mangled in every way, left for days without hardly a look. Some of us would snatch an hour to go over, and fetch them water–bind up simple wounds etc. etc.–but their misery was almost unmitigated. It was a heart rending sight to see them. Their appeals for help would have moved a heart of stone. . . . Many of the Confederates are gentlemen, evidently of good birth and education, and there are not a few pious men among them. There was one, a sweet handsome boy with beautiful deep eyes, with whom I fell in love. He was mortally wounded and for days bore his sufferings with most admirable fortitude. I procured a bed and a pillow for him and went to see him as often as possible. He possessed a most cheerful Christian spirit and was really a lovely character. One night I went to him, and was so touched by his nobleness that I stooped down and kissed him. The poor little fellow burst out crying. I buried him yesterday before I came away, and mourned for him sincerely.[33]

Twichell composed a letter to his mother five days later describing how the sights and sounds after a battle had become somewhat routine:

It seems almost impossible that I have become so accustomed to the miseries of life and the solemn mysteries of death. I can sleep the night through when the air is full of anguished cries, or witness the most rending agony, not unmoved but with composure. Once I could hardly bear the sight of a surgeon's knife. Now I can keep my finger calmly on a man's pulse while the keen blade is plunged into his quivering flesh. The horrible scenes of the late battlefield would have driven me crazy a year ago, and 1000 things I could never have dreamed before I went to the war are almost familiar. At the same time I am not aware that my sympathy with human suffering is any the less, and I certainly know better how to minister to it. If I live, my experience here will prove of great value to me as a clergyman.[34]

Twichell was mustered out with the regiment on July 30, 1864. He returned home and enrolled in Andover Theological Seminary to complete his studies. He graduated the following year and married Julia Harmony Cushman that November. They had eight children. He was installed as the first pastor of Asylum Hill Congregational Church in Hartford, Connecticut, where he ministered for forty-seven years. Twichell devoted himself to not only his congregation, but also to missionary work in China and Peru. He became a fellow at Yale University in 1874 and was awarded the honorary degree of Doctor of Divinity (against his wishes). He died on December 20, 1918, and is buried in Cedar Hill Cemetery in Hartford.

William Reed Eastman, 72nd New York Infantry

William Reed Eastman was born in New York City in 1836. After graduating from Yale in 1854, where he excelled in mathematics, he worked on the Erie Canal and surveyed the first railroad in Mexico City. In 1859, he enrolled in Union Theological Seminary in New York City, and after he graduated in 1862, he received a license to preach from the Presbyterian Church. That summer, he served as a first sergeant in the 22nd New York Militia, then as chaplain of the 165th New York Infantry. On January 1, 1863, he became chaplain of the 72nd New York Infantry, Third Excelsior Brigade.

The chaplains of the Excelsior Brigade were close friends, and Eastman described collegial times of conversation and gentle ribbing between them. They also spoke at length about the religious views of the man who had been at

Chaplain William Eastman of the 72nd New York Infantry. (from *History of the Third Regiment, Excelsior Brigade, 72nd New York Volunteer Infantry*)

various times their brigade, division, and corps commander, Daniel Sickles. Eastman recalled being at a recruiting station in New York City in May 1861 when men were being enrolled in the first two regiments of the Excelsior Brigade. Sickles presented the chaplains he had recruited for the regiments, and told the men, *"They represent the great Commander. Respect them. They are good men and they will do you good."*[35]

Eastman's recollections of Gettysburg focus more on his fellow Excelsior Brigade chaplains than on his own experiences. But several people testified to Eastman's remarkable experience on the battlefield. His story was included in a book describing incidents observed by members of the U.S. Christian Commission:

> *His horse plunging during the battle, struck him on the knee-pan. His leg swelled and stiffened until the pain became almost unendurable. When he could no longer stand, he gave his horse to a servant and laid himself down on the ground. He had to take a wounded soldier's place alone that night. As he lay suffering and thinking, he heard a voice, "O my God!" He thought, "Can anybody be swearing in such a place as this?"*
>
> *He listened again, and a prayer began; it was from a wounded soldier. How can I get at him? was his first impulse. He tried to draw up his stiffened limb, but he could not rise. He put his arm round a sapling, drew up his well foot, and tried to extend the other without bending, that he might walk; but he fell back in the effort, jarred through as if he had been stabbed.*
>
> *He then thought, I can roll. And over and over he rolled in pain and blood, and by dead bodies, until he fell against the dying man, and there he preached Christ and prayed.*
>
> *At length one of the line officers came up and said, "Where's the Chaplain? One of the staff officers is dying."*

Chaplain William Eastman was wounded late on July 3 and could not walk, but asked to be carried across the field so he could minister to wounded and dying men. (from *The Story of American Heroism: Thrilling Narratives of Personal Adventures During the Great Civil War*)

"Here he is, here he is," cried out the sufferer.

"Can you come and see a dying officer?"

"I cannot move. I had to roll myself to this dying man to talk to him."

"If I detail two men to carry you, can you go?"

"Yes."

They took him gently up and carried him. And that live-long night the two men bore him over the field, and laid him down beside bleeding, dying men, while he preached Christ and prayed. Lying thus on his back, the wounded Chaplain could not even see his audience, but must look always heavenward into the eyes of the peaceful stars–emblems of God's love which even that day of blood had not soiled nor made dim.[36]

After the war, General Howard praised Eastman's dedication to the wounded:

It has struck me that there was no display of self-abnegation and generous heroic conduct at Gettysburg superior to that of Chaplain William R. Eastman. Is not this a case of "Noblesse oblige"?[37]

Eastman mustered out with his regiment on June 19, 1864 and pastored several Congregational churches in Massachusetts and Connecticut. He married Laura Elizabeth Barnes on November 20, 1867; they had three daughters. In 1892, Eastman changed careers and became state inspector of the New York Public Library system. He wrote several books about library science and the construction of library buildings. He died of pneumonia in Washington, D.C., on March 25, 1925, and is buried in Albany Rural Cemetery in Menands, New York.

Third Brigade:
Colonel George C. Burling

The brigade under the command of Col. George Burling was detached from the rest of the corps on July 1 to remain near Emmitsburg with de Trobriand's brigade to watch for any Confederate movement through the mountain passes to the west. After settling in for what they believed would be a comfortable night, they received orders around 1:30 a.m. on July 2 to join the rest of the corps at Gettysburg. Because many of his units were widely dispersed on picket duty, Burling was not able to get them on the road for a couple of hours. They finally rejoined the corps in their bivouac south of Gettysburg midmorning on July 2.

Around noon, the brigade was ordered to form as a reserve near the woods along the Wheatfield Road. After spending some uneasy time in the Wheatfield, they pulled back to the relative safety of the woods. Almost immediately, Burling's regiments were peeled off to support other sections of the line including in the Wheatfield, along the Emmitsburg Road, by Devil's Den, and near the Peach Orchard. By the time the Confederate attack on the Wheatfield was heating up, Burling released the one regiment that had not been sent to another sector, and he reported to his commander, David Birney, to see if he could assist in some way. The regiments of Burling's brigade fought alongside those of other brigades and divisions and fell back with them when the Third Corps line collapsed.

The brigade reassembled in the Trostle Woods and rejoined the division the next day. It was sent along with other Third Corps units to support batteries during the Pickett-Pettigrew-Trimble charge, then rested in its original position with the rest of the corps until they left the battlefield on July 7.

The brigade included the 2nd New Hampshire, 115th Pennsylvania, and the 5th, 6th, 7th, and 8th New Jersey regiments. These units brought only three regimental chaplains with them to the field, none of whom left any written records of their time at Gettysburg.

Chapter 5:

The Fifth Corps

CORPS COMMANDER:

Major General George Sykes

The Fifth Army Corps camped near Frederick, Maryland, on June 28, 1863. That night, corps commander George Gordon Meade received orders to assume command of the Army of the Potomac in place of Joseph Hooker. Meade dutifully turned the corps over to First Division commander George Sykes and began planning the army's movement north into Pennsylvania.

After two more days of hard marching, including twenty-three miles on June 30, the Fifth Corps bivouacked near Bonaughtown, Pennsylvania (modern-day Bonneauville), on the evening of July 1. At daybreak, the corps approached Gettysburg via the Hanover Road and took a position along the road next to units of the Twelfth Corps. About two hours later, Sykes received orders to move the corps to a new position near the Baltimore Pike, where they would serve as the army's reserve. (One regiment would remain on the picket line along the Hanover Road for the time being.) Sometime after 4:00 p.m., the corps was ordered to support the left of the army amid the Confederate offensive, so they moved toward the southern end of Cemetery Ridge. As they passed Little Round Top, two brigades were diverted from the rest of the corps to defend the hill while the rest marched toward Stony Hill and the Wheatfield to support the beleaguered Third Corps units.

FIRST DIVISION:

Major General James Barnes

First Brigade:

Colonel William S. Tilton

Col. William Tilton's brigade included the 1st Michigan, 18th and 22nd Massachusetts, and 118th Pennsylvania regiments. When the men arrived near the battlefield early on July 2, they expected hostilities to resume soon. Instead, they had time to rest, eat, and even bathe in Rock Creek until midafternoon, when they marched to the southwest behind Col. Jacob Sweitzer's brigade. Both brigades took positions to the right of the Third Corps brigade of Col. Regis de Trobriand along the southern and western edges of the Stony Hill to protect that side of the Wheatfield. After a brief lull in the action, Tilton's and Sweitzer's brigades were attacked by South Carolinian troops approaching from the south and the west and Georgians who were close behind. In danger of being flanked, Tilton raised his concerns to division commander James Barnes, who told Tilton to withdraw his brigade if he thought it was necessary. Tilton, threatened by Confederate troops on three sides, pulled back, and Sweitzer soon followed.

Tilton reformed in the woods north of the Wheatfield facing west, but when the Federal batteries in line along the Wheatfield Road to his front began to withdraw, he decided he could not hold his position and pulled his regiments further back to Cemetery Ridge.

On July 3, Tilton's brigade was sent to relieve Col. Strong Vincent's brigade, now commanded by Col. James C. Rice, where they had a good view of the Pickett-Pettigrew-Trimble charge that afternoon. The next morning, the men were sent forward to "feel" for the enemy, which they discovered as they approached the Wheatfield. After trading some shots, the brigade pulled back again. On July 6, they joined the rest of the army in pursuit of the Army of Northern Virginia.

Only one of the regiments in Tilton's brigade—the 118th Pennsylvania "Corn Exchange" Regiment—was accompanied by a chaplain who left no record of his Gettysburg experience.

Second Brigade:
Colonel Jacob Sweitzer

The movements of Col. Jacob Sweitzer's brigade were similar to those of Tilton's brigade until both units had withdrawn from the Stony Hill. While Tilton's men faced west in the Trostle Woods north of the Wheatfield, Sweitzer's troops faced south, along the road. After Tilton started to pull back toward Cemetery Ridge, Sweitzer received a request from commander Brigadier General Joseph Caldwell to reenter the Wheatfield to support his Second Corps troops. Sweitzer balked, saying he would move only on the orders of his own commander, which was quickly arranged. As Sweitzer's three regiments marched south into the field (the fourth was coming back from picket duty on the Hanover Road), Caldwell's brigades began to retreat, being outflanked and outnumbered by Confederate troops. Sweitzer noticed that enemy soldiers were advancing over the Stony Hill on his right. He was severely overpowered and without support, and the fighting was close and fierce. Col. Harrison Jeffords of the 4th Michigan was mortally wounded by a bayonet thrust as he attempted to save the regiment's colors. Sweitzer's Brigade was shattered and withdrew under intense fire as other Union regiments entered the Wheatfield. They then joined Tilton's men along Cemetery Ridge.

Sweitzer's Brigade included the 9th and 32nd Massachusetts, 62nd Pennsylvania, and 4th Michigan regiments. Only the last of those had a chaplain at the time of the battle, and unusual circumstances prevented him from being present at Gettysburg.

John B. Seage, 4th Michigan Infantry

John B. Seage (pronounced "Sage") was born in 1809 in Tavistock, Devon County, England. He entered the ministry and served a church in Dover County, England from 1829 to 1834. While he was there, he married Mary Ann Creber on October 3, 1831. The couple, along with their young daughter, emigrated to Upper Canada sometime before 1835. For the next

Chaplain John Seage of the 4th Michigan Infantry. (Ron Coddington)

few years, they moved frequently, from Troy, New York, to Swanton, Vermont, and Staten Island, New York. In 1857, Seage took his wife and five children to Michigan to start a Baptist church in White Pigeon.[1]

On July 20, 1862, Seage was commissioned as a chaplain in the 4th Michigan Infantry, joining two of his sons who had already enlisted in the regiment: Henry and Richard, both serving as corporals in Company E. Reverend Seage replaced a chaplain who had evidently been dismissed for drunkenness and gambling, and he quickly became a popular chaplain and a *"caring but tough, no-nonsense preacher."*[2]

In June 1863, Seage headed toward Washington with the men's pay and a few watches that needed repair so they could be sent home. Seage described the events of that trip in a letter he wrote to the adjutant general on June 1, 1866:

> *I have the honor most respectfully to submit the following statement of the manner and occasions of my being wounded.*
>
> *I left the regiment, 4th Michigan volunteer infantry, in which I was a chaplain on the morning of the 8th of June at 4 o'clock under orders from Major General Meade then in command of our corps, the regiment was on duty at Kelly's Ford, Virginia, to proceed to Washington DC to transmit moneys for the officers and men to their families in Michigan. I had in my haversack about 6000 dollars beside several watches for repair. I was alone and on horseback when 12 miles from the camp near Deep Run Mill I was halted by a party of men who ordered me to halt and surrender. I asked by what authority? The leader replied in the name of Moseby's Cavalry. I replied, "I don't recognize that authority and shant surrender." They*

Corp. Henry Stark Seage, son of Chaplain Seage, served with his father in the regiment. (Steve Roberts)

2nd Lt. Richard Watson Seage, son of Chaplain Seage, was seriously wounded in the Wheatfield on July 2. (Steve Roberts)

fired and one ball went through my right wrist breaking the radius and cutting off the radial artery passed through my coat, vest and shirt causing a wound in the rib. Seeing if the gang was in front and rear I wheeled my horse or rather the horse turned when they fired again, one ball entering the point of the left shoulder breaking the clavicle. It was cut out 13 inches from the place of entry. My horse jumped across a ditch and they fired a third time. One ball cut open my left ankle and another made a flesh wound in my thigh.

My horse being one best got away from them. I found both arms useless and the blood from the severed artery springing out a stream. Our Division train and commissary was about a mile back thither horse took me.

The guards of the trains belong to our regiment. They seeing me coming and having heard the firing ran to meet me. My sight had gone from the loss of blood but I heard one exclaim "My God tis our dear Chaplain." I was taken from my horse and through kind and skillful treatment I was in a condition to be moved when the army went to head off Lee on his way to Gettysburg. I was in an ambulance to Manassas & from there to Washington where my wounds were dressed. The wrist put up in splints and both arms in slings I was sent home by the surgeon Dr. Clymer for 60 days.

P.S. I has [sic] forgotten to say I did not lose a cent or a cent worth of anything entrusted to me.[3]

The regular mail carrier for the brigade, Alexander Patrick, described the chaplain's unfortunate experience: *"When the reverend old gentleman took the road, well mounted, we thought at least his sacred cloth would be safe from our rapacious foe; but he had only been gone a few hours when his horse came bounding back with our priest severely wounded, almost riddled with the rebel irreligious bullets."*[4] Henry Seage learned of his father's wounding and *"was ordered to [. . .] report to Division Train to take Care of Father. Started with [brother] Dick about 2 P.M. Changed his Clothes & washed him."*[5] A week later, Henry accompanied his father first to Alexandria and then to Washington, where his wounds were rebandaged and his wrist set in a new splint. On June 19, the chaplain boarded a train for home, where he would spend the next two months recuperating.

Chaplain Seage missed the Battle of Gettysburg, but his sons were with the regiment when it entered the Wheatfield on July 2. Richard, by this time a second lieutenant, was severely wounded. His father described his son's misfortune in a letter to Michigan governor Austin Blair:

> *One ball entered the right breast, went through the right lung, came out near the spine, an explosive ball entered under the back of the left shoulder, came out under the right arm, balls passed through the left thigh, the calf of the right leg and left heel, and while lying on the field supposed by the enemy to be dead the next day, a rebel ran his bayonet through the upper part of the left thigh and came out under and inside the knee joint.*[6]

Richard was sent home to recover with his father.

The 4th Michigan Infantry mustered out at the end of its three-year term in June 1864 but was soon reorganized and mustered back into service in October 1864. Both Chaplain and Lieutenant Seage were back to serve in the new regiment, with the son being commissioned as quartermaster and his father serving first as a recruiting agent, then once again as the beloved spiritual guide for the men. Henry Seage survived the battle of Gettysburg and remained with the regiment until his term of enlistment expired in September 1864, then became an insurance adjuster in Lansing, Michigan. When the regiment finally mustered out on May 26, 1866, Richard and his father returned to Michigan. Richard, who had married in 1864, raised a family and worked in the insurance industry. John received a small disability pension for the wounds that left him unable to close his right hand or move his left shoulder. He spent time in Tennessee working for the Freedmen's Bureau, where he was well respected for exposing racial injustices. Upon returning to Michigan, he resumed his ministry and served as superintendent of the Detroit YMCA.

John and Mary Ann relocated to St. Louis, Missouri, to be near their two daughters, where John served as the superintendent of the Street Boys' home. While visiting his son Richard in New Jersey in 1883, John died on November 25 of chronic hepatitis. He is buried in Fountain Cemetery in West New Brighton, New York.

Third Brigade:
Colonel Strong Vincent

After an enthusiastic crossing from Maryland into Pennsylvania on July 1, Col. Strong Vincent's brigade marched toward Hanover, where Vincent, an ardent Pennsylvanian, exclaimed, *"What death more glorious can any man desire than to die on the soil of old Pennsylvania fighting for that flag?"*[7] It was midafternoon and the men were permitted to rest, and many of them prepared to spend the night. But they received orders to resume their march, and after covering twenty-two miles they reached Gettysburg at 1:00 a.m. on July 2. They rested again, expecting to be called into the fight soon. They continued to Powers Hill along the Taneytown Road, made a hasty breakfast, and then were shifted to various positions until they marched off at the head of their division toward the sound of the guns late that afternoon.

Accounts vary about what happened next and who gave orders to Vincent, but the brigade peeled off from the rest of the division and double-quicked up the slopes of Little Round Top, which was threatened with a Confederate attack and was manned only by members of the Signal Corps. Vincent quickly formed his brigade for defense as Alabamians and Texans advanced toward the hill. The brigade held against repeated attacks until the 140th New York, part of the corps' Second Division, arrived to finally repulse the Confederates on the northern portion of the brigade's line. On the southern slopes, the 20th Maine successfully countercharged against two regiments from Alabama, and by evening, Little Round Top, and the far left of the Union Army line, were secure. During the fighting, Vincent was mortally wounded.

That night, two regiments climbed Big Round Top and began a vigil from the summits of both hills, enduring sniper fire from Confederates at Devil's Den. By noon on July 3, the brigade had moved north on Cemetery Ridge, where they found refuge behind stone walls from the cannonade that preceded the Pickett-Pettigrew-Trimble charge. They played no part in the repulse of that charge.

On July 4, after carrying out a reconnaissance toward the Emmitsburg Road, the brigade returned to Little Round Top to bury the dead and build solid stone breastworks in case of another attack from Lee's army. The brigade, now under the command of Col. James

Rice, joined the Army of the Potomac in its pursuit of the Confederates on July 5.

Of the four regiments in the brigade—the 16th Michigan, 20th Maine, 44th New York, and 83rd Pennsylvania—three were accompanied by a chaplain, but a record of service at Gettysburg was found for only one of them.

Luther Pierce French, 20th Maine Infantry

Luther Pierce French was born in Solon, Maine, on May 2, 1812. At the age of twenty-three, he felt a call to ministry and enrolled in Maine Wesleyan Seminary. He was accepted into the Maine Conference of the Methodist Episcopal Church in 1839 and served several churches. Julia Ann Blunt became his wife in June 1844 and bore him one son before she died in February 1860.

In October 1861, French and two other pastors began raising companies for the 13th Maine Infantry with a newspaper article proclaiming that *"The ministers can do the war fighting, as well as the war preaching."*[8]

Luther's brother Joseph, who was also a minister, was a captain in Company B in the 14th Maine Infantry. On August 5, 1862, he lost a leg in fighting at Baton Rouge, Louisiana; while he was being transported with other wounded soldiers to St. James Hospital in New Orleans on August 7, the steamer *Whiteman* collided with the gunboat *Oneida* and sank. French, who was unable to swim, drowned. Two months later, perhaps motivated by his brother's death, Luther joined the 20th Maine Infantry as their chaplain. He married his second wife, Augusta Carter French, just two weeks before he was mustered in. She would eventually give birth to two children.

The only record we have of Chaplain French's experiences at Gettysburg comes from other sources. As the regiment was rushing up Little Round Top on July 2, Confederate shells were bursting all around them. French watched in horror as an officer's horse was beheaded by a shot, and he

Chaplain Luther French of the 20th Maine Infantry. (Maine State Archives)

ran to Capt. Atherton Clark of Company E, *"babbling about what he had seen. Clark interrupted French abruptly and shouted: 'For Christ sake Chaplain, if you have any business attend to it.'"*[9] Col. Joshua Chamberlain then asked French to help set up an aid station in preparation for the men who would soon need it. Before long, hospital steward Granville Baker, Colonel Chamberlain's brother John (who was at Gettysburg with the Christian Commission and was with the regiment), and Chaplain French *"had prepared a makeshift aid station in a 'sheltered nook' of the woods on the east side of the hill about one hundred yards behind the regimental line. From there, all that they knew of the fight was what they could hear."*[10]

At some point after the battle, French contracted an illness and resigned from the army on January 12, 1864. He returned to his ministry in Maine; Augusta died in 1874 and he married Mary Frances Leavitt a year later. He continued to suffer from his lingering illness and was granted "supernumerary" status by the church from 1875 to 1880, evidently supplementing his income by working as a harness maker. He left the ministry and applied for a disability pension in 1887, and died in Solon, Maine, on January 14, 1895, attended by his wife and younger son. He was laid to rest in Evergreen Cemetery in Solon.

SECOND DIVISION:

Major General Romeyn B. Ayres

First Brigade:

Colonel Hannibal Day

Second Brigade:

Colonel Sidney Burbank

The Second Division of the Fifth Corps included two brigades (ten regiments altogether) of United States Regulars. As such, these regiments had no chaplains because War Department orders made provisions for chaplains only for volunteer regiments. These brigades entered the Wheatfield (Burbank first, followed by Day) after the Second Corps units had pulled out, leaving Sweitzer's men in the field, and were crushed by an overwhelming force of Confederates who were pushing through the field from the west. Despite the odds, they held on and fought as long as possible, but at great cost. Burbank's brigade suffered the highest casualty rate (47 percent) of any Fifth Corps unit. After watching their performance in the Wheatfield, a witness said, *"For two years the U.S. Regulars taught us how to be soldiers. In the Wheatfield at Gettysburg, they taught us how to die like soldiers."*[11]

Third Brigade:
Brigadier General Stephen H. Weed

Like the men in Vincent's brigade, the soldiers of Brig. Gen. Stephen Weed's brigade were overjoyed to reach Pennsylvania after long and harsh marches in Virginia and Maryland. Reaching Hanover on July 1, their joy was quashed by the orders to strike the tents, which some men had started to pitch, and continue toward Gettysburg. The brigade rested along the Taneytown Road, with expectations of being sent to support the Third Corps that afternoon. When the summons came, Weed led his men south and then west toward the fighting. As they were hurrying to where they were needed, Maj. Gen. Gouverneur Warren, who was searching for reinforcements to aid Strong Vincent's lone brigade on Little Round Top, intercepted Col. Patrick O'Rorke of the 140th New York regiment and told him to climb the hill to support Vincent. Warren then rode off to find Weed. While meeting with Daniel Sickles, whose Third Corps Weed expected to reinforce, Weed received notice that his entire brigade was needed on Little Round Top. By the time the rest of the brigade reached the summit the Confederate attack had been repulsed, although sniper fire continued; one shot mortally wounded Weed.

That night, the brigade remained in position and built breastworks. The next afternoon they watched the Pickett-Pettigrew-Trimble charge from their position on Little Round Top. On July 4, they collected muskets and other equipment that was strewn on the ground below the hill. They moved off in pursuit of the enemy on July 5.

The brigade included the 91st and 155th Pennsylvania and 140th and 146th New York. Only one of the four units had a chaplain with it.

Albert Erdman, 146th New York Infantry

Chaplain Albert Erdman of the 146th New York Infantry. (from *Historical Sermon Preached in the South St. Presbyterian Church* by Albert Erdman)

Albert Erdman was born in Allentown, Pennsylvania, on October 28, 1838. He graduated from Hamilton College in 1858. The war began during his final year at Union Seminary in Manhattan, where his professors and classmates spent many hours watching the soldiers pass by on their way to the wharves. While serving a Congregational church in Deansboro, New York, Erdman made speeches encouraging people in the village to enlist until one day he realized he should join them. He hoped to serve as a chaplain but was not yet ordained, so he traveled to Philadelphia to receive ordination. He then resigned from his ministry, enlisted in the 146th New York Infantry, and was mustered in as chaplain on October 11, 1862.

Although it does not seem that he left a diary or letters about his experience at Gettysburg, he did give a talk at a gathering of veterans in Morristown, New Jersey, in 1887 called "A Chaplain's Experience." After describing the duties and challenges of chaplains in general, he turned to Gettysburg:

> *But let us go on to the Battle of Gettysburg. We were engaged in various minor engagements, but this was one of our two great battles during my connection with the regiment. Let me try and give you an idea of that battle. I used to think that a battle meant soldiers standing in line opposed to each other firing their guns and then with bayonets closing in deadly struggle, and that the scene of action was in some open place; but the Battle of Gettysburg was not such a one.*
>
> *In the afternoon of July 2nd, we moved on through the woods, and as we went forward the sound of battle came nearer and nearer, and as we came out of the woods we were hurried down a little declivity. I remember the first man who fell. A minie ball cut him right through the neck. We were then hurried forward to a little*

clump of trees, but an order came to go back, for by some error we had got beyond the place we were to occupy. Being directly under fire of the enemy many of our men fell, even before we had fired a shot, as we pushed on to take possession of Little Round Top. Longstreet's Corps made assault after assault, charging to the foot of the rocks. Men were mowed down by hundreds. Hundreds lay wounded and dead on the field below us, but fortunately we held our line. In a few minutes officer after officer was struck down and promotions made alas too rapidly.[12]

Chaplain Erdman recalled that the regiment was on Little Round Top near the high point where Gouverneur Warren and the Signal Corps had been positioned. (Sketch by Alfred Waud, Library of Congress)

The third day we lay on the rocks and could see the battle going on. From that high position which Gen. Warren occupied with the signal corps near him making known to him the various movements, we could see clearly. I shall never forget to the end of my life the close of that battle. The line of Confederates moved forward across the long plain, and as they came within short range of our batteries shot and shell were thrown amongst them. Whole lines withered away under that terrible fire, but the ranks were closed up and still they pressed forward. Now we could see the officers urging on their men. As they came nearer our musketry opened upon them. No force could stand that fire, and they scattered. Our men cheered as they never cheered before, for without knowing it we instinctively felt that that was the end of the battle.

All the night following we were caring for our wounded. I went down below Little Round Top and saw men who had been wounded early in the second day's fight, and had been without water for all that time. Some had been wounded over and over again as they lay there unable to move.

I remember one soldier brought back a little way from the battle shot through the body. As I leaned over him he gave me a few hurried messages and said: "Chaplain, will you pray with me." Kneeling down with Hell's work going all around, I offered prayer. While praying the poor fellow said "Amen" and fell dead.

The Chaplain after such a battle has plenty to do as you may readily imagine. I know my hands were not idle for a moment.[13]

One month after the battle, on August 3, Erdman was discharged because of an undisclosed injury he sustained during a march. He returned to New York and was soon called to serve the Stone Church in Clinton, which he guided as they changed from a Congregational to a Presbyterian form of church government. He courted one of his parishioners, Sarah Agnes Pinney, and they were married on September 13, 1865; they had nine children, including a son who died in infancy.

In 1869, Erdman accepted a call to the South Street Presbyterian Church in Morristown, New Jersey, where he served as a beloved pastor for thirty-eight years. Hamilton College conferred a Doctor of Divinity degree on him in 1881. To mark his twentieth year in ministry in 1889, his congregation gave Erdman and his wife a four-month tour of Europe and the Holy Land. Erdman finally retired in 1907, and the church bestowed on him both the honorific of pastor emeritus and a life annuity. "Al Erd," as he was lovingly known, died in Manhattan on January 24, 1918, after suffering heart problems. He is buried in Morristown.

THIRD DIVISION:

Major General Samuel W. Crawford

First Brigade:

Colonel William McCandless

Third Brigade:

Colonel Joseph Fisher

The two brigades of Maj. Gen. Samuel Wiley Crawford's division included nine regiments of Pennsylvania Reserve troops. They had performed extremely well on the Peninsula and at Second Bull Run and Antietam, but at a heavy cost. After the Battle of Fredericksburg, these depleted units were sent to help defend Washington and to rest and refit. When the men heard that General Lee was moving north toward their home state, they petitioned to rejoin the Army of the Potomac. Their request was granted, and they left Washington to join the army near Frederick, Maryland, on June 18, where they were assigned to the Fifth Corps. Marching was challenging for these men who had spent a few months in the relative ease of garrison duty, and they lagged somewhat behind the rest of the corps. But when the division finally crossed into their home state during the afternoon of July 1, the soldiers let loose with cheers, flying caps, and patriotic songs.

They stayed briefly at Hanover and then quickly marched toward Gettysburg with the rest of the corps. Some of the men in the 30th Pennsylvania (1st Pennsylvania Reserves) were from Gettysburg and passed by the homes of friends and loved ones as they moved toward the scene of the battle. The men finally had a chance to rest near where the Baltimore Pike crossed Rock Creek.

When the division was called to support the Third Corps late in the afternoon of July 2, the two brigades separated. Joseph Fisher's men headed up Little Round Top to support Weed and Vincent, although the worst of the fighting was over by the time they arrived. William McCandless's brigade, reinforced by one of Fisher's regiments, advanced across the northern slope of Little Round Top to confront the enemy troops that had pushed through the Wheatfield and were crossing the Plum Run valley. Charging down the slope in solid line, the Reserves surprised the exhausted Confederates with the deadly short-range fire from their smoothbore muskets. The gray tide soon retreated across the Wheatfield to the Stony Hill as the mass of Union men halted on the east side of the field. The fighting petered out and the two sides cautiously faced and sniped at each other for the rest of the battle, looking across that no man's land of death and destruction. Six men of the 6th Reserves were awarded the Medal of Honor for capturing Confederate soldiers who were shooting from within a house off to their left.

Some of Fisher's men were sent up Big Round Top in the evening, forcing enemy skirmishers to withdraw back down the hill. They remained there behind their breastworks until July 5 when the corps left the battlefield. Two of Fisher's regiments took position on the saddle between the two hills to protect the gap between the various Fifth Corps units on both hills.

On July 3, after the Confederate charge had ended, McCandless received orders to send his men to clear the Rose Woods in their front. After chasing out some Confederates, McCandless became aware of a larger body of enemy troops to his left, and he ordered his brigade to charge them. These Confederates were quickly overwhelmed and many of them were captured, along with a large number of rifles left behind by those who were able to get away. On July 4, McCandless returned from this advanced position and returned to the Wheatfield until they left the battlefield with the rest of the corps on July 5.

None of the regiments in McCandless's brigade, comprising the 1st, 2nd, 6th, and 13th Reserves (30th, 31st, 35th, and 42nd Pennsylvania Infantry), included a chaplain. Fisher's brigade included the 5th, 9th, 10th, 11th, and 12th Reserves (34th, 38th, 39th, 40th, and 41st Pennsylvania Infantry), three of which units were attended by chaplains; only one wrote about his experiences.

Adam Torrance, 11th Pennsylvania Reserves (40th Pennsylvania Infantry)

Adam Torrance was born in Westmoreland County, Pennsylvania, on April 24, 1801. His educational background is unknown. He began his ministry at a Presbyterian church in Ohio, and while there he married Elizabeth Graham in 1832. Several years later, he returned to Pennsylvania because of the poor health that plagued him throughout his life. On June 13, 1838, Torrance was installed as the first pastor of the Presbyterian Church in New Alexandria, Pennsylvania, where he ministered for thirty years. During his pastorate, in late 1862,

> *he and his people jointly gave a display of patriotic zeal that claims a passing notice. They for the time consented to forego his faithful services, and he as a sexagenarian encountered all the discomforts of camp, the trials of march, the perils of the battle-field, and the miasma of the swamps and hospitals to act as chaplain of the Eleventh Regiment of the Pennsylvania Reserve Corps. The consent of his people being obtained on Sabbath, he joined his regiment on Monday at Camp Wright. After the battle of Bull Run the officers of the regiment by a unanimous vote invited him to remain with them.*[14]

He was officially mustered in as chaplain on September 8, 1862. According to another historian, *"At the age of sixty-two years Chaplain Torrance followed the fortunes of that famous fighting regiment, and at Gettysburg, mounted on his white horse, accompanied the men into battle."*[15]

Chaplain Adam Torrance of the 11th Pennsylvania Reserves (40th Pennsylvania Infantry) (Library of Congress)

Torrance's regiment had been detached from Fisher's brigade and spent July 2 and 3 beside the other brigade in the division. While at Gettysburg, Torrance wanted to write a letter to his wife but was somewhat hampered by the regimental wagons having been left behind, leaving the chaplain without his usual writing paper. But he found paper and was able to compose his letter:

> *Battlefield near Gettysburg, Sat. July 5th*
>
> *My dear wife: I have neither paper nor envelopes as the regimental wagons were left 25 miles behind. So I commence writing on the leaves of my notebook, sitting on a stone, almost exhausted by hard work and want of rest . . . July 6th. An order to march obliged me to suddenly put up my notebook and mount my horse. We started from the battle ground 2½ miles from Gettysburg on the Tawny Town Road about 6:30 o'clock and continued our march till 12:00 o'clock. The road was rough and very muddy and the night cloudy and dark and the boys say it was the most exhausting march since we left Vienna [Virginia, outside Washington], but they endured it with remarkable fortitude and seemed cheerful this morning. Elly [the chaplain's son] overtook the regiment and came along side of me and spoke. I could not otherwise have recognized him. I took his gun and carried it the rest of the way . . . The newspapers will tell you that the battle at Gettysburg commenced on Thurs. the 2nd when that valuable officer Gen. Reynolds was killed* [sic]. *That day we performed a long and exhausting march and encamped at 2 o'clock in the morning within 4 miles of the battlefield. At 5 & 1/2 the division was again on the road. We rested in a field 1 mile from the scene of action 3 hours and took dinner. At 3 &*

1/2 o'clock the order was given to fall in. Hundreds of the men piled their knapsacks together & left them. The order to load was given. That peculiar silence in the ranks which I remarked on the morning of the 13th of Dec. [at the Battle of Fredericksburg] was equally manifest and impressive. About 4 & 1/2 o'clock our 2 brigades were formed in line of battle on the summit of the hill on which the advanced line of the grand Army of the Potomac was placed & from which our artillery was playing upon the enemy & was receiving a terrible fire from their batteries. Our division had not been formed more than 20 minutes before a large body of our regulars were being driven in confusion up the hills by the rebels, & a battery on the summit was in imminent danger of being captured. Our first brigade and the 11th of the 3rd brigade were immediately led forward to repel the rebels. This they did in a most handsome & gallant manner, driving them at the point of the bend down the hill, across a narrow valley & some distance up the opposite slope. This successful charge has been highly commended by all the troops on this part of the line. [. . .] A barn was selected by the chief surgeon of our division as our hospital. I had followed the regiment so far into the battle as to see the commencement of the charge. When the wounded began to be brought into the hospital, Dr. McClarren, Mr. McFarland [another chaplain in the brigade] found useful employments in caring for them. I did not lie down till 2½ o'clock Saturday morning, & was up at 4 & again among the sufferers.

Your affectionate husband, A. Torrance.[16]

Torrance's son Eliakim ("Elly") had enlisted with his parents' permission at the age of sixteen in the 9th Reserves in the same division as his father.[17] In a letter to his sister Mattie, young Elly poignantly described the scene around him as his regiment prepared to enter the battle on July 2:

We had just enough time to make a little coffee when a battery on a hill about a mile in front went bang-bang, which was immediately followed by another & another till almost 300 guns were sending their huge hissing, deadly missels into each others ranks; every heart beat faster & each face became more serious & you could see the poor fellows take their letters up & destroy them & read a hurried chapter from their well worn Bibles, trying to prepare for the very worst, & alas! Too many of them for the last time. Soon an aide comes riding along & in a minute we are on our way to the front.[18]

In October 1863, the Presbytery of New Salem, Pennsylvania, adopted a resolution approving a report submitted by Rev. Torrance describing his labors as an army chaplain. In this report, he provided some details about his experience at Gettysburg:

On the Field, the chaplain's labors, if properly directed, are of very great importance. When a wounded or dying soldier sees a chaplain approaching (whom he recognizes by his uniform, if not previously known to him) he always expects to find in him a friend, to whom be can speak with greater freedom than to any other, both of his bodily sufferings, and of the wants of his soul. And every act of kindness the chaplain performs, and every word of sympathy, counsel or prayer he may utter, is sure to be better received and more justly appreciated, than when done or spoken at any other time. For example, one wounded soldier on the field at Gettysburg, as he lay on the ground faint from the loss of blood, and while I kneeled at his side, near the hour of midnight, threw his arm around my neck and told me of his conscious lack of preparation for death, and of his solicitude about that event. And when I asked him to let me go that I might give my attention to others who lay near, and in like need, it was only on condition that I would promise soon to return to him, that he withdrew his arm from my neck. He died the tenth day after. Even the rebel soldiers, when wounded and fallen into our hands, expect to find in the union chaplain a friend. Of many instances of this, the following may serve as an illustration: I approached a rebbel [sic] soldier as he lay suffering from a wound which would evidently soon be followed by death, and having directed his attention to the dying Saviour, as the only hope for dying sinners, I was about turning away from him, when he beckoned me back and said: "Chaplain, I have been trusting in that Saviour for the last seven years, and feel assured that he will not leave me now. I leave in his care my wife and two children; I wish you to remember me in your prayers." I complied with his request, but the arrival of surgeons and their hurry in getting wounds examined and dressed, prevented me from doing so in his presence.[19]

The rigors of army life aggravated Torrance's health problems, and because of his age and concerns about another winter spent in camp, he resigned from the army on November 16, 1863. According to fellow chaplain John F. McLaren of the 10th Reserves, the men of the 11th who were out on picket duty hurried to camp once they were relieved so they could hear from him one last time:

> *The Chaplain's words were received by the Regiment, both officers and men, in a manner that gave evidence of the mutual interest and attachment subsisting between him and them. And as the officer, in charge of the picket, in a subdued tone gave the usual orders, it was evident, as they faced about and marched to their quarters, that these brave young men parted with their venerable Chaplain with sorrow.*[20]

Torrance returned to his church in New Alexandria, but his health grew even worse and in 1867, he resigned from the ministry after serving that congregation for almost thirty years. He died on October 18, 1881, and is buried in the New Alexandria Presbyterian Cemetery in Westmoreland County, Pennsylvania.

Chapter 6:

The Sixth Corps

CORPS COMMANDER:

Major General John Sedgwick

Although the Sixth Corps was the last of the Union forces to arrive on the battlefield, it earned fame for its grueling forced marches in June, including a thirty-five-mile trek from Manchester, Maryland, that took most of the night of July 1 and much of the day on July 2, for a total of eighteen hours of marching with very few opportunities to rest and only one hour-long stop to make coffee. This march was inadvertently extended when the corps took a wrong turn and had to countermarch a couple of miles to get to the Baltimore Pike, an occasion that caused much strong language and ill feelings among the soldiers. General Meade was much relieved as the vanguard of the Sixth Corps approached Gettysburg late in the afternoon of July 2, when the situation on the battlefield was desperate.

The corps stopped near Rock Creek for what turned out to be a brief break and were sent first to be in support of the Union center along Cemetery Ridge. A few brigades were soon sent to reinforce the left of the Union line, while others supported the right. By the end of July 3, some of the Sixth Corps' brigades held both the extreme right and extreme left of the fishhook line, with the rest in various locations along the line. All the brigades played supporting roles on the second and third days of the battle and led the Union army in the pursuit of the Confederates on July 5.

FIRST DIVISION:

Major General Horatio G. Wright

First Brigade:

Brigadier General Alfred T. A. Torbert

The brigade commanded by Brig. Gen. Alfred Thomas Archimedes Torbert was one of the few brigades in the Army of the Potomac that included regiments from one state: the 1st, 2nd, 3rd, and 15th New Jersey. The brigade had originally been commanded by Brig. Gen. Philip Kearney, who was killed at Chantilly, Virginia, after the Battle of Second Bull Run.

Torbert proclaimed in his official report that during their strenuous march on July 1 and 2, only twenty-five men had fallen out. When they were within a couple of miles of Gettysburg on July 2, they heard the sounds of battle and braced themselves for what lay ahead. The men reached Rock Creek and stopped to bathe their aching feet in the stream but were soon called to take up a position behind the main line north of Little Round Top, where they stayed in reserve but were not engaged. They spent the night there, sleeping on their arms.

On July 3, those who had fallen out during the march rejoined their comrades. The brigade was detached from the division and sent farther north between the First and Fifth Corps troops near the center of the line, where it was placed under the command of Maj. Gen. John Newton of the First Corps. The men crouched behind a stone wall to shield themselves from the Confederate cannonade but, other than picketing on their front, played no part in repelling the enemy during the Pickett-Pettigrew-Trimble charge. The men held their positions throughout July 4 while helping to care for the wounded. Early the next morning, Torbert's men joined the rest of the Sixth Corps and took the lead to follow the rebel army in its retreat.

All of the New Jersey regiments marched to Gettysburg accompanied by chaplains, but only two left a record of their experiences.

Robert Boyd Yard, 1st New Jersey Infantry

Robert Boyd Yard was born in Trenton, New Jersey, on January 9, 1828. He graduated from Pennington Seminary in 1848, was admitted into the

New Jersey Conference of the Methodist Episcopal Church, and served various churches in northern New Jersey. In 1851 he married Hannah A. Wilkins, who bore him two children before she died in 1855. Both of their children died in childhood. He married Sarah Purdue in 1856, and they had four children together, including one that died in infancy.

Chaplain Robert Yard of the 1st New Jersey Infantry.
(Lance Ingmire Collection)

Yard was deeply interested in the national situation regarding secession and the possibility of war, and when that time came, he enlisted in the 1st New Jersey Infantry on June 25, 1861.[1] He became endeared to the men in the regiment and was fiercely faithful to them and to his duty. Once, while Yard was attending to the wounded and dying at the front while the battle was still raging around him, an officer exclaimed, *"Chaplain, what in the world are you doing here?"* Yard simply replied, *"Doing my duty."*[2] As early as November 1861, Yard had gained the respect of Lt. Col. Robert McAllister, who wrote to his wife: *"We think we have the best chaplain of any of our regiments. He has done a grate [sic] deal of good here."*[3]

In early 1862, Yard acted as a correspondent for newspapers, and he wrote several letters describing the regiment's experiences on the Virginia Peninsula. He was careful to avoid writing *"anything [. . .] calculated to be of value to the rebels, should they see it,"* so instead of providing details about the *"forces and important movements,"* he portrayed scenes of the Virginia countryside and some of the Southern people they encountered along their marches.[4]

In June 1863, Yard sent a letter to a newspaper describing the condition of the troops and situation of the army:

> *Our splendid corps–the sixth–is lying in bivouac, on the Winchester turnpike about two miles beyond Fairfax Court House, and about 20 miles from Aldie. Every man is ready at five minutes notice to march to battle. We throw a blanket on the ground and sleep as soundly as you on your softer couches. Our wagons have been lightened by limiting officers strictly to twenty pounds of luggage, all told, save in the case of field officers, who are allowed thirty pounds. The reduction of baggage results in the material lessening of our*

wagon train. The Army is in better trim for rapid movement, long marches and, and earnest fighting than I have ever known it to be.

The privations are of course more severe. Supplies are limited to army necessaries. Sutler's stores are but seldom enjoyed, their teams not being allowed to encumber the roads. Hard-tack, pork and coffee are our reliance. Butter, bread, milk, canned meats, &c., are the rarely enjoyed luxuries. We cheerfully submit to all this, if it but prove the earnest of speedy victory.[5]

In the same letter, Yard recalled the difficulties of the marches and the various ways the soldiers had suffered in the previous two weeks:

I never saw such sufferings on a march before. Many fell from sun stroke, others wilted down panting and over-heated. Here was work for the merciful. The ambulances were soon filled. [A] chaplain was supporting a feeble man on his (the Chaplain's) horse, that he might not be left behind, alone, and to starve. Another Chaplain was leading his horse loaded with the knapsacks of weary and suffering men, who must otherwise be left behind. Surely the Chaplain's position is not a sinecure. Some of the noblest and best of men now fill this place in the Army, and in all my acquaintance I do not know an unworthy incumbent.[6]

Yard wrote another letter to the newspapers one month after the Battle of Gettysburg. Yet unlike his previous letters, which either lightheartedly helped families back home feel closer to their soldiers or recounted the misery of a campaign, this letter was a deeply theological reflection on how God had enabled the Army of the Potomac to be victorious during the Gettysburg campaign. Perhaps the horrific scenes Yard had witnessed, along with his increasingly poor health, caused him to offer this sermon on the nation's need to recognize the hand of Providence in the war:

I trust the time is at hand when throughout our nation, and in all our armies there shall have matured a full belief of the truth that this is God's war. I think I am not mistaken in saying that among the intelligent officers and soldiers of this army–and this class forms nearly the whole–there exists but a single feeling of submission to the clearly-defined objects of this war. Prejudice, party feeling hero worship, self-ease, are fast disappearing. Leaders may change, partisan platforms may form and dissolve, errors at the head of government may excite our attention, names like those of Lincoln, Burnside, M'Clellan, Hooker, Grant, and Meade may grow bright or fade, it makes little difference to us. God, truth, humanity, and Christianity abide and speak to us in the "stars and stripes," under which we toil.

We are not unmindful of the mercy which God has shown us in the present campaign. Our men have been able to make the most astonishing marching and to have overcome scores of miles of weary travel because the skies have been overcast and the scorching June and July suns have been hidden by His hand, when, otherwise, thousands must have failed by the way, and a victorious enemy would have despoiled our homes while our troops were sweltering, swooning, and lagging in weary pursuit.

Then, too, heavy rains which have refreshed us, or at the worst have only given us a wetting, providentially sent have helped to punish a proud and boastful enemy, and to complete the disaster with which our noble army of freedom overwhelmed the champions of slavery.

Nor should we fail to record the singular exhibition of God's hand in the great victory in Pennsylvania. Jealous of His name and glory, He gave his signal victory only when it would teach the nation its dependence on Him. In this victory, this victory Gen. Meade–all due honor to him–can claim but little, because he directed a veteran army appared [sic] to his hand by others. A combination of providential preparations, in which our past disasters contributed much resulted in the decisive and sweeping triumph [at] Gettysburgh.

A fact which has deeply impressed me is worthy of note. Perhaps nothing has more stirred our army with genuine indignation than the report generally credited that a distinguished commander had declared his determination to "go to Richmond in spite of Lee, or Davis, or the almighty." I heard from all classes of men, profane or Christian, but one alarmed, indignant, and discourged [sic] expression. Deep in the mind of these soldiers there exists a sense of divine care, and a looking for of a divinely ordered destiny.[7]

Chaplain Yard was intensely concerned about the men entrusted to his care. Before the Battle of Mine Run in December 1863,

[he] came down the Brigade line, giving to each man a slip of paper and a pin and instructed each man to write plainly his name,

regiment, company and home address on the slip and to pin it on the inside of his coat lapel. He had with him several haversacks, into which he put such valuables or trinkets as the men wanted sent home in case they were killed.[8]

Then, just before the men entered the fray, Yard approached the regiment with several canteens on his shoulders, some filled with water, and some with the whiskey he would use to *"succor the wounded."*[9]

In early 1864, Yard's health had worsened and he resigned from his beloved position as chaplain on March 7. The regimental historian described his leave-taking:

> *Before his departure the regiment was paraded, and formed in a hollow square. Chaplain Yard came to the centre with Lieutenant Colonel Henry and made an address to the men, bidding them good-bye. Colonel Henry, on behalf of the officers of the regiment, presented him with a gold watch. A sense of personal loss was felt by all, for the chaplain had been close to them, not only in quarters but on the battlefield, exposing himself with quiet unconcern of the danger, whenever there was need of his services.*[10]

Yard returned to his ministry in New Jersey, but his failing health forced him to retire from the pulpit after two years. In 1871, he felt strong enough to resume ministry and preached at several churches. Finally, while serving in Elizabeth, his disease, which was called "inflammation of the kidneys" and caused him much suffering, grew worse and he became partially paralyzed. He died at the age of fifty-seven on January 17, 1875, and was buried in Maplewood Cemetery in Freehold, New Jersey. Some of Yard's fellow ministers who had been selected to serve as pallbearers relinquished the honor to veterans of the 1st New Jersey who requested the privilege.

Alanson Austin Haines, 15th New Jersey Infantry

Alanson Austin Haines was born on March 18, 1830, in Hamburg, New Jersey. His father had served two terms as New Jersey governor and sat on the state supreme court at the outbreak of the war. Alanson attended the College of New Jersey, but poor health prevented him from completing his studies. He took up civil engineering and worked for the railroads, then enrolled in Princton Theological Seminary and graduated in 1858. That September, he was ordained at the Buckingham Presbyterian Church in Berlin, Maryland, and after two years there he filled the pulpit in a church in Amagansett, Long Island. He answered his country's call in late 1862 and was mustered into the 15th New Jersey Infantry on August 25.

Haines was noted for his bravery under fire by a newspaper correspondent who had observed the 15th New Jersey in action at Fredericksburg: *"I could not but admire the conduct of their chaplain, who by the way is a son of ex-Governor Daniel Haines of New Jersey. He had taken command of the drum crops of that regiment, and was constant in his efforts to minister to the welfare of any who might be wounded–exposing himself to the same dangers as the soldiers."*[11]

In 1862, the Haines family lost two of its young men to the war, both of whom served in the 1st New Jersey Cavalry. Capt. Thomas Ryerson Haines, a brother to Chaplain Haines, was killed in June during a cavalry battle at Harrisonburg, Virginia. His body, which had been shot and sabered, was brought back home to be buried in the family plot. Lt. Alanson Austin, who was a cousin to the chaplain, was mortally wounded by a shell in August during the Battle of Cedar Mountain, Virginia. Because of the Union army's retreat, his body was hastily buried by Confederates in an unmarked grave, which the family could not locate when they tried to bring him home. Chaplain Haines stayed with his regiment for the duration of his three-year term and wrote the regimental history, which was published in 1883.

The forced marches of the Sixth Corps became a part of Gettysburg legend. Haines described one particularly hard march:

> *The men fell out in squads; some fainted, some were sunstruck. The aides came riding back from our division commander, repeating orders to close up the ranks and hurry on the battalions. So the column was forced on and on, until only one man in ten remained with the brigade. There may have been great necessity for haste, but the attempted forced march accomplished nothing. Two miles from*

Capt. Thomas Ryerson Haines of the 1st New Jersey Cavalry, a brother to Chaplain Alanson Haines, was killed in June 1862 in Virginia. (US Army Heritage and Education Center)

During the Sixth Corps' long march to Gettysburg, Brig. Gen. Horatio G. Wright halted his division because so many men were falling out.
(Library of Congress)

Dumfries, General [Horatio] Wright, who was acting under orders to follow the army quickly, was forced to halt, for fear his whole command would leave him. The ambulances were crowded. Stragglers were brought up, forced along at the sword's point.[12]

The Sixth Corps rested in Manchester, Maryland, on July 1 but was ordered to continue their march late that evening:

We were moving all night, at times by forced marches, and when the roads were blocked, at slow and tedious pace. The troops were kept awake by music from the band and beating of drums from the drum corps. Our line of march was five miles southwesterly until we struck the Littlestown turnpike road; thence north-westerly across Pipe Creek and through Littlestown, reaching Gettysburg at 3 P.M, of the 2d of July. We had thus made a march of thirty-five miles within sixteen hours. We made no halt, excepting for a few minutes at a time, and were mostly without food. Only twenty-five men were reported absent from the entire brigade, and several of these came up a few hours later.[13]

As Maj. Gen. John Sedgwick brought his troops to Gettysburg on July 2, the men heard the roar of Confederate batteries that were opening against the Union left. The brigade stopped along the Baltimore Pike near Rock Creek:

The wearied men were resting and refreshing themselves, as best they could, after the terrible strain of the forced march of thirty-six miles. Some began making coffee; others, divested of much of their clothing, were stretched on the ground in almost sheer exhaustion. Others were bathing their bruised feet, and for the time all our thoughts were occupied with our own comfort. Suddenly the heavy musketry was heard to our left, towards the south, and rapidly approaching nearer. Directly an aide, covered with dust, came riding down to the hollow and asked for the headquarters of the Sixth Corps. He was pointed across the brook, where the corps flag was flying and some tents were going up. Hardly had he reached the General's tent before the bugle sounded the alarm. Our men had already gotten their traps together, and clothes and shoes on, and the order to fall in found them ready in their places.

Muskets were seized in haste, the companies formed, and we were hurried forward at the double quick, toward Little Round Top mountain–a distance of nearly a mile. As we went through the woods and over the fields, shells were bursting in the air and minnie balls singing close to our heads. Hundreds of fugitives were flying past. They had thrown down their arms and were pressing with all their might to the rear. Men with bleeding wounds were coming out of the battle, and the more severely wounded were carried by their comrades. These were the men from the Third Corps. Our forces on and around Round Top saw us coming, and it is probable the Confederates also, for the tide turned with our advance, and the enemy were driven from the mountain. We were not actually engaged, but no doubt the moral effect of our approach had its influence.[14]

After Union troops of the Fifth and Sixth Corps pushed the Georgians and South Carolinians back across the Wheatfield, and the fight on the Union left had slowed to skirmishing and picket fire, the New Jersey brigade took their place north of Little Round Top and in rear of the former position of the Third Corps.

We slept on our arms in the position we had taken. In the bright moonlight we slumbered soundly through the quiet hours. The stillness seemed the more intense after the uproar and excitements of the afternoon. Hundreds of the slain lay all about us; especially were they thick on the plain, in our immediate front, a part of which was the memorable wheat-field where Sickles suffered so much. Only a few wakeful ones among us heard the moans and cries of the wounded who lay between the two lines in front. They were begging piteously for water, and some that they might be carried off. The sad wail broke on the night air, and every now and then it came up like the whine of a dog. A few venturesome spirits, moved by humanity, carried water in canteens, and relieved those who could be reached. We were on the eve of a great battle and thousands of living men who slumbered with us on that long line were to taste of death before to-morrow's sun had set. Yet we enjoyed that night's repose, and slept as unconsciously of alarm as ever in all our lives.[15]

July 3 brought an early awakening for the New Jersey men as they were ordered to stand to arms. Haines described their morning activities:

> *Our brigade was moved early in the day, and a place assigned us in line to the north of Little Round Top, upon a little rocky knoll, whose westerly face was covered with timber, concealing us from the enemy's view. At the foot of the hill, and in the front line of battle, was the First New Jersey Regiment. A low line of stone wall formed a slight protection. The second line of battle was formed by the Fifteenth Regiment, along the brow of the hill. Before us, also, ran a low wall or stone row, which became a partial cover when the stones were laid up and the gaps filled. Cartridges were taken from the boxes and laid on the stones, extra muskets were picked up and loaded, and every preparation made for a stout resistance, and with the full determination not to be driven from our stony crest.*[16]

As the Confederate artillery opened the barrage prior to the Pickett-Pettigrew-Trimble charge, the New Jersey men crouched behind their stone walls and listened as *"the terrific rain of hundreds of tons of iron missiles was hurled through the air. The forests crashed and the rocks were rent under the terrible hail."*[17] But Haines noted that the men of the New Jersey brigade *"escaped wonderfully from the enemy's shells that frequently tore the trees and scattered their limbs upon us. Sometimes their missiles would strike the stones and make the pieces fly with great velocity. Only one man, John C. Conklin, of Company K, was seriously wounded, and he by a piece of shell which tore his back."*[18] When the Confederate artillery fire stopped,

> *we rose from our crouching position and looked over our slight parapet. As the dim war cloud rolled away and we could look out from our position, the sun shone out brightly, revealing the trees and the plain. Charging on came the mighty columns of the enemy. It was an imposing sight. The magnificent spectacle presented could not but awaken our admiration, even at that moment. We saw their lines plowed and pierced, but they pressed on still, with the same rapid pace. As they approached nearer and nearer we heard their yells, and saw their flags, and could distinguish officers from men.*[19]

Haines described the men as being disappointed in not being able to lend their strength and fire to the fighting:

> *All the fighting passed above to the right of our position. We longed for participation in the conflict, but, with the exception of firing on picket, were not permitted to use our muskets. We had been ordered to hold ourselves in readiness to assault the enemy's front, and fully expected to do so immediately after Pickett's defeat. Yet hour after hour passed until the sun went down and we did not move. The men of our corps were anxious for the conflict. Had the order come to advance they would have sprung forward with alacrity to obey it.*[20]

The men of the 15th stayed on their line throughout the night of July 3 and *"slept with less apprehension and were in better spirits."*[21] The next morning,

> *Colonel Penrose took the regiment down, a company at a time, to the scene of the conflict of July 2d, and each man supplied himself with an excellent Springfield musket from among the great number of arms left upon the field. When we marched from Gettysburg, we stacked our old Enfields on the ground, and left them behind. We were now better supplied with fire-arms of the approved make, yet numbers of our soldiers had learned to love the old Enfields, to which they had grown accustomed, and with which they fancied they could shoot farther, and with more certainty of aim.*[22]

That afternoon, it began to rain heavily, which the chaplain noted *"is frequently observed as following great battles. We were far from comfortable on our line, where we were restricted in providing for ourselves; and few overcoats and shelter tents remained after the march of the night of July 1st. We would have gladly welcomed another assault–confident in our ability to repulse any attack that might be made upon us."*[23] Despite the rain, the regiment spent most of July 4 caring for the wounded and burying the dead. Haines remembered the horrific scenes at the hospitals:

> *The human body was wounded and torn in every conceivable manner. No description can portray the work of the surgeons at the amputating table. All the nights of the three days, they were busy with their dreadful work. Limbs were thrown in piles outside the hospital tents, and the sufferers were at first stretched in the open air, side by side. There were men with both legs gone; men shot*

through the lungs; men with bullets in their brain, still living; men with their torn bowels protruding. On the floor of a crowded barn sat a man in gray coat, swaying his body back and forth, with both eyes shot out, and his face all mangled. The tide of human misery around the little town of Gettysburg swelled high as never before, perhaps, in all our land. We saw the horrors of war, enough to make the heart ache and revolt at the inhumanity of man to man. Yet all these ghastly wounds were received from the hands of their own countrymen. The surgeons were very humane in their treatment, and seemed, in the discharge of their work, to know no difference between Union and Confederate soldiers.[24]

Haines also spent time that day helping to bury the dead:

Every passing hour added new corpses to the vast number. They were so many that it seemed a gigantic task to the details that were largely drawn from the various regiments. Sometimes a grave was dug beside where the body lay, and it was merely turned over into the narrow pit. Sometimes long trenches were dug, and in single lines, with head to foot, one corpse after another was laid in; then the earth was thrown back, making a long ridge of fresh ground. Whenever names could be ascertained, each grave was marked by a head-board, with name and regiment of the dead soldier. All these dead, so rapidly consigned to earth, were living men but yesterday, or the day before, in full vigor of manhood. We had seen many of them marching in their youthful prime–the gallant soldiers of their country; while from the missiles of the others, the foemen from the South, we had shrunk in peril of our lives.[25]

As Chaplain Haines moved out with his regiment on July 5, they passed many scenes such as this. (*Unfit for Service*, Library of Congress)

Because the Sixth Corps had not been heavily engaged in the battle, Sedgwick received orders to pursue the enemy, and Haines noted that on the morning of July 5, the men observed ghastly sights as they moved west:

> *We were roused at 2 o'clock. An hour later we moved down the slope and across the flat to the foot of Seminary Ridge. Here we halted, and stood for two hours in the heavy pouring rain. At sunrise we threw out skirmishers and advanced up the ridge. No enemy was visible. All had gone, and the pursuit was now to begin. We were passing over the battle-fields of the second and third days, and saw many hundreds of the unburied dead. The bodies were often fearfully torn, and generally bloated and blackened past recognition. Dead horses were swelled to elephantine proportions, and dreadful effluvia tainted the air.*
>
> *It was evident that our artillery fire had been very destructive. The location of the enemy's pieces of artillery could be marked by the number of slain men and dead horses which encircled the spot. At one place a caisson-wagon had exploded, and around it were the dead horses which had drawn it, and sixteen bodies of the cannoneers. Some of the dead were lying across each other. One man in gray had a bullet in his forehead, and had lain there since the afternoon of the 3d. He was past consciousness, but that life was not extinct was shown by the convulsive kicking of his legs. A large barn had been burned, and we were told that it had been full of wounded men. We could distinguish the charred remains of several, but could not tell whether these had died in the barn, before the fire, or had perished in the flames. Some bodies, with clothing partially burned, were those of Union soldiers, probably wounded prisoners from the Eleventh Corps.*
>
> *In a small shattered house, we found in the loft above, an old man and woman, who had been there through all the terrors of the bombardment. They were heartily glad to be lifted down from their retreat, and to hear our assurance that the battle was all over and we were in pursuit of the enemy. We passed over many new-made graves, where Southern soldiers had left the bones of their comrades.*
>
> *We came upon the Confederate hospitals, where were left those too severely wounded to be transported in army wagons. Our men*

distributed much of their rations among them, though they said they had received plenty of food the day before. They seemed to have had good treatment and to have been well cared for by their own surgeons. Their wounds had been properly dressed, and there were many cases of amputation. Like those we left in Gettysburg, they were very helpless, and objects of commiseration.[26]

The chaplain remembered passing a farm during their pursuit of the Confederates, where they met a farmer who greeted them kindly:

We supposed that his politeness was intended as a sarcastic return for our wholesale destruction of his crops, but it appeared that he had been in rebel hands for a week, and had lost horses and everything beside that could be taken off, and they had finally left him with his barn full to overflowing with their wounded. His demonstrations had been only his expression of joy to see us. The sufferings of citizens had been very great, where they were overrun by the rebel army, and the invasion was a reign of terror to them.[27]

After Lee's army crossed the Potomac River near Williamsport, Maryland, the regiment marched another thirty-six miles before being granted three very welcome days of rest. Haines observed that throughout the Gettysburg campaign, the men *"had completed the long march of two hundred and fifty miles. We had suffered, without complaint, all the privations and severity of the toilsome round. We rejoiced in the success of the Union forces, and only regretted that the hostile army so often confronting us had not been entirely broken up."*[28]

Chaplain Haines remained with his regiment until they mustered out on June 22, 1865. He returned to New Jersey and was invited to pastor the North Hardyston Presbyterian Church in Hamburg. His congregation granted him leaves of absence in 1873 and 1876 to serve as an engineer with the American Palestine Exploration Society, where he surveyed Mount Nebo, the Sinai Peninsula, and other sites around the Dead Sea. After ministering to the congregation in Hamburg for twenty-five years, he resigned in 1890 because of poor health. He died after a lingering illness on December 11, 1891, and was buried in the North Hardyston Cemetery. He never married and had no children.

Second Brigade:
Brigadier General Joseph J. Bartlett

Brig. Gen. Joseph Bartlett's brigade included the 5th Maine, 95th and 96th Pennsylvania, and 121st New York regiments. Only the soldiers from Maine had a chaplain with them. When the brigade reached Gettysburg with the rest of the corps, they were sent to the left of the Union line and saw the Union troops in front (from the Third and Fifth Corps) heading to the rear. Bartlett ordered his men into a supporting line north of Little Round Top, to the right of Wheaton's Third Division brigade, but were prevented from advancing against the oncoming Confederates when Wheaton's men moved to the front and right of Bartlett's men.

Bartlett's brigade remained in this position throughout the night. In the late afternoon of July 3, Sedgwick ordered Bartlett to cooperate with the brigade of Pennsylvania Reserves to move against the Confederates that held the ground around Devil's Den and the west side of the Wheatfield. After some brisk skirmishing and the capture of some Confederates, the brigade fell back to a position a few hundred yards west of their original line.

On July 4, the brigade advanced with other troops some 500 yards on a reconnaissance to ascertain the position of the enemy. Then, early on the morning of July 5, Bartlett's men, along with those of Torbert's brigade, led the pursuit of General Lee's army.

John Ripley Adams, 5th Maine Infantry

John Ripley Adams was born in Plainfield, Connecticut, on March 20, 1802. When he was eight years old his family moved to Andover, Massachusetts. He was educated at the Phillips Academy, where his father served as principal. At the age of fifteen, he entered Yale College, and he graduated in 1821. After spending some time assisting his father at the academy, he enrolled in the theological seminary at Andover and received his degree in 1825. The following year he was licensed as a minster and moved to Waterville, New York, to work as an evangelist. He married Mary Anne MacGregor on February 19, 1833, and they had three children.

He was ordained and installed as pastor at the Presbyterian church in Londonderry, New Hampshire, in 1851, then accepted a call to the Congregational Church in Gorham, Maine. When Fort Sumter was attacked in April 1861, Adams was in New York City and was elected chaplain of the 4th New York regiment, but he declined because he wanted to serve among the men of his own state. So, he returned to Maine and, at the age of sixty, was elected chaplain of the 5th Maine Infantry in June 1861.

Chaplain John Ripley Adams of the 5th Maine Infantry (Maine State Archives)

When General Howard was wounded during the Battle of Seven Pines in May 1863, he went home to Maine to recover from the wound that cost him an arm. While there, he gave a talk to a large crowd during which he praised the "untiring energy" of fellow Mainer Adams, as reported in a local newspaper:

> *Chaplain J. R. Adams, who, unmindful of his own life, followed the soldier into the carnage of deadly strife, and who, while the swift shot and bursting shell were carrying death to many a heart, and sorrow to many a home, chose by his Christian impulses to prove to the people of Maine his readiness to do his duty under all and any circumstances. [He] was the only one out of four of his profession who followed the Brigade of General Howard into every battle, and through every deprivation, so attendant upon the life of a soldier. Truly, Maine has just cause to be proud of such sons.*[29]

Adams wrote many letters to his wife and children during his time with the army, which his daughter compiled into a memorial booklet that was published in 1890. In a letter dated July 1, he reported that the regiment was somewhere between Westminster and Manchester, Maryland, having marched continuously for ten days:

> *Some of the marches have been long and wearisome, but the men have stood it well. Day before yesterday we marched about twenty-five miles; this is a long march, and when the feet are blistered and sore, it is hard work. The inhabitants of Westminster were very glad to see us; they are mostly Union people; they gazed as though they had never supposed there were so many men in the world. Their*

houses were open, freely dispensing all manner of eatables, which we greatly enjoyed. Last Sabbath we marched early and late, and had no service; when the men halt, they throw themselves down and sleep if they can; when they camp, the first thing is supper.

This is a time when we need wise men at the helm. I hope the whole nation will be aroused on account of these raids. I have stood the march wonderfully well; my health was never better. I sleep in the open air, sometimes in the rain. The only trouble with us is that we do not get enough sleep, as we march by four in the morning; but we can take naps at our halts.[30]

In a letter dated July 10, Adams recounted the regiment's experience as they approached Gettysburg and entered the fray:

We are in the midst of exciting scenes, and have been for some time past. While we are halting for a time, I have opened my haversack, and, seated on the ground in the shade, with back against a rail fence, paper on knee, I will commence a few jottings to you, my dear wife.

The army has made long and forced marches. You have no conception of its toils or endurances. We marched all night, and when we halted for breakfast, instead of getting coffee, the word was given, "Fall in!" and again the men were on the march. It was trying, and some found fault, but we assured them there was a good reason for it; and so it proved; for, as we neared Gettysburg, we arrived in season to support the Fifth Corps, who had made a charge. The result was glorious; the men forgot their fatigue for joy; they had marched thirty-five miles since eight o'clock of the afternoon preceding, and all this after the forced marches of nearly a week.

Upon the arrival of the corps at Gettysburg a short halt was made for rest, and then they were at once pressed forward into position, the Fifth Maine in advance. As our lines came up, the news spread like wildfire throughout the army, and cheer after cheer ran along the lines. The men seemed wild with excitement. Drums beat, colors were flying; it was a season of rejoicing. Vigorously our regiment leaped forward at the word of command, and at once took up the position indicated to them, forming themselves into line of battle, the left of the regiment resting upon the side of Little Round Top, a point which was very prominent on this battlefield. As our corps came up; the enemy fell back, and hence a position was gained with comparatively little difficulty. The work was principally to hold it.

Our boys felt proud that, at almost the turning-point in the fortunes of the day, the arrival of the Sixth Corps, they should lead that noble body of soldiery into action, and thus become the first regiment under fire. That night was a good time to give thanks. I mounted a flat rock, and made a short address, and offered prayer. It was a scene for a painter. Groups of men were lying amid the rocks on rough ground, in battle line ready for action, hushed to silence after the thunders of the day's fight had ceased, and yet imploring God's blessing, and thanking Him for the success of our arms.[31]

In the same letter, Adams expressed a common sentiment of soldiers: *"I cannot give the particulars of the battle at Gettysburg, or of the field as we passed over it. Personal observations I cannot impress on a letter-sheet; men must see for themselves, to understand what a battlefield is when the din of arms has ceased."*[32]

Adams described the scenes as the army continued in its pursuit of the Confederates:

As our corps moved on, we passed over the ground recently occupied by the Rebels. We had proof that they left in a hurry, for they left their wounded on our hands; hospitals and barns were filled with them. I visited several of them, and conversed with officers and men. They acknowledged that the Army of the Potomac are good fighters; they did not expect us, for they had been told by Lee that they would find nothing but militia; and they wondered how we got here so soon.[33]

The regiment passed over South Mountain at night in a drenching rain, which caused certain challenges for the men and Chaplain Adams:

In going up the mountain my saddle slipped, and came over the rear of the horse; dark as pitch, road rough and stony, troops passing, it was no easy thing to disentangle, and set things to rights; but this I did, and rejoined the men, as they had orders to rest when they chose. Early in the morning we resumed the march to the top of the mountain; while there we were in the clouds, and the rain poured in floods; I threw my shelter-tent over my shoulders and let it pour. I was not saturated as some were who had no overcoats to protect them.[34]

When the 5th Maine's three-year term of service expired in June 1864, there were not enough men and officers left to form a veteran unit, and all were mustered out. Adams immediately received an invitation to serve as chaplain from the 121st New York Volunteers, and he remained with them until he was discharged on June 25, 1865.

After the war, Joshua L. Chamberlain (commander of the 20th Maine at Gettysburg) recommended Chaplain Adams for a "brevet" promotion. (Library of Congress)

Adams returned to Gorham and accepted a commission from the Maine Missionary Society to serve as a missionary among destitute churches. In April 1866 he suffered from exhaustion and nervous prostration. He was diagnosed with "typhomania," or acute inflammation of the brain, as a result of his four strenuous years of service in the army. On April 25, he died at the age of sixty-four at the North Hampton Lunatic Hospital and was buried in the Phillips Academy Cemetery in Andover, Massachusetts.

Chaplain Adams was dearly loved and respected. In 1867, Governor and Brevet Maj. Gen. Joshua Chamberlain, former commander of the 20th Maine Infantry, extolled Adams in a letter to Joseph Wilson, publisher of the *Presbyterian Almanac*:

> *My admirable friend, Rev. Dr. John R Adams, was well known throughout the Army of the Potomac, and probably there has not been any chaplain in the service more highly commended in "the field" and at home. I happened to become acquainted with some acts of gallantry on his part "in action"–such as rallying our broken lines and reviving the courage of our men by the noble example of his own–and I felt it my duty to recommend him for a brevet promotion "for meritorious and efficient service in the line of his duty, and for gallant conduct in battle during the war." It was an extraordinary thing to recommend a chaplain, who has no recognized rank as a surgeon has, for a "brevet," and I do not know whether the War Department acted in the case.*[35]

When the GAR in Gorham was mustered in January 1884, the members honored the chaplain by adopting his name for their John R. Adams Post 101.

Third Brigade:
Brigadier General David A. Russell

The brigade commanded by Brig. Gen. David Russell reached Gettysburg along with the Sixth Corps late on July 2, and early the next morning it was positioned at the extreme left of the Union line behind the Round Tops. Later in the day, it was moved to help support the center of the line against an anticipated attack by the enemy. However, the brigade was not actively engaged and suffered no casualties. On July 4, the brigade relieved part of the Fifth Corps on the slopes of Little Round Top until it was ordered to join the rest of the corps in pursuit of the Confederate army on July 5.

Russell's command included the 49th and 119th Pennsylvania, 5th Wisconsin, and 6th Maine Infantry regiments; only two regiments were accompanied by chaplains, and no record of their service has been located.

SECOND DIVISION:
Major General Albion P. Howe
First Brigade:
Colonel Lewis A. Grant

After arriving on the field late on July 2, the Vermonters of Col. Lewis Grant's brigade were moved to different positions along the left of the Union line until they were finally sent to the right of Russell's brigade, with its right resting on the reverse slope of Big Round Top and its left on the Taneytown Road. It remained in this position throughout July 3. The next day, one of the brigade's regiments was ordered to feel for the position of the enemy and had a slight skirmish with Confederate pickets, which resulted in the brigade's only casualty at Gettysburg. On July 5, it joined the corps in its pursuit of the Army of Northern Virginia.

Five Vermont regiments constituted this "First Vermont Brigade": the 2nd, 3rd, 4th, 5th, and 6th Vermont Infantry. Chaplains accompanied the 3rd and 6th regiments, but neither left writings about Gettysburg.

Third Brigade:
Brigadier General Thomas H. Neill

Brig. Gen. Thomas Neill had five regiments plus a small detachment of a sixth with him at Gettysburg: the 7th Maine, 43rd, 49th, and 77th New York, and the 61st Pennsylvania, plus about sixty men from the 33rd New York. When the brigade arrived at Gettysburg on July 2, Meade sent it first to Powers Hill to support a battery; then, at midnight, Twelfth Corps commander Henry Slocum moved it to the far right of the Union line, east of Rock Creek, where it skirmished with Confederates until the end of the battle.[36] All of the regiments except the 61st Pennsylvania and the detachment of the 33rd New York had chaplains with them, and one recorded his experiences.

Norman E. Fox, Jr., 77th New York Infantry

Chaplain Norman Fox of the 77th New York Infantry. (Green-Wood Cemetery)

Norman E. Fox was born in Glens Falls, New York, on February 13, 1836. He earned a degree from the University of Rochester in 1855 and from Rochester Theological Seminary two years later. He followed his father and grandfather into ministry in the Baptist Church and served at Whitehall, New York, from 1859 to 1862, when he enlisted as chaplain of the 77th New York Infantry (known as the "Bemis Heights Battalion"). He was one of four brothers who served in the Civil War.

Fox wrote letters to his family and friends while he was serving as chaplain, but none of them described the Battle of Gettysburg. However, the chaplain gave a speech at the dedication of the monument to the 77th Volunteers on Powers Hill at Gettysburg on October 16, 1889, in which he recounted the regiment's experiences:

> *The Gettysburg campaign must ever hold a prominent place in our recollections of army life [. . .] We marched all that night and on the next day till late afternoon [June 25]. That day was one of the hottest of the season, and the forced march in the intense heat made it one of the severest in the whole regimental experience. Scores fell by the wayside, overcome with sunstroke, their faces purple with*

the overpowering heat and fatigue. After a night's rest we started early in the morning for another long day's march, which was relieved by a halt in the late afternoon at Occoquan Creek, where all were ordered to go in swimming. It was a novel sight to see such multitudes splashing in the waters. Refreshed by the bath the men fairly danced the remaining hour or two of their tramp.

After a short stay at Fairfax Court House we marched northward again, crossing the Potomac at Edwards Ferry [June 27]. One of my recollections of General Sedgwick is of his standing in the rain at the end of that pontoon bridge, yelling at the teamsters to hurry them up, the long trains requiring so much time to cross. He wore that little round hat and a private's blouse. There was nothing in his dress to indicate his rank; but when he shouted at a slow teamster, it was apparent that he was a man to be obeyed. Glorious old "Uncle John!" He was a noble soldier, and of so kind a heart that every man in the corps loved him. He was always mindful of the comfort of his followers, and every wounded man called forth his sympathy.

The weather on that march through Maryland was showery. Each night we were too tired to put up tents, and so we used to sleep beneath the open sky. Each night there would be showers, and in the morning we would fold up our wet blankets, which, of course, would not dry during the day, and at night we would wrap ourselves again in their soggy folds and lie down with no trouble from insomnia. We were at Manchester in Maryland, when one evening was sounded the order to fall in. We marched all night, and, after a short halt in the morning to make coffee, we marched on. In the early forenoon [July 2] a farmer by the wayside told us that there had been a fight the day before at Gettysburg, a town of which not many of us had ever heard; and that General Reynolds had been killed. It was evident that Gettysburg was our destination.

At 2 or 3 in the afternoon as we went over some of the ridges of the Baltimore Pike we could look forward and see the valley some miles before us filled with smoke. A regiment was always a walking debating society, and the boys began to discuss what made that smoke. Some said it was only a farmer burning fallow. But before long we could see the white cotton balls in the air, and this smoke of bursting shells showed the real state of affairs. It was perhaps 4 o'clock when our brigade reached the margin of the field, the second day's battle being then at its height.

The men had marched nearly forty miles, and were turned aside into a field to rest a little. They had had nothing to eat since their coffee in the morning, and they went to work frying their pork and boiling their coffee in the most unconcerned manner, paying no attention to the fact that there, but a little distance in front, hundreds of cannon were thundering, and there were being enacted scenes which would form one of the great turning points of history.

And after all such unconcern is not strange; for the true man attends simply to what is before him, taking each duty only as it comes. There is a great deal of the hum-drum in heroism. The man who made the good soldier was not the swaggering swash-buckler, not the street brawler, but the respectable plain man who at home had always done his duty, faithfully, whatever it might be. The man who being set to hoe corn on a hot day would hoe his row without watching, even when the day was hot, was the man who, when assigned a station on the field of battle, would stay there till recalled, even though it was apparent that the recall would be given only by the resurrection angel.

The part assigned to the Seventy-seventh at Gettysburg was not one of especial danger. Its service on that field was for the most part only to "stand and wait." But it stood ready for any duty which might arise; and, had occasion demanded, it would have taken the same part in that deadly melee which it bore in so many other terrible conflicts.[37]

Fox mustered out on December 13, 1864. He spent several years traveling and studying and served as editor of *The Central Baptist*. He also taught religious history at William Jewell College of Theology in Missouri and devoted himself to writing and to the cause of temperance. In the late 1880s he settled in Morristown, New Jersey and became active in local politics. His work was so well respected that he was elected mayor of the town in 1990. He authored several books, served as a board member for the New Jersey State Village for Epileptics near Princeton, and received a Doctor of Divinity degree from Rochester University in 1887.

Fox married three times: in 1868 to Julia McKnight, who died the following year after giving birth to a son; in 1874 to Jane B. Bleecker, with whom he had four children and who died in 1880; and in 1906 to Martha Dimmock. While Martha and Norman were traveling in Europe on their honeymoon, he became ill, and just one week after returning to the United States, he died of appendicitis on June 8, 1907. He is buried in Green-Wood Cemetery in Brooklyn.

THIRD DIVISION:

Major General John Newton / Brigadier General Frank Wheaton

First Brigade:

Brigadier General Alexander Shaler

The brigade under the command of Brig. Gen. Alexander Shaler included three New York and two Pennsylvania regiments. On the evening of July 2, it was held in reserve on the left of the Union line, in front of the brigade of Col. Henry Eustis. Early the next morning, when fighting broke out on Culp's Hill, the brigade moved to support the Twelfth Corps, where, under the command of Brig. Gen. John W. Geary, it helped man the breastworks to hold off the repeated attacks by Confederates, and to give the tired men of the Twelfth Corps a respite from their fighting. Shaler's Brigade was sent off the hill in midafternoon to rejoin the Sixth Corps. Meade placed it behind the Third Corps troops near the center of the line and under the command of Maj. Gen. John Newton of the First Corps. It remained there until the morning of July 4, when it rejoined its division.

The 23rd Pennsylvania and 65th New York regiments had chaplains, one of whom recorded the story of his experience at Gettysburg; the 67th and 122nd New York and the 82nd Pennsylvania did not.

James Gallagher Shinn, 23rd Pennsylvania Infantry

James Gallagher Shinn was born in Philadelphia on March 13, 1822. After graduating as valedictorian from the University of Pennsylvania in 1844, he attended Princeton Theological Seminary, completing his studies in 1847, and was immediately licensed to preach by the

Presbyterian Church. A friend and fellow minister from Philadelphia was visiting in Burlington, Iowa, and recommended Shinn to a congregation there that was searching for a pastor. Shinn went west and was ordained in November 1848. That same year, he married Eliza Davis, with whom he had eight children, three of whom died as infants. He stayed at the church in Iowa for three years, then returned east when Eliza became ill.

Chaplain James Shinn of the 23rd Pennsylvania Infantry (from *History of the Twenty Third Pennsylvania Volunteer Infantry*)

On August 31, 1861, Shinn was mustered into service as chaplain in the 23rd Pennsylvania Infantry. He was beloved by his men for the ways he cared for them and taught them to be careful with their money. At one point, he was granted ten days' leave to take more than $18,000 to the soldiers' families at home.[38]

The regimental history of the 23rd includes an interesting story about Chaplain Shinn: The regiment *"had a fire-dog called 'Dash;' he seemed to know all the boys and was in his element when under fire. At Fair Oaks he and the chaplain were captured, but during the night both got back to the lines."*[39]

Shinn did not leave any writings during his time at Gettysburg, but he did give a lengthy oration at the regimental reunion held in Philadelphia in July 1888. In his speech, he described the Gettysburg campaign in detail, including the movements of both armies, but he also provided some specifics of what his own regiment experienced. On July 1 and 2, he recalled,

> *the Sixth Corps, at Manchester, thirty-six miles distant, by the most strenuous efforts, marching a day, a night and the greater part of the following day, from early on the first through to the afternoon, late, on the second, arrived just in time to render much needed help. But, as we all well know, Uncle John Sedgwick, as he was familiarly called, and his boys of the Sixth Corps could do great things in times of great emergencies.*[40]

As the regiment marched into Pennsylvania on July 2, the men

> *received strength as they touched their native soil. They were energized with new vigor and fired anew with the just ambition*

of defending their friends and their homes. Never did the men of the Twenty-third Pennsylvania Volunteers march better or perform better work than when their faces were turned North and their own Pennsylvania called forth their loyal zeal and hearty service. That march was made by some of you, as your Chaplain can testify, with bare and bruised and bleeding feet and yet never did the men of the Twenty-third march better. And this is applicable to the Sixth Corps and of other Corps.

The long march from Manchester to Gettysburg, thirty-six miles, increased to forty miles by mistaking the road, occupied all the daylight of July 1st, all that night, and nearly all the day of July 2d. Our regiment reached the battlefield near Little Round Top, as the big red sun was fast declining to his setting and then, after such a continuous march, with a hurrah, went directly to the front to the support of the Fifth Corps.[41]

On the morning of July 3, the 23rd was sent, along with the rest of its brigade, to reinforce the Twelfth Corps on Culp's Hill against attacks from Confederate troops. Shinn described the action there:

The shock and clash of arms is terrific. A desperate struggle takes place among the rocks. Upon the positions exposed all the artillery opens fire. The contest continues and yet loses none of its desperate character. General Stonewall Jackson's old soldiers are not willing

This painting by Edwin Forbes depicts the fighting on Culp's Hill the morning of July 3 from the Confederate side at the eastern base of the hill. (Library of Congress)

to back down even though the contest is against them. At last after seven hours' fighting they determined to make a most determined effort to break Geary's lines so as to reach the Baltimore Pike. But they find that not only are Geary's troops steadfast but that these have been re-enforced by General Kane's brigade and our own brigade under General Shaler. The rebel General Stewart having extended his line to the Creek heads the assault and his men follow into the concentrated fire–Ruger's skirmishers on their flank open a murderous fire, while Geary's troops strengthened by others steadfastly resist the assault. They are repulsed. Then immediately Ruger crosses the stream against the enemy while Geary makes a direct advance into the wood, and the enemy is driven out of the entrenchments. Three stands of colors and 500 prisoners prove the success of this combined movement–Culp's Hill is cleared.[42]

Shinn mustered out with the regiment on September 8, 1864. Over the course of three years, he had sent many personal belongings and notes with the last words of dying soldiers home to their families. Just one week after completing his service with the 23rd, he applied for and received a commission as chaplain of Satterlee U.S. Hospital in Philadelphia. His wife died in 1867, and in 1873 he returned to the pulpit and served churches in New Jersey and Pennsylvania. He married Mary Shoemaker in 1887, and at some point they moved to Atlantic City, New Jersey, where Shinn died on October 26, 1903. He is buried in Laurel Hill Cemetery in Philadelphia.

Second Brigade:
Colonel Henry Eustis

Col. Henry Eustis brought the 2nd Rhode Island and 7th, 10th, and 37th Massachusetts infantry regiments to Gettysburg. Upon reaching the field on July 2, the brigade bivouacked on the northeast slope of Little Round Top. The next morning, it was moved to the center of the Union line and was held in reserve. Although not actively engaged in repelling the enemy, artillery fire from the cannonade preceding the Pickett-Pettigrew-Trimble charge wounded several men while they were marching along the Taneytown Pike to their new position. July 4 was spent tending to the wounded and burying the dead, and the brigade joined its corps as it moved out after the Confederate army on July 5. Only one chaplain accompanied the brigade, and he left no record of his experience at Gettysburg.

Third Brigade:
Brigadier General Frank Wheaton / Colonel David Nevin

When division commander John Newton was ordered to take command of the First Corps on July 1, Brig. Gen. Frank Wheaton assumed command of the division and turned over his brigade to Col. David Nevin. Late in the afternoon of July 2, soon after having arrived on the field, Nevin's men formed a line to the north of Little Round Top just as Union troops were retreating through and past their line. They moved up to support the Pennsylvania Reserves and helped repulse the enemy and recapture Union guns that had been overrun. They remained in this position, to the right of the Reserves, until late on July 3, when they were sent on a reconnaissance with some of the Reserves. They assisted in the capture of many enemy soldiers and the recapture of one gun that had been abandoned the day before. The next morning they were sent to support another reconnaissance by Fifth Corps troops, and they joined the corps on July 5 as they headed out to follow General Lee's army.

The brigade included the 62nd New York and the 93rd, 98th, and 139th Pennsylvania regiments. The 102nd Pennsylvania was left in Westminster, Maryland, to guard the trains and sent fewer than one hundred men with the brigade to Gettysburg. All of the regiments except the 98th Pennsylvania brought chaplains with them on the campaign; two of them left a record of their time as chaplain.

Joseph Sylvester Lame, 93rd Pennsylvania Infantry

Joseph Sylvester Lame was born on September 17, 1831, in Philadelphia. He was educated in public schools and by private instruction, was licensed to preach by the Philadelphia Conference of the Methodist Episcopal Church in May 1852, and was fully ordained three years later. That same year, he married Hannah Ann Thompson, who bore three children, two of whom died young. Lame's first pastoral charge was the Radnor

Circuit outside Philadelphia, but he was soon moved to a church at Cambridge on Maryland's Eastern Shore. Although he had not held strong opinions on slavery to this point, his exposure to the slave-keeping actions of fellow church members and ministers drove him to admit that slavery was *"utterly repugnant to the teachings of the Bible."*[43] When Lame was appointed to the Snow Hill circuit in southern Maryland in 1857, he began writing letters under a pseudonym to *Zion's Herald*, an antislavery newspaper in Boston, exposing the injustices he witnessed among the slaveholding Methodists.[44] Once Lame's identity was discovered, he was charged with being an abolitionist by church members, who threatened to burn down the parsonage if he did not leave the area. He and his wife and son returned to Pennsylvania, where he was appointed to churches near Philadelphia.

Chaplain Joseph Lame of the 93rd Pennsylvania Infantry. (Mt. Moriah Cemetery)

Rev. James M. McCarter was colonel of the 93rd Pennsylvania Infantry and invited his friend and colleague Joseph Lame to join the regiment as chaplain. (Library of Congress)

One of Lame's colleagues and a fellow abolitionist, the Rev. James M. McCarter, was serving as colonel of the 93rd Pennsylvania Infantry. The regiment's first chaplain, Rev. John Quimby, had died of typhoid in August 1862. McCarter invited Lame to become the new chaplain; he accepted and was mustered in on October 8. Lame proved to be diligent in his service and was greatly respected for his devotion to the soldiers' mental, physical, and spiritual well-being. He remained with the regiment until they mustered out on June 27, 1865.

Lame left no writings during his time in the army, but he did give an address at the dedication of the regimental monument at Gettysburg on September 11, 1889. His speech covered the entirety of the regiment's service throughout the war. What follows are his recollections of Gettysburg.

While the two great armies, during the month of June, were manoeuvring for position to fight a mighty duel–to ascertain the enemy's position, the regiment crossed the Rappahannock, when it was developed that Lee had pushed the head of his column northward for an invasion of Pennsylvania. The march for Pennsylvania now commenced, the regiment moving by way of Manassas and Centerville. The Sixth Corps formed the right wing of the army.

On the 1st of July, [the regiment] arrived at Manchester, Maryland. During all the preceding day the regiment had trod the dusty heated highway. At 9 o'clock in the evening, worn with the long and weary march, they stretched their aching limbs in the shelter of a friendly forest. Scarcely had they thrown themselves upon the ground, when an aide-de-camp arrived from the bold-baptized heights of Gettysburg, announcing the death of General Reynolds, and that the stupendous conflict had commenced, and requesting regimental commanders to address their troops in language becoming the grandeur of the crisis, and bearing an order for the immortal Sixth–a corps that had never failed to achieve the possible, to hasten to the defense, to strike for their altars and their fires, God and their native State. The drums beat–"Fall in," leaped from lip to lip, and the host is all astir, swords and belts are buckled on, knapsacks slung, weapons grasped, and forming into a solid square, they stand determined, defiant. But who shall address them? Where are the souls of fire and tongue of flame? They are there. Colonel McCarter, though now an invalid [he had been wounded at Seven Pines], the genius of eloquence had touched his lips and bade them speak. His rostrum was a war-steed, the silence was profound and painful, not a foot rose or fell, breathing seemed suspended, all nature appeared as awe-struck at the sublimity of the scene, stood silent, solemn, listening. He who was to interpret and give tongue to this tremendous silence, began in tones low and tremulous, his voice acquiring force and volume as he proceeded, rang out on the evening air, solemn and sepulchral as a trumpet from the skies, as if God had recommissioned the immortal Moses to reinflame the serried hosts of the Lord God about to march to the valley of decision for the dread battle of Armageddon.[45]

Lame recited the colonel's stirring speech in full, then continued:

Not a cheer arose, not a murmur was heard; feeling too profound for speech filled all hearts. Silently, solemnly and majestically as the ocean tide the men move through the aisles of the forest.

The corps marched until midnight, when it was found that through a mistake in the wrong road had been taken, and that it had marched several miles out of their way. These miles had to be remarched by the footsore and weary troops. At break of day, a short halt being called, a few fires were kindled and an attempt made to secure a rude breakfast. Some were trying to boil coffee when the order sounded "Fall in," and some lingering a few moments around the fires, officers approached and kicked over the coffee pots and all. Again the weary march was taken up in heat and dust. Many fell fainting in their tracks, these were loaded into the ambulances until they were full, others were pulled aside into the shade and left, some possibly to revive and rejoin the regiments, others to be overtaken and overwhelmed by bushwhackers. At 9 in the morning, the booming of cannon from the distant field was distinctly heard. At 10 the regiment crossed the State line. She unfurled her colors, beat her drums, came to a quickstep and sang "Home, Sweet, Sweet, Home."

About 3 p.m. a halt was ordered, the men too much exhausted to eat, threw themselves wearily to the ground and lay like logs. In an hour an order came to advance into the battle. The corps were promptly in motion, the Ninety-third leading the column to the support of the Third and Fifth corps which were then hard pressed, Colonel David J. Nevin, of Sixty-second New York, being in command of the brigade. The Ninety-third being in the advance, was the first regiment of the corps to get into action. Major Nevin in command, General Sedgwick in person led the brigade and formed on the brow of a low rocky knoll covered with scattered trees, just to the right of Little Round Top, the left of the brigade joining with the Pennsylvania Reserves. It got into position just as the troops which had been contesting the ground in the open fields along the Emmitsburg pike, broken and almost annihilated, were coming back in disorder, followed by the exultant enemy.

The command was ordered to lie down and to withhold its fire until the enemy was close upon it. Had this order been heeded, the whole rebel line could easily have been captured. A premature fire was opened from a part of the line which checked the advance. The whole brigade then advanced and after a short contest the rebel line was driven in tumult. In the charge the Ninety-third took twenty-five prisoners. Just before nightfall, the regiment was ordered forward with a regiment of Reserves to retake a battery, which had been lost in the early part of the day, but the guns having been removed it returned. At night, the men slept for a few hours in the line of battle but spent most of the time in removing the wounded who strewed the fields in front. Since 8 o'clock on the previous evening the regiment had marched thirty-nine miles, had fought three hours and passed an almost sleepless night and nearly without food.

On the afternoon of the 3d the Confederates opened with all their batteries. For two hours, from a space less than two miles, there was an incessant cannonade from two hundred guns of the enemy. Upon no battlefield of the world's history had such a bombardment ever been witnessed. During this terrible cannonade the men partly sheltered by a stone wall, rocks and trees, hugged closely the ground, and at the conclusion of the charge on the left center renewed the picket firing and kept it up until dark. During the night the regiment was engaged in burying the dead and bearing off the wounded. The fourth of July was celebrated at the front, the men being ordered on the skirmish line on the extreme left where it suffered some loss. At two in the afternoon it was relieved.

On the 5th it was ascertained that the enemy had retreated and pursuit was at once begun. The Ninety-third was detached to guard the corps artillery and assist in taking it across the mountains. The duty proved a difficult one, the men suffering much from the hardships it imposed.

The Ninety-third Regiment Veteran Volunteers has a reputation that no member of that organization need by ashamed of. Nay, she has won a grand historic position that the great Keystone State and the nation at large can well be proud of. It was composed chiefly of the middle classes of society, yeomen, men that sprang spontaneously and patriotically to their country's call.[46]

After the war, Lame returned to Pennsylvania and served several churches for the next forty years until, at his last charge in Tamaqua, he grew too weak to preach and was put on the "superannuated" or retired list of clergy. His health continued to decline and he died on December 15, 1895. He is buried in the "Preacher's Burial Lot" at Mount Moriah Cemetery in Philadelphia, next to the grave of his three-year-old son Alfred Cookman Lame, which was the first burial in the cemetery.

Alexander M. Stewart, 102nd Pennsylvania Infantry

Alexander M. Stewart, or A. M. Stewart as he preferred, was born on January 22, 1814, in Beaver County, Pennsylvania. He graduated from Franklin College in New Athens, Ohio, and then completed his studies for ministry at Western Theological Seminary in 1843. After he was licensed to preach, he traveled throughout the country, doing church work in Ohio, Kentucky, Tennessee, Alabama, and Mississippi. In 1845, he accepted the role of pastor of the Reformed Presbyterian Church in Chicago, but he resigned ten years later to care for his health. Two years later, he moved to Pittsburgh to serve as pastor of the Second Reformed Presbyterian Church. He married Nancy E. Hadley in 1847; after bearing a son and a daughter, she died in 1860.

Chaplain Alexander Stewart of the 102nd Pennsylvania Infantry. (U.S. Army Heritage and Education Center)

When war broke out in April 1861, he immediately responded by writing a letter to offer his services as chaplain to any regiment that would accept him (see sidebar). When he was mustered in to the 13th Pennsylvania Infantry, a three-month regiment, he became the first volunteer chaplain to enter the U.S. Army. At the end of their term, the 13th was reorganized as the 102nd Pennsylvania Infantry, although many members still referred to their unit as the "Old Thirteenth."

According to his obituary in the Pittsburgh *Weekly Gazette*, Stewart had been offered various commissions as a higher-ranking officer but had repeatedly turned them down. In a letter dated February 5, 1862, he explained, *"The conviction has been deliberately formed that a minister of the gospel ought not to leave the exercise of his sacred calling, and accept a military commission"* because *"such a course proves injurious to the minister himself, often destroying the minister without making the officer."*[47]

Throughout his three and a half years with the regiment, Stewart sent sketches of the soldiers' experiences to newspapers back home almost every week. In 1865, these letters were published as *Camp, March, and Battlefield*, a regimental history that focused less on the military operations of the unit and more on the effect of army life on ordinary men. He wrote no letters for more than six weeks after May 13, 1863, as he explained in his next letter, dated July 28: *"During the past forty-five days, since finally breaking up our old camp at Falmouth, it may be literally, without figure of speech, asserted, no time has been allowed for writing."*[48] The regiment had been almost constantly marching during that time, and at Gettysburg they had been detached to guard the corps trains at Westminster.[49] His letter vividly described the effect of those long marches on the soldiers of the 102nd:

> *GETTYSBURG AN EPISODE–That harvest of death and mutilation at Gettysburg, the gleanings of which the benevolent have been so industriously and kindly gathering up, and binding, constitutes, after all, but an episode in this late campaign. The Herculean labors and untold fatigues uncomplainingly endured by the soldiers, are not likely ever fully to be written. Those, having never seen nor felt, could hardly be made to understand these by any labored description.*
>
> *THE MARCH–Those, who have been most carefully noted, estimate that during this time, beside the fighting, together with other multiplied duties and toils, our 6th corps–and this is an average of others–has marched three hundred and fifty miles.*[50] *Marched? What is comprehended in the march of a great army under the burning suns of July? Will our rugged farmers, who sweat in the harvest field, or tradesmen who daily put forth strong muscular effort at the ordinary business, believe me when assuring them, that were the strongest from among their number for the first time to be arrayed with what each soldier daily and for long hours and many miles carries–knapsack, haversack, gun, ammunition box, canteen, tin cup, coffee boiler with various other et cetera, weighing in all about as much as a bushel of wheat and he thus accoutered started at the middle of a hot July day, on a dusty road, amid a thick and smothering crowd of men, horses, mules, and*

wagons; in less than a mile he would fall prostrate to the earth and perhaps never rise again. It has, however, taken two years of terrible practice to inure these iron men to undergo this wonderful physical endurance. Nor must it be forgotten, that in the hardening process, two out of three have sunk under the toil and exposure, and have disappeared from the army.

MODE OF MARCHING.–Our mode of marching for many days, during the late campaign, has been after the following fashion. Stretched out in a single road and in close marching order, the army of the Potomac with its infantry, cavalry, artillery, ambulances, and wagon trains, would extend a distance of forty miles; so where the front may now be, it would, in ordinary marches, take several days for the rear to reach. In order to facilitate matters, keep the army more compact, and be able to act more speedily in concert, as lately at Gettysburg, several columns usually start together on different roads leading in the same general direction. Not only this, but of late it has been usual for the artillery, ambulances and wagons to take the road, and if a turnpike or wide thoroughfare, wagons and artillery go abreast, and the infantry column take a course in the vicinity and parallel with the road–through fields and woods, down into deep glens and hollows, up steep bluffs and over high hills, through unbridged marshes, ponds and creeks. Along such a course it is often quite as easy for the footman as for us who are on horseback.

INTERESTING–The eye never wearies in its interest with ever-varying scenes constantly presenting themselves on these marches. Long miles of artillery–a cannon with its six horses followed by its caisson and its six horses, and others, and others–strings of neat two-horse ambulances reaching out of sight, and army wagons without seeming number or end–with those on foot; great streams of living men, which those remaining stationary sometimes imagine will never all pass. A strange fascination has it, at least to the writer, often on the march when getting on some eminence and looking forward for miles at that dark column, four abreast, winding down into valleys; up over hills, across fields, orchards and meadows–away, away, and hiding itself in some dense woods far off. Looking back, the same curious bewitching vision meets the eye. A vast living moving anaconda, encircling and seemingly about to crush the earth within its folds. At a mile's distance the motion of the column cannot readily be discerned; but fixing the eye on a stationary object in close proximity, you at cone discern that it actually lives and moves.[51]

When the Sixth Corps was moved to Washington in July 1864 to support the troops there against the advance of Jubal Early's Confederate forces, the regimental surgeon ordered Stewart to take a season of rest, and since his term as chaplain for the 102nd was nearing its end, he was assigned to be chaplain at an army hospital in the city. Although he found the work there to be rewarding, he wrote in his final letter, *"A longing desire is frequently felt for a renewal of the trying, difficult, yet deeply interesting labours of the camp, on the march and battle-field, in behalf of our brave, yet too often wicked soldiers, for whom the writer continues to yearn with an unspeakable affection."*[52]

At the end of the war, Stewart mustered out of service and accepted the position of pastor of two churches in Chester County, Pennsylvania. He had married his second wife, Josephine A. Malcom, in February 1864, and five years later the couple moved to the Pacific coast, where Stewart served as district secretary of the Board of Home Mission in California. His last pastorate was in Chico, California, which he held until his death on February 24, 1875. He is buried in Allegheny Cemetery in Pittsburgh.

Chapter 7:

The Eleventh Corps

CORPS COMMANDERS:

Major General Oliver Otis Howard
Brigadier General Carl Schurz

The Eleventh Corps was the smallest corps in the Army of the Potomac and included the highest number of German immigrants, thus giving the Eleventh the name "the German Corps." By 1863, it had become not just an ethnic moniker, but a derisive slur against the corps that had broken when it was attacked on the flank at Chancellorsville. Several regiments in the corps were predominantly German, while others were mixed with Irish, German, and what were then called "native American" soldiers.

The Eleventh Corps was part of the "left wing" of the army, which also included the First and Third Corps, under the command of Maj. Gen. John Reynolds. On the night of June 30, the men bivouacked near Emmitsburg, Maryland, and orders arrived the next morning to march toward Gettysburg. Once they crossed into Pennsylvania, they received news of a battle near that town. With the death of Reynolds earlier that morning, Maj. Gen. Oliver Otis Howard assumed command of the left wing and Brig. Gen. Carl Schurz was placed in command of the corps. The Eleventh arrived at Gettysburg just after noon on July 1 during a lull in the fighting. Two divisions were ordered to form a line to the right of the First Corps while the Third Division and two batteries were held in reserve on Cemetery Hill.

This line north of town proved to be untenable because the right flank was in the air and because the attacking Confederate forces outnumbered the Union soldiers by almost 2 to 1. Around 4:00 p.m. both the Eleventh and First Corps lines were outflanked and retreated through town to their fallback position on Cemetery Hill. The men of the Eleventh took positions from the west to the east side of the hill. For the next two days, the units on the west side of the hill engaged in heavy skirmishing with Confederates in town and to the west of it. On the evening of July 2, those regiments on the east side of the hill, with support from some Second Corps regiments, fought off an attack by two Confederate brigades that briefly climbed the hill and overran some batteries. July 3 was spent sniping and resting, and the corps joined the Army of the Potomac in its pursuit of Lee's army on July 5.

FIRST DIVISION:

Brigadier General Francis Barlow / Brigadier General Adelbert Ames

First Brigade:

Colonel Leopold von Gilsa

Brig. Gen. Francis Barlow commanded the First Division. He was a strict disciplinarian who did not hide his disdain for the "Dutchmen" under his command.[1] The first brigade in the division was commanded by Brig. Gen. Leopold von Gilsa. His men moved toward Gettysburg on the Emmitsburg Road, but their march was slowed by the wagons of the First Corps that were clogging the road ahead of them. When they reached the field, the men first formed a line on the right of the corps' Third Division. But Barlow noticed a small eminence in front of his division that he believed would give his men a better position, so he ordered his brigades forward to Blocher's Knoll, now called Barlow's Knoll. The division's right flank was in the air near the Harrisburg Road, down which Maj. Gen. Jubal Early's Confederate division was marching. Gilsa's men were positioned at the top of the knoll and down toward the road. Although they fought well, they were quickly outflanked and driven back with severe losses. Barlow was wounded during the melee and was taken to a field hospital by his Confederate captors. As the division rallied on Cemetery Hill, Brig. Gen. Adelbert Ames assumed command of the division.

On July 2, the depleted ranks of the division held a thin line near the eastern base of Cemetery Hill and came under fire from Confederate artillery on Benner's Hill and suffered severely. That evening near sunset, two of General Early's brigades attacked the eastern face of the hill, and although the line briefly broke, the Eleventh Corps repulsed the Confederates with assistance from other regiments, and the men returned to their original positions. They spent July 3 under fire from snipers in town and Confederate artillery during the bombardment preceding the Pickett-Pettigrew-Trimble charge. The next day, they were sent into town and captured almost three hundred prisoners before returning to East Cemetery Hill. Finally, their long ordeal over for the time being, they left Gettysburg with the rest of the army to follow Lee's men back toward Virginia.

All four of the regiments in the division, the 41st, 54th, and 68th New York and 153rd Pennsylvania, were accompanied by chaplains. Three of the chaplains were German and were well suited to minister to the German soldiers in their units. One recorded his experiences in a diary. Another was the first Jewish regimental chaplain in the Army of the Potomac; he was wounded during the fighting on July 1 but left no record of his service.

Philip Weller Melick, 153rd Pennsylvania Infantry

Philip Weller Melick was born on February 29, 1824, in Columbia County, Pennsylvania. After completing his education at Lafayette College and Princeton Seminary, he was ordained in the Presbyterian Church. He served various parishes until 1857, when he was assigned as pastor of the Mount Bethel Presbyterian Church. Mary Ellen Camden became his wife on July 3, 1860, and they had four children.

Chaplain Philip Melick of the 153rd Pennsylvania Infantry (from *History of the One Hundred and Fifty-third Regiment Pennsylvania Volunteers Infantry* by Rev. W. R. Kiefer)

Chaplain Melick was tending to the wounded of the Eleventh Corps in the German Reformed Church on Stratton Street until he had to leave when the town was overrun by the Confederates late on July 1. (Library of Congress)

In October 1862, Melick responded to Governor Andrew Curtin's call for nine-month regiments and enlisted as chaplain in the 153rd Pennsylvania Infantry. Melick kept a diary in which he briefly described each day of the march to Gettysburg. On June 21, he recorded hearing the sounds of firing, which he correctly surmised came from the cavalry battle at Aldie, Virginia. Four days later as the corps was crossing the Potomac River, he reported the *"large Brigade Medical Wagon team went off the pontoons and all were lost."*[2] On July 1, he wrote, *"Marched at 8-1/4 for Gettysburg. Arrived about or a little after noon. 1st Corps was engaged with the enemy when we arrived. Our boys went right on without dinner."*[3] He listed the casualties, including the capture of regimental surgeon Dr. Abraham Stout, then continued, *"Was here, there, and all over. Went to hospital but had to leave it in the hands of the Rebs. Slept or rather staid with the Regt."*[4] The hospital was most likely at the German Reformed Church; see the note for the surgeon's account.

Melick's diary entries for the next two days read:

> *Thursday July 2nd (1863)*
>
> *Left camp about break of day. Went out the Baltimore road to Mr. Henry Spangler's where I left my carpet satchel last night. Rode back to Regt. saw preparation for holding the position. Some picket firing in the night, and some cannonading by our side, but not answered except by a few sharp shooters. Gen. Reynolds of the 1st Corps killed yesterday. Am writing on a porch of a house on Baltimore road [likely the site of regimental or brigade headquarters]. Hope we will drive the Rebs. out of town. Heard the citizens are ordered to leave the town, but think it doubtful, as there are but a few passing.*

Still rainy weather. Went down in the meadow laid some rails on the fence for a bed along the end. Went to the hospital, found 12 of our wounded boys there. Back to regt. and gave Major Lt. R. & M. dinner [most likely Major Adam Reisinger, with whom Melick often shared a tent, and Lt. Jonathan Moore] and took dinner with them. Left and went down to Mr. Spangler's wagon house a kind of Sub. look-out hospital; made a bed, lay down, took a nap. Chaplains of 41st & 54 present. Wrote a letter to Ellie [his wife] but know of no way to send it. About the time I had finished it the shell from the enemy began to come in and we hurried off. Some were wounded near by. Rebs. tried to flank us, and I suppose take our train. Most terrible fighting for about 3 hours commencing about 4 o'clock P.M. Felt very sorry for the alarmed and distressed citizens who have been very kind to us. Retreated on the Baltimore turnpike a few miles built up a house of rails and invited Chaplain Dr. Bogan [of the 41st New York] to share it. Each joined in prayer as we lay down. Slept well until around about 2 o'c. packed up and then scarcely knowing where to go stopped in an oat field,

July 3, 1863.

Still near Gettysburg. Returned almost to Mr. Spangler's in hopes of getting the things I left there and also my haversack & two canteens left in the wagon house yesterday, and also to get something for the mess, but cannot pass the firing. The Rebs. attained possession of some of the works of the 12th and our batteries and musketry all driving them out. Some of the most determined on both sides I have ever seen. Tried several times to go to the front and at last succeeded in getting up to within one town lot of the 153rd which was their former position, when in the lot which lay before the one I finally got into I was told that it was not safe to go any further. I thought I was now so near I would at least try to make it. I led Charley [his horse] over the stone fence got on him and went up to the corner of the next lot where I expected to meet my regt. but soon the whizzing of bullets over my heard plainly told me that the sharpshooters had their eyes on me and Charley and perhaps mistook us for a mounted commanding officer. I concluded not to go any further in that direction but went up to the entrance to the cemetery, took my horse down the road, left him in charge of one of our men and went back to the Cem. gate intending to go to my Regt. Met Col. Von Gilsa who said he wished me to be with the Regt. the most of the time, but that I had better not go to the Regt. then, on account of the sharpshooters, so I do not get to the Regt. Went back to headquarters by the barn on the Baltimore Road. Had a good nights rest.[5]

Melick continues his daily entries, noting on July 4 that he *"attended to the wants of the wounded soldiers in the barn as well as I could. Still searching for hospital [. . .] Took the mess something to eat. Went to hospital [. . .] got back late–very dark and rainy. Had prayer in barn during rain."*[6]

Some of the men in the regiment evidently did not care for their chaplain's aversion to drinking alcohol and to his passing judgment on those who did imbibe. On July 5, Melick went to the field hospital to lead a service and got down on his knees to offer prayer when some soldiers started yelling for him to leave. To his credit, though, Melick worked hard in the days immediately following the battle to find what he called "mess," or food, for the wounded men in the hospital. He made several trips into town and went from wagon to wagon to beg for food for his men. His perseverance and success served the wounded soldiers well.

Melick mustered out with his regiment on July 24, 1863, and returned to Pennsylvania, where he served several churches. In 1870, he moved to North Carolina, resigned from the ministry, and opened a general supply and furnishing house that proved to be successful. After a period of illness, he died on February 24, 1902, and is buried in Old Hollywood Cemetery in Elizabeth City, North Carolina.

Second Brigade:
Brigadier General Adelbert Ames / Colonel Andrew Harris

Brig. Gen. Adelbert Ames commanded the second brigade of the First Division and followed the brigade of Colonel von Gilsa into Gettysburg and to the fields beyond. After a short rest in the fields near the Adams County Almshouse, some men were sent out to secure a bridge across the Harrisburg Road while others were sent to support Lt. Bayard

Wilkeson's battery. Confederate guns opened on the brigade almost immediately and they were pushed forward along with von Gilsa's men to the knoll in their front. Overwhelming numbers of Confederates attacked from the front and both flanks, and they soon were forced to retreat along with the rest of the Eleventh Corps. It was not a "rout," however. Many soldiers stopped and turned to fire at their pursuers, even in the town.

Once on Cemetery Hill, the brigade formed a line next to von Gilsa's brigade and spent a restless night, waiting for an attack that came the next evening. Although when the Confederates attacked, some of von Gilsa's men broke up the hill to the rear, others held their position along the stone wall near the bottom of the hill's eastern side. Hand-to-hand fighting by these two brigades, supported by Second Corps regiments, pushed the Confederates away from the batteries and off the hill.

July 3 brought no fighting, but the men were exposed to Confederate artillery fire. They were briefly sent into town with von Gilsa's men on July 4, then joined the pursuit of Lee's army on July 5. Because Ames took over the division after Barlow was wounded, Col. Andrew Harris assumed command of the brigade.

There were four regiments in the brigade: the 17th Connecticut and the 25th, 75th, and 107th Ohio. Only two of them had chaplains with them and neither left a written witness to the battle.

SECOND DIVISION:

Brigadier General Adolph von Steinwehr

First Brigade:

Colonel Charles Coster

The divisions of Brig. Gen. Adolph von Steinwehr and Maj. Gen. Carl Schurz marched into Gettysburg on the Taneytown Road to avoid the congestion on the Emmitsburg Road. While Schurz led his men north of town, von Steinwehr held his division in reserve on Cemetery Hill. Once the divisions of Schurz (now commanded by Brig. Gen. Alexander Schimmelfennig) and Barlow began to break, Col. Charles Coster's brigade was sent out to form a rear guard to help their comrades safely retreat through town and to the hill. Three of Coster's regiments took a line near a brickyard north of town and were attacked by two brigades of Confederates. Being outnumbered by more than three to one, the line fought as long as it could but had no choice but to retreat. One of the regiments in the brigade, the 154th New York, suffered one of the highest casualty rates of any Union regiment at Gettysburg: Almost 84 percent of the men were killed, wounded, captured, or reported missing, leaving only three officers and fifteen men who made it back to Cemetery Hill.[7]

During the Confederate attack on the evening of July 2, two of the regiments in the brigade helped repulse the enemy from around the battery of Capt. Michael Wiedrich, while the other two were in support. The morning of July 3 was quiet, but the brigade came under severe fire from the Confederate cannonade that afternoon. The two Pennsylvania regiments were sent to support the Union line near Zeigler's Grove but were not needed, and they returned to East Cemetery Hill. The men joined those of Barlow's (Ames's) division skirmishing through the town on July 4, and after capturing some prisoners, built barricades on some of the streets. On July 5, they left Gettysburg with the rest of the army.

The brigade included two New York regiments, the 134th and 154th, and two from Pennsylvania, the 27th and 73rd. Of the two chaplains with the New York men, one wrote about his experiences.

Henry Dyer Lowing, 154th New York Infantry

Henry Dyer Lowing was born in East Gainesville, New York, on May 29, 1827. After attending the Kingsville Academy, he taught for twelve years. He and Nancy J. Pierce were wed on April 21, 1853; they had seven children, one of whom died in infancy. Lowing studied law for a while then was appointed professor and assistant principal of the Academy in Randolph, New York. He received a call to preach and served Congregational churches first in Pierpont, Ohio, and then at Napoli, New York, where he was ordained in 1858. He was well known for his abolitionist and temperance advocacy. After seven years at Napoli, he enlisted as chaplain in the 154th New York infantry on September 23, 1862.

Chaplain Henry Lowing of the 154th New York Infantry. (from *History and Genealogy of the Lowing Family*)

Lowing wrote to his father on July 22 from the West Branch of Goose Creek near the Alexandria and Winchester Turnpike in Virginia (near Leesburg), and reported (in a letter full of misspellings):

> *I can hardly be reconciled to the sad failure [of allowing the Confederates to recross the Potomac] but we had every reason to believe that the ammunition of the Rebs after the battle of Gittisburg was nearly exhausted. We should have been out of it had not been for the fresh supplies constantly coming in and we knew that they had no such facilities for getting it. Our prisoners said that the ferry boats which carried them across the river were loaded back with ammunition but that was a slow way of supplying a large army. But for some good reason but yet to be seen and over ruling Providence permitted them to escape.*
>
> *We ought to be thankful that he gave us the victory at Gittisburg and yet has not given us anything to boast of. We had a narrow escape at Gittisburg. The first day of the fight we were whipped and they drove us out of the town and we were compelled to fall back to our position on the hights East of the Town. This in the end proved to be our salvation. Gittisburg is in a valley the mountains on the West gradually though unevenly sloping down to within a mile or so of the town on the West and nearer on the North and then rising on the East. Perhaps a rough drawing will help to give an idea of the situation.*[8]
>
> *The first day's fight was on the West of the town. If we had held the ground and fought the battle there we should have been routed. On the first day of the fight (Wednesday) our Brigade was sent through the town to take a position and in 15 minutes after they got into position they were flanked and nearly all taken prisoners some wounded and a few killed. Only about 20 of our Regt came out. 50 of our Regt have been sent out on Reconnaissance and were not in so that after the battle we had only about 70 men. Some convalescents have returned to the Regt from Washington but we have only a little over 100 now. Doctor [Cordon C.] Rugg was three days a prisoner in Gettisburg but was treated like a gentleman and had full liberty to do all he could for the wounded. 150 of our Regt are prisoners in the hands of the enemy and 130 in Alexandria. When they are exchanged we shall have quite a Regt again. The talk is now that these Regiments are all to be filled up with drafted men.*[9]

After the convalescents and exchanged prisoners rejoined the regiment, it was sent to Tennessee in October 1863. Lowing was discharged for disability less than three months later, on January 3, 1864. He returned to Pennsylvania and served as pastor of the Conneaut Center church and as postmaster for Centre Road Station, and then pastored churches in Ohio and Missouri. During the four years he was in Neosho, Missouri, Lowing became aware of the need for a Congregational college in the western part of the state and was instrumental in the founding of Drury College in Springfield. Although members of the community had tried to persuade Lowing to serve as president of the new school, he declined and moved his family back to Pennsylvania, where he was pastor of his old church in Conneaut Center for an additional twenty-one years.

Lowing ran for the Pennsylvania Legislature and served from 1878 to 1881; he later ran for Congress but failed to win election. A strong temperance man, he presented bills to limit the sale and manufacture of liquor; although the Pennsylvania House supported them, they never passed in the Senate. In 1881, Lowing worked with his son Frank to publish the *Linesville Herald*, in which he published many editorial columns on behalf of the Republican Party. Lowing died on the family farm in Conneaut Township on November 9, 1903, and is buried in the Conneaut Center Cemetery in Crawford County, Pennsylvania.

Second Brigade:
Colonel Orland Smith

The brigade commanded by Col. Orland Smith arrived in Gettysburg via the Taneytown Road around midday on July 1 and marched through Evergreen Cemetery and rested. When the rest of the Eleventh Corps was retreating toward the hill, Smith's men prepared for a possible Confederate attack by forming a line on the western side of the hill, along the Taneytown Road. When the anticipated attack did not come, Smith threw out a skirmish line close to enemy forces both in town and west of it. It proved to be some of the most deadly and prolonged skirmishing to take place during the battle, not ending until late on July 3. The regiments rotated in and out of the skirmish line, and in the afternoon of July 2 some men from one regiment drove out Confederate snipers from a house between the lines but were later captured.

One of the regiments, the 33rd Massachusetts, had been sent to East Cemetery Hill to support batteries. During the Confederate attack in the evening of July 2, this regiment was in good position to fire on the flanks of the rebels. The rest of the brigade was exposed to severe shelling during the cannonade on July 3, but did not actively engage in repelling the Pickett-Pettigrew-Trimble charge. On July 4, all the regiments were reunited and served on picket duty, and they followed the army out of Gettysburg on July 5.

The 33rd Massachusetts and 55th Ohio regiments brought their chaplains to Gettysburg, while the 73rd Ohio and 136th New York had no chaplains at the time. Only the Massachusetts chaplain left a written record.

Daniel Foster, 33rd Massachusetts Infantry

Daniel Foster was born in Hanover, New Hampshire, on December 10, 1816. He attended Kimball Union Academy and was one of seven Foster brothers to attend Dartmouth College. He left before he graduated and moved to Kentucky to teach school for two years. While there, he was exposed to what he called the "inherent sinfulness" of slavery, which led him to become an ardent abolitionist. He returned to New England and continued to teach until he finished his degree at Dartmouth in 1845. Two years later, he was ordained as a Congregational minister (as were six of his brothers), and he moved to Salem, Massachusetts, to organize an antislavery congregation. After one year, he moved to Danvers and was ordained in the Methodist Episcopal Church. He served several churches but ran into trouble because of his passionate preaching on the evils of slavery. He wrote articles for William Lloyd Garrison's *The Liberator* and participated in demonstrations against the Fugitive Slave Law. Although he eventually converted to Unitarianism, he became so radical in his antislavery views that he could not find a congregation to serve. In 1857, he was appointed chaplain of the Massachusetts House of Representatives, where he heard John Brown deliver a speech about the problems in Kansas. Foster was so moved by the battle over slavery in that territory that he moved to Kansas to support Brown in his activities. Foster traveled between Kansas and Massachusetts for a few years to lecture and raise money for the Free-Soilers in Kansas.

Foster had married Deborah Taylor Swift (called "Dora") in 1850. In 1862, Foster moved his family, which now included five children, back to Massachusetts so he could enlist as chaplain in the 33rd Massachusetts Infantry, mustering in on August 10. Foster proved to be one of those chaplains who stayed close to their men even in the midst of battle. When his regiment was on East Cemetery Hill in Gettysburg on July 2, the chaplain walked along the lines and told the men, *"If any of you want to write a letter I will take it and after the battle mail it for you."*[10]

On July 5, 1863, Foster wrote a letter to *The Liberator* and described the regiment's experience at Gettysburg:

> *I took my pen to give my friends, through your paper, some idea of what we have been doing for the last month. We left our camp near Aquia Creek at 5 P. M. the 6th of June, and marched all night. We went in the fight at Beverly's Ford, and the 33d regiment, which had been chosen by Gen. Howard from the 11th corps, for that expedition, behaved most nobly under a severe fire. After that battle, we were joined by the whole army of the Potomac, and then commenced a march which has rarely, if ever, been equalled in the movement of a large army. Through intense heat and blinding dust for the first few days, then through rain and mud, and wet to the skin, loaded with bed and board and ammunition, the army marched from twenty-five to thirty miles per day. It was often past midnight before we lay down, and then we would start at daylight.*

This view from the crest of East Cemetery Hill shows the fields over which the Confederates attacked in the evening of July 2. The 33rd Massachusetts was positioned behind a stone wall at the base of the hill and poured a devastating fire into the flanks of the attacking lines. (Library of Congress)

We had, at one time, over a hundred men who had fallen out from sheer exhaustion by the wayside, with a permit from the surgeon. They would rest, and then push on, and when we finally stood in position on the battle-field, our men were all on hand, save about a dozen, who came up afterwards. We marched three hours through a heavy rain and swamping mud, without a rest, as fast as we could hurry on, to get upon the field in time for the fight, after the booming of cannon was first heard.

We did not get in a moment too soon. It was the 11th corps, too, let it be remembered, which came up in time to turn the tide, when defeat was apparently inevitable. Gen. Howard chose the position and placed his men in line where the great battle of this war has been fought. As the other corps came pressing in, they took their positions. Our artillery was massed in splendid positions, and the line of battle promptly formed. The rebels were present in full force, with a hundred and sixty cannon. These they got into position, and on Thursday afternoon, the artillery opened with shell, solid shot, and grape and canister. Our regiment lay near the battery, about the centre of the line of battle, exposed to a cross fire from two powerful batteries of the enemy. The shelling continued three hours. Our oldest artillery men say it was as hot a fire as they ever saw. It was a fearful ordeal, but our boys stood it without flinching. The rebels made their first charge on the left. They fought desperately, but in vain. Our soldiers hurled them back, and inflicted fearful loss on them.

Just at dark, Jackson's old corps, under Ewell, charged with fierce impetuosity upon our right. Prisoners taken in that charge say that Ewell came on in hot haste, with full confidence of piercing our line. He made three separate charges before he gave it up, the last one directly into the face of the 33d, as we lay behind a stone wall. But all in vain. Our batteries played on his columns with terrific effect, and when the head of his column came within range of our rifles, an incessant storm of bullets was poured into it. The column reached the wall, and a few men tried to break through, but were bayonetted on the spot. Then, with a wild yell of despair, the enemy broke and fled to the cover of the woods. The first day's work was over, and well done.

At daylight the next morning, the cannonading opened again. The rebels had their guns all in position. The prisoners had assured us that Lee would make every possible effort to cut our lines. The cannonading and infantry firing lasted without cessation for eight hours, when the rebels stopped from sheer exhaustion. They made a later and final effort,–a despairing but desperate charge on the left. They only dashed themselves to pieces in vain.

I never saw men fight with more enthusiasm than our whole army has done all through this terrific battle or series of battles. As the men got out of cartridges, they would rush eagerly to the point of supply for more, and hurry back to the fearful conflict. Indeed, they were animated with a spirit which made victory certain.

We have met the enemy and conquered them. The 11th army corps fought as well as men ever did or could; just as they had done before under Sigel, and as they will do again under anybody who leads them as well as Howard has done this time. We have lost in killed and wounded, out of the 33d, between thirty and forty men. What our whole loss is I cannot say. You will know that and the loss of the enemy before this reaches you.

In helping off wounded men from the field, we took the rebels and cared for them as for our own men. I talked with men who declared that they were forced into the fight, and had no heart in it–that they still loved the old flag. From all I can learn, I am satisfied the Southern masses are ready to yield. Let slavery be ended, and we shall become one people, the freest and happiest in the world. Before this comes to hand, I hope you will hear of the utter rout and dispersion of Lee's army. The Lord hath prepared His throne in the heavens, and His kingdom ruleth over all.[11]

One month later, Foster wrote another letter to *The Liberator* in which he expressed his admiration for U.S. Colored Troops who were fighting for the Union:

As I read with a thrilling heart of their noble daring and heroic achievements, I deeply regret that I am not associated with them in their grand work.[12]

His regret was short-lived: He resigned as chaplain of the 33rd on November 16, 1863, to accept a position as captain of Company B in the 3rd North Carolina Colored Infantry, soon renamed as the 37th Regiment of U.S. Colored Troops. In the fall of 1864,

Foster's company was about 10 miles outside of Richmond at a place called Chapin's Bluff. On September 30, his company was sent forward to test the enemy lines but when the retreat was sounded some of his men were too far forward to hear it. Foster jumped on his horse and rode forward to bring his men back. As he approached the enemy lines he was shot in his left side, just above the hip. He managed to stay on his horse and return to the Union lines, where his men took him down and laid him on the ground. He asked them to turn him around, as he had vowed that he would die facing the enemy. He died a few moments later. His men and fellow officers raised enough money to have his body sent back to his wife Dora.[13]

Daniel Foster is buried in Merrimack Cemetery in West Newbury, Massachusetts. His gravestone includes plaque that reads, *"Greatly beloved and respected by the Officers of the Reg. and by his own men. Friend of the poor and needy. 'Inasmuch as ye have done it unto one of the least of these my brethren, ye have done it unto me.'"*[14]

In the fall of 1864, Daniel Foster was killed in action near Chapin's Bluff, Virginia (pictured) while serving as a captain in the 37th Regiment of US Colored Troops. (Library of Congress)

Capt. Daniel Foster's name is included on a bronze plaque on the Soldier's Monument in Concord, Massachusetts, as one of those who "died for their country in the War of the Rebellion." (Kimball Union Archives)

THIRD DIVISION:

Major General Carl Schurz / Brigadier General Alexander Schimmelfennig

First Brigade:

Brigadier General Alexander Schimmelfennig / Colonel George von Amsberg

The first brigade of the Third Division was commanded by Brig. Gen. Alexander Schimmelfennig, but when General Reynolds was killed General Howard took command of the left wing, Maj. Gen. Carl Schurz moved up to command the corps, and Schimmelfennig took over the division. This left Col. George von Amsberg leading the brigade, which arrived on the field before Barlow's First Division. When the brigade reached Gettysburg, Howard ordered it to occupy Oak Hill on the north side of the town, but Confederates had already taken position on the hill, so Schimmelfennig ordered his division to extend the line of the First Corps near the Mummasburg Road; however, enemy artillery fire prevented them from connecting with the First Corps, and they instead took positions north of the road. Colonel von Amsberg's brigade was attacked along with the rest of the Eleventh Corps line from the flank and front, and once the brigade to their left broke, von Amsberg's men had no choice but to retreat through the town, dodging enemy musket fire and losing many men as captives to the pursuing Confederates. Once on Cemetery Hill, they assumed a position on the northwest corner behind a stone fence.

On July 2, just before Confederates launched their attack on East Cemetery Hill, four of von Amsberg's regiments were sent to Culp's Hill to assist the one brigade of Twelfth Corps troops that was defending the upper portion of the hill. They remained there during the night, and sometime the next morning they rejoined their Eleventh Corps comrades on Cemetery Hill, where they suffered under Confederate artillery fire on July 3, then joined the march toward Emmitsburg on July 5.

When General Howard once again assumed command of the Eleventh Corps, Schurz moved back to division command. However, during the retreat, Schimmelfennig had been caught for three days behind enemy lines and von Amsberg retained command of the brigade.

Only two regiments, the 82nd Illinois and the 157th New York, had chaplains on their staff and only one wrote about his experiences during the campaign. The other three regiments, the 45th New York, 61st Ohio, and 74th Pennsylvania, had no chaplains.

Ova Hoyt Seymour, 157th New York Infantry

Ova Hoyt Seymour, who preferred the moniker O. H. Seymour, was born on September 14, 1826, in Syracuse, New York. He received degrees from Michigan University and Union Theological Seminary and accepted a position as pastor of the Presbyterian Church in Cortland, New York, in January 1858. Mary L. Blodgett became his wife in late 1857, but after bearing a son, she died in 1862. Seymour left his ministry to enlist as chaplain of the 157th New York Infantry and was mustered in on March 7, 1863.

Seymour was not with his regiment at Gettysburg because he had become severely ill in early June, although he joined them on July 10 during the pursuit of the Confederate army. In letters he wrote to his family between June and early August (which included many misspellings and abbreviations), he described the heartache of not being with his men. On June 5, the last day of a furlough he had been granted, he reported from the Officer's Hospital near Camack's Woods in Philadelphia, where he had gone to visit some sick men and fell ill with dysentery and a high fever. Five days later, he was doing better but still in the hospital, and he indicated that the soldiers and hospital personnel were feeling anxious but hoping that Hooker would not let Lee rest. Seymour was still recuperating on June 21 when he wrote,

> *I may start for Va tomorrow night, & find my Regt if I can. I am very sorry to be away from them just now for I don't want the boys to get an impression that I want to escape marching and battle etc. I had rather be absent from them when all is quiet. And I am getting homesick to see them all.*[15]

On July 5, Seymour made it as far as Frederick, Maryland, where he wrote to his brother:

> *I must go on tomorrow if at all consistent, for I ought to be with the Regt. It has Suffered sadly I fear, & as I cannot hear direct from it, I want very much to be there & help in some way. The 11th Corps*

has now fully redeemed itself. It fought to the death, & our Regt was placed in a place of great responsibility. You cannot tell how much I desire to be with them. It is my present home & we like to be at home when there is trouble there & we can aid.

This city is a Sort of Depot of Supplies. Has about 8000 inhabitants, union & rebel. Our Flags were thick from the windows yesterday & the boys enjoyed the day. The city is very full of troops. Thousands of Cavalry have been here today, they came last night & go tonight it is said to cut off Lee's retreat. May he be kept this side of the Po[tomac] till he is ruined, & there is real danger to him. His position at one point (Falling waters) was destroyed yesterday.

Yesterday a few rebel cavalry came near here & caused a great fight. I think the majority would prefer our occupation of the city.[16]

The chaplain finally rejoined his regiment on July 10 near Sharpsburg after an arduous two-day journey from Fredrick by ambulance, mule train, and foot. He reported that he slept one night near South Mountain, then

started out on foot & walked over the mountain & on beyond Boonsboro a little ways where I had the happiness of finding my Regt. and yet it was a sad happiness, so decimated, not a Capt. present, Lieut. Col. killed & hundreds of our poor boys gone. But many will report before long we hope.

We have marched a few miles today. We have heard our guns in front. We may have a battle tomorrow. Great confidence in Genl. Mead. May the Lord keep him & us all & our cause.[17]

Seymour wrote again on July 22 from the Army's camp near Goose Creek, Virginia:

We arrived here night before last & do not move today I conclude. We enjoy the rest wonderfully. After an army has march from Falmouth to Gettysburg & there fought one of the most terrible battles on recent, then chased the enemy to the river, & then followed him back as far as here, you can well imagine that the great cry is for rest.

No one can be more disappointed than we at the escape of Lee. Burnside & Hooker escaped from Lee & he was greatly chagrined at it and so he escaped from McClellan & from Meade. Such things will occur. Some newspaper reporters are a worse scourge than the locusts of Egypt. They tell you Lee is cornered, has no boats, the river is so high that pontoons cannot live on it &c. &c. The most of Lee's men actually waded the river just above Williamsport. I [went] down to the town & to the river. A miserable village. We supposed we were to pursue him at once, & our counter marches looked like it, till now we are resting. The men want clothes & shoes & money. Where our Cavalry are I do not know. Moseby's Cavalry are near us & captured some of our sutlers & stragglers yesterday & we captured some of them.[18]

In mid-July, Seymour wrote a letter to a newspaper back home to defend his beloved Eleventh Corps: *"If the 11th corps lost any renown at Chancellorsville, it won more than it ever had, at Gettysburg. But the 11th corps has been meanly belied by interested parties. It did just what any other corps would have done under similar circumstances."*[19]

After mustering out with the regiment on July 10, 1865, Seymour returned to New York and held pastorates at the churches in Hammondsport, Trumansburg, Port Byron, and Onondaga Valley. He married Harriet Hoes in 1866, and they had two daughters. In 1875, he was elected as a commissioner to Auburn Theological Seminary. He died at the age of sixty-nine at his home in Onondaga Valley on September 8, 1889, and is buried in Cortland Rural Cemetery.

Second Brigade:
Colonel Col. Wladimir Krzyzanowski

Col. Wladimir Krzyzanowski's brigade followed the first brigade of the division through Gettysburg on July 1 and took a position in reserve, just north of the town. When Barlow's men on the knoll came under attack, General Schurz sent Krzyzanowski's brigade out to support Barlow's left flank. They fought in close contact with two brigades of Georgian troops, but were soon overwhelmed by the Confederate assault and joined their comrades in retreat. The brigade was the last to enter Gettysburg and was the last of their corps to leave the field of battle on July 1. They rallied behind von Amsberg's men on the western side of Cemetery Hill.

July 2 exposed them to almost continuous sniper fire from enemy troops hidden in some buildings in town and from artillery fire from Seminary Ridge. At least one of the regiments in the brigade assisted in repulsing the Confederate attack against East Cemetery Hill that evening. Early on July 3, some soldiers were sent to clear out some houses on Baltimore Street that harbored enemy snipers. That afternoon, they were exposed to and lost a few men to the cannonade preceding the Pickett-Pettigrew-Trimble charge, but otherwise, their activity in the battle had come to an end. They left Gettysburg with the rest of their corps on July 5.

The brigade included five regiments: the 58th and 119th New York, 75th Pennsylvania, 26th Wisconsin, and 82nd Ohio. Three of them were accompanied into the battle by chaplains, none of whom left a record of their experiences.

Chapter 8:

The Twelfth Corps

CORPS COMMANDERS:

Major General Henry Slocum
Brigadier General Alpheus Williams

The Twelfth Corps crossed into Pennsylvania on the morning of June 30 and spent the night near Littlestown, about ten miles southeast of Gettysburg. The next morning, the corps marched up the Baltimore Pike and stopped near Two Taverns around noon, despite a plea for assistance from Maj. Gen. Oliver Otis Howard, then in command of the field. Maj. Gen. Henry Slocum, who believed he was the commander of the "right wing" of the army, has been criticized for not moving more quickly toward the sound of the guns.[1] The corps finally marched the remaining five miles and arrived on the field around 4:00 p.m., too late to assist the First and Eleventh Corps. Slocum had been directed to send one of his divisions to the right and the other to the left. The division under Brig. Gen. Alpheus Williams had planned to attack the Confederate left near Benner's Hill but was ordered back once it was learned that the Eleventh Corps had retreated. Williams led his troops to a bivouac near Wolf's Hill. Slocum's other division, under Brig. Gen. John Geary, was sent by General Hancock, who had arrived on the field by this time, to the far left of the Union line, near the Round Tops.

Early on July 2, Williams, commanding the corps while Slocum exercised command of the right wing of the army, received orders to move both divisions to Culp's Hill. Joining with the right of Wadsworth's division that was in line on the western slope of the hill, the Twelfth Corps formed a line along the eastern slope from the crest of the upper hill to near the base of the lower hill. At the suggestion of Brig. Gen. George Sears Greene, the men spent most of the day building formidable breastworks along the line. Toward evening, all but Greene's brigade was sent off the hill to support the Union left, leaving Greene's men to defend against attacks later that evening. When the corps returned to the hill that night, they found their works occupied by Confederate forces and waited until morning to reclaim their positions. Remaining on Culp's Hill on July 4, they joined the army in its pursuit of Lee's army the next day.

FIRST DIVISION:

Brigadier General Alpheus Williams / Brigadier General Thomas Ruger

First Brigade:

Colonel Archibald McDougall

When the First Division arrived on the field on July 1, the men were given time to rest and have breakfast the next morning. Midmorning, they moved to Culp's Hill and took a position to the right of Geary's division and joined the rest of the corps in felling trees and building sturdy works. Around 6:00 p.m., they were ordered to support the Union left against Longstreet's assault. But by the time they arrived, the Confederate attack had already been stalled and pushed back, so Col. Archibald McDougall's men were ordered back to Culp's Hill. They learned that their works had been appropriated by Confederates, and when some soldiers were sent forward as skirmishers to probe the enemy position, a few got too close and were captured. The rest of the brigade pulled back to a field near the Baltimore Pike, where the men rested on their arms.

Early on July 3, Union artillery opened on the Confederates on the eastern side of Culp's Hill, during which some soldiers in McDougall's brigade were killed or wounded. This barrage kicked off a long struggle for the Union soldiers that lasted the rest of the morning as they sought to push the enemy off the hill once and for all. Finally, by about 11:00 a.m., the works were retaken and the longest sustained fight of the three days came to an end.

When the Confederate artillery barrage began that afternoon, the men suffered as some shot and shells fell among them on the hill. The brigade was once again ordered to support the Union line, this time near the center, but after waiting in reserve behind the Second Corps, they were ordered back to the hill because the Pickett-Pettigrew-Trimble charge had been repulsed. One regiment, the 5th Connecticut Infantry, was ordered out the Hanover Road to support the Union cavalry in its fight against Maj. Gen. J. E. B. Stuart's rebel troopers.

On July 4, three regiments were sent on a reconnaissance around the town. After marching eight miles, they saw no enemy, then returned to Culp's to help bury the dead and collect arms and other equipment that was strewn across the slopes of the hill. On July 5, the regiments joined the rest of the corps as it started after the retreating Confederates.

McDougall commanded six regiments: the 3rd Maryland, 5th and 20th Connecticut, 123rd and 145th New York, and 46th Pennsylvania. Only two chaplains, in the 5th and 123rd, were present with their regiments. Neither left a written record, but one had an experience during the battle that is worth telling.

Moses Cook Welch, 5th Connecticut Infantry

Moses Cook Welch was born in Mansfield, Connecticut on July 31, 1827, and was named after his grandfather, who served in the Revolutionary War and the War of 1812. He received degrees from Yale College in 1850 and Yale Divinity School in 1853. After working as a tutor at Yale, he moved to Kansas in 1856 to serve a Congregational colony at Waubonsee. When the war broke out, he enlisted on June 26, 1861, as a private in Company B of the 2nd Kansas Infantry, a three-month regiment. He served with Brig. Gen. Nathaniel Lyon's brigade in Missouri but fell ill near the end of his term and was mustered out on October 31, 1861. He returned to Connecticut to recuperate, and when he was well enough he enlisted in the 5th Connecticut Infantry on October 16, 1862. But because he was not yet ordained, he could not yet be commissioned as chaplain. So, in November 1862, he received his ordination at the Congregational Church at Wethersfield, Connecticut, one of the oldest congregations in the country, dating from 1635.

Although Welch left no record of his time with the regiment, he had an interesting experience at Gettysburg. The chaplain was not one to stay in the rear during a battle, as noted by Sgt. Harlan P. Rugg of

Company I in a diary entry on July 2, 1863: *"Chaplain goes with us everywhere."*[2] And Col. Warren W. Packer praised his chaplain in a report to the governor of Connecticut:

> *I cannot conclude this report without calling your especial attention to the conduct and good deeds of the esteemed chaplain of this regiment, Rev. M. C. Welch, who, totally regardless of self or personal safety, was invariably found in the front, whenever the regiment or any portion of it occupied a position of danger or responsibility, encouraging the men by his presence, [and] doing all in his power to relieve the wounded.*[3]

Welch's tendency to be near the front with his men proved to be dangerous at Gettysburg. When the regiment was returning to Culp's Hill late in the evening of July 2, they did not realize that their former position behind the breastworks on the lower hill had been occupied in their absence by Confederate soldiers. As Colonel Packer noted in his diary, *"Chaplain Welch and others in advance [were] taken prisoners. We did not attempt to regain them but remained in bivouac [just west of Spangler's Spring] all night under a heavy picket fire."*[4]

Packer noted that he had sent fourteen volunteers to reconnoiter the breastworks, and five enlisted men plus their chaplain were captured. Welch either escaped his captors (as per his colonel's report) or was released on account of his status as a noncombatant, and he returned unscathed to his regiment by July 4. It seems the other five captives were quickly paroled and all six were saved a trip to Libby Prison in Richmond.

The 5th Connecticut was in bivouac near Spangler's Spring on Culp's Hill the night of July 2. (New York Public Library Digital Collections)

Welch remained with the regiment until illness forced him to resign on July 5, 1864. He married Sarah Dwight Mills on September 15, 1864, with whom he had three children, then entered the service of the U.S. Christian Commission in Nashville, Tennessee, for several months. Returning to Connecticut, he pastored the Congregational Church in Mansfield, following the path of his father and grandfather who had served the church for a total of almost fifty years. After ten years in Mansfield, he moved to Pomona, Florida, and organized a new church, which he served for nearly thirty years. He also served as chaplain for the local GAR post. After retiring from the ministry, he moved back to Windsor, Connecticut, where he died on April 7, 1913. He is buried in the Palisado Cemetery in Windsor.

Second Brigade: Brigadier General Henry Lockwood

Brig. Gen. Henry Lockwood commanded a brigade of three regiments, none of which had been in battle before Gettysburg. Because of seniority, Lockwood was placed in "independent command," although his brigade was assigned to the First Division of the Twelfth Corps. Two of his regiments joined the corps on Culp's Hill when they arrived on the field on July 2 (the third was still marching toward Gettysburg). When they were sent with the rest of the corps late that afternoon in support of the Third Corps, they found themselves facing the hard-hitting Mississippians who had broken through the Union line along the Emmitsburg Road. Lockwood first ordered his men into line of battle to the left of Col. George Willard's Second Corps brigade, then ordered them to fix bayonets and charge. They helped push the Confederate tide back (although some reports have the enemy already in retreat by the time Lockwood's men began their charge), and recovered and pulled off three Union guns that had been overrun near the Trostle Farm. By about 9:00 p.m., the brigade was ordered back to Culp's Hill, but stopped along the Baltimore Pike to support two Union batteries.

The third regiment arrived early on July 3, and each of the regiments played a role in pushing the Confederates off the hill, performing admirably for troops that had never been in battle. They accompanied McDougall's brigade in support of the Union center that afternoon but did not take part in the defense. After spending July 4 helping to bury the dead and manning rifle pits, the brigade marched off to Littlestown on July 5 as the Army of the Potomac left Gettysburg.

The brigade included the First Maryland Potomac Home, First Maryland Eastern Shore, and 150th New York regiments. The latter two had chaplains with them, but only one wrote about the Battle of Gettysburg.

Thomas Edwin Vassar, 150th New York Infantry

Chaplain Thomas Vassar of the 150th New York Infantry. (courtesy of Jeff Donaldson)

Thomas Edwin Vassar was born in Poughkeepsie, New York, on December 3, 1834, into a well-known family that included a relative who founded Vassar College in 1861. After working as a dentist for a while, Thomas entered the ministry and was ordained in 1857 as a Baptist pastor even though he received his theological education under a private tutor and not in a seminary. He married Tamma Guernsey Sackett in October 1861; four of their children survived to adulthood. While Vassar was serving the Baptist Church in Amenia, New York, his congregation granted him a one-year leave of absence so he could serve as chaplain for the 150th New York Infantry; he was mustered in on October 11, 1862. His younger brother James also enlisted, and because he was musically inclined he was detailed to serve as leader of the regimental band, a position he held until the 150th mustered out at the close of the war.

Vassar left a large corpus of letters, articles, a diary, and a chapter in the regimental history in which he described his year of service with the regiment. Because the 150th had been on garrison duty outside Baltimore, the call to join the Army of the Potomac on the way to Gettysburg was the soldiers' introduction to the rigors of being on campaign. On June 26, 1863, Vassar wrote in his diary: *"Marched through rain and mud, [the] distance said to be twenty-seven miles. I never saw men so exhausted, and at intervals I put several of them on my horse and walked by the side. When shoes and stockings were pulled off at night I saw great strips and patches of skin come off the feet."*[5]

From July 1 to 3, his diary recorded the regiment's experience at Gettysburg:

> *Wednesday, July 1st–Made sixteen miles and got within eight miles of Gettysburg. As we were lying down for the night orders came to move at midnight.*

> *An hour or more after midnight we fell into line, and silently as a company of shadows the men got into their places, with not a joke, not a laugh, and not a snatch of song. Word reached us that the fight had begun, that General Reynolds had been killed, our forces worsted, and that the whole Army of the Potomac was hurrying to the field.*
>
> *Thursday, July 2nd–Halted near Round Top, and Little Round Top, at sunrise, meeting loads of half-crazed women and children escaping from their homes. We did not get into the battle until afternoon, when we were ordered to the support of the 3rd Corps, which was hard pushed.*
>
> *Little Round Top was very quiet when we passed it in the early morning, but before sundown it belched flame like a veritable volcano. Let me mention one humorous occurrence just here. Sometime in the early hours of the day, and before the action had become general, I was lying with the regiment in a wheat field. The grain had been cut, and with some of the sheaves for pillows we were talking or drowsing. All of a sudden there came screeching over our heads a shell that buried itself a rod or two away, and sent up earth and stone like a water-spout.*
>
> *It was the enemy's salute to the 150th, and in its immediate vicinity there was such an exhibition of fluttering coat-tails as is rarely witnessed. It might be a bit of exaggeration to say that we made a quarter of a mile in a single minute, but the action was surely swift. We got more used to that sort of thing before night.*
>
> *Friday, July 3rd–Got into battle early. I helped our surgeons to care for the wounded in an old stone barn on the Baltimore pike, and kept at it until night.*[6]

In the regimental history, Vassar shared some painful memories of that one great battle to which he was a witness. Late on July 2, the 150th had been sent forward to recover some cannon that had been overrun in the afternoon's Confederate assault.[7] The chaplain described his experience:

> *We were pushing over ground littered with the wounded, the dying and the dead, and my horse, not yet become accustomed to such sights, stopped short. Dismounting I tied him to a tree, proposing to follow on foot. Hardly was I out of the saddle than those nearest me, who were least injured, began their pitiful cries for help. "Water! Water!*

Chaplain; for God's sake!" This was the cry on every side. Seeing a small house a fourth of a mile away I ran toward it, hoping to fill a few canteens and furnish some relief. I found a well there, but it was absolutely surrounded with wounded men, some of whom must evidently have crawled thither on their hands and knees. Some that could stand had so drained the well that what now came up was so thickened with mud as to be of the consistency of cream; but even these nauseous driblets were clamored for with passionate agony.

I stood beside that same well in the summer of 1902 when Nature all around was robed in her fairest hues and forms, and very vividly stood out that summer night of thirty-nine years earlier, when the heavens were lit with trailing fire, the soil around drenched with blood, and the air rent with shrieks and groans.[8]

While trying to find water for the wounded, Vassar became separated from his regiment, and he did not find them again until midnight, when they were resting along the Baltimore Pike at the far right of the army.

The pastoral heart of a chaplain came through in his account of late afternoon on July 4. Some men of the regiment came to him,

saying that they had found a dead soldier near a fence between Culp's Hill and the Baltimore Pike, and did not know whether he was a member of our regiment or not. He was lying there all by himself, and they wished me to go and see him. Some thoughtful survivor had drawn a covering over the dead man's face to protect it from discoloration under the hot summer sun. Turning the covering down we looked on a countenance utterly unknown, but singularly impressive in all its lines. Death had not marred a feature; if carved in marble they could hardly have been more fair. It was the expression on the face however that fixed all our eyes. It was not triumph; that could be seen on other brows. It was not peace; one often sees that when death has done its work. There was no trace of earthly passion in the half-closed eyes, but there was such a smile as one would imagine might have been caught if a glimpse of some thing bright on beyond had gleamed on the dying vision as mortality was swallowed up in life.

Perhaps it is mere conjecture on my part, but I believed then, and I believe now, that our fellow-soldier glimpsed an opening heaven when his call came. Some will declare this all imagination, but those who stood over the dead man that Independence Day saw a look that was not of earth. Why should anyone who has faith in immortality question my interpretation of this expression?[9]

Later that same evening, Vassar walked along the lines where his regiment had fought the day before and recalled,

> *I found that our regimental dead, and twice as many more of our brigade, yet lay unburied. I had gathered them up and labelled them early in the day. On reporting this to General Lockwood he gave me a detail of twenty-one men, with a request that I would superintend the interment. After a long hunt for picks and shovels we got at the job. The graves were dug in a bit of thinly-wooded ground, not far, I think, from where our regimental monument now stands. I am not positive as to the precise location, for in none of my later visits to Gettysburg have I been able to fix upon the spot. It was so dark that we required light to do the work, and there was no way of getting it excepting by building a fire out of the dead twigs and branches; but the blaze drew on us an occasional shot from Confederate sharpshooters.*
>
> *The gruesome and somewhat dangerous task was not finished until midnight. As the bodies had been lying out in the fierce summer heat from twenty-four to forty-eight hours their condition can be imagined; It need not be described. When these and other bodies were removed to the National Cemetery the autumn following but two of the regimental dead that we buried were missing, and the head-board inscriptions I had so hastily penciled were all distinct enough to read. I lay down that night between two dying men, so utterly fagged out that I could hardly have tramped a mile further.*[10]

In addition to keeping a diary, Vassar wrote to newspapers in Dutchess County. On July 9, he sent a lengthy and descriptive letter to the *Amenia Times*, in which he recounted both the regiment's march to and action at Gettysburg:

> *When one is on the march from dawn to darkness he feels decidedly more inclined to slumber than to write, but now while we are halting on a hillside for dinner, I place a sheet upon my knee to jot down some incidents of the eventful two weeks past, persuaded that though they may come a little behind time to some they will be welcome still.*

Monday morning [June 29] early orders came attaching us to the 12th army corps, and bidding us go on to join it. A few hours after we caught up, and on Thursday morning came in sight of Gettysburgh [sic]. Again and again while on the route I wished that those at home who complain of the slowness with which the army moves could look on and see what moving the army really means. Not one person in a thousand at the north has the slightest conception of the magnitude of the work. Ambulances, provision trains, artillery, caissons, ammunition wagons, horses, men, all to be pushed along together, is an undertaking of no ordinary kind. Of course the highways will not give space sufficient for this moving throng, and roads are speedily made through meadows and fields of wheat and corn along which the hosts surge.

But let us come to Gettysburg. It is a pleasant little village of eight thousand [sic] inhabitants, lying among Pennsylvania hills. Approaching it from the south there is quite an elevation to ascend. Off to the north, the east, and west, stretch heavy pieces of timber, in which the rebels at the time of our arrival chiefly laid. The northern part of the town they also held, while the other side we yet kept. We found pretty heavy skirmishing going on, but the general engagement for that day had not begun. The corps of which the 150th is a part was ordered to hold itself as a reserve. From the cemetery at the top of the hill I witnessed the skirmishing for two hours, till the balls of the rebel sharpshooters commencing to fly unpleasantly thick there, I returned to our camp. Toward the latter part of the afternoon the corps was called out to reinforce Gen. Sedgwick on the left of the line, a most furious engagement having there set in. The response was prompt. It was sundown, however, by the time our line of battle was formed. A perfect shower of shells fell all around as through the twilight woods our regiment pushed up. Steadily they advanced, the rebels faltered and fell back. For a mile we drove the fugitives, and then it being too late further to continue the chase, one of our companies laid hold upon four guns which had been captured from us during the day, and brought them off. None that night were hurt.

As I went over the dusky, blood-stained field, sad was the sight and sadder still the sounds. Again and again I was stopped by men writhing in their last great agony, and besought in God's name to do something for them if it was only to bring a draught of water. But even dying men I was compeled [sic] to turn away from, only able to promise that ambulances would soon be brought.

Our wearied men having regained their camp slept upon their arms. At two o'clock we were aroused. The rebels had massed in the woods upon the left. Soon after daylight we were called to support a battery for two hours, and after this ordered into the rifle pits. I went down with the men. In the edge of a heavy piece of woods breastworks built of fallen trees had been thrown up for more than a mile, and in front of these the Confederate forces laid with sharpshooters posted in the thick trees. To the place assigned them our men marched with three rousing cheers. Minnie balls buzzed around us like a swarm of bees. Soon after the commencement of the firing I retired, conscious that my services would be needed elsewhere, and in a large stone barn near the field which was used as a temporary hospital waited the bringing of the wounded in.

The uniform testimony of those who witnessed the fight is that the Dutchess regiment deported itself nobly–so nobly as to earn the warmest commendations from officers whose opinions are regarded as of the highest worth. Twice for more than two hours each time it stood without flinching under the hottest fire, and from the number of dead gathered up opposite that point on the following morning, there is reason to believe that they left their mark. It was not long before the services of the attending surgeons were in demand. Our band had been detailed as an ambulance corps and upon stretchers soon began to bring the victims in–some rebels, some Union boys. After being temporarily attended to, they were placed in ambulances and carried to the hospitals of the different corps.

Soon after noon the rebels began to shell the rifle pits where our men laid, and the batteries nearer to the left. Two of the batteries were near the barn where we were receiving the wounded, and of course the missiles of death fell round us a perfect storm. Two burst within six or eight feet of me. Language is powerless to describe the fury of this cannonade. One hundred pieces were playing without intermission for hours till the solid earth seemed to shake. But vain were the rebels most desperate attempts. Nowhere could they break our lines, and by night they had fallen back at every point, thousands being taken prisoners, among them a small detachment which surrendered to our own boys. The rebel wounded with whom I had anything to do all admitted heavy losses. Several of them were officers, gentlemanly in their manners, and very grateful for every attention shown.

On Saturday morning I went over the battlefield gathering up and labeling the dead of our own regiment, and looking at the same time upon the slain on the other side. Few if any of their dead had been removed, and at points it would hardly be exaggerating to say that the ground was covered. That portion of the field over which I passed certainly had five rebel dead to one of our own. The scene was too sickening to describe–its memory will remain with me forever. Enough to say that bodies mangled, swollen, discolored and horribly offensive littered that beautiful forest from end to end. Saturday night, at the request of our Brigadier-General, I superintended the burial of the dead of the 150th. Close by the edge of the woods we dug their graves. The flicker of the dying camp fires streamed up amid the deep darkness as we wrapped around our heroes their blankets for a winding sheet, and silently laid back earth to earth, ashes to ashes, and dust to dust.

Sunday morning I had commenced looking up the wounded at the general hospital, when I received orders to rejoin the regiment at once, as it was about to leave. Since then we have constantly been upon the march, attempting to intercept Lee, and are now said to be within six or eight miles of a portion of his army. Our men, though tired, are in good spirits, and ready again to meet the enemy at five minutes notice.

O, if this impending battle might but be the final blow, what thanksgivings would go up from the land–aye, and from the hearts of homesick, weary soldiers too. While the army is willing to keep at its work till that work is done, I suspect there are few in it but would leap up for gladness could they hear their country say, "you are no longer needed, strife is over, soldier, go home."[11]

Two weeks later, Vassar wrote another letter from Sandy Hook, Maryland, to report on the failure of the army to capture the Confederates before they crossed the Potomac:

Though weary, there was on the part of the Union forces a universal desire for a fight, with a confident expectation of being able to finish up, on the banks of the Potomac, what had been begun ten days previously among the hills of Pennsylvania. Anxiously we waited orders for the attack to begin. Toward night, however, instead of moving upon the foe, the command was given to commence throwing up breastworks; and all day Monday the great army was kept thus engaged. Soldiers could see no reason for this, but supposed that their officers could, and so of course pushed the job along; and, while thus employed, Lee quietly moved his frightened men safely across the river, the last going over as the light of Tuesday morning dawned.

By noon the report became generally that the prey, which seemed within our grasp had effected an escape. Never have I witnessed manifestations of deeper disappointment or burning rage. That army which had so often defeated, baffled or eluded us, but of whose destruction we had been all but sure, had again slipped away when its overthrow seemed ordained.

Wednesday morning we started upon the track of the runaways. Terrible was the trail which they had left. In the barns lay unburied putrefying dead. By the road side used up horses were scattered all along. Growing crops were trampled flat, fences stripped away, houses pillaged, stables and stalls and poultry yards left empty–ruin on every side.[12]

Chaplain Vassar is the only chaplain named on a regimental monument at Gettysburg. The monument to the 150th New York sits near the top of Culp's Hill. (Author's collection)

When the Eleventh and Twelfth Corps were sent to the west after Gettysburg, Vassar resigned due to poor health on August 8 and returned to his church in Amenia. Over the next four decades he served churches in Lynn, Massachusetts; Flemington and Newark, New Jersey; and Kansas City, Missouri. Madison (present Colgate) University conferred on him the honorary degree of Doctor of Divinity in 1882. After he retired from ministry, he made himself available as "supply" preacher for vacant pulpits, and was actively engaged in veteran gatherings. His lecture "The Battle of Gettysburg" won him fame throughout the states. He wrote a biography of his uncle John Ellison Vassar, a well-known evangelist who worked for the American Tract Society and often found himself within the lines of his nephews' regiment (see sidebar). Chaplain Vassar died on July 2, 1918, in Elizabeth, New Jersey, and is buried in Evergreen Cemetery in Hillside. The monument to the 150th New York on Culp's Hill at Gettysburg is the only regimental monument that includes the name of the chaplain who shared in the trials of the battle.

John Vassar, the uncle of Chaplain Vassar, was known by his many friends as "Uncle John." He worked for the American Tract Society distributing books and Bibles to men in the army. Joining his nephew and other friends of the 150th in late June 1863, he marched with them toward Gettysburg. Following the battle, he had a most interesting experience. When he became separated from Union troops, he was captured by Confederate troopers from J. E. B Stuart's cavalry. When he was brought to Stuart and questioned as a suspected spy, he repeatedly asked Stuart, "General, do you love Jesus?" Then,

> *The puzzled officer [Stuart] was relieved by the suggestion of those who had arrested Uncle John.*
>
> *"General," said they, "take the man's promise that he will not tell of our whereabouts for twenty-four hours, and let us see him out of our lines, or we will have a prayer-meeting from here to Richmond."*
>
> *And so it was decided. He made his way back into the Union lines, and was once more among friends.*[13]

John was unanimously elected to be regimental chaplain after Thomas Vassar resigned. But because he was not ordained, he could not officially serve in the capacity. After remaining in Gettysburg for two weeks to care for the wounded, he returned to his former occupation as "colporteur" (or distributing agent) for the Tract Society, although he did not see his Dutchess County soldier friends again until the war was over.

"Uncle" John Vassar delivered bibles and tracts to soldiers and was beloved by the men in the 150th New York Infantry. (*Uncle John Vassar* by T. E. Vassar)

Third Brigade:
Brigadier General Thomas Ruger / Colonel Silas Colgrove

Col. Silas Colgrove commanded the brigade of Brig. Gen. Thomas Ruger, who took over command of the division at Gettysburg. On July 2, they marched to Culp's Hill and formed the far right of the Union line, near the bottom of the lower hill and Rock Creek. When they were ordered to the Union left that afternoon, they waited to be sent into action, but only received orders to return to their earlier position. Colgrove cautiously sent skirmishers out, and they returned with twenty-three prisoners and confirmation that Confederates held the works, so the men spent the night in McAllister's Woods.

When fighting broke out the next morning, Colgrove's men did not charge the works as did their comrades in other brigades. Rather, they spent most of the morning firing in the direction of the enemy they couldn't see. But about midmorning, Colgrove received orders to send out skirmishers to probe the enemy strength, and then, if possible, launch a full-scale attack against the works. However, this order was somehow miscommunicated, and two regiments were immediately sent forward across an open meadow to storm a much larger foe secured behind the works. The result was swift and disastrous. The remnants of the two regiments returned to the safety of the woods, where they turned and successfully fought off a counterattack by some Virginians. The rest of the morning was spent suffering from sniper fire, and when the fighting ended by midday, one regiment was sent to occupy the now vacant breastworks. Another regiment was sent to support the cavalry out on the Hanover Road.

The brigade was ordered to make a reconnaissance on July 4 through and around Gettysburg. Only dead and wounded enemy soldiers were discovered. The brigade left Gettysburg on July 5 with the rest of the army.

Colgrove commanded five regiments. The 3rd Wisconsin and 27th Indiana regiments did not have chaplains, while the 13th New Jersey and 107th New York were accompanied by their chaplains. The chaplain of the 2nd Massachusetts was not with his regiment at Gettysburg, but he wrote the regimental history and composed letters regarding the battle that he did not personally witness.

Alonzo Hall Quint, 2nd Massachusetts Infantry

Alonzo Hall Quint was born in Barnstead, New Hampshire, on March 22, 1828. He graduated from Dartmouth College in 1846, intending to pursue a career in medicine, but enrolled in Andover Theological Seminary and received his divinity degree in 1852. The next year, he was ordained and began his ministry at the Mather Congregational Church in Jamaica Plain, Massachusetts. He also served as a member of the State Board of Education, the Massachusetts Historical Society, and the New England Historic Genealogical Society. Rebecca Page Putnam became his wife in 1854, and they had three children.

On June 20, 1861, after receiving a two-year leave of absence from his congregation, he was commissioned as chaplain for the 2nd Massachusetts Infantry and was quickly invited to be a war correspondent for the *Congregationalist* weekly paper. After he left the service, he compiled his letters to the paper, along with additional commentary, as *The Potomac and the Rapidan*. He also wrote the regimental history.

Just as the regiment was preparing to support the cavalry at Culpeper, Virginia, on June 6, Quint became seriously ill because of "exposure in the line of duty," and the regimental surgeons sent him home. He was not with his regiment at Gettysburg, much to his dismay. *"After a tedious illness and slow recovery, after losing the historical days of Gettysburg, after restlessly mourning over the gallant sufferers whom I could not see, and the gallant dead none shall see here,"* he returned to the regiment by the middle of August, although he never fully recovered from his illness.[14] His account of the Battle of Gettysburg in the regimental history is taken not from his own eyewitness experiences, but from a careful examination of *"the note-books of officers and enlisted men, [. . .] private letters, and letters in newspapers."*[15] His letters, however, demonstrate his attempts to learn about and comment on the battle from a more personal viewpoint. In a letter dated August 24, he reported, *"there are some things I want to write. Some work of our brigade and regiment at Gettysburg. I have picked up*

Chaplain Alonzo Hall Quint of the 2nd Massachusetts Infantry
(courtesy of Ron Coddington)

what ought to be chronicled; for when a regiment loses a hundred and thirty odd out of less than three hundred, and presses on and fights on without a wavering, it ought to be recorded."[16] The quotes that follow reveal what Quint had gleaned from his comrades and thought was most important to preserve for the sake of *"men to whom every date is a scene, and every name a comrade; for widows and orphans, and for childless parents."*[17]

> *On Thursday, the 2d, the line moved forward a short distance, found the enemy in force, withdrew, and the whole corps made a detour by the left, to hills near Rock Creek, and threw up intrenchments; the brigade was, about four P. M., ordered to the left of the whole line, but was sent back directly, and found the enemy in the works which General Geary had erected.*[18]
>
> *It was in obedience to the order to retake these works, about seven the next morning, that our regiment lost one hundred and twenty-six, killed and wounded, out of two hundred and ninety-four enlisted men, and ten officers out of twenty-two officers. Three color bearers were killed, and two wounded. Passing down a straight slope, across an open meadow, up to the edge of the other hill, in the face of a terrible fire, the men found some shelter behind works, and a portion of the front of the curving breastworks, still continuing the fire. But troops which should have supported on the right failed to do it, and the enemy were flanking the regiment in that direction, and after holding the position for some time, the general ordered it back to the place it had left. Need I say that no man flinched in the deadliest storm?*[19]

The 2nd Massachusetts Infantry made a deadly charge across Spangler's Meadow on July 3. Their regimental monument, the first to be erected on the field, is on the left. (*Historic Views of Gettysburg* by Robert Miller, 1906)

Following the battle, in late 1863, the regiment was sent west to join the Army of the Cumberland. During the Atlanta campaign the following spring, on the advice of the regimental surgeon, Quint was mustered out on May 25, 1864. He returned to Massachusetts and accepted a position with the North Congregational Church in New Bedford. Dartmouth College awarded him a Doctor of Divinity degree in 1866. In 1881, he served the Broadway Church in Somerville, and five years later, he was sent to pastor a new church at Allston. He was a member of the New Hampshire Legislature from 1881 to 1885, served as manager of the Congregational Publishing Society for twenty-one years, as a director of the American Congregational Association twenty-five years, and as secretary of the Massachusetts General Association twenty-five years. Quint was the first chaplain-in-chief of the GAR.

Quint died at the age of sixty-eight on November 4, 1896, of "neuralgia of the chest," and is buried in Pine Hill Cemetery in Dover, New Hampshire. His body was escorted first to the church and then to the cemetery by a large delegation from the GAR, many local political and religious leaders, and a cornet band.

SECOND DIVISION:

Major General John W. Geary

First Brigade:

Colonel Charles Candy

After reaching Gettysburg late on July 1, the brigade of Col. Charles Candy halted and spent the night just north of Little Round Top, with two regiments sent out on picket duty in the fields to the west. Early the next morning, the brigade joined the rest of its division on Culp's Hill and formed a line behind the other two divisions on the upper hill. Around 4:00 p.m., they marched off with the five other brigades to support the Union left. But because they left the hill after Colgrove's division, they missed a turn off the Baltimore Pike and continued marching south to Rock Creek, where they remained until about midnight. Then came a treacherous march in the dark and, reaching the area of the Spangler Farm along the Pike about 90 minutes later, they were allowed to grab whatever rest they could.

The next morning, two regiments were facing the Confederates across a small field, while the other three were in a hollow, ready to support General Greene's brigade when needed. Throughout the morning, these regiments were sent forward to relieve other units. One regiment was sent to the crest of the upper hill to form a line perpendicular and downslope of Greene's men, where they could pour a devastating flanking fire in the Confederates attacking up the hill. About 10:30 a.m., during the final Confederate attack of the morning, the two regiments on the brigade's right swept the enemy away as they rushed across the open field, later named "Pardee Field" in honor of one of the regimental commanders. Candy's regiments were sent to various locations on the hill throughout the rest of the day and into the night.

The men spent July 4 attending to the wounded, burying the dead, and collecting equipment, then left Gettysburg with the rest of the army on July 5.

The brigade included six regiments: the 5th, 7th, 29th, and 66th Ohio, and the 28th and 147th Pennsylvania. Only two of the Ohio regiments, the 29th and 66th, were accompanied by chaplains, with only one keeping a record of his experiences.

Lyman Daniel Ames, 29th Ohio Infantry

Lyman Daniel Ames was born in Royalton, Vermont, in 1813, one of nine children. We know little about his upbringing and education, but at some point, he was ordained in the Baptist Church (although some accounts list him as a minister in the Christian Church, or Disciples of Christ).[20] In 1842, Ames married Clara G. Carr, who gave birth to one son. Ames served churches in Vermont and New Hampshire, and when the war broke out, he was pastor of a congregation in Conneaut, Ohio. On February 18, 1863, he enlisted in the 29th Ohio Infantry.

Although Ames kept a diary throughout his time as chaplain, his entries for the Gettysburg campaign are sparse because he became very ill in late June. For ten days beginning on June 20, he rode in an ambulance that followed his corps on the march north, which bothered him greatly: *"I endure but do not enjoy this march. To enjoy, one wants to feel well and keep his place; to be able to do his duty."*[21] On July 1, he wrote, *"We move towards Gettysburg. Enemy in town in force. Fighting going on all day. Alarm among the people. Keep along with ambulance train but ride my own horse."*[22] The next morning, he *"found [the regiment] in line of battle ready for any call of duty. Fighting continued all day. Our men held their ground."*[23] Once the men entered the fray, Ames went to the corps hospital as the wounded came in. He noted a *"glorious victory"* on July 3, when the *"battle raged through the day terribly [and] closed by the enemy retiring from the field."*[24]

On July 5, *"the great body of the Army of the Potomac, including the 29th, moved in pursuit of Lee's retreating army."*[25] Ames gathered the names of the wounded so he could send a letter to the newspaper back home before he became exhausted and found a bed to sleep on. In that letter, he wrote,

> *The rebels seemed inspirited with their usual confidence in their ability to whip the army of the Potomac, anywhere and everything, and they were desperately determined to break through our well formed lines, and after trying at all points for three days, acknowledged their defeat by withdrawing from the field, our lines remaining unbroken. Our wounded are having the best care circumstances will admit of.*[26]

As the army left Gettysburg, he remained behind and, although he was still very weak, he continued to work at the corps hospital, which was located on the farm of George Bushman, on present-day Hospital Road. He noted on July 8, *"Feel very weak, appetite poor. God is my only hope and help. He restores my soul and body to soundness."*[27] Over the next few days, he reported that wounded men were dying every day, and many were being sent to the regular hospital that had been established on the York Pike. On Sunday, July 12, he and other Twelfth Corps chaplains held services for the wounded and the medical personnel in Mr. Bushman's barn and at the tents, after which he visited all the wounded of his regiment.

On July 15, he wrote *"Mrs. Mason's son died this morning. She has been here for a few days. A sad blow to her! God pity the afflicted."*[28] Ames watched as visitors came to the battlefield, some to claim the bodies of their family members and some to find wounded friends. By July 19, his health had improved and he was encouraged that some of the wounded men were feeling cheerful and one proclaimed he wanted to live a better life. As soldiers were moved to the general hospital, Ames stayed at the corps hospital and buried an increasing number of men, including several Confederates. On July 23, he felt strong enough to walk over the ground where his corps fought on Culp's Hill; then, after paying Mr. Bushman for three weeks' board of $10.50, he moved to the general hospital, which he found to be quite pleasant and comfortably located. Two days later, he reported, *"Rested in my quarters very well. Called upon many of the wounded; found appreciation of kind acts and words. Been hard at work all day among the wounded–there is much to be done. Efforts rightly applied are very beneficial."*[29] By July 27, he noted that most of the wounded were in good spirits, although some were *"sinking fast,"* and wounded were coming in from other corps in great numbers, including more Confederates who were *"failing and must go down."*[30] The next day he wrote, *"Many once hopeful cases fail and die. The struggle of mind is often great when compelled to give up hope of recovery! A majority of cases give evidence of sincere penitence and of humble hope. What a blessing to man is the gospel. Daily deaths occur."*[31] He noted the morning report of July 29, which included 307 rebel and 308 Union wounded men in the hospital, with more coming in each day, and total provisions being made for 1,500. The same day, there was *"some excitement occasioned by the presence of Ladies from Baltimore of supposed South sympathies."*[32]

By Saturday, August 1, he was preparing to rejoin the regiment and went to town to procure some supplies for his trip. He and the regimental surgeon were relieved from hospital duties on August 3, and he *"sent my horse overland–took cars myself. I left camp unceremoniously. Did not see all again as I hoped. Must trust then with God."*[33] He reached Washington by August 4 and stayed there for several days, visiting some Twelfth Corps men in local hospitals, drawing his pay and sending some home to his wife, and attending church with fellow brigade chaplains Wilson Parsons of the 66th Ohio and Moses Welch of the 5th Connecticut. He crossed the river into Alexandria, Virginia, on August 8, where he met a man who had been acquainted with George Washington in the latter part of the general's life. Finally, on August 11, he and Chaplain Welch boarded a train to Manassas Junction, where they mounted horses and rode on to the brigade camp near Kelly's Ford. He reported, *"New officers–new arrangements. Everything seems like being with strangers."*[34]

The 29th was soon sent to New York City to help control the draft riots, after which they joined the Army of the Cumberland in the west for the remainder or the war. Chaplain Ames stayed with the regiment until he resigned and was mustered out on June 26, 1865. He returned to Ohio, feeling unsettled and troubled about his future.[35] He moved to Pennsylvania to try his hand at the oil business, but failed. He eventually returned to his ministry in Vermont and assumed the pastorate of the Christian Church in West Randolph. Shortly after retiring from active ministry, Ames died of pneumonia on January 22, 1879, and was buried in South View Cemetery in Randolph.

The 29th Ohio was one of several regiments that were sent to New York City after the Battle of Gettysburg to help control the draft riots. (*The Illustrated London News*)

Second Brigade:
Colonel George Cobham / Brigadier General Thomas Kane

Brig. Gen. Thomas Kane was suffering from pneumonia, and although he was present at Gettysburg the command of his brigade fell to Col. George Cobham. When the other two brigades of Geary's division marched to Gettysburg on July 1, Cobham's men stayed behind at Two Taverns, beside the Baltimore Pike and only two miles from the battlefield, and slept on their arms. On the morning of July 2, the brigade rejoined its division when it reached Culp's Hill. Two regiments formed a line to the right of Greene's brigade while the third was in the rear. When most of the corps marched off to support their comrades against Longstreet's attack, Cobham's men followed Candy's and missed the same turn. About 9:00 p.m., Cobham's brigade backtracked toward Culp's Hill but pulled back to the Baltimore Pike after several men were hit by a Confederate volley fired from the captured breastworks. Some skirmishers strayed too close to enemy lines and were captured or fired upon. The brigade then moved toward the "saddle" between the upper and lower hills and spent an uneasy night in close proximity to Confederate troops.

Skirmishing opened very early on July 3 as Confederates started to advance toward Cobham's men in the darkness. Throughout the morning, the regiments moved back and forth from the works to safety of the hollow, where they cleaned their guns, replenished their ammunition, and took a bit of rest. When the Confederates launched a major attack up the hill later that morning, Cobham's soldiers first fired too high, over the enemy's heads, then corrected their aim, which successfully repulsed the charge, the last one of the day on Culp's Hill.

The brigade spent the rest of the day dodging enemy sniper fire from behind their recovered breastworks. The next morning, July 4, they discovered the Confederates had left their position. As they moved down the hill in front of them, they saw many dead and wounded enemy soldiers dotting the slope. The rest of the day was devoted to burying the dead and caring for the wounded before leaving Gettysburg on July 5.

Kane and Cobham commanded three Pennsylvania regiments: the 29th, 109th, and 111th, and the only chaplain, in the 29th, left no record.

Third Brigade:
Brigadier General George Sears Greene

Brig. Gen. George Sears Greene, the oldest of the Union commanders and beloved by his men (who called him "Pap" Greene), brought much experience as an engineer to his position with the army. After spending the night of July 1 near Little Round Top, his brigade marched to Culp's Hill early the next morning and set right to work following Greene's directive to build breastworks along their line, which extended along the eastern slope from the crest of the upper hill to the lower hill. Confederate artillery opened on their position that afternoon, but the shelling was brief and did little damage.

When the bulk of the Twelfth Corps marched south to assist the Union troops at the far left, Greene's men were tasked with defending the hill by themselves. Greene extended his line to occupy the breastworks to his right, and almost immediately, Confederates attacked the very thin Union line. The Federals repulsed three consecutive assaults, but during a fourth attempt, the regiment at the right of Greene's line was forced to pull back to a traverse that was perpendicular to the line of breastworks and that Greene had wisely included in his plans. Assisted by troops from the First Corps, Greene's men held off further Confederate attacks and held their position throughout the night.

When fighting broke out early on July 3, the Union men were ready. Now supported by the rest of their corps, they fired down the hill on advancing Confederates from behind the works, then took a break in the shelter of the hollow when other units relieved them. By about 11:00 a.m., they could see the Confederates falling back and watched as some groups of rebel soldiers waved pieces of white cloth as a sign of surrender.

Greene and his men won fame for their dogged defense of the Union right flank on Culp's Hill against far superior numbers. The regiments involved in this action were all from New York and included the 60th, 78th, 102nd, 137th, and 149th. Chaplains were present with three units; only one of them wrote about his regiment's experience at Gettysburg.

Eli Fuller Roberts, 137th New York Infantry

Eli Fuller Roberts, more commonly known as E. F. Roberts, was born in Honesdale, Pennsylvania, on March 26, 1826. After losing his father at the age of ten, he was left mostly to his own devices even though his uncle provided him with shelter. He converted to the Christian faith at the age of twenty, and three years later, on September 20, 1849, he married Catherine DeWitt, with whom he had four children.

He received an exhorter's license in the Methodist Episcopal Church and served several churches in Pennsylvania, and was ordained in 1858. In 1862, he had been serving the church in Candor, New York, for less than a year when he stepped forward to enlist and organize Company H of the 137th New York Infantry. First mustered in as the company's captain in September 1862, he was promoted to chaplain two months later. In that capacity, he won admiration even though his attempts to hold divine services each Sunday were often interrupted by drilling and other military business. A captain remembered that after this happened several times, *"the duties of the Chaplain were largely confined to that of post-master. He was known to handle 800 letters in a day and was always cheerful and obliging and a favorite with the men. He was also ready to help a poor fellow on the march by taking his knapsack and gun and was often seen with about as many guns, and knapsacks on his horse as he could carry."*[36]

Roberts wrote several letters to newspapers to keep the people at home informed about the regiment. His first letter after the Battle of Gettysburg, dated July 5, included a lengthy list of casualties and his assurance that

> *nobly did our brave men do their duty in this the hardest fought battle of the Potomac army, and the greatest victory. Our loss is great, as a regiment, but greater to dear ones at home, with whom I sympathize in their deep affliction. The dead of this brigade were buried in a field near the place where they fell, three-fourths of a mile east of Gettysburg, and one and one-eighth of a mile from the turnpike running from Gettysburg to Little Town.*[37]

Over the next couple of months, Roberts wrote regularly to *"give the friends at home a short report of our journeying, fighting, and suffering; and, above all, the joy of victory that gladdens our hearts."*[38] He recounted the regiment's experiences in the campaign and included insights into army life, reflections on the different places his brigade visited, and some humorous anecdotes. In one letter, he reported on the orders to march even after the brigade expected some time to rest, and noted, *"One thing the soldier soon learns after he enters the service of the country, i.e., that many things are uncertain, save that he is a soldier, and military law knows of no compromise, and is only satisfied by strict obedience to orders."*[39]

Many wounded men were sent to Armory Square Hospital in Washington.
(Library of Congress)

When the sudden order came to strike tents on June 13 and be ready to march on a moment's notice, he wrote,

> *the order was complied with as far as practicable, for many were sick and unable to go any farther. These were sent to the hospital at Washington, while the rest of our regiment fell into line in a few minutes–it now being dark–and marched a short distance when they were halted to wait for our supply trains to pass. The toils of the day had exhausted our men, and no sooner were they halted, than they sunk down in the arms of sleep on the green grass. But how long they remained, I don't know, for nature's sweet restorer had stolen my senses away, and held me so securely with Drs. Farrington and Elmore, [the regimental surgeons] that when the regiment moved we did not awake to obey orders, "forward march." As day dawned, I awoke, looked around, and found all had gone save the two Doctors and my faithful horse who lay sleeping at my side. I can assure you no time was lost in waking all sleepers, and giving chase after the regiment, which we found near Stafford Court House.*[40]

The next morning, the regiment was in line, ready to march, by 2:30 a.m. Roberts related, *"I thought I had seen what is called a forced march, but at no time have the men suffered from the extreme heat as they did this day. Many of our own regiment fell out overcome by pure exhaustion and heat, unable longer to keep their places in the ranks."*[41]

In a letter written on August 2, he remarked on the Virginia countryside through which the men marched: *"Most of the country [. . .] needs only northern enterprise to make it all that could be desired, but at present it bears the marks of war, which is devastation and ruin, accompanied with extreme poverty on the part of poor families, and the loss of many comforts to the rich."*[42] Roberts also told the story of three men in the First Division of his corps who were shot for desertion while the corps was at Leesburg. Although many in the regiment expected a last-minute pardon, this was not to be. The soldiers were drawn up to witness the execution of *"their comrades who had turned their back upon their country in its hour of peril, and had shown themselves unworthy any longer to live in it, and hence the government was about to give them a place under it."*[43]

Roberts continued his narrative in a letter dated August 25 in which he described the army's movement into Maryland and Pennsylvania:

> *After crossing the Potomac into the state of Maryland, our hearts were cheered and nerves strengthened by the exhibitions of loyalty*

and a Good speed, such as we had not witnessed while marching through any part of Virginia, and it made us rejoice with joy unspeakable to see the fair ones of the country towns and city through which we were passing, throwing the old flag, under which we were fighting, to the breeze, inscribed upon its ample folds, "The Union Unsevered." The change was perfectly electrifying to our brave soldiers, and cheer after cheer would go up in response to every show of true loyalty to our country, and as if by the power of magic, every man felt he was equal to two of the invading foe.

The day we crossed the line from Maryland into Pennsylvania, I think I realized to some extent the love that one has for the land of his birth. Pennsylvania was my native state; I had shared her fortunes and misfortunes for some years, and in obedience to the voice of my church had but just passed beyond her lines for a short time, when I enlisted at the urgent call of my country, in the defence of all that is dear to me as such.

As the infantry columns passed the line marking the boundaries of the two states, their flags were unrolled from their several staffs, and sent floating upon the gentle breeze that was just then fanning our weary soldiers in their forced march to meet and repel the invading foe. As I reviewed the whole train thus in motion, I strangely felt a disposition to alight from my horse, in my spirit of sadness, and weep on the soil of my native state, in view of the coming event, for it needed not the eye of any prophet to look into the future, and that, too, not many days hence, when her soil would be drinking the baptism that was being prepared for her by the misled rebels.

Yes, the hour was coming and near at hand, when we crossed the Pennsylvania line, when the blood of thousands of true patriots, both of her own and other states, would mingle and commingle together upon the battlefield, in reconsecrating its soil to freedom with a baptism of blood that should forever insure it to be the Keystone State of this Union unsevered.[44]

In his final letter in this serialization of the regiment's experiences during the Gettysburg campaign, Roberts reported:

In my last letter, I parted with you at Littletown [sic], Pa. Our reception by the citizens of the village was hearty, and praise worthy.

The heat at midday was extreme, and in the rapid movement of our troops, the appetite thirst made large demands for water. This was understood by the gentlemen and ladies of the town, both old and young, who stood with pail and cup in hand to meet the weary and fainting patriots. Three cheers for the citizens of Littlestown, Pa.

Tuesday June 30th at 3 o'clock P.M. the regiment was filed into a field one mile north of said town for the purpose of resting and attending to what proved to be the last roll call to many of our brave men.

It was mustering day and every man's name must be called by the Colonel, whether present or absent. I called to mind, as I retrospect that day of muster, over one hundred braves who will never respond again to the call of the mustering officer of the 137th Regiment, N.Y.V. It was to them, their last.[45]

In the evening of June 30, Roberts and eight officers of the regiment gathered at a house in Littlestown, waiting for the woman of the house to finish baking bread for them. Roberts noted,

the fact could not be disguised from them, of the impending battle that must come, far from the distant roar of artillery which we had been hearing during the afternoon. It was clear our cavalry had advanced [and] had come up with the enemy and in all probability ere another day should pass [these officers] would see the smoke of battle, if they did not participate in it. Yet how could the army of the Potomac fight this battle now pending without the aid of the 12th Corps and its able General?[46]

He noted the officers,

talked of the dangers of battle and its dreadful results, which they had previously seen, and passed through. Lee had made a bold push in his invasion of Pennsylvania, and it was clear to this group of officers, that a general who would venture so far from his base of supplies, must intend to fight desperately when attacked by General Meade. A proper time for reflection. Hence, the question was asked by one of the members, "Where shall we all be tomorrow night, and shall we live thro' the coming battle?"[47]

The officers ate the bread and returned to camp and slept. Then, *morning came, and with it, the duties of another day. Eight o'clock, A.M., the bugle sends out its shrill notes, "fall in line, for march." This was the first day of July, also the first day of the Gettysburg battle.*

The first night after this social gathering, you might have seen [the officers] one half mile to the left of the cemetery, at Gettysburg, in a wheat field. With the coming light of July 2d, came also another order to change position to the right of the centre, which order was readily obeyed by the 12th Army Corps. A position was well chosen by Gen. Gary [sic] on the brow of a hill, where breast works were thrown up as a line of defence by the second division of this corps. Their preparations being completed by noon, our men rested until the battle opened in the afternoon, and as the darkness of night gathered over the battle field of July 2d.[48]

Roberts related how he and others searched for these officers late on July 2, but found four of them wounded, three mortally, at field hospitals. The next morning, another officer was killed instantly and one more seriously wounded. *"What a lesson on the fate of battle, for out of eight was six killed and wounded."*[49] That was the last the chaplain wrote of the Gettysburg campaign.

Roberts stayed with his regiment until they mustered out on June 9, 1865. Returning to Pennsylvania, he served several churches over the next decade. A colleague noted how Roberts spoke often of Col. David Ireland of the 137th, who died of disease in Atlanta in the spring of 1864, and of *"the other boys of his regiment from whose cold lips he had heard the faint, 'God bless you, Chaplain,' and whose eyes he had lovingly closed in death."*[50] Roberts became ill and died at the age of fifty-five on January 21, 1882, in Meshoppen, Pennsylvania, where he helped build the Methodist Episcopal Church in which his funeral service was held. He is buried in Overfield Cemetery in Meshoppen.

Chaplain Roberts credited Maj. Gen. John W. Geary with choosing a good position on Culp's Hill. (Library of Congress)

Chapter 9:

The Cavalry Corps

CORPS COMMANDER:

Major General Alfred Pleasonton

The three divisions of Federal cavalry under Maj. Gen. Alfred Pleasonton saw much action in the weeks before the Battle of Gettysburg, including the large clash at Brandy Station, actions at Aldie, Middleburg, and Upperville in Virginia's Loudoun Valley, and skirmishes at Westminster, Maryland, and Hanover, Pennsylvania. During the first three days of July, the cavalry was engaged at Hunterstown, Brinkerhoff's Ridge, Fairfield, East Cavalry Field, and South Cavalry Field. The troopers played a significant role in the pursuit of General Lee's army July 4–14, including battles at Monterey Pass, Pennsylvania; Hagerstown, Maryland; and around Williamsport, Maryland.

FIRST DIVISION:

Brigadier General John Buford

Two of the brigades of cavalry in the division commanded by Brig. Gen. John Buford were the first Federal units to engage the enemy at the Battle of Gettysburg. On June 30, Colonels William Gamble and Thomas Devin led their troopers into Gettysburg, where Buford gathered intelligence and set up vedette posts (small outposts of four or five troopers) to the west and north of town. The next morning, the horsemen positioned along the Chambersburg Pike saw a large dust cloud approaching from the west. About 7:30 a.m., a trooper in the 8th Illinois Cavalry fired toward Confederate soldiers on a ridge in what many have accepted to be the first shot of the battle. For almost three hours, Buford's troopers fought a delaying action against the Confederate advance by falling back from ridge to ridge, but the Union horsemen were desperately outnumbered and needed infantry support. By midmorning, Union First Corps brigades arrived in support. The horsemen spent the rest of the day guarding the flanks of the Union line until the Confederates pushed the Federal line back through town late that afternoon.

That night, the brigades of Devin and Gamble formed a picket line from Evergreen Cemetery to Little Round Top, and the next morning, they pushed out to the Emmitsburg Road near the Peach Orchard. About midday, some of the troopers supported the reconnaissance of Third Corps men who were sent into Pitzer's Woods to feel out the enemy thought to be massing there. At some point that afternoon, Buford's men were relieved and sent first to Taneytown to refit, then to Westminster to guard the trains. Their actions in the three days of battle were done.

First Brigade:
Colonel William Gamble

Col. William Gamble's brigade included the 3rd Indiana, 8th New York, and 8th and 12th Illinois regiments, but only the 8th New York was accompanied by a chaplain who left no record.

Second Brigade:
Colonel Thomas Devin

Col. Thomas Devin's brigade consisted of the 3rd West Virginia, 6th and 9th New York, and 17th Pennsylvania Cavalry, but only the New York units had chaplains at the time of the battle, and neither left any writings about Gettysburg.

Third Brigade:
Brigadier General Wesley Merritt

The brigade of newly minted Brig. Gen. Wesley Merritt spent the first two days of the battle picketing and patrolling roads through the mountains in Maryland. On July 3, the brigade marched to Gettysburg and took a position on the far Union left, along the Emmitsburg Road. Merritt sent one regiment, the 6th United States, to Fairfield to locate Confederate wagons that were reported to be in the area. This regiment was cut to pieces in a brutal battle during which they were severely outnumbered. The other regiments participated in the advance against enemy infantry at the southernmost end of the battlefield during the late afternoon of July 3.

The only chaplain in Merritt's brigade was with the 6th Pennsylvania Cavalry; none of his United States cavalry regiments, the 1st, 2nd, 5th, and 6th, had chaplains.

Samuel Levis Gracey, 6th Pennsylvania Cavalry

Samuel Levis Gracey was born in Philadelphia on September 8, 1835. He received his education at Boston University, was ordained as a Methodist Episcopal deacon in 1857, and served two churches in quick succession. He married Leonora Thompson in November 1860, and they had four children. After being appointed to the church at Media just weeks before the war broke out, *"nearly all the male members of his church enlisted in the army, [and] he was constrained to follow them."*[1] He was commissioned as a chaplain in the 6th Pennsylvania Cavalry (known as "Rush's Lancers") on November 20, 1861. He returned to Philadelphia briefly in March 1862 to be ordained as an elder, then rejoined the regiment.

Chaplain Samuel Levis Gracey of the 6th Pennsylvania Cavalry. (State Library of Massachusetts)

Gracey wrote a well-regarded history of Rush's Lancers in 1868 in which he combined newspaper reports, interviews with comrades, and his own observations about their time of service. He only briefly mentioned the cavalry battles at Aldie, in which his regiment fought, and those at Middleburg and Upperville in which the other regiments in the brigade were engaged.

The brigade spent two days guarding trains along the road from Hagerstown to Baltimore, then moved to Emmitsburg on July 2. The next morning, the troopers advanced to Gettysburg and took a position near the Emmitsburg Road at the extreme left of the Union line. Gracey described what happened when they arrived:

> *The Sixth Pennsylvania, having the advance of our brigade, was the first of the cavalry to become engaged. The men were dismounted, led horses taken to the rear, when we were pushed forward to meet the infantry line of the enemy. The men deployed as skirmishers, and went up boldly over ground intersected by stone walls and fences, but on rising the crest of a hill, they were saluted by a storm of balls that checked their advance. A stone house within range of our men was filled with the sharp shooters of the enemy, doing great mischief to our advancing lines. A section of artillery was immediately brought into position, and opened on the building, causing hasty evacuation of the premises by the enemy. A brisk skirmish was kept up until about 1 o'clock in the afternoon.*[2]

Although the position of his cavalry regiment would not have allowed the troopers to witness the advance of the Confederates that afternoon, they did see and hear the cannonade prior to the Pickett-Pettigrew-Trimble charge, and Gracey provided vivid details about it:

> *First, one great gun spoke; and then, as though it had been the signal for the commencement of an artillery conversation, the whole hundred and twenty or more opened their mouths at once, and poured out their thunder. A perfect storm of shot, shell, and ball, rained upon and about us. Every possible shelter was gained behind barricade and stone wall, while the movements of the enemy were carefully watched, and every ordinary advance promptly checked. Our own batteries were splendidly served in reply to the enemy, while the earth trembled beneath the unearthly roar and tumult. The air seemed full of fragments of bursting shell and ball, while the sounds peculiar to the several projectiles told of the determination of the attack. There was the heavy whoo! whoo!–who-oo! Of the round shot. The "which-one? which-one?"*

Chaplain Gracey described the sounds of the shells fired from these "fiendish" Whitworth guns. *(Historic Views of Gettysburg)*

> *of the fiendish Whitworth gun, the demoniac shriek of "what-you-doing-here?" of the shells, and the buzzing Minie, all combined to give it the character of a high carnival of powers infernal.*[3]

Merritt's brigade did not participate in the cavalry charge ordered by Brig. Gen. Judson Kilpatrick late that afternoon, but the dismounted troopers engaged with Texans at the far right of the Confederate line: *"Our force, which was at first to the west of the Emmettsburg [sic] Road, was forced back a considerable distance, but our thin line was extended, and every foot of ground fought for desperately."*[4] Their line held, and throughout the night the troopers *"stood to horse, and although we were worn out, by long marches and hard fighting on less than half rations, we were started by 5 o'clock on the morning of the 4th, on a forced march of over seventy miles."*[5] The fourth proved to be a strenuous day for both the men and their horses. As they passed through Emmitsburg that afternoon in drenching rain, the march was

> *necessarily very slow. Both men and horses were tired and jaded. For five days we had been without forage for our horses, and in almost constant motion. Hundreds of horses dropped down on this march, and were left on the road with their saddles, blankets, and bridles upon them. Men, whose horses "played out," trudged along*

on foot through muddy roads and swollen streams without food; the night coming on rapidly, and no shelter from the merciless storm that beat upon us the entire day and night.[6]

That evening, they arrived at Mechanicstown, and

a halt was ordered for four hours. As soon as the column halted, the men dismounted, and lay down in the muddy roads or fields, with bridle tied to wrist, and utterly exhausted, were soon asleep, and were aroused with great difficulty to pursue the march twelve miles further in dense darkness and heavy rain, halting at 3 o'clock, A.M. after being eighteen hours in the saddle. The ground, though thoroughly saturated, was not more so than the troops, and without tents, fire, or food, we threw ourselves upon the ground to rest.[7]

The men and their mounts were finally supplied with rations and forage when they arrived at Frederick on July 5, and *"took a new lease on life."*[8] The 6th continued in pursuit of General Lee's army and participated in several cavalry engagements over the next week, and the Gettysburg campaign came to an end on July 14 when they attacked the rear guard of the Confederate army as it crossed the Potomac River to safety in Virginia.

Gracey remained with the regiment until he was assigned to duty as post chaplain at the prison camp in Rock Island, Illinois. He rejoined the 6th Pennsylvania Cavalry in June 1865, when the 6th was consolidated with two other cavalry regiments to form the 2nd Provisional Pennsylvania Cavalry, which mustered out of the army a month later. Gracey returned to ministry first in Delaware, and then in New England, where he became active in local politics and was twice elected to the Massachusetts State Legislature. In 1890, President Benjamin Harrison appointed Gracey to serve as U.S. consul to Foochow, China. After being recalled briefly, he was reappointed, and in addition to the duties of his office, he also aided various missionary societies. His wife, Leonora, died in 1897, and Gracey married Corda Pratt three years later.

By 1911, Gracey's health was failing, and while he was a patient at a sanitarium near Boston, he took a razor and cut his throat. He is buried in the Ministers' Lot of Mount Moriah Cemetery in Philadelphia, under a stone that reads, "Soldier—Clergyman—Diplomat."

SECOND DIVISION:
Brigadier General David McMurtie Gregg

Brig. Gen. David McMurtie Gregg commanded three brigades of cavalry. The first and third brigades, under Colonels John B. McIntosh and J. Irvin Gregg, arrived on the field at Gettysburg on July 2 and took a position on the extreme right of the Union line. Some regiments engaged Confederates on Brinkerhoff Ridge and managed to drive them back. The next day, with a large force of enemy cavalry reported to be moving toward their position, Gregg was reinforced by the Third Division brigade of Brig. Gen. George Armstrong Custer. When an attack was imminent, Custer agreed to remain with Gregg instead of rejoining his division on the far left of the line. The combined Union forces fought a fierce battle at East Cavalry Field and managed to force the Confederate cavalry to withdraw that evening. The brigade of Col. Pennock Huey had been detached at Hanover Junction on July 1 and did not rejoin the division until July 9.

First Brigade:
Colonel John B. McIntosh

Four of Col. John B. McIntosh's cavalry regiments had chaplains: the 1st Maryland, 1st and 3rd Pennsylvania, and 1st New Jersey. His other two regiments were the 1st Massachusetts and the 3rd Pennsylvania Heavy Artillery battery unit. Only one of the chaplains left a record.

Henry Rogers Pyne, 1st New Jersey Cavalry

Henry Rogers Pyne was born in Middletown, Connecticut, on August 3, 1834. After completing his education at St. James College in Maryland and General Theological Seminary in New York, he was ordained in December 1858 at Grace Episcopal Church in Baltimore. He was soon appointed as the rector of St. Stephen's Episcopal Church in Crownsville, Maryland, but because most of his parishioners supported the South, Pyne, who was a strong Unionist, submitted his resignation and enlisted as a chaplain in the 1st New Jersey Cavalry on September 16, 1861.

Pyne wrote a history of the regiment that was published in 1871. He described the regiment's engagement in the cavalry battle at Brandy Station in detail. During the fight the 1st New Jersey participated in several charges and took a number of prisoners; the regiment then played only a supporting role in the rear during the other three battles in late June at Aldie, Middleburg, and Upperville. The regiment was the last unit of the Army of the Potomac to cross the Potomac at Edward's Ferry on June 27. Upon entering Maryland, Pyne observed,

Chaplain Henry Pyne of the 1st New Jersey Cavalry.
(Ron Coddington)

> *The transition from a region inhabited by active or secret enemies, to one where every village poured out a throng of enthusiastic friends, was one that delighted and inspired the war-worn veterans of the army. No longer scowled at as invaders, or repaid by hate when they sought to supply their necessities, the march of the cavalry through the fertile country was one long series of ovations, a succession of grateful greetings. All along the road, the inhabitants came thronging out to gaze upon the hardy figures and weather-beaten visages of the troops who had defeated the famed cavalry of the South, and with shouts and joyful tears they cheered us forward in the pursuit. From doorways, windows, balconies, handkerchiefs and scarfs were waved in welcome; young girls saluted us with patriotic songs; matrons brought out abundant provision for our refreshment; men opened barns, and granaries, and store-rooms, with one impulse of zeal for the glorious standard of the nation, displayed upon every house. Not a village in that noble little State of Maryland, whose sympathies the rebels claim to be with them, allowed the soldiers of the Union to pass without a tribute of hearty sympathy and unrestrained applause.*[9]

The situations in Westminster and Manchester were even better:

> *From the cellars where they had been secreted from the marauding Southern horsemen, casks of beer and ale were rolled into the street; and as the men marched past, the owners offered to each trooper a brimming glass of the strengthening and refreshing beverage.*

At Manchester, near the Pennsylvania line, wreaths of flowers were thrown down upon the dusty and haggard soldiers, while the hands that had woven these graceful tokens of welcome were quickly busied in providing a more substantial tribute. In those few hours of halt, feelings of gratitude and affection were aroused in the hearts of men hardened to cold looks and bitter words, which have survived the hardships and privations of all the succeeding campaigns, to endure long after the war shall be a thing of the past-when the fierce struggles of the battle-field shall have softened into subjects of pleasant recollection.[10]

He contrasted the goodwill of Marylanders with the more practically minded citizens of Pennsylvania that they met later: *"Though of the rich northern inhabitants of Pennsylvania, many gazed stolidly upon their defenders, and with a sordid spirit of extortion drained from them their few hard-earned dollars for the supply of their simplest wants."*[11]

Pyne reported that the troopers reached Gettysburg early in the morning of July 2 and were sent to the far right, *"the infantry posted there being removed to strengthen other points,"* where the horsemen dismounted to *"lay in wait for any advancing enemy."*[12] This would have been the skirmish at Brinkerhoff's Ridge. However, at this point in his history, Pyne seems to switch suddenly to a narrative of the battle on what came to be known as East Cavalry Field.[13]

He continues the story by describing a detachment of 150 men from the 1st New Jersey who were *"sent forward as a forlorn hope, to give time for the rest of the division to come up with unblown horses, [and] by their undaunted bearing and their steady fire, staggered the troops that by a single charge could have ridden over them."*[14] When this small band of men were recalled to be relieved, they steadfastly refused to leave their hazardous position: *"The Third Pennsylvania came upon the line, and the First Jersey was at liberty to retire from the action. But no! They sought every method to avoid falling back. Borrowing ammunition from the Pennsylvanians, they kept their boldly-won position, and cheering like mad, defied the efforts of the enemy."*[15] The Jersey men eventually pulled back, and with the grand charge by the Michigan and Pennsylvania troopers, the clash on the field was over. But *"the First New Jersey had work still to do. Guarding the line and picketing far to the front, they watched through the night upon the bloody ground, until the welcome light of the birthday of the nation permitted them to seek a brief season of repose."*[16] The cavalry left Gettysburg late in the afternoon of July 4 and Pyne recounted that the 1st New Jersey engaged in several skirmishes over the next few days while in pursuit of the Confederate army.

Pyne mustered out of service on September 20, 1864. A year later, he married Elizabeth Ann Frailey, with whom he had four children, and they first settled in Holland Patent, New York. They moved next to Nebraska, where he served briefly as president of Nebraska College. Their next homes were in Washington and Hamilton, New York. Pyne then accepted the pastorate of two different churches in Eastport and Wiscasset, Maine, where he remained for a total of sixteen years. He served as general secretary for The Conference of Church Workers Among Colored People, an organization that sought to fully integrate black Episcopalians into the life of the church. In 1889 he returned to Washington, where he died on April 12, 1892. He is buried in Washington's Congressional Cemetery.

Second Brigade:
Colonel Pennock Huey

None of Col. Pennock Huey's regiments—the 2nd and 4th New York, 6th Ohio, and 8th Pennsylvania—were accompanied by chaplains.

Third Brigade:
Colonel J. Irvin Gregg

Col. J. Irvin Gregg, a cousin of his division commander, had only one regiment with a chaplain, the 10th New York, who left no record of his service. Gregg's brigade also included the 1st Maine and 4th and 16th Pennsylvania.

Third Division:
Brigadier General Judson Kilpatrick

Brig. Gen. Judson Kilpatrick commanded two brigades under two new brigadiers, Elon Farnsworth and George Armstrong Custer. Both brigades were engaged in the battles at Hanover on June 30 and at Hunterstown on July 2. Early the next morning, Kilpatrick received orders to move his division to the far left of the Union line, but Custer's brigade was ordered to report to General Gregg, where he played an important role in the battle at East Cavalry Field. Farnsworth led his men in a disastrous attack against the Confederate right in which the young brigadier was mortally wounded.

First Brigade:
Brigadier General Elon Farnsworth

Brig. Gen. Elon Farnsworth's brigade included the 1st West Virginia, 1st Vermont, 5th New York, and 18th Pennsylvania cavalry regiments. Only the first three were accompanied by chaplains and only the New Yorker wrote not only about the regiment's participation at Gettysburg, but also about his remarkable experiences after the battle.

Louis Napoleon Beaudry, 5th New York Cavalry

Louis Napoleon Beaudry (sometimes spelled Boudrye) was born August 18, 1833, in Highgate, Vermont. His parents were French Canadians, and when he was five, the family moved to Quebec and ran a bakery for six years. They moved back to Vermont and then to Ticonderoga, New York. Beaudry was raised in the Roman Catholic Church, but his intense study while at the Keeseville Academy led him to the Protestant faith. He then entered Troy University, was ordained in the Methodist Episcopal Church, and taught school for a few years. Beaudry was a scholar and fluent in French and English and could converse in Spanish and German. He married Celeste G. Gallyianx in 1858, but she died the next year, and in October 1860, Pearlie Schermerhorn became his wife. Together they had four children.

Chaplain Louis Beaudry of the 5th New York Cavalry. (Wheaton College)

Beaudry responded to the call of his country and received a commission as chaplain of the 5th New York Cavalry (known as the Ira Harris Guard) on January 31, 1863. Before he left for the war, he wrote a letter to a newspaper in Albany, New York assuring his students that they would be well cared for in his absence.

He wrote two books about the unit's experiences: a regimental history and his personal war journal. Most of the following quotes are taken from his journal, which are written from his personal point of view. In describing the regiment's arrival at Littlestown, Pennsylvania, on June 29, he wrote, *"Great demonstrations of joy were made in this village. Children sitting on a high balcony sang patriotic airs, while cheers from the men made the welkin ring."*[17]

The next day, they moved to Hanover, where the citizens provided them with another joyous welcome and provided much food and coffee. But,

> *while we were thus feasting gayly and sumptuously, a charge of rebel cavalry was made upon us, mostly in the train, while a battery, before concealed, opened with shot and shell upon us. Nothing could have been more surprising nor could take us at a more inopportune moment for us. The rebels were within three rods of me, while pistol balls, shot and shell flew in every direction. I turned out of the village with the 5th N.Y. in the rear of which I was marching, where they formed in line and charged the enemy. Having no arms, but a pocket pistol, I followed the non-combatants.*[18]

After caring for some wounded Confederate prisoners, Beaudry went to the Union hospital in town and ministered to his own men. He spent most of July 1 at the hospital, where he could *"distinctly hear the fight in the direction of Gettysburg. This evening, assisted by citizens and soldiers, we buried eighty men killed yesterday, all in one grave. It was a solemn time under the moonlight. I made some remarks and prayed."*[19]

The Battle of Hanover took place on July 2, with Union and Confederate cavalry fighting in close quarters in the center of town. (The Hanover Centennial Committee, 1915)

On July 2, the regiment moved to Gettysburg and entered the battle, and his contemporaneous daily entries ended until he could resume his journal in the fall of 1863 using notes and personal memories. Of July 2, he recalled that he remained at the hospital and cared for some Confederates, one of whom *"remarked that he was treated better than he expected and was perfectly satisfied."*[20] Although he could clearly hear the sounds of the battle and could see smoke rising from the field, he heard *"only contradictory rumors of the tide of battle. But our hearts were often uplifted by the God who watches over the destinies of nations."*[21]

The 5th New York moved from the right to the left flank of the army, near Little Round Top, early on July 3, where they were joined by Wesley Merritt's brigade. Beaudry and the others who had stayed behind in Hanover left for Gettysburg late that afternoon. *"There were times when the booming of cannon was continuous, with no intermission. The road [toward Gettysburg] was filled with carriages and wagons bringing the wounded to the rear and many wounded were on foot. It was a sad time."*[22] When they arrived on the field about 5:00 p.m., they saw about 3,000 sorry-looking rebel prisoners, then went back to Littlestown to spend the rainy night in a house. Beaudry surmised that the heavy rain *"was in accordance to the theory that heavy cannonading always produced rain! There is doubtless truth in it."*[23]

Later that afternoon, the troopers headed toward Emmitsburg and then Monterey Pass in their pursuit of the Confederate army. Just after daybreak on July 5, Beaudry, Chaplain Oliver Taylor of the 5th Michigan Cavalry, and several other "defenseless ones" were surrounded by a detachment of Confederate general J. E. B Stuart's horsemen and were taken prisoner and marched off to Libby Prison in Richmond.

While he was there, he collected articles, poems, and other items written by his fellow prisoners and combined them into a weekly "newspaper" called *The Libby Chronicle, Devoted to Facts and Fun*, as an attempt to raise the spirits of his comrades while suffering the effects of prison life. Beaudry read these submissions every Friday morning to his fellow prisoners, and he published them as *The Libby Chronicle* in 1889. Here is his account of his capture from the *Chronicle*:

> *HOW I WAS CAPTURED AND THEN BROUGHT TO LIBBY PRISON.*
>
> *Gettysburg! Three bloody days! Then Rebellion's desperation and folly rose to flood tide and Pickett's Division made its awful*

The Libby Chronicle.

DEVOTED TO FACTS AND FUN.

EDITOR-IN-CHIEF, LOUIS N. BEAUDRY, CHAPLAIN FIFTH N. Y. VOL. CAVALRY.

VOL. I. LIBBY PRISON, RICHMOND, VA., AUGUST 21, 1863. NO. I.

While he was in prison, Chaplain Beaudry complied articles from his fellow prisoners into *The Libby Chronicle* to help bolster morale. He published the *Chronicle* after his release from prison.

charge and was annihilated! Scarcely had the echoes of the last gun of that memorable cannonade reverberated among the hills of the "Keystone" State that General Meade ascertained that the enemy was already retreating toward his own place. Accordingly General Kilpatrick, commanding the Third Division of the Cavalry Corps was ordered around the Rebel right to intercept their flying trains in the passes of the mountains.

During the night of Saturday the Fourth of July, in the midst of a torrential rain storm (great storms seem to have followed quickly on the heels of great battles), Kilpatrick attacked Ewell's train at the Monterey Pass. Here he captured over two hundred wagons laden with stolen property from the stores and granaries of Pennsylvania, and about 1,500 prisoners fell into his hands. It was during the latter part of the night that at least fifty of us were surrounded by a force of Stuart's Cavalry. It is hard enough for any Yankee, and harder still, I think, for a Yankee Frenchman, to say to a hated enemy, "I surrender." But this had to be done. A Rebel lad was taking possession of my horse. I had a splendid charger, the pride of my heart and a favorite with the regiment. I said to the Rebel: "Young man, I am a Chaplain, and that horse is my own and not the Government's. Will you not respect my private property?" He answered me with a piquant sneer. Soon the officer in command made his appearance. To him also I made an appeal. To my surprise he turned to the lad and said: "Let that horse alone, sir." Then turning to me he added, "Take your own horse, Chaplain, saddle and mount him, and when you reach General Stuart's headquarters, you shall be released."

Bowing him my thanks and it may be inferred how polite a Frenchman could be under such circumstances–I gathered up my "traps," and was soon riding among the "Johnnies."

After riding a few hours we reached the anticipated headquarters, of course, in the saddle, near a place called Mechanicville. On arriving, according to the promise made me at time of capture, I was immediately "released"–of my horse and of all hopes of liberty. This was a serious contrecoup. A personal interview with General Stuart, before whom I laid all my rights and complaints availed me nothing. With my hand upon his horse's shoulder, I looked up into his bright blue eye and saw clearly the terrible agitation of his mind. When he learned that I belonged to Kilpatrick's troops, he nervously inquired: "Where is Kilpatrick?" "I don't know, sir." He eyed me closely as if to see whether or not I was answering honestly. "How many men has Kilpatrick?" "I can't tell you." Had I known, he would not have been any wiser for it. He wore a slouched hat adorned with a black plume, and carried an ivory-handle bowie-knife, fastened with a gold chain to his belt. Our interview was brief and away he rode toward the head of his column.

The griefs of that Sabbath day can never be recounted. Lugging my equipage I was compelled to walk through deep mud and across swollen and unbridged brooks, paddling along as best I could with my great awkward cavalry boots. All this while a Rebel provost-marshall (Lieutenant Ball) rode my beautiful horse. Up and down the lines of prisoners he often passed, as if anxious to increase my sorrows. On one occasion, he accosted me by saying, "Do you know, Chaplain, how much this horse is worth to me?" On answering that I did not know, he added, "He is worth $500." This was poor consolation.

Confederate general J. E. B. Stuart questioned Chaplain Beaudry about the location of Union cavalry, and then refused to release him, against the chaplain's protests. (Library of Congress)

Our captors paid no attention to our physical wants. No rations were issued to us during the day. All would have fainted by the way, as a few actually did, had not the Union ladies along our route come to our relief. As soon as they could recognize us, they brought us bread, cake, cold meats, pies, etc., pressing through the guards who at times threatened to bayonet them, while with tears at our sufferings and prayers for our safety, they bid us God-speed.

About sun-down Kilpatrick made an attack upon Stuart. How we prayed that he would demolish him and release us! But darkness soon put an end to the contest and we were left with the enemy. Near midnight we arrived in the valley of the Potomac. Footsore and weary we were driven into a damp field where we spent the remainder of the night.

We were marched and countermarched much of the day and after sundown driven into a field, where we supposed we would spend the night. Darkness had come and I had fallen into a dose [sic], *when I heard a call: "Chaplain, Fifth New York Cavalry." Springing to my feet I saw a Rebel lieutenant standing near with whom I had had some conversation during the day. He held in one hand a piece of warm bread and in the other a cup of smoking hot coffee. In an undertone he remarked, "Chaplain, I thought you might be hungry, and I've brought you this for your supper." I was well-nigh overwhelmed at the unexpected act of kindness. This was a noble fellow, worthy of a better cause. Glad am I to testify to the nobility of character wherever I find it.*

We reached and crossed the Potomac at Williamsport. The Rebel army was in a most deplorable condition. There is little doubt that had General Meade closely followed up his victory he would have nearly, if not quite, annihilated his antagonist. All Rebel hopes had been blasted. The feeling of their rank and file was well expressed by one of the officers of the guard. On reaching the sacred soil of Virginia, he flung his sabre down exclaiming with much emotion, "Lie there! and never again will I cross this river, God helping me, on an expedition of this kind."

A change of guard was here made and a striking episode occurred. By the outgoing commander we were introduced to the new provost-marshall. As my turn came I was presented as "Chaplain Beaudry of the Fifth New York Cavalry." "To what denomination do you belong?" inquired the talkative provost-marshall. "I am a Methodist, sir."

"So am I," smilingly added my interlocutor. "I am very sorry to find you where you are," I said half earnestly and half jokingly.

"Ditto! ditto!" almost screamed out the Rev. Mr. Linthicum of the Baltimore Conference into whose hands at I was both prisoner and guest. This passage at arms–with words not swords–served me a good turn. He treated me with kindness and at times with condescension.

On Friday, July 10, we all suffered terribly from the excessive heat of the day. Many even of the guards gave out completely. If infantrymen, accustomed to the climate and hardship of the march, failed, it may be inferred how much cavalrymen, unused to the foot march, suffered. Before night my feet were terribly wounded with blisters under each heel half the size of an egg. I had perspired so much and was so nearly exhausted that cold flashes shot up my hips and back, indicating that I was in a critical condition indeed. We bivouacked that night near the Washington Springs, not far from Winchester, where we remained to rest until the following Sunday.

Here we heard through Rebel sources of the fall of Vicksburg. Had it not been for Rebel bayonets all around us we would have cheered lustily. Like our Quaker friends we endured our joy in silence. "Gettysburg! Vicksburg! Vicksburg! Gettysburg!" were often passed from lip to lip like a draught of nectar to the Union prisoners, but like gall and vinegar to the Rebel guards.

Two hundred miles of travel brought us at length to Staunton, Va., at the head of the beautiful Shenandoah Valley. Here we struck the Virginia Central Railway. On the morning of the 18th of July we took cars for the Rebel Capital.

There were about 4,000 Union soldiers captured in the Gettysburg campaign. Of these about two hundred were officers. The first dispatches published in Richmond gave 40,000. The city was jubilant at the news, while our poor fellows in Libby Prison were terribly dejected. The second day's news showed that one zero too many had been given in previous dispatches. "Look on this picture and on that." The thermometer went down below zero outside the prison when it was ascertained that at least 17,000 Rebels had been captured, that General Pickett's Division was obliterated, and that General Lee was flying back to recross the Potomac with the dispirited and broken remnant of his lately proud Confederates.[24]

Chaplain Beaudry was marched to Libby Prison in Richmond, where he and the other chaplains who had been captured during the Gettysburg campaign remained for several months until they were paroled in October. (Library of Congress)

Beaudry was one of nine Union chaplains at Libby, including seven who had been captured during the Confederate advance north at the second Battle of Winchester in June. As noncombatants, they should have been released as per Confederate General Order 46, issued on July 1, 1862, which ordered that *"all chaplains taken prisoners of war by the armies of the Confederate States while in the discharge of their duties will immediately and unconditionally be released."*[25] However, an article in the *Chronicle* noted that the breakdown in prisoner exchanges had begun in early June because the Confederacy refused to exchange certain officers who were known to have strong influence in the North. The suspension of exchanges hardened when the Confederacy treated captured black Union soldiers not as prisoners of war, but as escaped slaves.

All the chaplains, except Chaplain Charles McCabe of the 122nd Ohio Infantry—who had been taken at Winchester and was recovering from illness in a hospital—were released from Libby in October 1863. Before leaving the prison, Beaudry stuffed his handwritten files of the *Chronicle* in his boots, along with letters from fellow prisoners. To his relief, his captors did not search him and he was able to carry all the precious documents home to New York.

After spending some time with his family to recover, Beaudry returned to his regiment in January 1864 and mustered out on July 19, 1865. He resumed his ministry near Albany, New York, and in 1876 moved to Montreal to work with French Canadians until 1887, when he returned to New York to be appointed as a superintendent of French evangelical work. He was working as a missionary in Chicago when he died on January 3, 1892. Beaudry had been active in the George H. Thomas No. 5 Post of the GAR, and members of the post escorted his body to Oak Woods Cemetery in Chicago, where he was laid to rest.

The chaplains who had been captured at Winchester in June 1863 included:

James Harvey, 110th Ohio Infantry; George H. Hammer, 12th Pennsylvania Cavalry; E. W. Brady, 116th Ohio Infantry; D. C. Everhart, 87th Pennsylvania Infantry; E. C. Ambler, 67th Pennsylvania Infantry; J. T. Brown, 6th Maryland Infantry; and Charles McCabe, 122nd Ohio Infantry. They were joined by Chaplains Oliver Taylor, 5th Michigan Cavalry, and Louis Beaudry, 5th New York Cavalry, who were captured on July 5.

In *The Libby Chronicle*, Beaudry included a story, as later told to him, about how the prisoners observed July 4, 1863:

> *Let us see how these heroes celebrated the 4th of July in Libby Prison in 1863. It is certainly the most pathetic celebration ever recorded in the annals of American history. As the day approached, it was felt that the occasion must not be allowed to pass without some kind of demonstration. Consequently, committees were appointed to arrange a program and select the personae dramatis. As perfectly as possible the Declaration of Independence was to be recited. Orators were to expatiate on the history and memories of the day. Chaplain McCabe was charged with the responsibility of the musical entertainment. Thus far the work of the committees was quite simple and satisfactory.*
>
> *The great thing wanting, however, was a suitable stand of colors. "How can a genuine flag be procured?" was on the lips of all. There were a few Union flags, captured in battle, in the rebel office below. Could not one of those be obtained? If love failed, might not money secure one? But where was the money? All suggestions and plans looking in this direction seemed futile. At length a happy thought occurred: "Let us make our*

own flag." But where was the bunting or other material for this purpose? All the stores, except of Yankee ingenuity, were about exhausted. After a careful search, or inventory, one of the prisoners exclaimed: "take the flap of my nether garment." No sooner said than done. Threads drawn from the same stuff supplied the sewing. If more nimble fingers ever manufactured a flag, certain are we that no more loyal hearts ever guided the operation. Material, such as it was, was contributed for stars and stripes, and the work went briskly forward.

The glorious day came but too tardily. No jubilant boom of cannon nor other demonstration of joy in and about Richmond ushered its dawn. In the midst of the awful stillness in this Sahara of Rebeldom, the only oasis of loyalty to freedom was Libby Prison. There the day we celebrate received merited attention. The arrangements for the occasion were duly prepared. This was in the upper west room, where were quartered Col. Streight and his officers, on this occasion reinforced by the unfortunate officers of Gen. Milroy's command, who occupied the room below. At the proper time, and in the presence of a crowd nearly frantic with excitement, the newly-made flag was hoisted into position amid "salvos" of manly voices. The enthusiasm knew no bounds–the cheers somewhat suppressed at first, soon broke out into thunderous applause. Men wept and laughed, and stamped and clapped and shouted. The old walls echoed and trembled, and for awhile, like those of ancient Jericho, seemed ready to tumble down. No one, surely, will ever contradict this assertation: that no flag ever had a more unique history, and that no 4th of July ever witnessed a more loyal demonstration.[26]

Second Brigade:
Brigadier General George Armstrong Custer

Three of the Michigan cavalry regiments of Brig. Gen. George Armstrong Custer's brigade, the 1st, 5th, and 6th, had chaplains, while the 7th did not, but none of them left a record of their time with their units at Gettysburg.

Appendix I

Union Chaplains at Gettysburg by Brigade

Those chaplains whose stories are included in this book are marked in **bold**.

First Corps (20)

Brigadier General Solomon Meredith

7th Wisconsin .... **Samuel W. Eaton**, Congregational
19th Indiana .... **Thomas Barnett**, Methodist
24th Michigan .... **William C. Way**, Methodist

Brigadier General Lysander Cutler

No chaplains

Brigadier General Gabriel Paul

94th New York..................... **Philos G. Cook**, Presbyterian
16th Maine .... George Bullen, Baptist
104th New York................... **Ferdinand D. Ward**, Presbyterian
107th Pennsylvania............. William T. Campbell, unknown

Brigadier General Henry Baxter

11th Pennsylvania............... **William H. Locke**, Methodist
88th Pennsylvania............... Charles W. Clothier, unknown
90th Pennsylvania............... **Horatio S. Howell**, Presbyterian
97th New York..................... **John V. Ferguson**, Methodist

Colonel Chapman Biddle

142nd Pennsylvania............ William P. Moore, Presbyterian
151st Pennsylvania .... Thomas F. McClure, Methodist

Colonel Roy Stone

149th Pennsylvania.............**James F. Calkins**, Presbyterian
150th Pennsylvania............. William McCormick, Methodist

Brigadier General George Stannard

12th Vermont .... Lewis Brastow, Congregational
13th Vermont ....Joseph Sargent, Universalist
14th Vermont .... **William S. Smart**, Congregational
15th Vermont .... Ephraim Cummings, Congregational
16th Vermont .... **Alonzo Webster**, Methodist

Second Corps (20)

Colonel Edward Cross

148th Pennsylvania............. **William H. Stevens**, Methodist
61st New York..................... Henry Vogel, Baptist
81st Pennsylvania .... Stacy Wilson, Methodist

Colonel Patrick Kelly

88th New York.................... **William Corby**, Roman Catholic

Brigadier General Samuel Zook

52nd New York................... Peter Steffen, Lutheran

Colonel John Brooke

64th New York.................... Oliver Hibbard, Presbyterian
2nd Delaware .... George Condron, Baptist
145th Pennsylvania.............**John H. W. Stuckenberg**, Lutheran

Brigadier General William Harrow

1st Minnesota .... **Francis A. Conwell**, Methodist
19th Maine .... George Hathaway, Congregational

Brigadier General Alexander Webb

72nd Pennsylvania.............. Gamaliel Collins, Universalist

Colonel Norman Hall

No chaplains

Colonel Samuel Carroll

4th Ohio .... Daniel Strong, Methodist
8th Ohio .... Alexander Miller, Presbyterian
14th Indiana .... Elias Sabin, Methodist

Colonel Thomas Smyth

108th New York.................. Thomas Grassie, Dutch Reformed
1st Delaware .... **Thomas G. Murphey**, Presbyterian
14th Connecticut................ **Henry S. Stevens**, Baptist

Colonel George Willard

111th New York.................. **John N. Brown**, Methodist
125th New York.................. **Ezra D. Simons**, Baptist
126th New York.................. **T. Spencer Harrison**, Baptist

Third Corps (22)

Brigadier General Charles Graham

57th Pennsylvania............... William T. McAdam, Presbyterian

Brigadier General Hobart Ward

20th Indiana .... William C. Porter, Presbyterian
86th New York.................... Jonathan Watts, Methodist
124th New York.................. Thomas S. Bradner, Presbyterian
3rd Maine .... **Stephen F. Chase**, Methodist
4th Maine .... **Benjamin A. Chase**, Methodist
2nd U.S. Sharpshooters...... **Lorenzo Barber**, Methodist

Colonel Regis De Trobriand

40th New York.................... William H. Gilder, Methodist
17th Maine .... Jeremiah Hayden, Baptist
5th Michigan .... Benjamin F. Pritchard, Methodist

Brigadier General Joseph Carr

1st Massachusetts................ **Warren H. Cudworth**, Unitarian
26th Pennsylvania............... Charles A. Beck, Church of Christ
12th New Hampshire .... Thomas Ambrose, Church of Christ
11th Massachusetts............. Elisha Watson, Episcopal

Colonel William Brewster

71st New York..................... **Joseph H. Twichell**, Congregational
72nd New York................... **William R. Eastman**, Congregational
73rd New York ....Joseph O'Hagan, Roman Catholic
74th New York.................... Robert Littler, Baptist
120th New York.................. Foster Hartwell, Baptist

Colonel George Burling

5th New Jersey.................... Thomas Sovereign, Methodist
6th/8th New Jersey .... Samuel T. Moore, Methodist
7th New Jersey....................Julius Rose, Episcopal

Fifth Corps (9)

Colonel William Tilton

118th Pennsylvania............. William O'Neill, Methodist

Colonel Jacob Sweitzer

4th Michigan ....**John B. Seage**, Baptist

Colonel Strong Vincent

83rd Pennsylvania .... Orson Clark, Universalist
44th New York.................... Cyrus Crain, Presbyterian
20th Maine .... **Luther P. French**, Methodist

Colonel Hannibal Day

No chaplains

Colonel Sidney Burbank

No chaplains

Brigadier General Stephen Weed

146th New York.................. **Albert Erdman**, Presbyterian

Colonel William McCandless
No chaplains

Colonel Joseph Fisher
9th Pennsylvania Reserves..James McFarland, Presbyterian
10th Pennsylvania Reserve.John McLauren, Presbyterian
11th Pennsylvania Reserves **Adam Torrance**, Presbyterian

Sixth Corps (20)

Brigadier General Alfred T. A. Torbert
1st New Jersey .... **Robert B. Yard**, Methodist
2nd New Jersey.................... Robert R. Proudfit, Presbyterian
3rd New Jersey ....Joseph H. James, Methodist
15th New Jersey.................. **Alanson A. Haines**, Presbyterian

Brigadier General Joseph Bartlett
5th Maine ....**John R. Adams**, Congregational

Brigadier General David Russell
6th Maine .... Moses Kelley, Baptist
119th Pennsylvania............. Benjamin Miller, Methodist

Colonel Lewis Grant
3rd Vermont .... Daniel Mack, Methodist
6th Vermont .... Edward Payson Stone, Congregational

Brigadier General Thomas Neill
7th Maine .... Collamore Purington, Baptist
49th New York.................... Henry Benson, Presbyterian
43rd New York .... Corra Osborne, Baptist
77th New York.................... **Norman E. Fox Jr.**, Baptist

Brigadier General Alexander Shaler
23rd Pennsylvania ....**James G. Shinn**, Presbyterian
65th New York.................... Peter H. Burghardt, Presbyterian

Colonel Henry Eustis
37th Massachusetts............. Frank C. Morse, Methodist

Brigadier General Frank Wheaton

62nd New York....................John Harvey, Methodist
93rd Pennsylvania ....**Joseph S. Lame**, Methodist
102nd Pennsylvania............ **Alexander M. Stewart**, Presbyterian
139th Pennsylvania............. Robert McPherson, Presbyterian

Eleventh Corps (15)

Colonel Leopold Von Gilsa

41st New York...................... Frederick Bogen, Lutheran
54th New York..................... Ferdinand L. Sarner, Jewish
68th New York..................... William Mussehl, Lutheran
153rd Pennsylvania .... **Philip W. Melick**, Presbyterian

Brigadier General Adelbert Ames

17th Connecticut................ William K. Hall, Congregational
107th Ohio .... Robert Kabus, Jerusalem Reformed

Colonel Charles Coster

134th New York.................. Frank Fletcher, Baptist
154th New York.................. **Henry D. Lowing**, Congregational

Colonel Orland Smith

33rd Massachusetts .... **Daniel Foster**, Unitarian
55th Ohio .... Alfred Wheeler, Methodist

Brigadier General Alexander Schimmelfennig

82nd Illinois........................ Emanuel Reichhelm, Disciples of Christ
157th New York.................. **Ova Hoyt Seymour**, Presbyterian

Colonel Wladimir Krzyzanowski

26th Wisconsin .... William Vette, unknown
82nd Ohio ....John Burke, unknown
119th New York.................. Ezra Sprague, Universalist

Twelfth Corps (13)

Colonel Archibald McDougall

5th Connecticut.................. **Moses C. Welch**, Congregational
145th New York.................. Martin Dean, Congregational

Brigadier General Henry Lockwood

1st Maryland Eastern Shore Thomas Poulson, Methodist
150th New York.................. **Thomas E. Vassar**, Baptist

Brigadier General Thomas Ruger

2nd Massachusetts.............. **Alonzo H. Quint**, Congregational
13th New Jersey.................. Theodore Beck, Dutch Reformed
107th New York.................. Ezra Crane, Baptist

Colonel Charles Candy

29th Ohio .... **Lyman D. Ames**, Church of Christ
66th Ohio .... Wilson Parsons, Methodist Protestant

Colonel George Cobham / Brigadier General Thomas Kane

29th Pennsylvania............... Benjamin Sewell, Methodist

Brigadier General George Sears Greene

102nd New York................. Thomas Drumm, Episcopal
137th New York.................. **Eli F. Roberts**, Methodist
149th New York.................. Arvine Bowdish, Methodist

Calvary (15)

Colonel William Gamble

8th New York......................John Van Ingen, Episcopal

Colonel Thomas Devin

6th New York...................... George Crocker, Baptist
9th New York...................... Charles Keyes, Baptist

Brigadier General Wesley Merritt

6th Pennsylvania................ **Samuel L. Gracey**, Methodist

Colonel John McIntosh

1st Maryland .... Arthur Brickman, Lutheran
1st Pennsylvania ....James H. Beale, Presbyterian
1st New Jersey .... **Henry R. Pyne**, Episcopal
3rd Pennsylvania .... Moses H. Hunter, Episcopal

Colonel Pennock Huey

No chaplains

Colonel J. Irvin Gregg

10th New York.................... Robert Day, unknown

Brigadier General Elon Farnsworth

5th New York...................... **Louis N. Boudrye**, Methodist
1st Vermont ....John Woodward, Congregational
1st West Virginia................. F. W. Vertican, Methodist

Brigadier General George A. Custer

1st Michigan........................Jonathan Hudson, Methodist
5th Michigan .... Oliver Taylor, Episcopal
6th Michigan .... Stephen Greeley, Congregational

Number of Chaplains by Denomination

Denomination	Number
Methodist	39
Presbyterian	26
Baptist	19
Congregational	16
Episcopal	7
Unitarian	6
Lutheran	5
Unknown	5
Church of Christ	3
Roman Catholic	2
Dutch Reformed	2
Disciples of Christ	1
Methodist Protestant	1
Jerusalem Reformed	1
Jewish	1

Notes

Chapter 1

1 St. Clair A. Mulholland, *The Story of the 116th Regiment Pennsylvania Volunteers* (Philadelphia, 1903), 407. Other sources situate Corby's absolution earlier in the day. These will be explored in the chapter on the Second Corps.

2 William Corby, *Memoirs of Chaplain Life* (Chicago, 1893), 184.

3 Mulholland, *The Story*, 408.

4 Ibid., 407–8 (translated from the Latin).

5 Corby, *Memoirs*, 184.

6 Mulholland, *The Story*, 408.

7 Roy J. Honeywell, *Chaplains of the United States Army* (Washington, DC, 1958), 37.

8 Rollin W. Quimby, "Congress and the Civil War Chaplaincy," in *Civil War History* 10, no. 3 (Sept. 1964): 246.

9 U.S. War Dept., *War of the Rebellion: A Compilation of Official Records of the Union and Confederate Armies* (Washington, 1880–1901), Serial III, I, 154. Hereafter cited as *OR*, with all references to Serial III.

10 "Father Joseph B. O'Hagan," *The Woodstock Letters* 8, no. 3 (Maryland Province of the Society of Jesus, 1879), 178.

11 Henry Wilson, *Military Measures of the United States Congress 1861–1865* (New York, 1866), 2.

12 Ibid., 3. During the Mexican-American War, chaplains were expected to be Protestant. But the increasing number of Roman Catholic soldiers began a series of discussions about this policy, which was still in effect in 1861. In 1850, Archbishop John Hughes of New York delivered an address in which he proclaimed. "The object we hope to accomplish is to convert all Pagan nations, and all Protestant nations [. . .] including the inhabitants of the United States—the people of the cities, and the people of the country . . .

the Legislatures, the Senate, the Cabinet, the President, and all!" This only served to increase existing anti-Catholic sentiments toward new immigrants, especially the Irish (McPherson, *Battle Cry of Freedom*, [New York: Oxford University Press, 1988],132).

13 Act of Congress, approved July 22, 1861: Section 9.

14 *The Buffalo Commercial*, Jan. 17, 1862.

15 *The Buffalo Commercial*, Jan. 23, 1862.

16 A. W. Bartlett, *History of the Twelfth Regiment, New Hampshire Volunteers in the War of the Rebellion*, 54. The "Army of Flanders" was renowned for its ill-disciplined activity off the battlefield.

17 A. M. Stewart, *Camp, March and Battlefield* (Philadelphia,1865), vi.

18 Augustus Woodbury, *Second Rhode Island Regiment: A Narrative of Military Operations* (Providence, RI: Valpey, Angell and Company, 1875), 213.

19 Robert Hunt Rhodes, ed., *All for the Union: The Civil War Diary and Letters of Elijah Hunt Rhodes* (New York: Orion Books, 1985), 123–24.

20 Lowing may have been influenced in his decision to resign as chaplain by the malicious actions of more "irreligious members" of the regiment, who "squirted mule urine on the attendees at prayer meetings in Chaplain Henry Lowing's large wall tent, and broke up on such gathering by dropping cartridges down the chimney into the fire. The resulting explosion scattered the worshipers and burned holes in Lowing's tent" ("Undated interview notes in E. D. Northrup Papers," *Edwin Dwight Northrup Papers*, no. 4190, Division of Rare and Manuscript Collections, Cornell University Library).

21 Mark H. Dunkelman, *Brothers One and All: Esprit de Corps in a Civil War Regiment* (Baton Rouge, 2006), 176.

22 Ibid., 180.

23 Ibid., 177.

24 John J. Ryder, *Reminiscences of Three Years' Service in the Civil War by a Cape Cod Boy* (New Bedford, MA: Reynolds Printing, 1928), 47.

25 Ibid.

26 "Army Christian Association," *The Potter Journal and News Item* (Coudersport, Pennsylvania), Feb. 18, 1863, 2.

27 Woodbury, *Second Rhode Island Regiment*, 213.

28 Louis Napoléon Beaudry and Richard E. Beaudry, ed., *War Journal of Louis N. Beaudry, Fifth New York Cavalry: The Diary of a Union Chaplain, Commencing February 16, 1863* (Jefferson, NC, 1996), 25.

29 H. Clay Trumbull, *War Memories of an Army Chaplain* (New York, 1898), 107.

30 "Army Chaplains," *The Buffalo Commercial*, Jan 23, 1862.

31 Alonzo Quint, *The Potomac and the Rapidan* (Boston, 1864), 13.

32 James I. Robertson Jr., ed., *The Civil War Letters of General Robert McAllister* (New Brunswick, NJ, 1965), 136.

33 Stewart, *Camp, March, and Battle-field*, 12.

34 Ibid.

35 Ibid., 256.

36 W. O. Stoddard, "White House Sketches." *New York Citizen*, Oct. 6, 1866, quoted in David R. Barbee, "President Lincoln and Doctor Gurley," *Abraham Lincoln Quarterly* (March 1948): 7.

37 Henry N. Blake, *Three Years in the Army of the Potomac* (Boston: Lee and Shephard, 1865), 306.

38 *The Army and Navy Journal*, January 24, 1885. Quoted in Herman Norton, *The U.S. Army Chaplaincy, 1791–1865*, 86.

39 Although chaplains were considered to hold the rank of captain based on the congressional bill that set their pay at the rate of a captain of cavalry, that bill was amended in March 1864 to officially recognize "the rank of chaplain in the regular and volunteer service of the United States," stipulating that "Chaplains shall be borne on the field and staff-rolls next after the surgeon, and shall be subject to the same rules and regulations as other officers of the army" (No. LXIII. The Bill to amend Section Nine of the Act approved July seventeenth, 1862, "to Define the Pay and Emoluments of certain Officers of the Army," in Wilson, *Military Measures of the United States Congress*, 62).

40 David Power Conyngham, *Soldiers of the Cross, the Authoritative Text* (Notre Dame, IN, 2019), 149.

41 Quint, *The Potomac and the Rapidan*, 68–69.

42 Frederic Denison, *A Chaplain's Experience in the Union Army* (Providence, 1893), 22.

43 Edwin C. Bennett, *Musket and Sword, or The Camp, March, and Firing Line in the Army of the Potomac* (Boston, 1900), 179. Although wary of chaplains in general, Bennett admitted that the chaplain who joined his regiment, the Rev. C. M. Tyler, "was very companionable, and finely equipped mentally. He contributed much to the social and religious life of the regiment during the winter, and was a wise and kindly adviser to those who sought his counsel."

44 Section 8 of "An Act to define the Pay and Emoluments of certain Officers of the Army, and for other purposes," approved July 17, 1862.

45 *OR*, Series III, II: 278.

46 Ibid.

47 Ibid.

48 *Army and Navy Journal*, December 5, 1863.

49 Roy J. Honeywell, *Chaplains of the United States Army*, 6.

50 Maj. Abner Small, *The Sixteenth Maine Regiment in the War of the Rebellion* (Portland, 1886), 86.

51 Rev. J. J. Marks, *The Peninsular Campaign in Virginia* (Philadelphia, 1864), 46.

52 Edward P. Stone, correspondence to family, The University of Vermont Libraries Digital Collections, https://cdi.uvm.edu/manuscript/uvmcdi-93760.

53 William Eastman, "The Army Chaplain of 1863," *Personal Recollections of the War of the Rebellion*, MOLLUS, New York Commandery, Fourth Series (New York, 1912), 340.

54 Denison, *A Chaplain's Experience in the Union Army*, 16.

55 Thomas Wentworth Higginson, *Massachusetts in the Army and Navy During the War of 1861–65*, vol. 1 (Boston: Wright & Potter Printing Co., 1896), 141–42.

56 "Volunteer Chaplains for the Army," *United States Christian Commission, First Annual Report* (Philadelphia, 1863), 115. Emphasis original.

57 J. Pinkney Hammond, *The Army Chaplain's Manual* (Philadelphia, 1863), vii.

58 Ibid.

59 W. Y. Brown, *The Army Chaplain: His Office, Duties, and Responsibilities, and the Means of Aiding Him* (Philadelphia, 1863), 3, 82.

60 Ibid.

61 J. W. Muffly, ed., *The Story of Our Regiment: A History of the 148th Pennsylvania Vols.* (Des Moines, 1904), 343.

62 Trumbull, *War Memories*, 76–77.

63 Richard Eddy, *History of the Sixtieth Regiment New York State Volunteers* (Philadelphia, 1864), 88.

64 J. Chandler Gregg, *Life in the Army* (Philadelphia, 1866), 89.

65 Trumbull, *War Memories*, 106–7.

66 Sgt. William W. Bailey letter home, September 25, 1862, quoted in Charles J. LaRocca, *The 124th New York State Volunteers in the Civil War: A History and Roster* (Jefferson, NC: McFarland and Co., 2012), 34.

67 LaRocca, *The 124th New York*, 34.

68 William Putnam, "Army chaplains' work in time of war," MOLLUS, Michigan Commandery, 1901, 3.

69 John L. Cunningham, *Three Years with the Adirondack Regiment, 118th New York Volunteers Infantry* (Norwood, MA, 1920), 38.

70 Trumbull, *War Memories*, 4.

71 Thomas Wentworth Higginson, *Massachusetts in the Army and Navy During the War of 1861–65*, vol. 1 (Boston: Wright & Potter Printing Co., 1896), 141–42.

72 How the relationships between chaplains, soldiers, and the soldiers' families were affected in the postwar period is the topic for another study.

73 Chaplains were required to submit a quarterly report to the regimental commander on "the moral and religious condition of the regiment, and offer such suggestions as may conduce to the social happiness and moral improvement of the troops" (Act of Congress, approved Jul 22, 1861: Section 9). But such reports were often forgotten or went unread by the commander.

74 David Power Conyngham, *Soldiers of the Cross, the Authoritative Text* (Notre Dame, IN: University of Notre Dame Press, 2019), 149. Emphasis original.

75 William Eastman, "The Army Chaplain of 1863," *Personal Recollections of the War of the Rebellion*, MOLLUS, New York Commandery, Fourth Series (New York, 1912), 340.

76 John H. W. Stuckenberg, "The Effect of a Battle on a Man's Religious Views and Feelings," *The Lutheran Observer*, March 6, 1863.

77 Stewart, *Camp, March and Battlefield*, vi.

78 Ibid.

79 Frances Vinton, *The Christian Idea of Civil Government* (New York, 1861), 11. Emphasis original.

80 Trumbull, *War Memories*, 66.

81 "Captain Samuel A. Craig's Memoirs of Civil War and Reconstruction," *Western Pennsylvania Historical Magazine* 13, no. 4 (October 1930): 233. Emphasis original.

82 Eastman, "The Army Chaplain of 1863," 349.

83 Trumbull, *War Memories*, 76.

84 Drew Gilpin Faust, *This Republic of Suffering: Death and the American Civil War* (New York: Vintage Books, 2009), 20.

85 Trumbull, *War Memories*, 253. There are many stories about soldiers who died in peaceful resignation and acceptance of their fate. See, for instance, A. S. Billingsley, *Christianity in the War* (Philadelphia: Claxton, Remsen & Haffelfinger, 1872).

86 Faust, *This Republic*, 21.

87 Horatio Hackett, *Christian Memorials of the War: Scenes and Incidents Illustrative of Religious Faith and Principle, Patriotism and Bravery in Our Army* (Boston: Gould and Lincoln, 1864), 94.

88 Stuckenberg, "The Effect of a Battle."

89 "At a time of imminent danger [. . .] where a priest is present, and general absolution if given, imperfect contrition [that is, sorrow for sin out of fear of punishment] will suffice, provided the penitent resolves, if he escapes death, to confess his sins to a priest." *Memorial of the Monument* (Catholic Alumni Sodality of Philadelphia: Allen, Lane & Scott, 1911), 8.

90 "Mathew Andrew Dunn Letters," *Journal of Mississippi History* 1 (1939), 119.
91 Stuckenberg, "The Effect of a Battle."
92 Trumbull, *War Memories*, 5.
93 Stewart, *Camp, March and Battlefield*, vi.
94 C. A. Stevens, *Berdan's United States Sharpshooters in the Army of the Potomac* (St. Paul, MN, 1892), 276. According to the regimental historian, "being one of our best marksmen, and on account of his exposure and bravery in the late battle [Chancellorsville] where he was not obliged to go, from that time on [Chaplain Barber] never failed to have a large audience when he officiated as preacher" (275–76).
95 Ronald C. White, *Lincoln's Greatest Speech: The Second Inaugural* (New York, 2006), 101.
96 The Executive Committee, Maine Commissioners, *Maine at Gettysburg* (Portland, ME, 1898), 558.
97 Joseph W. Sanderson, "Chaplains and Chaplains," (paper read May 1, 1900), *War Papers, Commandery of Wisconsin, Military Order of the Loyal Legion of the United States*, vol. 3 (Milwaukee, 1903), 373–74. Emphasis original.
98 Allen R. Thompson, *In the Shadow of the Round Tops: Longstreet's Countermarch, Johnston's Reconnaissance, and the Enduring Battles for the Memory of July 2, 1863* (New York: Permuted Press, 2023), 8.
99 Some portions of regiments were on detached duty, and it cannot be ascertained whether their chaplains were at Gettysburg or with the rest of the regiment at Westminster or elsewhere.
100 Eastman, *The Army Chaplain*, 350.

Chapter 2

1 Maj. Gen. Abner Doubleday was acting commander of the First Corps on July 1, with Brig. Gen. Thomas Rowley assuming command of Doubleday's Third Division.
2 Harry W. Pfanz, *Gettysburg: The First Day* (Chapel Hill, NC, 2001), 77. General Meade replaced Doubleday as commander of the corps on the evening of July 1 with Maj. Gen. John Newton of the Sixth Corps.
3 Brig. Gen. George Stannard's brigade had been detached to guard the corps' trains in Westminster and did not reach the field until after the bulk of the fighting had finished for the day.
4 The 6th Wisconsin, which had been held back in reserve by the Seminary, participated with regiments from Brig. Gen. Lysander Cutler's brigade to capture Confederates who had advanced into the open railroad cut north

of the Chambersburg Pike. The regiment stayed with Cutler for the rest of the day's battle. The 6th Wisconsin did play a role on the night of July 2 in keeping the Confederates from advancing into the rear of the Union troops on Culp's Hill. By morning, they rejoined their brigade.

5 Edward Dwight Eaton, *Two Wisconsin Pioneers: Sketches in Remembrance, Samuel Witt Eaton, Catherine Demarest Eaton* (Cambridge, MA, 1933), 21–22.

6 Alan T. Nolan, *The Iron Brigade: A Military History* (Bloomington, IN: Indiana University Press, 1961), 203.

7 Samuel W. Eaton, "Some Sketches From a Three Years' Experience in the Army," Manuscripts and Archives, Yale University Library, MS 972, series I, box 1, folder 5a, 8.

8 Ibid.

9 Ibid.

10 Samuel W. Eaton to Catherine Eaton, July 21, 1863, in Edward Dwight Eaton Papers, Wisconsin Historical Society, Division of Library, Archives, and Museum Collections.

11 Eaton, "Some Sketches," 8–9. Pvt. Alexander P. Alcorn of 1st Pennsylvania Light Battery B (Cooper's Batter) was killed on July 1.

12 Ibid., 9–10. The total number of casualties for any unit (always an educated guess because of incomplete records) includes those killed, wounded, captured, and missing.

13 Ibid., 9–10.

14 Ibid., 10.

15 Ibid., 17.

16 "Report of Col. Robinson to the Governor," *Quiner Scrapbooks: Correspondence of the Wisconsin Volunteers, 1861–1865*, vol. 8, Wisconsin Historical Society (May 12, 1863), 153a. https://content.wisconsinhistory.org/digital/collection/quiner/id/18297/rec/4. Accessed Sept. 17, 2022.

17 Edward Eaton, *Two Wisconsin Pioneers*, 23.

18 Eaton, "Some Sketches," 17. Emphasis original.

19 "Late from the Iron Brigade," *Wisconsin State Journal*, December 16, 1862, 2.

20 Thomas Barnett, "The Losses of the 19th Indiana," *Indianapolis Daily Journal*, July 13, 1863, 2. The total number of casualties for the three days of fighting was 210 out of 308 men engaged, a 68.2 percent loss. See Steven Floyd, *Commanders and Casualties at the Battle of Gettysburg*, 7.

21 Ibid.

22 Alan D. Gaff, *On Many a Bloody Field: Four Years in the Iron Brigade* (Indianapolis: Indiana University Press, 1996), 371.

23 In 1871, Reverend Barnett "surrendered his parchments and withdrew from the church." In *A History of the North Indiana Conference of the Methodist Episcopal Church* (Indianapolis, 1917), 112. The charges were not specified.

24 "Resolution of Respect and Condolence," *The Fort Scott Republican*, June 24, 1904, 4.

25 *Journal and Reports of the Forty-First Annual Session of the Detroit Conference of the Methodist Episcopal Church* (Detroit, 1896), 46.

26 Bruce Catton, *Glory Road* (Garden City, NY, 1952), 12.

27 Donald L. Smith, *The Twenty-Fourth Michigan of the Iron Brigade* (Harrisburg, PA, 1962), 9.

28 O. B. Curtis, *History of the Twenty-fourth Michigan of the Iron Brigade* (Detroit, MI, 1891), 137.

29 Smith, *The Twenty-fourth Michigan*, 121

30 Curtis, *History of the Twenty-Fourth Michigan*, 155.

31 "From the 24th Michigan," *Detroit Advertiser and Tribune*, July 16, 1863.

32 Wills was a lawyer who played a prominent role in the creation of the National Cemetery at Gettysburg. He hosted President Lincoln at his home the night before the president gave his Gettysburg Address in November 1863.

33 "From the 24th Michigan," *Detroit Advertiser and Tribune*, July 16, 1863.

34 Ibid.

35 L. S. Trowbridge and Fred E. Farnsworth, *Michigan at Gettysburg* (Detroit, 1889), 64.

36 "From the 24th Infantry," *Detroit Advertiser and Tribune*, July 24, 1863. Emphasis original.

37 Ibid. The "various associations" include the U.S. Sanitary Commission and the Christian Commission, which sent agents to Gettysburg to care for the wounded. Hospital nurses were often soldiers from the regiment who were detailed for the duty.

38 Ibid.

39 Ibid. John Burns was a Gettysburg citizen and veteran of the War of 1812 who had joined the Iron Brigade on July 1 armed with his old flintlock musket.

40 Ibid.

41 *Detroit Advertiser and Tribune*, letter dated August 7, 1863 (date of publication unknown).

42 Ibid.

43 Ibid.

44 Ibid. Emphasis original.

45 William C. Way letter to Capt. A. M. Edwards, August 10, 1863, Michigan Civil War Collection, https://micivilwar.us/document.php?doc=William-Way-1863-08-10, accessed April 26, 2023.
46 Quoted in John Robertson, *Michigan in the War* (Lansing, MI, 1880), 271
47 *Detroit Free Press,* July 18, 1863, 1.
48 *Journal and Reports of the Forty-first Annual Session of the Detroit Conference of the Methodist Episcopal Church* (Detroit, 1896), 47.
49 The quotes in the following paragraphs are from William C. Way letters to the Ryder family, July 9, July 12, and July 19, 1863, Bentley Historical Library, University of Michigan.
50 The 7th Indiana was on detached duty and did not reach the field until the end of the day on July 1.
51 Andy Ward, "The 16th Maine Infantry at Gettysburg," *Gettysburg Magazine* no. 37 (July 2007), 36.
52 The grand Confederate advance on July 3 is more commonly known as Pickett's Charge, but "Pickett-Pettigrew-Trimble" more accurately includes the divisions, other than that of Maj. Gen. George Pickett, that took part in the charge.
53 "Good Life Ended," *The Buffalo Weekly Express,* June 27, 1895, 2.
54 Ibid.
55 Ibid.
56 July 14, 1863, letter to the *Buffalo Christian Advocate,* July 23, 1863, 2.
57 July 15, 1863, letter to the *Northern New York Journal,* July 21, 1863, 2.
58 July 14, 1863, letter to the *Buffalo Christian Advocate,* July 23, 1863, 2
59 July 15, 1863, letter to the *Northern New York Journal,* July 21, 1863, 2.
60 July 14, 1863, letter to the *Buffalo Christian Advocate,* July 23, 1863, 2.
61 Ibid.
62 Ibid.
63 July 15, 1863, letter to the *Northern New York Journal,* July 21, 1863, 2. Cook claimed that "it was while running this gauntlet that nearly all the casualties of the regiment occurred."
64 July 14, 1863, letter to the *Buffalo Christian Advocate,* July 23, 1863, 2.
65 July 15, 1863, letter to the *Northern New York Journal,* July 21, 1863, 2.
66 Ibid.
67 "Letter from Colonel Root," July 14, 1863, *The Buffalo Commercial Advertiser*, July 18, 1863, 2. This unique parole situation may not have been legal or valid, which might have jeopardized the men's chance to be duly exchanged. The conditions of this parole were that the prisoners detailed to care for the wounded "will not attempt to escape nor take up arms against the

Confederate States, nor give any information that may be prejudicial to the interests of the Confederate States until regularly exchanged, and should the United States Government refuse to consider this parole as valid and binding, and refuse to exchange the prisoners, then the prisoners are to remain prisoners of war to the Confederate States Government until regularly exchanged after returning within Confederate lines, and this detail of prisoners are to be subsisted by the Confederate States Government so long as they remain within its lines. Col. Adrian Root, 94th N. Y. V. (wounded) is permitted to take charge of the detail upon the above conditions" (July 15, 1863, letter to the *Northern New York Journal*, July 21, 1863, 2).

68 July 15, 1863, letter to the *Northern New York Journal*, July 21, 1863, 2. A "nullity" is a thing that is not legally valid.

69 July 14, 1863, letter to *The Buffalo Commercial Advertiser*, July 18, 1863, 3.

70 Ibid.

71 Ibid.

72 July 22, 1863, letter to the editor of the *Express* (unknown date of publication), cited in New York State Military Museum and Veterans Research Center, https://museum.dmna.ny.gov/index.php/?cID=2557.

73 August 7, 1863, letter to *The Buffalo Christian Advocate*, August 20, 1863, 2.

74 It is interesting to note that their son, Ferdinand Ward Jr., was responsible for creating the company that functioned like a Ponzi scheme and that bankrupted former president Ulysses S. Grant in 1884.

75 At Gettysburg, Brig. Gen. James Wadsworth commanded the First Division of the First Corps.

76 Geoffrey C. Ward, *A Disposition to be Rich* (New York, 2012), Kindle edition, location 1680.

77 *Livingston Republican*, January 18, 1863.

78 "The Late Battle—104th N.Y.S.V.," *Livingston Republican*, July 23, 1863.

79 Ibid.

80 Letter to the *Union and Advertiser*, August 12, 1863. http://www.13thmass.org/1863/rappahannock.html#mozTocId181097.

81 Ibid.

82 Ibid.

83 Ibid.

84 Ferdinand Ward to Sarah Ward, August 24, 1863, MSS 0453, Brinton family papers, Special Collections, University of Delaware Library, Newark, Delaware.

85 *Livingston Republican*, July 23, 1863.

86 When the regiment was being reorganized, the state tried to designate it as the Fifty-first, perhaps out of pride to demonstrate how many regiments the state could muster in, but the men wanted to retain their honorable number of the Eleventh. The issue was decided in the soldiers' favor in late October.
87 William Henry Locke, *The Story of the Regiment* (Philadelphia, 1868), v.
88 Ibid., 212.
89 Ibid., 214.
90 Ibid., 221.
91 Ibid., 224.
92 Ibid., 224–25.
93 Ibid., 226.
94 Ibid., 229.
95 Ibid., 231–32.
96 By late in the afternoon of July 1, four Confederate brigades had not yet reached the town.
97 William Henry Locke, *The Story of the Regiment* (Philadelphia, 1868), 233–34.
98 Ibid., 233.
99 Ibid., 234.
100 Ibid.
101 Ibid., 235.
102 Ibid.
103 Ibid.
104 Ibid., 236–37.
105 Ibid., 236.
106 Ibid., 237–38.
107 Ibid., 238.
108 Ibid.
109 Ibid., 239.
110 Ibid., 238–39.
111 Ibid., 240.
112 Ibid., 240–41.
113 Ibid., 241. The quartermaster mentioned forced his way into a local home on the night of July 3 and was promptly captured the next morning by Union soldiers. At Fredericksburg, Union soldiers ransacked the town and destroyed or carried off many possessions of private citizens.
114 Ibid., 242.
115 Ibid., 254–55.
116 New York Monuments Commission, *Final Report on the Battle of Gettysburg*, vol. 1 (Albany, 1900), footnote on 24.

117 May Gerlach Hoffman, "Gettysburg Terrors Made to Live Again in Woman's Account of Great Battle," *Philadelphia Inquirer*, June 27, 1938, 2 (memoir of Mary McAllister as told to Hoffman in 1903).

118 Jeffrey I. Richman, *Final Camping Ground: Civil War Veterans at Brooklyn's Green-Wood Cemetery in Their Own Words* (Brooklyn, 2007), 155.

119 Charles P. Potts, "A First Defender in Rebel Prison Pens," in *Publications of the Historical Society of Schuylkill County*, vol. 4 (Historical Society of Schuylkill County, 1914), 343.

120 A. J. Sellers and the Survivors Association, "Reunion of the Survivors of the Ninetieth Penna. Vols. on the Battle-field of Gettysburg" (Philadelphia, 1889), 65–66.

121 John V. Ferguson letter to Kate. May 4, 1862. All letters cited were transcribed by Leith Regan and accessed at https://museum.dmna.ny.gov/application/files/4215/5309/0175/97thInfFergusonLetters.pdf.

122 John V. Ferguson letter to Kate, July 11, 1863.

123 Ibid.

124 Ibid.

125 Ibid.

126 John V. Ferguson letter to Kate, July 28, 1863.

127 Ibid.

128 Ibid.

129 John V. Ferguson letter to Kate, August 8, 1863. Colonel Wheelock had returned home by that time to see to the new conscripts.

130 Ibid.; John V. Ferguson letter to Kate, August 25, 1863. A "soger" is a soldier who is always trying to evade his share of work.

131 John V. Ferguson letter to Kate, October 6, 1864.

132 Col. Roy Stone had recruited the original Bucktails (the 42nd Pennsylvania) earlier in the war and was asked to form more regiments of these excellent marksmen, who wore bucktails on their hats as a symbol of their skill with a musket.

133 Orrin G. Cocks, *An Informal History of the First Presbyterian Church of Wellsboro, Pennsylvania* (1937), 20–21.

134 "Army Christian Association," *The Potter Journal* (Coudersport, Pennsylvania), February 18, 1863, 2.

135 "Letter from Rev. J. P. Calkins," *The Wellsboro Gazette* (Tioga County, Pennsylvania), July 29, 1863, 2.

136 Ibid.

137 Ibid.

138 "Rev. J. F. Calkins and His Church," *The Tioga County Agitator*, January 6, 1880, 2.

139 The First Vermont Brigade was part of the Sixth Corps. It was commanded by Col. Lewis A. Grant and included the 2nd, 3rd, 4th, 5th, and 6th Vermont regiments.

140 "From the 14th Regiment," *Rutland Weekly Herald* (Rutland, VT), July 16, 1863, 8.

141 Ibid.

142 Col. G. G. Benedict, *A Short History of the 14th Vermont Reg't* (Bennington, VT, 1887), 44–45.

143 Ibid. Meade wasn't the only general who lauded the Vermonters' efforts on July 3. Colonel Benedict reported that when Abner Doubleday saw the charge of the Vermont brigade, he cried, "Glory to God, glory to God! See the Vermonters go it!" (478).

144 Ibid., 45.

145 "From the Sixteenth Vermont Regiment, First Letter," *The Vermont Christian Messenger* (Montpelier, VT), July 16, 1863, 2.

146 Ibid.

147 Ibid.

148 Ibid.

149 Ibid. The First Vermont Brigade, consisting of the 2nd, 3rd, 4th, 5th, and 6th Vermont Infantry, was in the Sixth Corps under the command of Col. Lewis A. Grant. They arrived on the field late in the afternoon of July 2 and took a position behind Little Round Top.

150 "From the Sixteenth Vermont Regiment, Second Letter," *The Vermont Christian Messenger* (Montpelier, VT), July 16, 1863, 2.

151 Ibid.

152 "From the Sixteenth Vermont Regiment," *The Vermont Christian Messenger* (Montpelier, VT), July 23, 1863, 2.

153 Ibid.

154 "From the Sixteenth Vermont Regiment," *The Vermont Christian Messenger* (Montpelier, VT), July 30, 1863, 2.

155 Ibid. Some citizens of Baltimore had attacked Union soldiers who were marching through the city on their way south in April 1861.

156 Ibid.

157 Ibid.

158 Ibid.

159 "Our Wounded at Gettysburg," *The Vermont Christian Messenger* (Montpelier, VT), August 27, 1863, 2.

160 Ibid.

Chapter 3

1 Rev. Emory M. Stevens, "Story of the Chaplain," in *The Story of Our Regiment: A History of the 148th Pennsylvania Vols.*, ed. J. W. Muffly, 193.

2 Stevens evidently wrote letters to his wife throughout his term of service, and although his son included excerpts in his "Story of the Chaplain," the letters themselves are lost in the Stevens family records.

3 Stevens, "Story of the Chaplain," 197.

4 Ibid., 198.

5 Ibid., 197.

6 Ibid., 198.

7 Ibid.

8 Ibid. The "butterfly" was the Second Corps symbol of a trefoil.

9 Ibid., 202.

10 When he arrived home, Stevens craved green vegetables, but his physician said that eating them would hasten his death. He begged his wife for some sliced radishes she was preparing for supper, and after eating a few, he collapsed and his family began his death vigil. But after a few hours, he awoke and proclaimed, "I am not going to die. My work is not done yet." When he returned to the regiment, he told the surprised surgeon that the men would suffer less illness if they had more green bulky matter to eat (Stevens, "Story of the Chaplain," 213).

11 At Gettysburg, the entire brigade counted about 530 men, just a bit bigger than most regiments.

12 William Corby, *Memoirs of Chaplain Life* (Chicago: La Monte, O'Donnell & Co., 1893), 176. It is commonly accepted that the advance of the Sixth Corps on July 2, a total of thirty-eight miles from Manchester to Gettysburg, was the longest and most epic march of the campaign, if not the war.

13 Corby, *Memoirs*, 178.

14 Ibid., 179.

15 Ibid., 180.

16 Ibid., 181.

17 Ibid. The details of this absolution are given in chapter 1.

18 Ibid., 185.

19 Ibid., 186. In the years leading up to the Civil War, there was quite a lot of prejudice against both the Irish and Roman Catholics.

20 Ibid., 187.

21 Ibid., 192.

22 Ibid. The location of this bullet today is unknown.

23 John O. Evjen, *The Life of J. H. W. Stuckenberg* (Minneapolis, MN: The Lutheran Free Church Publishing Company, 1938), 101.

24 *The John Henry Wilbrand Stuckenberg Papers*, which includes his *July 29, 1863 to September 10, 1863 Diary as Chaplain of the 145th Regiment PA Volunteers* and his *January 6, 1864 Lecture on the Battle of Gettysburg*, are in the Special Collections of Musselman Library at Gettysburg College. His two diary manuscripts were later published by David T. Hedrick and Gordon Barry Davis, Jr., eds., as *I'm Surrounded by Methodists* (Gettysburg: Thomas Publications, 1995), but the lecture is unpublished.

25 Stuckenberg diary, 14.

26 Ibid., 14–15.

27 Ibid., 15.

28 John H. W. Stuckenberg, *July 29, 1863 to September 10, 1863 Diary as Chaplain of the 145th Regiment PA Volunteers*, *The John Henry Wilbrand Stuckenberg Papers*, Special Collections, Musselman Library, Gettysburg College, 15–16.

29 Ibid.

30 Ibid., 16–17.

31 Ibid., 17.

32 Ibid., 18–19. The route Stuckenberg took with the surgeon appears to be from the division hospital at the Granite School House, then west on the Granite School House Lane, south on Taneytown Road, and west on the Trostle Lane to the George Weikert Farm, the first house he mentions, which sits at the intersection of modern-day United States and Hancock Avenues. Then they probably continued south to the John T. Weikert Farm, which would have been very close to both the Union picket line and rebel pickets on Stony Hill.

33 Ibid., 19.

34 Ibid., 20.

35 Ibid., 21.

36 Ibid., 22. Captain Hilton recovered and was present at Gettysburg for the dedication of the regiment's monument in 1889.

37 Ibid., 24.

38 Ibid.

39 Ibid., 24–25.

40 Ibid., 27.

41 Ibid., 28.

42 Ibid., 28.

43 Letter to "Respected Pastor," September 2, 1863, John Henry Wilbrand Stuckenberg Papers, Special Collections, Musselman Library, Gettysburg College.

44 "January 6, 1864 Lecture on the Battle of Gettysburg," John Henry Wilbrand Stuckenberg Papers, Special Collections, Musselman Library, Gettysburg College.

45 George Ross Mather, *The Story of the Pioneer Congregations of Fort Wayne, Indiana, 1820-1860* (Fort Wayne, Indiana: Allen County-Fort Wayne Historical Society, 1992), 49.

46 Francis's nephew and namesake, Francis Asbury Shoupe, shocked his Indiana friends and family when he moved south and attended the Secession Convention in South Carolina in December 1860. He went on to become a Confederate general, the only one from Indiana.

47 "Letters from Adjt. McCallum and Chaplain Conwell to Mrs. Messick, on the Death of her Husband," *Faribault Central Republican*, August 5, 1863, 1.

48 "From the First Minnesota," *The Saint Paul Daily Press*, November 4, 1863, 2.

49 Ibid.

50 Ibid.

51 Widow's Pension Record, National Archives, Rev Francis Conwell. The original account dates this event to the time of the Peninsula Campaign in 1862, but Conwell had not yet joined the regiment at that time. It most likely took place in October 1863 when the regiment was camped near Kelly's Ford, Virginia.

52 John W. Simon, ed., *The Papers of Ulysses S. Grant, Volume 24: 1873* (Carbondale: Southern Illinois University Press, 2000), 48.

53 Ibid., 49.

54 His name was also spelled "Murphy" in various records.

55 Thomas G. Murphey, *Four Years in the War, The History of the First Regiment of Delaware Veteran Volunteers* (Philadelphia: James S. Claxton, 1866), prefatory.

56 Ibid., 114.

57 Ibid., 115.

58 The Bliss Farm buildings changed hands several times throughout the day, until Brig. Gen. Alexander Hays of the Third Division ordered them burned by the 14th Connecticut Infantry about midday on July 3.

59 Murphey, *Four Years*, 116–17.

60 Ibid., 118.

61 Ibid., 118–19.

62 Ibid., 120–21.

63 Ibid., 123.

64 Ibid., 125.
65 Ibid., 126.
66 Ibid., 124.
67 Ibid., 124.
68 Murphey, *Four Years*, 126.
69 Ibid.
70 Ibid., 126–27.
71 Ibid., 128.
72 Ibid., 119.
73 Henry S. Stevens, *Address Delivered at the Dedication of Monument of the 14th Conn. Vols. at Gettysburg* (Middletown, CT: Pelton & King, 1884), 12.
74 Ibid., 12–13.
75 Ibid., 15.
76 Ibid., 15–16. The division commander was Brig. Gen. Alexander Hays.
77 Ibid.
78 Ibid.
79 Ibid., 17. According to the official report of Capt. John Hazard, chief of artillery for the Second Corps, three limbers of Lt. Alonzo Cushing's 4th U.S. Artillery, Battery A, were exploded on the morning of July 3, but he makes no mention of Capt. William Arnold's battery.
80 Ibid.
81 Ibid., 18–19.
82 Ibid., 19.
83 Ibid., 20. The sound of the hexagonal bolts from the English Whitworth guns was unique and unmistakable.
84 Ibid., 21.
85 Ibid., 21–24. According to the final tally, by the end of the Pickett-Pettigrew-Trimble charge, the 14th claimed more than two hundred prisoners and five captured battle flags.
86 Henry S. Stevens, *Souvenir of Excursion to Battlefields by the Society of the Fourteenth Connecticut Regiment* (Washington: Gibson Bros., 1893), 31.
87 Ibid., 24.
88 Ibid., 25.
89 Ibid., 37.
90 Arabelle Willson, *Disaster, Struggle, Triumph*, 169.
91 *Official Journal and Minutes of the Eighty-Sixth Session of the Genesee Conference of the Methodist Episcopal Church* (Buffalo: S. McGerald & Son, 1895), 129.

92 He was elected historian of the regiment in 1888 and began working on a regimental history, most likely using his diary as a source, but like the diary, that history has not been located.

93 W. G. Lightfoote, *Proceedings of the Reunion of the Veterans of the 111th and the 126th Reg'ts N.Y. Vols.* (Canandaigua, NY: Times Book and Job Print. House, 1886), 36.

94 Ibid., 38.

95 *Auburn Weekly Democrat*, October 25, 1888. The soldier mentioned was most likely Edgar Proseus, a private in Company E who was wounded on July 3. His older brother Augustus, a first lieutenant in the same company, was killed in action on July 2.

96 New York Monument Commission, *Final Report on the Battle of Gettysburg*, vol. 2 (Albany, NY: J. B. Lyon Co., 1900), 801.

97 *Official Journal and Minutes of the Eighty-Sixth Session of the Genesee Conference of the Methodist Episcopal Church* (Buffalo: S. McGerald & Son, 1895), 129.

98 Ibid. The regimental monument was dedicated on June 26, 1891 and sits near the spot where the color bearers were killed on July 3.

99 He said that over the course of fifty years in the ministry, he served twenty-one churches plus his three years as chaplain.

100 Ezra D. Simons, *A Regimental History: The One Hundred and Twenty-Fifth New York State Volunteers* (New York: The Judson Printing Co., 1888), 75–76.

101 Ibid., 76. "Bandbox" and "white glove" were derisive terms given to inexperienced troops by veterans.

102 Ibid., 102.

103 Ibid.

104 Ibid., 103.

105 Ibid.

106 Ibid., xix.

107 Ibid., 111–12.

108 Ibid., 105.

109 The Bliss Farm was directly in the regiment's front, yet Simons makes no mention of the farm or its burning on the morning of July 3 in his regimental history, thus suggesting that he was not actually with his men on the front line that day. Nevertheless, his account of the day's events is worth including here.

110 Simons, *A Regimental History*, 136–38.

111 Ibid., 146.

112 "From the Wounded of the One Hundred and Twenty-fifth," *The Troy Daily Times*, July 29, 1863, 3.

113 New York Monuments Commission, *Final Report on the Battlefield of Gettysburg*, vol. 2 (Albany: J. B. Lyon Company, 1902), 892.

114 T. Spencer Harrison, "126th Regiment!" *The Geneva Daily Gazette*, July 17, 1863.

115 Ibid.

116 Arabella M. Willson, *Disaster, Struggle, Triumph, the Adventures of 1000 "Boys in Blue," from August, 1862 to June, 1865* (Albany, NY: The Argus Company, 1870), 194.

117 Ibid., 365.

Chapter 4

1 "From the Third Maine," *The Maine Farmer*, July 7, 1863, 2.

2 S. Freeman Chase letter to Lizzie, July 24, 1863, Paul W. Bean Papers, Special Collections, Fogler Library, University of Maine, Orono, Box 279, folder 25. Emphasis original.

3 Henry Dill Letter, August 14, 1863, quoted in Charles LaRocca, *The New York 124th State Volunteers in the Civil War* (Jefferson, NC: McFarland & Co., 2012), 161.

4 Sgt. Walter W. Smith, Co. H, 2nd USSS, letter to his sister, date unknown, quoted in Jeffery D. Marshall, *A War of the People: Vermont Civil War Letters* (Lebanon, NH: University Press of New England, 1999), 196.

5 Charles H. Weygant, *History of the One Hundred and Twenty-Fourth Regiment, NYSV* (Newburgh, NY: Journal Printing House, 1877), 109.

6 C. A. Stevens, *United States Sharpshooters in the Army of the Potomac, 1861–1865* (St. Paul, MN: The Price-McGill Co., 1892), 276.

7 "From the 2d Reg. U.S. Sharpshooters," August 28, 1863, 2. There were no "large forces" of J. E. B. Stuart's cavalry near Emmitsburg at the end of June. But some of Albert Jenkins's mounted men were near there on or before June 30, and these could easily have been mistaken for Stuart's troopers.

8 C. A. Stevens, *Berdan's United States Sharpshooters in the Army of the Potomac, 1861–1865* (St. Paul, MN: The Price-McGill Company, 1892), 540.

9 "From the 2d Reg. U.S. Sharpshooters," August 28, 1863, 2.

10 Because his regimental history was written so soon after the war, it contains descriptions of events that do not align with the *Official Reports of the Battle of Gettysburg*, which were published in 1889. Some of his descriptions confuse which corps participated in certain actions, or conflate the actions of July 2 and 3, or add details that are incorrect or overdramatized. Nevertheless, as a

primary source from an eyewitness to the battle, and from a chaplain, it is a valuable resource.

11 Letter to "My Dear Bradlee," Governor's Island, N.Y. Harbor, August 12, 1863, in Angeline M. Cudworth, *A Memorial of Rev. Warren H. Cudworth* (Boston: D. Lothrop and Company, 1884), 108.

12 Warren H. Cudworth, *History of the First Regiment, Massachusetts Infantry* (Boston: Walker, Fuller, and Company, 1866), 7.

13 Letter to "My Dear Mother," Bivouac at Gum Spring, June 22, 1863, in Angeline M. Cudworth, *A Memorial of Rev. Warren H. Cudworth* (Boston: D. Lothrop and Company, 1884), 106–7.

14 Ibid., 390.

15 Ibid., 392–93.

16 Ibid., 393.

17 Ibid., 393–94. His description of cavalry bringing word of the rebel concentration in the front of the Third Corps is mistaken; the cavalry had left the area earlier in the day. He makes no mention of the Second and Fifth Corps units that had been sent out to reinforce the Third Corps line during the Confederate attack.

18 Ibid., 396–97.

19 Ibid., 400.

20 Ibid., 406.

21 Ibid. It is uncertain what he means by "defeat of Lee twice in succession," since the two battles previous to Gettysburg had been Confederate victories.

22 Ibid., 407–8.

23 Ibid., 409.

24 Angeline M. Cudworth, *A Memorial of Rev. Warren H. Cudworth* (Boston: D. Lothrop and Company, 1884), 300.

25 Joseph H. Twichell, letter to his father, April 22, 1861, Joseph Hopkins Twichell Papers, Beinecke Rare Book and Manuscript Library, Yale University, New Haven, Connecticut.

26 Joseph H. Twichell, letter to Dear Mother, June 30, 1863, Joseph Hopkins Twichell Papers, Beinecke Rare Book and Manuscript Library, Yale University, New Haven, Connecticut.

27 Ibid. Twichell was fond of Sickles and defended the general's controversial actions on July 2 at Gettysburg. Sickles sent a note to Twichell sometime after the fiftieth reunion at Gettysburg, asking the clergyman to speak at his funeral and to read a letter from Gen. James Longstreet that said if it had not been for Sickles's action, the fight would have gone the other way (Steve

Courtney, *Joseph Hopkins Twichell* [Athens, GA: University of Georgia Press, 2008], 271).

28 Joseph Hopkins Twichell, Letter to "My darling sis," July 5, 1863, Joseph Hopkins Twichell Papers, Beinecke Rare Book and Manuscript Library, Yale University, New Haven, Connecticut.

29 Ibid.

30 Ibid.

31 Ibid.

32 Ibid.

33 Joseph Hopkins Twichell, letter to "Dear Ned," July 15, 1863, Joseph Hopkins Twichell Papers, Beinecke Rare Book and Manuscript Library, Yale University, New Haven, Connecticut.

34 Joseph Hopkins Twichell, letter to "Dear mother," July 20, 1863, Joseph Hopkins Twichell Papers, Beinecke Rare Book and Manuscript Library, Yale University, New Haven, Connecticut.

35 William R. Eastman, "The Army Chaplain of 1863: Read Before The New York Commandery, December 13, 1911" in Titus Munson Coan, *Personal Recollections of the War of the Rebellion: Addresses Delivered Before the New York Commandery of the Loyal Legion of the United States,* 1883 (New York: Knickerbocker Press, 1912), 338.

36 "A Rolling Chaplain," in Rev. Edward P. Smith, *Incidents Among Shot and Shell* (Philadelphia: Edgewood Publishing Company, 1868), 164.

37 Oliver Otis Howard, "Minor Incidents Amid Great Events," in *The Story of American Heroism: Thrilling Narratives of Personal Adventures During the Great Civil War* (Springfield, OH: J. W. Jones, 1897), 338–39.

Chapter 5

1 Seage had evidently been a member of the Methodist Episcopal Church when he emigrated from England but withdrew from the Methodist connection in 1851 to join the Baptist Church.

2 Martin N. Bertera and Kim Crawford, *The 4th Michigan Infantry in the Civil War* (East Lansing: Michigan State University Press, 2010), 150.

3 John Seage, letter to Jonathan Robertson, Adjutant General, June 1, 1866, https://4thmichigan.wordpress.com/john-seage/.

4 Jonathan Robertson, *Michigan in the War, Part II* (Lansing, Michigan: W. S. George and Co., 1880), footnote, 73.

5 Henry Seage journal, Tuesday, June 9, 1863, from the collection of Steven Roberts.

6 John Seage, letter to His Excellency Gov. Blair, December 23, 1863, https://4thmichigan.wordpress.com/john-seage/. Richard Seage was one of the lieutenants that Col. Harrison Jeffords had asked to help recover the regiment's national flag during the intense hand-to-hand fighting in the Wheatfield. Jeffords was mortally wounded by a bayonet, the highest-ranking officer to die in this way, and Richard fell next to his colonel, his body riddled by bullets and a bayonet thrust; it is not known what happened to the flag they fought to defend. Richard was brevetted captain and then major after the war.

7 Oliver Wilcox Norton, *The Attack and Defense of Little Round Top, Gettysburg, July 2, 1863* (New York: The Neale Publishing Co., 1913), 285.

8 *Lewiston Sun-Journal*, October 28, 1861, 3.

9 Glenn W. LaFantasie, *Twilight at Little Round Top: July 2, 1863–The Tide Turns at Gettysburg* (New York: Vintage Books, 2007), 109.

10 Thomas A. Desjardin, *Stand Firm Ye Boys from Maine: The 20th Maine and the Gettysburg Campaign* (New York: Oxford University Press, 1995), 50.

11 American Battlefield Trust, "The 16th Infantry Regiment, United States Army," July 7, 2017 (updated November 1, 2023), https://www.battlefields.org/learn/articles/16th-infantry-regiment-united-states-army.

12 Albert Erdman, "A Chaplain's Experience," in *War Talks by Morristown Veterans* (Morristown, NJ: Vogt Bros., Publishers, 1887), 41–42.

13 Ibid.

14 George Dallas Albert, *History of the County of Westmoreland, Pennsylvania: With Biographical Sketches of Many of Its Pioneers and Prominent Men* (Philadelphia: L. H. Everts & Company, 1882), 594.

15 Rev. Marion Daniel Shutter, ed., *History of Minneapolis, Gateway to the Northwest* Vol. 3 (Chicago: The S. J. Clarke Publishing Co, 1923), 4.

16 Adam Torrance, Letter to "My Dear Wife," U.S. Army Heritage and Education Center, Robert L. Brake Collection.

17 At one point during the war, three Torrance brothers and their father were in the army at the same time.

18 Elly Torrance, letter to "My dear Sister Mattie," September 21, 1863, Gettysburg National Military Park Library.

19 "Letter from Rev. A. Torrence, Camp Near Rappahannock Station, Va., September 11, 1863," *Presbyterian Banner*, October 28, 1863, 1.

20 John F. McLaren, "Chaplain's Farewell," *Presbyterian Banner*, December 23, 1863, 1.

Chapter 6

1 Robert was one of five Yard brothers who served during the war. All of them survived.

2 "Rev. Robert Boyd Yard," in C. R. Barnes, ed., *Minutes of the Eighteenth Session of the Newark Conference of the Methodist Episcopal Church* (New York: Nelson and Phillips, 1876), 50.

3 James I. Robertson Jr., *The Civil War Letters of General Robert McAllister* (New Brunswick, NJ: Rutgers University Press, 1965), 95.

4 "Our Army Correspondence From the 1st N.J. Volunteers," *Monmouth Democrat* (Freehold, NJ), June 26, 1862, 1.

5 "Army Correspondence from the 1st Reg't. New Jersey Vols.," June 22, 1863, *Monmouth Democrat* (Freehold, NJ), July 2, 1863, 1.

6 Ibid.

7 Robert B. Yard, "Letter from the Army," *Rockland County Mesenger*, August 6, 1863, 1.

8 Camille Baquet, *History of The First Brigade, New Jersey Volunteers* (Trenton, NJ: MacCrellish & Quigley, 1910), 106.

9 Ibid., 107.

10 Ibid., 109.

11 "Bravery of Army Chaplains," *The Monmouth Inquirer* (Freehold, NJ), June 18, 1863, 1.

12 Alanson A. Haines, *History of the Fifteenth Regiment New Jersey Volunteers* (New York: Jenkins and Thomas, 1883), 72. The distances of the forced marches were: eighteen miles on June 28, twenty-two miles on June 29, twenty-three miles on June 30, and the epic thirty-five-mile march on July 1.

13 Ibid., 79–80. The Sixth Corps column is estimated to have been about ten miles long.

14 Ibid., 84.

15 Ibid., 85.

16 Ibid., 86–87.

17 Ibid., 88.

18 Ibid., 92.

19 Ibid., 90.

20 Ibid., 92.

21 Ibid., 94.

22 Ibid.

23 Ibid., 95.

24 Ibid., 94–95.

25 Ibid., 95.

26 Ibid., 96–97. The small shattered house may have been the home of John and Mary Wentz, which sat just to the north of the Peach Orchard along the Emmitsburg Road, or it might have been another home in the area.

27 Ibid., 97.

28 Ibid., 102.

29 "The Christian Warrior," *The Portland Daily Press*, June 27, 1862, 3.

30 John R. Adams, *Memorial and Letters of Rev. John R. Adams, D.D.* (Cambridge: John Wilson and Son, 1890), 115–16.

31 Ibid., 116–17.

32 Ibid., 117.

33 Ibid., 117–18.

34 Ibid., 118.

35 Joseph M. Wilson, *The Presbyterian Historical Almanac, and Annual Remembrancer of the Church for 1867* (Philadelphia: Joseph M. Wilson, 1867), 120. There is no evidence that the War Department granted the brevet promotion.

36 Thus, the Sixth Corps had the distinction of guarding both extreme flanks of the Army of the Potomac.

37 "Oration by Rev. Norman Fox, D.D.," *New York Monuments Commission, Final Report on the Battlefield of Gettysburg* (Albany: J. B. Lyon, 1900), 621–23.

38 "Rev. Jas. Shinn Dies at the Ripe Age of 81," *Press of Atlantic City*, October 27, 1903, 1.

39 *History of the Twenty-Third Pennsylvania Volunteer Infantry, Birney's Zouaves*, compiled by the Survivors Association (Philadelphia: 1904), 136.

40 Ibid., 393.

41 Ibid., 392.

42 Ibid., 402.

43 Laura M. DiPaolo, "God's Forgotten Acre," *Journal of the Historical Society of the Eastern Pennsylvania Conference*, 2011, 80.

44 These letters were later published in full, along with a detailed description of his church trial and explusion, as *Maryland Slavery and Maryland Chivalry* (Philadelphia: Collins, Printer, 1858).

45 *Pennsylvania at Gettysburg*, Vol. 1, 507–9, 510. Colonel McCarter was with his men at Gettysburg, but due to a lingering illness from the wound he received a year earlier, he was not in command of the regiment.

46 Ibid.

47 Rev. A. M. Stewart, *Camp, March, and Battlefield* (Philadelphia: Jas. B. Rodgers, 1865), 107.

48 Ibid., 323.

49 Three officers and one hundred men were sent to Gettysburg with the supply train and was posted in line with the rest of the brigade on July 3. The remainder of the regiment picketed the roads between Gettysburg and Westminster and joined the Sixth Corps for the pursuit of the Confederates on July 5.

50 This includes the marches of the entire campaign.

51 Stewart, *Camp, March and Battlefield*, 324–36.

52 Ibid., 408.

Chapter 7

1 During the march to Gettysburg, a soldier in the 17th Connecticut Infantry stepped out of line to draw some water from a creek. When an aide reported this to General Barlow, he placed Lt. Col. Douglas Fowler under arrest. Once they reached the field Fowler appealed to General Schurz, who restored Fowler to his command.

2 Philip Melick diary, Easton Area Public Library, Easton, Pennsylvania, 130.

3 Ibid.

4 The regimental history includes an account by Dr. Stout: "I was captured between the Poor House [County Alms House] and the town. Col. D. P. Penn, of the 7th Regiment of the [Louisiana] Tigers, saw me and dismounted. He walked by my side and asked me who I was and then told me I was his prisoner, taking me to the German Reformed Church [on Stratton Street], when he said to me: 'You ought to take this church for a Hospital.' I said, 'Yes, if it is not locked.' 'Well,' said the Colonel, 'if it is we can soon open it.' But we found the doors unlocked, and took possession. In less than half an hour it was filled with wounded men, mostly Union men. I was in attendance there three days." Rev. W.R. Keifer, *History of the One Hundred and Fifty-third Regiment Pennsylvania Volunteers Infantry* (Easton, PA: The Chemical Publishing Company, 1909), 131. Stout was put in charge of all wounded at the church, Union and Confederate.

5 Ibid., 131–3.

6 Ibid., 133–4.

7 Two hundred men had been detached from the 154th New York and rejoined the regiment on the morning of July 2.

8 Lowing included a very rough sketch of the area where his unit fought west of Gettysburg. Unfortunately, the sketch is very faded and cannot be adequately reproduced here.

9 Henry D. Lowing, letter to "Dear Father," July 22, 1863, courtesy of the Mark H. Dunkelman and Michael J. Winey Collection, St. Bonaventure University Archives. The 154th New York Infantry suffered an 84 percent casualty rate, one of the highest of all the Union regiments at Gettysburg.

10 John J. Ryder, *Reminiscences of Three Years' Service in the Civil War* (New Bedford, MA: Reynolds Printing, 1928), 36.

11 "Letter from Rev. Daniel Foster," *The Liberator,* July 17, 1863, 3.

12 "Letter from Rev. Daniel Foster," *The Liberator*, August 21, 1863, 3.

13 "The Fighting Chaplain of the Massachusetts 33rd," *Chester Historical Society* 4, Issue 2, October 2005, 5.

14 Ibid.

15 O. H. Seymour letter, "Dear Brother Lou," June 22, 1863, O. H. Seymour Papers, Record Group 0306, Accession 99-113, Special Collections and Archives at Auburn University Libraries. Seymour prefaces these sentences with the warning, "N. B. Not to be read aloud." Perhaps he didn't want his family to worry about his desire to rejoin the regiment while they were on the march.

16 O. H. Seymour letter, "Dear Bro," July 5, 1863, O. H. Seymour Papers, Record Group 0306, Accession 99-113, Special Collections and Archives at Auburn University Libraries.

17 O. H. Seymour letter, "Dear Bro," July 10, 1863, O. H. Seymour Papers, Record Group 0306, Accession 99-113, Special Collections and Archives at Auburn University Libraries.

18 O. H. Seymour letter, "Dear Bro," July 22, 1863, O. H. Seymour Papers, Record Group 0306, Accession 99-113, Special Collections and Archives at Auburn University Libraries. Emphasis original.

19 "Letter from Rev. O. H. Seymour," July 18, 1863, *The Gazette and Banner* (Cortland, NY), from New York State Military Museum (museum.dmna.ny.gov).

Chapter 8

1 Slocum may have had General Meade's Pipe Creek circular in mind, and had no orders from him to advance to Gettysburg. Slocum also was senior to Howard and may not have felt a need to respond to his plea for help. He received the nickname "Slow Come" for his hesitancy to advance.

2 Harlan P. Rugg, diary entry July 2, 1863, Harlan P. Rugg Papers, Archives and Special Connections, University of Connecticut Library.

3 Report of Col. Warren W. Packer to Governor William Buckingham, August 7, 1863, in Edwin E. Marvin, *The Fifth Regiment Connecticut Volunteers: A History Complies from Diaries and Official Reports* (Hartford, CT: Press of Wiley, Waterman, and Eaton, 1889), 382–83.

4 Col. Warren Packer diary, entry for July 2, 1863, in Edwin E. Marvin, *The Fifth Regiment Connecticut Volunteers: A History Complies from Diaries and Official Reports* (Hartford, CT: Press of Wiley, Waterman, and Eaton, 1889), 275.

5 Edward O. Bartlett, *The "Dutchess County Regiment" in the Civil War, Its Story as Told by its Members* (Danbury, CT: The Danbury Medical Printing Co., 1907), 188.

6 Ibid., 189–90.

7 After helping to recover Capt. John Bigelow's abandoned guns near the Trostle farm, the 150th charged the retreating Mississippians toward the Emmitsburg Road.

8 Bartlett, *The "Dutchess County Regiment"*, 192–93.

9 Ibid., 193–4.

10 Ibid., 194–5.

11 "Our Army Correspondence: On the march through the Boonsboro Valley," July 9, 1863, *Amenia Times* (publication date unknown).

12 "Our Army Correspondence," July 17, 1863, *Amenia Times* (publication date unknown).

13 Thomas E. Vassar, *Uncle John Vassar; or The Fight of Faith* (New York: American Tract Society, 1879), 88–89.

14 Alonzo H. Quint, *The Potomac and the Rapidan* (Boston: Crosby and Nichols, 1864), 320–21.

15 Alonzo H. Quint, *The Record of the Second Massachusetts Infantry, 1861–65* (Boston: James P. Walker, 1867), v.

16 Quint, *The Potomac and the Rapidan*, 325.

17 Quint, *The Record of the Second Massachusetts Infantry*, vi.

18 Quint, *The Potomac and the Rapidan*, 329–30.

19 Ibid.

20 See James T. Fritsch, *The Untried Life: The Twenty-Ninth Ohio Volunteer Infantry in the Civil War* (Athens, OH: Ohio University Press, 2012), note 44, page 429.

21 Lyman Ames diary, entry for June 30, 1863, Lyman Daniel Ames papers, Ohio State Archives, VFM 2972 A.

22 Ames diary, entry for July 1, 1863.

23 Ames diary, entry for July 2, 1863.

24 Ames diary, entry for July 3, 1863

25 Ames diary, entry for July 5, 1863.

26 "Losses of the 29th Ohio," *Cleveland Daily Leader*, July 18, 1863, 3.

27 Ames diary, entry for July 8, 1863.

28 Ames diary, entry for July 15, 1863. There is no soldier with the last name of Mason in the 29th who was recorded as dying from wounds received at Gettysburg.

29 Ames diary, entry for July 25, 1863.

30 Ames diary, entry for July 27, 1863.

31 Ames diary, entry for July 28, 1863.

32 Ames diary, entry for July 29, 1863.

33 Ames diary, entry for August 3, 1863.

34 Ames diary, entry for August 12, 1863.

35 Ames diary, entry for June 19, 1865.

36 Capt. Geo. K. Collins, *Memoirs of the 149th Regt. N.T. Vol. Inft.* (Syracuse: published by the author, 1891), 34.

37 "Names of the Killed and Wounded in the 137th Regiment N.Y.V.," *The Owego Times*, July 16, 1863, 2. The field he describes is most likely present-day "Pardee Field" on Lower Culp's Hill, near where the 137th defended the Union flank on July 2.

38 "Camp 137th Reg. N.Y.S.V. July 29," *The Owego Times*, August 6, 1863.

39 Ibid.

40 Ibid.

41 Ibid.

42 "Letter from the 109th [sic], August 2, 1863" *The Owego Times*, August 20, 1863.

43 Ibid. The men were two privates from the 46th Pennsylvania Infantry, and one from the 13th New Jersey regiment.

44 "Camp 137th Regiment N.Y.V., August 25, 1863," *The Owego Times*, September 3, 1863, 2.

45 "Letter from Chaplain Roberts," September 14, 1863, *The Owego Times*, September 24, 1863, 2.

46 Ibid. Roberts was a strong supporter of Maj. Gen. Henry Slocum of the Twelfth Corps. In the same letter, he wrote, "My honest convictions are, and was at the time of the Chancellorsville fight with its shameful retreat, had Gen. Slocum been in the place of power, as the commander of this army, Richmond would be held by our forces."

47 Ibid.

48 Ibid.

49 Ibid.

50 *Minutes of the Wyoming Annual Conference of the Methodist Episcopal Church, Thirty-first session* (Elmira, NY: Steam Printing House, 1882), 44.

Chapter 9

1 *Official Minutes of the One Hundred and Sixteenth Session of the New England Conference of the Methodist Episcopal Church* (Boston: Murray and Emery Company, 1912), 132.
2 Samuel L. Gracey, *Annals of the Sixth Pennsylvania Cavalry* (Philadelphia: E. H. Butler and Co., 1868), 179.
3 Ibid., 179–80.
4 Ibid., 181.
5 Ibid., 181–82.
6 Ibid., 182.
7 Ibid.
8 Ibid.
9 Henry R. Pyne, *The History of the First New Jersey Cavalry* (Trenton, NJ: J. A. Beecher, 1871), 162.
10 Ibid., 163.
11 Ibid., 162.
12 Ibid., 164.
13 Pyne may have conflated the East Cavalry Field action with the skirmish at Brinkerhoff's Ridge. In both actions, the 1st New Jersey and the 3rd Pennsylvania cavalry fought side-by-side, with the Pennsylvanians being sent forward to relieve the New Jersey men. But at this point, Pyne mentions the Michigan troopers, who were not at Brinkerhoff's Ridge on July 2.
14 Pyne, *The History of the First New Jersey Cavalry*, 164.
15 Ibid., 165.
16 Ibid., 166.
17 Richard E. Beaudry, ed., *War Journal of Louis N. Beaudry, Fifth New York Cavalry* (Jefferson, NC: McFarland & Co., 1996), 48.
18 Ibid., 49.
19 Ibid. The actual number of men killed at Hanover was a little more than forty.
20 Ibid., 50.
21 Ibid.
22 Ibid.
23 Ibid.
24 Louis N. Beaudry, *The Libby Chronicle* (Albany, NY: C. F. Williams, 1889), 41–43.

25 *War of the Rebellion: A Completion of the Official Records of the Union and Confederate Armies*, Series II, vol. IV (Washington D.C.: Government Printing Office, 1899), 269.

26 Louis N. Beaudry, "A Unique Celebration: How the 4th of July, 1863, was Spent in Libby Prison," *National Tribune*, December 19, 1889.

Bibliography

Books

17th Connecticut Volunteers at Gettysburg, June 30th, and July 1st, 2d and 3d, 1884. Bridgeport, CT: The Standard Association, 1884.

Albert, George Dallas. *History of the County of Westmoreland, Pennsylvania: With Biographical Sketches of Many of Its Pioneers and Prominent Men*. Philadelphia: L. H. Everts & Company, 1882.

Bachelder, John B. *The Bachelder Papers: Gettysburg in Their Own Words*, vol. 1. Ohio: Morningside House, 1994.

Bancroft, Emily Adams. *Memorial and Letters of Rev. John R. Adams, D.D.* Cambridge, MA: John Wilson and Son, 1890.

Baquet, Camille. *History of The First Brigade, New Jersey Volunteers*. Trenton, NJ: MacCrellish & Quigley, 1910.

Barbee, David R. "President Lincoln and Doctor Gurley," in *Abraham Lincoln Quarterly*, March 1948.

Bartlett, Asa W. *History of the Twelfth Regiment New Hampshire Volunteers in the War of the Rebellion*. Concord, NH: Ira C. Evans, 1897.

Bartlett, Edward O. The "Dutchess County Regiment" in *The Civil War, Its Story as Told by its Members*. Danbury, CT: The Danbury Medical Printing Co., 1907.

Bates, Samuel P. *History of Pennsylvania Volunteers, 1861–5*. Harrisburg, 1870.

Beaudry, Louis Napoléon. *The Libby Chronicle*. Albany, NY: C. F. Williams, 1889.

Beaudry, Louis Napoléon, and Richard E. Beaudry, ed., *War Journal of Louis N. Beaudry, Fifth New York Cavalry: The Diary of a Union Chaplain, Commencing February 16, 1863*. Jefferson, NC: McFarland and Co., 1996.

Benedict, Col. G. G. *A Short History of the 14th Vermont Reg't.* Bennington, VT: C. A. Pierce, 1887.

Bennett, Edwin C. *Musket and Sword, or The Camp, March, and Firing Line in the Army of the Potomac.* Boston: Coburn Publishing, 1900.

Bertera, Martin N., and Kim Crawford. *The 4th Michigan Infantry in the Civil War.* East Lansing: Michigan State University Press, 2010.

Blake, Henry N. *Three Years in the Army of the Potomac.* Boston: Lee and Shephard, 1865.

Bowen, James L. *History of the Thirty-Seventh Regiment Mass. Volunteers, in the Civil War of 1861–1865.* Holyoke, MA: Clark W. Bryan & Co., 1884.

Brown, W. Y. *The Army Chaplain: His Office, Duties, and Responsibilities, and the Means of Aiding Him.* Philadelphia, William S. & Alfred Martien, 1863.

Catholic Alumni Sodality of Philadelphia. *Memorial of the Monument Erected on the Battlefield of Gettysburg to Very Rev. William Corby, C.S.C.* Philadelphia: Allen, Lamb & Scott, 1911.

Catton, Bruce. *Glory Road.* Garden City, NY: Doubleday, 1952.

Chiniquy, Rev. Charles. *Fifty Years in the Church of Rome, Fifteenth Edition.* Chicago: Adam Craig, 1888.

Coan, Titus Munson. *Personal Recollections of the War of the Rebellion: Addresses Delivered Before the New York Commandery of the Loyal Legion of the United States, 1883.* New York: Knickerbocker Press, 1912.

Cocks, Orrin G. *An Informal History of the First Presbyterian Church of Wellsboro, Pennsylvania.* 1937.

Coco, Gregory A., *A Strange and Blighted Land, Gettysburg: The Aftermath of a Battle.* Gettysburg: Thomas Publications, 1988.

Collins, Capt. Geo. K. *Memoirs of the 149th Regt. N.Y. Vol. Inft.* Syracuse: published by the author, 1891.

Conyngham, David Power. *Soldiers of the Cross, the Authoritative Text.* Notre Dame, IN: University of Notre Dame Press, 2019.

Corby, William. *Memoirs of Chaplain Life.* Chicago: La Monte, O'Donnell & Co., 1893.

Courtney, Steve. *Joseph Hopkins Twichell.* Athens, GA: University of Georgia Press, 2008.

Cross, Andrew B. *Battle of Gettysburg and the Christian Commission.* Baltimore, 1865.

Crowell, Joseph E. *The Young Young Volunteer: The Everyday Experiences of a Soldier Boy in the Civil War.* New York: G. W. Dillingham Company, 1906.

Cudworth, Angeline M. *A Memorial of Rev. Warren H. Cudworth*. Boston: D. Lothrop and Company, 1884.

Cudworth, Warren H. *History of the First Regiment, Massachusetts Infantry*. Boston: Walker, Fuller, and Company, 1866.

Cunningham, John L. *Three Years with the Adirondack Regiment, 118th New York Volunteers Infantry*. Norwood, MA: The Plimpton Press, 1920.

Curtis, O. B. *History of the Twenty-fourth Michigan of the Iron Brigade*. Detroit: Winn and Hammond, 1891.

Denison, Frederic. *A Chaplain's Experience in the Union Army*. Providence: Published by the Society, 1893.

Desjardin, Thomas A. *Stand firm ye boys from Maine: the 20th Maine and the Gettysburg Campaign*. New York: Oxford University Press, 1995.

DiPaolo, Laura M. "God's Forgotten Acre." *Journal of the Historical Society of the Eastern Pennsylvania Conference*, 2011.

Dreese, Michael A. *An Imperishable Fame: The Civil War Experience of George Fisher McFarland*. Mifflintown, PA: Juniata County Historical Society, 1997.

Dunkelman, Mark H. *Brothers One and All: Esprit de Corps in a Civil War Regiment*. Baton Rouge: Louisiana State University Press, 2006.

Eaton, Edward Dwight. *Two Wisconsin Pioneers: Sketches in Remembrance, Samuel Witt Eaton, Catherine Demarest Eaton*. Cambridge, MA, 1933.

Eddy, Richard. *History of the Sixtieth Regiment New York State Volunteers*. Philadelphia, 1864.

Erdman, Albert. "A Chaplain's Experience," in *War Talks by Morristown Veterans*. Morristown, NJ: Vogt Bros., 1887.

Evjen, John O. *The Life of J. H. W. Stuckenberg*. Minneapolis: The Lutheran Free Church Publishing Company, 1938.

Faust, Drew Gilpin. *This Republic of Suffering: Death and the American Civil War*. New York: Vintage Books, 2009.

Floyd, Fred C. *History of the Fortieth (Mozart) Regiment New York Volunteers*. Boston: F. G. Gilson Company, 1909.

Fraser, Wallace. *A History of the Presbytery of Clarion of the Presbyterian Church of the United States of America*. Presbytery of Clarion, 1940.

Fuller, Charles A. *Personal Recollections of the War of 1861*. Sherburne, NY: News Job Printing House, 1906.

Gaff, Alan D. *On Many a Bloody Field: Four Years in the Iron Brigade*. Indianapolis: Indiana University Press, 1996.

Gettysburg Battle-field Commission. *Pennsylvania at Gettysburg: Ceremonies at the Dedication of the Monuments Erected by the Commonwealth of Pennsylvania to Mark the Positions of the Pennsylvania Commands Engaged in the Battle*. Vol. 2. Harrisburg: E. K. Meyers, 1893.

Gilbert, Sr., Daniel R., ed. *Freddy's War: The Civil War Letters of John Frederick Frueauff*. Bethlehem, PA: Moravian College, 2006.

Gilder, Richard Watson. *The Poems of Richard Watson Gilder*. New York: The Riverside Press Cambridge, 1908.

Gracey, S. L. *Annals of the Sixth Pennsylvania Cavalry*. Philadelphia: E. H. Butler & Co., 1868.

Gregg, J. Chandler. *Life in the Army: Life in the Army in the Departments of Virginia*. Philadelphia: Perkinpine & Higgins, 1866.

Hackett, Horatio. *Christian Memorials of the War: Scenes and Incidents Illustrative of Religious Faith and Principle, Patriotism and Bravery in our Army*. Boston: Gould and Lincoln, 1864.

Haines, Alanson A. *History of the Fifteenth Regiment New Jersey Volunteers*. New York: Jenkins & Thomas, 1883. Hammond, J. Pinkney *The Army Chaplain's Manual*. Philadelphia: J. B. Lippincott & Co., 1863.

Higginson, Thomas Wentworth. *Massachusetts in the Army and Navy During the War of 1861–65*. Vol. 1. Boston: Wright & Potter Printing Co., 1896.

History of the First Reg't Pennsylvania Reserve Cavalry. Philadelphia: King & Baird Printers, 1864.

Honeywell, Roy J. *Chaplains of the United States Army*. Washington, D.C.: U.S. Government Printing Office, 1958.

Howard, Oliver Otis. "Minor Incidents Amid Great Events," in *The Story of American Heroism: Thrilling Narratives of Personal Adventures During the Great Civil War*. Springfield, OH: J. W. Jones, 1897.

Ide, Horace Knights. *History of the First Vermont Cavalry Volunteers in the War of the Great Rebellion*. Baltimore: Butternut and Blue, 2000.

Judson, A. M. *History of the Eighty-Third Regiment Pennsylvania Volunteers*. Erie, PA: B. F. H. Lynn, 1865.

Keifer, Rev. W. R. *History of the One Hundred and Fifty-third Regiment Pennsylvania Volunteers Infantry*. Easton, PA: The Chemical Publishing Company, 1909.

Kepler, William. *History of the Three Months' and Three Years' Service from April 16th, 1861, to June 22d, 1864, of the Fourth Regiment Ohio Volunteer Infantry in the War for the Union*. Cleveland, OH: Leader Printing Co., 1888.

LaFantasie, Glenn W. *Twilight at Little Round Top: July 2, 1863–The Tide Turns at Gettysburg*. New York: Vintage Books, 2007.

LaRocca, Charles J. *The 124th New York State Volunteers in the Civil War: A History and Roster*. Jefferson, NC: McFarland and Co., 2012.

LaRocca, Charles J., ed. *This Regiment of Heroes*. Montgomery, NY: C. J. LaRocca, 1991.

Lightfoote, W. G. *Proceedings of the Reunion of the Veterans of the 111th and the 126th Reg'ts N.Y. Vols*. Canandaigua, NY: Times Book and Job Print. House, 1886.

Locke, William Henry. *The Story of the Regiment*. Philadelphia: J. B. Lippincott & Co., 1868.

Maine Commissioners The Executive Committee. *Maine at Gettysburg*. Portland, ME: The Lakeside Press, 1898.

Marks, Rev. J. J. *The Peninsular Campaign in Virginia*. Philadelphia: J. B. Lippincott & Co., 1864.

Marshall, Jeffery D. *A War of the People: Vermont Civil War Letters*. Lebanon, NH: University Press of New England, 1999.

Martin, James M. et al. *History of the Fifty-Seventy Regiment, Pennsylvania Veteran Volunteer Infantry*. Meadville, PA: McCoy & Calvin, n.d.

Marvin, Edwin E. *The Fifth Regiment Connecticut Volunteers: A History Compiled from Diaries and Official Reports*. Hartford, CT: Press of Wiley, Waterman, and Eaton, 1889.

Mather, George Ross. *The Story of the Pioneer Congregations of Fort Wayne, Indiana, 1820–1860*. Fort Wayne, Indiana: Allen County-Fort Wayne Historical Society, 1992.

MOLLUS (Military Order of the Loyal Legion of the United States), New York Commandery, Fourth Series. New York, 1912.

Muffly, J. W., ed., *The Story of Our Regiment: A History of the 148th Pennsylvania Vols*. Des Moines: The Kenyon Printing & Mfg. Co., 1904.

Mulholland, St. Clair A. *The Story of the 116th Regiment Pennsylvania Infantry*. Philadelphia: F. McManus, Jr. & Co, 1899.

Murphey, Thomas G. *Four Years in the War, The History of the First Regiment of Delaware Veteran Volunteers*. Philadelphia: James S. Claxton, 1866.

Murphy, T. L. *Kelly's Heroes: The Irish Brigade at Gettysburg*. Gettysburg: Farnsworth House Military Impressions, 1997.

New York Monuments Commission, Final Report on the Battle of Gettysburg, Vols. 1 and 2. Albany: J. B. Lyon Co., 1900.
Nicholson, Lt. Col. John P. *Pennsylvania at Gettysburg, Vol. 1*. Harrisburg: Wm. Stanley Hay, 1904.
Nolan, Alan T. *The Iron Brigade: A Military History*. Bloomington: Indiana University Press, 1961.
Norton, Herman. Struggling for Recognition: The U.S. Army Chaplaincy, 1791–1865. Washington, D.C.: U.S. Government Printing Office, 1977.
Norton, Oliver Wilcox. *The Attack and Defense of Little Round Top, Gettysburg, July 2, 1863*. New York: The Neale Publishing Co., 1913.

Official Records of the Union and Confederate Armies, Reports Addendum, Series I, Vol. 27. Wilmington, NC: Broadfoot Publishing Company, 1995.
Osborn, Captain Hartwell et al. *Trials and Triumphs: The Record of the Fifty-fifth Ohio Volunteer Infantry*. Chicago: A. C. McClurg & Co., 1904.

Park Congregational Church: The Story of One Hundred Years 1836–1936. Grand Rapids: Park Congregational Church, 1936.
Pfanz, Harry W. *Gettysburg: The First Day*. Chapel Hill: University of North Carolina Press, 2001.
Pyne, Henry R. *The History of the First New Jersey Cavalry*. Trenton, NJ: J. A. Beecher, 1871.

Quimby, Rollin W. "Congress and the Civil War Chaplaincy," in *Civil War History* 10, no. 3 (Sept. 1964).
Quint, Alonzo. *The Potomac and the Rapidan*. Boston: Crosby and Nichols, 1864.
Quint, Alonzo H. *The Record of the Second Massachusetts Infantry, 1861–65*. Boston: James P. Walker, 1867.

Regimental History Committee, *History of the Third Pennsylvania Cavalry*. Philadelphia: Franklin Printing, 1905.
Rhodes, Robert Hunt, ed. *All for the Union: The Civil War Diary and Letters of Elijah Hunt Rhodes*. New York: Orion Books, 1985.
Richman, Jeffrey I. *Final Camping Ground: Civil War Veterans at Brooklyn's Green-Wood Cemetery in Their Own Words*. Brooklyn: Green-Wood Cemetery, 2007.
Robertson, Jr., James I., ed., *The Civil War Letters of General Robert McAllister*. New Brunswick: Rutgers University Press, 1965.
Robertson, Jonathan. *Michigan in the War, Part II*. Lansing, Michigan: W. S. George and Co., 1880.

Rusling, James Fowler. *Men and Things I Saw in Civil War Days*. New York: The Methodist Book Concern, 1914.

Ryder, John J. *Reminiscences of Three Years' Service in the Civil War by a Cape Cod Boy*. New Bedford, MA: Reynolds Printing, 1928.

Sanderson, Joseph W. "Chaplains and Chaplains," *War Papers*, Commandery of Wisconsin, Military Order of the Loyal Legion of the United States. Vol. 3. Milwaukee, 1903.

Sawyer, Franklin. *A Military History of the 8th Regiment Ohio Vol. Inf'y: Its Battles, Marches and Army Movements*. Cleveland, OH: Fairbanks & Co., 1881.

Sellers A. J. and the Survivors Association, *Reunion of the Survivors of the Ninetieth Penna. Vols. on the Battle-field of Gettysburg*. Philadelphia: John W. Clark, 1889.

Sewell, Rev. Benjamin T. *Sorrow's Circuit*. Philadelphia: Jesper Harding & Son, 1859.

Shutter, Rev. Marion Daniel. ed. *History of Minneapolis, Gateway to the Northwest*. Vol. 3. Chicago: The S. J. Clarke Publishing Co, 1923.

Simon, John W., ed. *The Papers of Ulysses S. Grant*. Vol. 24, *1873*. Carbondale: Southern Illinois University Press, 2000.

Simons, Ezra D. *A Regimental History: The One Hundred and Twenty-Fifth New York State Volunteers*. New York: The Judson Printing Co., 1888.

Sleight, Rev. C.L. "A Man Among Men." *American Agriculturist Weekly*, Feb. 6, 1904.

Small, Maj. Abner. *The Sixteenth Maine Regiment in the War of the Rebellion*. Portland, ME: B. Thurston and Co., 1886.

Smith, Donald L. *The Twenty-Fourth Michigan of the Iron Brigade*. Harrisburg, PA: Stackpole, 1962.

Smith, Rev. Edward P. *Incidents Among Shot and Shell*. Philadelphia: Edgewood Publishing Company, 1868.

Stevens, C. A. *Berdan's United States Sharpshooters in the Army of the Potomac*. St. Paul, MN: Price-McGill Company, 1892.

Stevens, Rev. Emory M. "Story of the Chaplain" in *The Story of Our Regiment: A History of the 148th Pennsylvania Vols.*, ed. J. W. Muffly. Des Moines: The Kenyon Printing & Mfg. Co., 1904.

Stevens, Henry S. *Address Delivered at the Dedication of Monument of the 14th Conn. Vols. at Gettysburg*. Middletown, CT: Pelton & King, 1884.

Stevens, Henry S. *Souvenir of Excursion to Battlefields by the Society of the Fourteenth Connecticut Regiment*. Washington: Gibson Bros., 1893.

Stewart, A. M. *Camp, March and Battlefield*. Philadelphia: Jas. B. Rodgers, 1865.

Survivors Association. *History of the 118th Pennsylvania Volunteers, Corn Exchange Regiment*. Philadelphia: J. L. Smith, 1905.

Survivors Assocation, *History of the Twenty-Third Pennsylvania Volunteer Infantry, Birney's Zouaves, compiled by the Survivors Association*. Philadelphia: 1904.

Thompson, Allen R. *In the Shadow of the Round Tops: Longstreet's Countermarch, Johnston's Reconnaissance, and the Enduring Battles for the Memory of July 2, 1863.* New York: Permuted Press, 2023.

Tompkins, Charles H. "With the Vermont Cavalry, 1861–2," *The Vermonter* 17 (1912).

Toombs, Samuel. *Reminiscences of the War, Comprising a Detailed Account of the Experiences of the Thirteenth Regiment New Jersey Volunteers in Camp, on the March, and in Battle*. Orange, NJ: Printed at the Journal Office, 1878.

Trowbridge, L. S., and Fred E. Farnsworth. *Michigan at Gettysburg*. Detroit: Winn and Hammond, 1889.

Trumbull, H. Clay. *War Memories of an Army Chaplain*. New York: Charles Scribner's Sons, 1898.

Vassar, Thomas E. *Uncle John Vassar; or The Fight of Faith*. New York: American Tract Society, 1879.

Vinton, Frances. *The Christian Idea of Civil Government*. New York: G. F. Nesbitt, 1861.

Ward, Geoffrey C. *A Disposition to be Rich*. New York: Alfred A. Knopf, 2012.

Washburn, George H. *A Complete Military History and Record of the 108th Regiment N.Y. Vols*. Rochester: E. R. Andrews Press, 1894.

Weygant, Charles H. *History of the One Hundred and Twenty-Fourth Regiment, NYSV*. Newburgh, NY: Journal Printing House, 1877.

White, Ronald C. *Lincoln's Greatest Speech: The Second Inaugural*. New York: Simon and Shuster, 2006.

Willson, Arabella M. *Disaster, Struggle, Triumph, the Adventures of 1000 "Boys in Blue," from August, 1862 to June, 1865*. Albany: The Argus Company, 1870.

Wilson, Henry. *Military Measures of the United States Congress 1861–1865*. New York: D. Van Nostrand, 1866.

Wilson, Joseph M. *The Presbyterian Historical Almanac, and Annual Remembrancer of the Church for 1867*. Philadelphia: Joseph M. Wilson, 1867.

Woodbury, Augustus. *Second Rhode Island Regiment: A Narrative of Military Operations*. Providence: Valpey, Angell and Company, 1875.

Newspapers and Magazines

The Akron Beacon Journal
Albany Weekly Ledger
Altoona Times
Amenia (NY) Times
Army and Navy Journal
Auburn (NY) Weekly Democrat

Bangor Daily Whig and Courier
Buffalo Christian Advocate
Buffalo Commercial Advertiser
Buffalo Courier
The Buffalo Daily Republic
Buffalo Weekly Express
Burlington Weekly Sentinel

Cleveland Daily Leader

The Daily Evansville Journal
The Daily Green Mountain Freeman (Montpelier, VT)
Daily Review (Hayward, CA)
The Daily Times (New Brunswick, NJ)
The Delaware (OH) Gazette
Detroit Advertiser and Tribune
Detroit Free Press

Elmira Daily Gazette and Free Press

Faribault (MN) Central Republican
Fort Scott Republican

Gazette and Banner (Pittston, PA)
Geneva (NY) Daily Gazette
The Goshen (NY) Democrat

The Hornellsville (NY) Weekly Tribune

Indianapolis Daily Journal

Lewiston Sun-Journal
The Liberator (Boston, MA)
Livingston (NY) Republican

Maine Farmer (Augusta, ME)
The Marysville (OH) Tribune
Monmouth Democrat
Monmouth Inquirer

National Tribune (Washington, D. C.)
New York Tribune
Northern New York Journal (Watertown, NY)

Orange County (NY) Telegraph
The Owego (NY) Times

Philadelphia Inquirer
Pittsburgh Post-Gazette
Portland Daily Press
Potter Journal (PA)
Presbyterian Banner (Pittsburgh, PA)
Press of Atlantic City

Rockland County Mesenger
Rutland Weekly Herald

The St. Johnsbury (VT) Caledonian
Saint Paul Daily Press
Sioux City Journal
Sunbury (PA) American
The Sunbury (PA) Gazette

Tioga County (NY) Agitator
Troy Daily Times

Union and Advertiser (Detroit)
Urbana (OH) Citizen and Gazette
The Utica Daily Observer

Vermont Christian Messenger (Montpelier, VT)

The Weekly Republican (Plymouth, IN)
Wellsboro (PA) Gazette
Wisconsin State Journal

Denominational Journals and Minutes

Barnes, C. R., ed., *Minutes of the Eighteenth Session of the Newark Conference of the Methodist Episcopal Church.* New York: Nelson and Phillips, 1876.

Keeler, Ralph Welles, ed., *Minutes of the Sixty-sixth session of the New York East Annual Conference of the Methodist Episcopal Church.* New York, 1914.

Journal and Reports of the Forty-First Annual Session of the Detroit Conference of the Methodist Episcopal Church. Detroit, 1896.

Minutes of the Central Ohio Conference of the Methodist Episcopal Church, Forty-Seventh Session, Daniel Carter, ed. Cincinnati: Western Methodist Book Concern Press, 1902.

Minutes of the Fifty-Seventh Session of the Erie Annual Conference of the Methodist Episcopal Church. Cleveland, OH: The Cleveland Printing and Publishing Co., 1892.

Minutes of the New York East Conference of the Methodist Episcopal Church, Fifty-Second Session. New York: Press of Eaton and Mains, 1900.

Minutes of the Wyoming Annual Conference of the Methodist Episcopal Church, Thirty-first session. Elmira: Steam Printing House, 1882.

Official Journal and Minutes of the Eighty-Sixth Session of the Genesee Conference of the Methodist Episcopal Church. Buffalo: S. McGerald & Son, 1895.

Official Minutes of the One Hundred and Sixteenth Session of the New England Conference of the Methodist Episcopal Church. Boston: Murray and Emery Company, 1912.

Protestant Episcopal Church, Diocese of New Jersey, Journal of Proceedings of the Seventy-Eighth Annual Convention. Philadelphia: J. B. Chandler, 1861.

Seventeenth Session of the New York East Annual Conference of the Methodist Episcopal Church. New York: Wynkoop & Hallenbeck, 1865.

Articles

"Captain Samuel A. Craig's Memoirs of Civil War and Reconstruction," *Western Pennsylvania Historical Magazine* 13, no. 4 (October 1930).

"Mathew Andrew Dunn Letters," *Journal of Mississippi History* 1 (1939).

Potts, Charles P. "A First Defender in Rebel Prison Pens," *Publications of the Historical Society of Schuylkill County* 4 (1914).

Ward, Andy. "The 16th Maine Infantry at Gettysburg," *Gettysburg Magazine*, no. 37 (July 2007).

Collections

Bentley Historical Library, University of Michigan

Brinton family papers, Special Collections, University of Delaware Library, Newark, Delaware

Chemung County Historical Society collection

Edward Dwight Eaton Papers, Wisconsin Historical Society, Division of Library, Archives, and Museum Collections

Edwin Dwight Northrup Papers, Division of Rare and Manuscript Collections, Cornell University Library

Elial T. Foote Papers, McClurg Museum, Chautauqua County Historical Society

Gettysburg National Military Park Library

Harlan P. Rugg Papers, Archives and Special Connections, University of Connecticut Library.

The John Henry Wilbrand Stuckenberg Papers, Special Collections, Musselman Library, Gettysburg College

Joseph Hopkins Twichell Papers, Beinecke Rare Book and Manuscript Library, Yale University, New Haven, Connecticut

Lyman Daniel Ames papers, Ohio State Archives, VFM 2972 A.

Manuscripts and Archives, Yale University Library

Mark H. Dunkelman and Michael J. Winey Collection, St. Bonaventure University Archives

Michigan Civil War Collection, http://micivilwar.com/

New York State Military Museum

O. H. Seymour Papers, Auburn University Libraries, Auburn, Alabama

Paul W. Bean Papers, Special Collections, Fogler Library, University of Maine, Orono

Philip Melick papers, Easton Area Public Library, Easton, Pennsylvania

Quiner Scrapbooks: Correspondence of the Wisconsin Volunteers, 1861–1865. Vol. 8. Wisconsin Historical Society (May 12, 1863)

Robert L. Brake Collection, US Army Heritage and Education Center

Steven Roberts Collection, Henry Seage journal

U.S. National Archives and Records Administration

The University of Vermont Libraries Digital Collections, https://cdi.uvm.edu/manuscript/uvmcdi-93760

The Woodstock Letters. Vol. 8, No. 3. Maryland Province of the Society of Jesus (1879)

Websites

Digital Public Library of America, https://dp.la

The Fourth Michigan Infantry in the American Civil War, https://4thmichigan.wordpress.com

"Gilder Family," https://helenadekaygilder.org/gilderfam/index.htm

John Banks' Civil War Blog, https://john-banks.blogspot.com

New York State Military Museum and Veterans Research Center, https://museum.dmna.ny.gov

The Odessa File, http://web.archive.org/web/20050306190513/http://www.odessafile.com/features.htm

"The 16th Infantry Regiment, United States Army," American Battlefield Trust, https://www.battlefields.org/learn/articles/16th-infantry-regiment-united-states-army

The Valley of the Shadow: Two Communities in the American Civil War, https://valley.newamericanhistory.org

Index

Units

People

About the Author

Nancy Jill Hale is a United Methodist pastor and a Union chaplain reenactor. Three of her ancestors fought at Gettysburg. She is the author of the Civil War novel *Faith and Duty*. She is also a Licensed Battlefield Guide at Gettysburg.